Experiencing Modern Management
A Workbook of Study Activities

Sixth Edition

for

Certo
Modern Management
Diversity, Quality, Ethics, and the Global Environment

Sixth Edition

Lee A. Graf
Illinois State University

Samuel C. Certo
Roy E. Crummer Graduate School of Business
at Rollins College

Allyn and Bacon
Boston•London•Toronto•Sydney•Tokyo•Singapore

CONTENTS

4   ORGANIZATIONAL OBJECTIVES 58

5   FUNDAMENTALS OF PLANNING 73

6   MAKING DECISIONS 85

APPENDIXES 388

TO THE INSTRUCTOR

This workbook of study activities is designed to supplement the text, *Modern Management: Diversity, Quality, Ethics, and the Global Environment,*[*] Sixth Edition, by Samuel C. Certo. Therefore the chapter titles of the two books correspond. While the framework of this workbook remains basically the same as in the first five editions, some significant changes have been made. While many of these changes are a result of your suggestions, others are a result of the major new emphases in the text. These include very significant changes in the production management and control (chapter 18) and quality (chapter 21) chapters, and the new chapter on managing diversity (chapter 22).

Of the many changes made in this edition the most noteworthy are:

(1) *Two completely new experiential exercises:*

Experience 22-1 Managing Diversity *Will* Be Your Business
Exposes students to their own shortcomings regarding judging what different employee groups really want or value out of work and personal relationships

Experience 22-2 Moving Your Company Toward A True "Multicultural Organization"
Asks students to ponder and debate the characteristics of a true or "ideal" multicultural organization and suggests to students that such a set of "ideal" characteristics can serve as the standard against which to compare all activity related to "multiculturizing" an organization.

(2) *Improvements to many other exercises* to accommodate colleague suggestions

(3) *Significantly expanded instructor's materials including many new transparency masters.* Call your Allyn and Bacon representative to obtain your copy.

(4) *Now 72 experiential exercises from which to select.* With this number and variety of exercises, you have the option to vary your assignments each semester.

For those of you who have not previously used *Experiencing. . .* each workbook chapter begins with a "Chapter Summary." Chapter summaries are organized around *Student Learning Objectives* specified at the beginning of each text chapter.

The summary is followed by a section entitled "Knowing You Know." This section provides students with twenty-five learning assessment activities or self-test questions. Answers to self-test questions and the text page numbers where the questions can be quickly referenced are provided for students at the end of the workbook. Students also are told how to evaluate their performance on the self-test (for more details, see the "To the Student" section that follows). While the "Knowing You Know" section was designed specifically for students it also can be valuable to instructors who encourage students to use it fully. For example, proper use of the "Knowing You Know" section frequently reduces the amount of class time spent answering student questions on subjects well covered in the text. In addition, positive self-test results make students more confident of their understanding of the subject matter and increase their willingness to participate in relevant class discussion.

The final section of each chapter "Applying What You Know," consists of 72 different experiences designed to spur student interest and support the text material. These experiences which range from critical incidents to experiential learning exercises are of varying length and difficulty.

Figure 1 indicates how each experience can be utilized effectively. Experiences designated as *individual assignments* often are good for introducing topics and frequently provide an excellent basis for class discussion. They also can assess (test) whether students have kept up with reading assignments and have an adequate understanding of chapter concepts.

---

[*]Samuel C. Certo, *Modern Management: Diversity, Quality, Ethics, and the Global Environment,* 6th ed., (Boston: Allyn and Bacon, 1994).

Small-group assignments are frequently more experiential in nature and are designed to be completed by groups of five to ten students. *Large-group activities* can be used effectively in mass lecture arrangements.

While the matrix in figure 1 suggests that some experiences be assigned on an individual basis and others be used in small-group settings, many of these experiences also can be utilized effectively in larger classes. For example, the instructor teaching a large class may wish to assign individual experiences to initiate discussion. Experience 9-1 has been assigned on an individual basis with a class of 220 students to introduce important organizing concepts, it generated an excellent discussion. Other individual and small-group activities also have been assigned as special projects to be prepared and then presented to the class--an excellent vehicle for helping students to improve oral communication and presentation skills. Annotations appearing in the margins of the accompanying *Instructor's Annotated Edition* indicate when an instructor should introduce selected exercises.

We would like to thank you once again for not only utilizing our workbook, but also for the contributions you have made to the evolution of the entire package. We are certain that the above mentioned changes will make the workbook/activity manual an even more dynamic supplement in your fundamentals of management course. With your assistance we will continue to meet the needs of the managers of the future--**our current students**.

TO THE STUDENT

This workbook was designed specifically for you, not for your instructor. If used as suggested in figure 2, the workbook should make you more self-confident of your newly developed knowledge base and also give you a number of opportunities to apply this knowledge.

Each chapter is divided into three sections. The **"Chapter Summary"** is an in-depth review of the major subject areas of the text and should refresh your memory of the material you read in the text chapter. The **"Knowing You Know"** section provides a solution for a common problem faced by almost every student. You probably have said to yourself: "I think I know the material in that chapter well enough to do well on the exam, but I just wish there was some way of *knowing that I know it well enough*." The "Knowing You Know" section is a series of objective questions (true/false, multiple-choice, matching, or completion) that you can use to test your understanding of the text and to identify the weaknesses in your knowledge base. The correct answer to each question and the corresponding text page number where the correct answer can be found are provided at the end of the workbook so that you can quickly reference areas of weakness. This section also should help you become more familiar with the type of examination questions asked at many schools. The activities and projects in the **"Applying What You Know"** section provide you with the opportunity to apply chapter concepts. Your instructor will select activities for individual and group analysis. You should regard these projects as job assignments by an employer, rather than as just classroom assignments. Full expenditure of effort is necessary if you hope to master the concepts of the modern management system.

The following step-by-step explanation indicates how to use this workbook in conjunction with your text (see figure 2):

Step 1 Read the chapter in the text. A good grasp of the text material is the starting point for understanding the modern management system. Highlighting, underlining, or note taking frequently improves comprehension because these methods reexpose you to the text after the initial read-through.

Step 2 Have you met the student learning objectives? Student learning objectives are identified at the beginning of each text chapter and restated in the "Action Summary" section at the end of each chapter. You can assess whether you have met each objective successfully by answering the questions related to each objective statement and then checking your answers with the "Action Summary Answer Key" provided at the end of the chapter. For each missed question, reread the section or sections of the text that are applicable to that objective.

Step 3 Can you answer the questions in "Issues for Review and Discussion?" You should be able to successfully answer these questions at the end of each text chapter. If you feel uncomfortable with a particular question (or questions), refer to that section in your text. At this point you probably will think that you know the text material, but there is a significant difference between *thinking you know* and *knowing that you know*.

Turn to the chapter in this workbook that corresponds with the text chapter you just studied and:

Step 4   Read the extended chapter summary. This section is designed to give you a quick review of the "meat," the major "nuts and bolts" of the chapter.

Step 5   Test your knowledge and understanding of the concepts in the chapter. Answer the questions in the "Knowing You Know" section. If you cannot answer a particular question, refer to the text page cited at the end of the workbook to find the correct response.

Step 6   Is your understanding adequate? If you answered nineteen or more questions correctly, your understanding of the text is probably above average. Reread only those pages of the text that correspond to missed questions. You should feel quite confident in knowing that you know the material. If you missed more than six questions, your understanding of the text is probably below average and you should repeat steps 1-5. However, since you already know the correct answers to the questions in the "Knowing You Know" section, on a separate sheet of paper write an explanation for each answer. For example, if the answer to a true/false question is "false," explain why it is false. Check your answer with the text. Because the questions cover many of the more important text concepts, when you have successfully explained each question you should fee confident of your understanding of the text material.

Step 7   Work through one or more experiences as assigned by your instructor. These tasks support your new knowledge base and help you to apply what you know. After completing an exercise, you might want to note (in your text margins) any concepts applied or additional insights gained from the exercise that might support statements in the text or be helpful for exam preparation.

Figure 1. Matrix of suggested activity groupings

EXPERIENCES:	Individual	Small Group	Large Group
Experience 1-1 Chairman of the Dance Committee	X	X	X
Experience 1-2 Burger Chef Versus Buster Brown		X	X
Experience 1-3 The Effectiveness and Efficiency of Your Study Habits	X	X	
Experience 1-4 Planning For Career Success: Is Where You Are Going Where You Want To Be?	X	X	
Experience 2-1 Analyzing a Baseball Swing	X		
Experience 2-2 Applying the Triangular Management Model	X	X	
Experience 2-3 The Interrelatedness of Parts in a System	X	X	
Experience 3-1 Who Is Responsible		X	
Experience 3-2 Mishap at Three Mile Island		X	
Experience 3-3 The Ethics of Various Business Practices	X	X	
Experience 3-4 Assessing Your Ethnicality	X		
Experience 4-1 Establishing and Operationalizing Objectives	X	X	X
Experience 4-2 Reevaluating Organizational Objectives	X	X	
Experience 4-3 The Objective-Setting Interview (MBO)	X	X	
Experience 4-4 Balancing Multiple Objectives		X	
Experience 5-1 Planning for a Weekend Trip	X	X	
Experience 5-2 Developing Planning Premises	X	X	
Experience 5-3 The Problem with Planning at Eastern Electric	X	X	
Experience 6-1 Individual Versus Group (Consensus) Decision-Making		X	
Experience 6-2 The Missing Keys: Evaluating a Decision-Making Process	X	X	X
Experience 6-3 A New Plant or Plant Expansion	X		
Experience 6-4 Personnel Promotion Decision		X	
Experience 7-1 Identifying Environmental Threats and Opportunities	X	X	
Experience 7-2 Identifying Grand Strategies by Type	X	X	X
Experience 7-3 Operational Planning		X	
Experience 8-1 Effective Scheduling: The Gantt Chart	X		
Experience 8-2 Changing a Flat Tire: PERT	X	X	
Experience 8-3 Selecting a Plant Site: An Application of the Planning Process	X	X	
Experience 8-4 Policy, Procedure, or Rule?	X		X
Experience 9-1 Diagnosing Organizational Problems from the Organization Chart	X		
Experience 9-2 A More Effective Organizational Design for Lavern County Farmers' Service Company	X	X	
Experience 9-3 Organization Chart Analysis--Wee-Fold-Up Company	X	X	X
Experience 10-1 Fecke & Company: Understanding Authority Relationships	X	X	X
Experience 10-2 Decentralization: Fact or Fiction at Dynamic Industries?	X	X	
Experience 10-3 First Among Equals	X		
Experience 11-1 Recruitment	X	X	

Figure 1. (continued)

EXPERIENCES:	Individual	Small Group	Large Group
Experience 11-2 Loaded or Blank?		X	
Experience 11-3 Role Playing: An Analysis of the Appraisal Interview		X	
Experience 12-1 Unexpected Relief		X	
Experience 12-2 Behavioral Change at Telectrics, Incorporated		X	
Experience 12-3 Coping with Stress	X	X	
Experience 13-1 Communication: One-Way Versus Two-Way		X	X
Experience 13-2 Giving and Getting Information		X	X
Experience 13-3 Effective Listening: A Key to Managerial Success		X	X
Experience 13-4 Interpreting Nonverbal Communication: Can You "Read" These Classic Smiles?		X	
Experience 14-1 Looking at Ourselves as Leaders	X	X	
Experience 14-2 Effective Leader Behaviors		X	
Experience 14-3 Leadership Effectiveness: Fiedler's Contingency Theory	X	X	
Experience 14-4 Leadership and Decision Styles In "Operation Desert Storm": The Vrom-Yetton-Jago Model	X	X	
Experience 15-1 What Do Employees Want from Their Jobs:		X	
Experience 15-2 Job Enlargement or Job Enrichment	X	X	
Experience 15-3 Easy-Does-It Can Opener Company--A Case in (De)Motivation	X		
Experience 16-1 What to Look for in Groups		X	
Experience 16-2 Using Sociometry		X	
Experience 16-3 The Work Group at Laird's Steak House	X	X	X
Experience 17-1 Fare Discrepancies on Bus 41	X	X	X
Experience 17-2 Correcting without Punishment		X	
Experience 18-1 Quality is Job 1: An Introduction to Statistical Process Control		X	
Experience 18-2 Using Materials Requirements Planning	X	X	
Experience 18-3 Solve the Dilemma of the Management Club with Break-Even Analysis	X	X	X
Experience 18-4 J. R. Manufacturing Company	X	X	
Experience 19-1 DC-10 Disaster in Chicago: FAA Information		X	
Experience 19-2 Information Loss?	X		
Experience 19-3 The Office of the Future: The Impact of Innovations in Information Technology		X	
Experience 20-1 Planning for International Operations		X	
Experience 20-2 Kuwait or Not?	X	X	
Experience 20-3 Preparing Managers for Overseas Assignments		X	
Experience 20-4 Organizatinal Structures for International Operations		X	
Experience 21-1 Harley-Davidson Builds in Quality to Beat Back the Japanese	X	X	
Experience 21-2 The Real Estate Development Project: An Integrative Exercise with an Emphasis on Quality		X	X
Experience 22-1 Managing Diversity Will Be Your Business		X	
Experience 22-2 Moving Your Company Toward A True "Multicultural Organization"		X	

Figure 2. From "Thinking You Know" to "Knowing You Know" to "Applying What You Know."

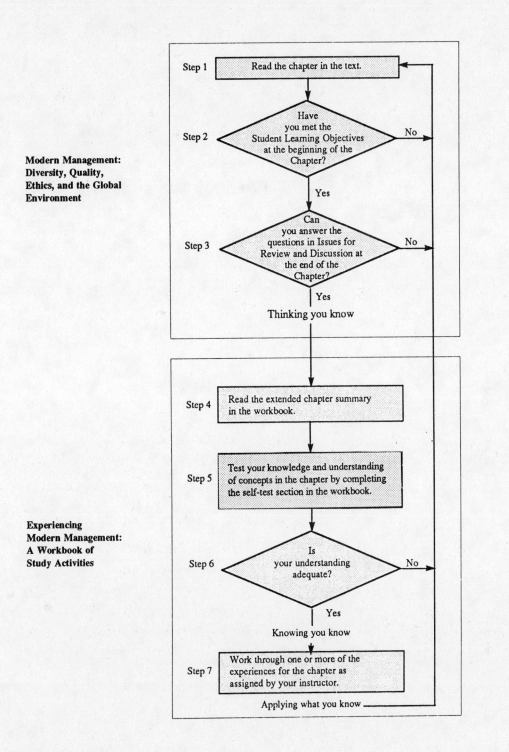

1 MANAGEMENT AND MANAGEMENT CAREERS

Chapter Summary

In this chapter, management is defined through a discussion of the importance of management both to society and to individuals, a description of the management task, a discussion of the universality of management, and insights about management careers.

Learning Objective 1   *An understanding of the importance of management to society and individuals*

Management is a function important to society in general and also to the livelihood and existence of many individuals. Society as it is known today simply could not exist without a steady stream of managers to guide its organizations. Management is also important because from 10 to 18 percent of the work force in the United States earn their living by being managers. Managerial positions can yield competent managers many returns, such as high salaries, status, interesting work, personal growth, and intense feelings of accomplishment.

Learning Objective 2   *An understanding of the role of management*

To understand the significance of being a manager, one must know what the management task entails. Essentially, the role of a manager is to guide an organization toward goal accomplishments. Management moves organizations toward achieving these purposes or goals by assigning organization members activities to perform.

Learning Objective 3   *An ability to define management in several different ways*

The term management can be and often is used in several different ways. Management can refer to the process managers follow to accomplish organizational goals. Management also can refer to a body of knowledge that furnishes managers with insights on how to manage. In addition, management is an identifying term for the specific group of people who guide and direct organizations, Lastly, management can designate the specific career devoted to the task of guiding and directing organizations. In this text, however, **management** is defined as the process of reaching organizational goals by working with and through people and other organizational resources.

Learning Objective 4   *An ability to list and define the basic functions of management*

The management process consists of the following four basic **management functions:** (1) planning, (2) organizing, (3) influencing, and (4) controlling. **Planning** involves choosing tasks that must be performed to attain organizational goals, outlining how the tasks must be performed, and indicating when the tasks should be performed. Planning activity focuses on attaining goals. **Organizing** can be thought of as assigning the tasks developed during planning to various individuals and/or groups within the organization. Organizing involves creating a mechanism to put plans into action. **Influencing** is the process of guiding the activities of organization members in appropriate directions to meet organizational goals and, ultimately, increase productivity. **Controlling** involves gathering information to measure recent performance within the organization, comparing present performance with pre-established performance standards, and from this comparison, determining if the organization should be modified to meet these pre-established standards.

Planning, organizing, influencing, and controlling are integrally related activities and cannot be separated. These functions are interrelated because the performance of one depends on the performance of the others.

Learning Objective 5   *Working definitions of managerial effectiveness and efficiency*

General standards exist that can be used to describe the quality of managerial performance, regardless of the type of organization being managed. These standards relate to the concepts of **managerial effectiveness and managerial efficiency**. As managers use their **organizational resources** (human resources, monetary resources, raw materials resources, and capital resources), they must strive to be both effective and efficient. If an organization is using its resources to attain its goals, the managers in the organization are effective. The closer an organization comes to achieving its goals, the more effective the managers of the organization are said to be. Managerial efficiency is the proportion of total organizational resources that contribute to productivity during the manufacturing process. Management is inefficient if a very small proportion of total resources contributes to productivity during the manufacturing process, while management is efficient if a very large proportion contributes.

Learning Objective 6   *An understanding of basic management skills and their relative importance to managers*

Management skills, perhaps the primary determinant of how effective and efficient managers will be, are also important organizational resources. If managers have necessary management skills, they probably will perform well and be relatively successful. Three types of primary skills are important for successful management performance: **technical skills, human skills, and conceptual skills.** Technical skills are mostly related to working with "things"--processes or physical objects; human skills involve working with people; and conceptual skills involve the ability to see the organization as a whole. As one moves from lower management to upper management, conceptual skills become more important and technical skills become less important. Human skills, however, are critical at all organizational levels.

Learning Objective 7   *An understanding of the universality of management*

Management principles are universal, or applicable to all types of organizations (business organizations, churches, sororities, hospitals, etc.) and organizational levels. Naturally, a manager's job is somewhat different in each of these organizations because each organization requires the use of specialized knowledge, exists in unique working and political environments, and uses different technology. However, job similarities also exist because of the common basic management activities necessary in all organizations: planning, organizing, influencing, and controlling.

Learning Objective 8   *Insight concerning what careers are and how they evolve*

A **career** is an individual's perceived sequence of attitudes and behaviors associated with the performance of work-related experiences and activities over the span of the person's working life. Careers evolve through a series of stages. During the **exploration stage** individuals analyze themselves and available jobs. Individuals experiencing this phase of career evolution are generally about 15 to 25 years old and commonly involved in some type of formal training like college or vocational education. It is during this phase that individuals typically pursue part-time employment to gain a richer understanding of what it might be like to have a career in a particular organization or industry.

The **establishment stage** is the second step of the career evolution process. This stage generally involves individuals who are about 25 to 45 years old. Employment sought during this stage is naturally guided by what was learned during the career exploration phase. Here jobs sought are usually full-time. Individuals in this stage commonly move to different jobs within the same company, within different companies, or even different industries. It is during this career stage that individuals typically start to become more productive or higher performers.

The **maintenance stage** is the third stage of career evolution. This stage typically involves individuals from 45 to 65 years old. This stage can be characterized by **career growth** (individuals whose performance continues to increase), **career maintenance** (individuals whose performance stabilizes), or **career stagnation** (individuals whose performance decreases). It is generally desirable during this career stage for employees to avoid career maintenance or stagnation, and to emphasize career growth. In an attempt to eliminate career plateauing, a number of the larger companies have begun providing career development guidance, identifying company job openings, and specifying available avenues for self development.

The **decline stage**, the last stage of career evolution, generally includes people of about 65 years of age and older whose productivity seems to decline somewhat naturally as they approach retirement. Individuals in this stage of career evolution commonly find it difficult to maintain prior performance levels because they begin to lose interest in their careers or haven't continually updated job skills necessary to remain productive. As society moves toward longer and healthier lives, more people in this life stage are becoming part-time workers.

Practicing managers as well as management scholars generally agree that the careful formulation and implementation of appropriate tactics can enhance the **success of management careers.** Planning your career path, the sequence of jobs that you will do along the course of your working life, is your first step in promoting your career. Career planning should be an ongoing process, beginning with the early phases of the career and continuing throughout the career. In promoting their careers, managers must be proactive and see themselves as businesses that they are responsible for developing. Set your career goals and continually revise and update these goals as your career progresses and take the steps necessary to accomplish these goals. While having a manager interested in the career development of employees is an important ingredient which will contribute favorably to career success, taking a proactive rather than reactive stance may be equally important. A proactive stance simply means demonstrating one's abilities and accomplishments. Individuals attempting to foster their careers must have a clear idea of the next position they are seeking, the skills they must acquire to function appropriately in that position, and a plan for how they will acquire those skills. In addition, individuals must have a clear idea of the ultimate position they are seeking and the sequence of positions they must hold in order to gain skills and attitudes necessary to qualify for that position.

Because **women** have only recently begun to join the ranks of management in large numbers, they often lack the social network systems and mentor relationships that are so important in the development of a management career. However, Tom Peters, author of *In Search of Excellence*, believes that women may have an enormous advantage over men in future management situations. Women's inherent strengths, which include placing a high priority on interrelationships, listening, and motivating others, will be the dominant virtues in the corporation of the 90s.

Recent growth of number of women at work, has forced many organizations to consider how **dual-career couples** affect the work force. Issues such as whose career takes precedence if a spouse is offered a transfer to another city, or who takes the ultimate responsibility for family concerns, points up the fact that dual-career relationships involve trade-offs and that it is very difficult to "have it all." The dual-career couple must work out coping mechanisms such as negotiating child care or scheduling shared activities in advance to better manage their work as well as family responsibilities. These couples often find that they must limit their social lives and volunteer responsibilities in order to slow the pace of their lives. They also must take steps to consciously facilitate their mutual career advancement.

Even a broader issue than dual-career couples is the increasing number of minority groups represented in the workforce and, more specifically entering management ranks. The workforce is fast becoming **multicultural**. The term "multicultural" refers to the mix of many different ethnic groups that will be working in American business in the 1990s. Minority groups are still underrepresented in management. One reason is a lack of education in the fields most in demand by businesses: hard sciences, business administration, and engineering. As a result, many minority members end up in staff rather than line positions, and are consequently more likely to be laid-off in the event of a downturn. Also, a lack of support for affirmative action by the Reagan and Bush administrations and in some instances discrimination may be responsible for minority workers being passed over for promotion.

The first step a company can take to address the above issues is to help minorities find the company by building community visibility. Also, managers can look within the firm for people who can be promoted. Firms may need to conduct their own training and education programs to provide these workers with the skills they need to join the ranks of management. Instead of looking for people who fit into the existing corporate culture, managers should look for talent and diversity.

Knowing You Know

True/False   *Directions: On the lines provided, place a "T" for true or an "F" for false for each of the statements that follow.*

_____1.   Planning can be thought of as assigning tasks to various individuals or groups within the organization.

_____2.   As used most commonly in the text, management is the process of reaching organizational goals by working with and through people and other organizational resources.

_____3.   One of the steps in promoting one's own career involves planning your career path.

_____4.   Management is probably the main resource of developed countries but is far less important in developing countries.

_____5.   Managers influence all aspects of modern organizations.

_____6.   Conceptual skills are mostly related to working with "things"--processes or physical objects.

_____7.   Management principles are universal, or applicable to all types of organizations and organizational levels.

_____8.   Dual-career couples often find that they must limit their social lives in order to slow the pace of their lives.

_____9.   If an organization is using its resources to attain its goals, the managers of the organization are efficient.

_____10. In reality, the four management functions are integrally related and cannot be separated.

_____11. As managers advance in an organization, human skills become increasingly important.

_____12. Instead of looking for talent and diversity, managers should look for people who fit into the existing corporate culture.

_____13. The establishment stage of career evolution is experienced by individuals generally about 20 to 35 years old.

14. The four basic types of organizational resources that managers must activate during the production process are:
    a. human resources, conceptual resources, monetary resources, and raw materials resources
    b. capital resources, human resources, monetary resources, and technical resources
    c. human resources, monetary resources, capital resources, and raw materials resources
    d. human resources, technical resources, conceptual resources, and capital resources
    e. none of these four basic types is correct

15. Which statement is *not* true of managerial efficiency?
    a. Efficiency is defined in terms of the proportion of total organizational resources that contribute to productivity during the manufacturing process.
    b. Managerial effectiveness and efficiency are related.
    c. If an organization is using its resources to attain its goals, it is efficient.
    d. Both *b* and *c* are *not* true statements.
    e. All of these are true statements.

16. Basically, as one moves from lower management to upper management
    a. conceptual skills become more important and technical skills become less important
    b. technical skills become more important and human skills become less important
    c. human skills become more important and conceptual skills become less important
    d. technical skills become more important and conceptual skills become less important
    e. none of the above

17. According to Katz, which of the following is a type of primary skill for successful management performance?
    a. managerial skills
    b. technical skills
    c. communication skills
    d. decision-making skills
    e. according to Katz, all of these are primary skills

18. Which of the following is *not* a step in the control process?
    a. gather information to measure recent performance within the organization
    b. determine if the environment allows people to satisfy their human needs through their work and work environment
    c. determine if the organization should be modified to meet the pre-established standards
    d. compare present performance to pre-established performance standards
    e. all of these are steps in the control process

19. The four basic functions or activities that make up the management process are
    a. producing, controlling, organizing, and financing
    b. planning, organizing, selling, and controlling
    c. organizing, planning, influencing, and controlling
    d. controlling, organizing, planning, and financing
    e. planning, organizing, influencing, and financing

20. Management is
    a. the process managers follow to reach organizational goals
    b. a body of knowledge
    c. a specific group of people
    d. a career
    e. all of these definitions are correct

21. Essentially, the *role* of a manager is to
    a. represent the organization in labor negotiations
    b. analyze the efficiency of employees
    c. guide the organization toward goal accomplishments
    d. control the rate of use of raw materials
    e. all of these are correct roles

22. In the long run, managerial positions can yield
    a. high salaries
    b. status and interesting work
    c. personal growth
    d. a feeling of accomplishment
    e. all of these statements are correct

23. Government statistics show that management positions have increased from____ percent to____ percent of the work force since 1950?
    a. 10 to 18 percent
    b. 2 to 3 percent
    c. 5 to 7 percent
    d. 15 to 20 percent
    e. none of the above

24. Which of the following are considered to be types of organizational resources?
    a. human resources
    b. raw materials
    c. capital resources
    d. money
    e. all of the above

25. Which of the following is not a characteristic of an excellently run company, according to Peters and Waterman?
    a. autonomy and entrepreneurship
    b. diversity of products
    c. a simple form with a lean staff
    d. productivity through people
    e. all of the above are characteristics of excellently run companies

Applying What You Know

Experience 1-1   Chairperson of the Dance Committee*

Introduction

The incident that follows permits you to apply your knowledge of the management process to a situation you may have already experienced or one in which you might well find yourself as you progress through college. Fraternities, sororities, clubs, and residence-hall associations frequently sponsor similar social activities. Read the incident and then complete the exercises as directed.

---

*Source of Experience 1-1: From Farmer, Richard N., Barry M. Richman, and William G. Ryan, *Incidents in Applying Management Theory.* © 1966 Wadsworth Publishing Company, Belmont, CA. Reprinted by permission of the authors.

Incident

The Student Executive Council of State College is responsible for planning and running four major dances for the student body during the academic year. The college administration has consented to provide the gymnasium for these dances, but it will assume no responsibility for the dances themselves.

Light refreshments soft drinks, coffee, milk, sandwiches, cake, cookies, etc. customarily either are sold at such dances or included free if the price of general admission covers such expenses. Kitchen facilities are available in the gymnasium building for preparing many of the refreshments to be served, and the Dance Committee usually makes use of these facilities rather than have all of the refreshments catered by an outside firm. The committee also generally uses the gymnasium's checkroom facilities, because there are several months of snow, as well as a rainy season, in this state. Two of the dances are held during the winter months; one is held in April, when there is generally quite a bit of rain.

Tickets for each dance usually go on sale at least a month before the dance. Tickets are available through the ticket offices located in the gym and in the students' union building. Large blocks of tickets also are distributed and sold through fraternities and sororities.

A band or orchestra must be obtained for each dance. It is also customary to provide other professional entertainment, such as a singer, comedian, and/or dance team. Souvenir programs usually are distributed or sold at the dances. Advertisements for these programs generally are solicited from local firms, student organizations, and the general public. The revenues derived from such advertisements are used by the Student Executive Council to finance student activities and new facilities and, if necessary, to offset the costs incurred in running each dance. The Student Executive Council is responsible for decorating the gymnasium for these dances and for general cleanup after each dance.

Assume that the Student Executive Council has elected you chairperson of the Dance Committee and has placed you in complete charge of the dances for the coming year. Some of the other Student Executive Council members are willing to assist you as Dance Committee members, but you also will need to obtain a number of other students to help with the planning and running of the dances.

The college administration is to receive 20 percent of any profits derived from the dances in payment for the use of the gymnasium and other facilities. The remaining profits go to the Student Executive Council, which has agreed to give you 25 percent of its net profits because your job as chairperson of the Dance Committee will require considerable personal time and effort.

The Student Executive Council hopes that each dance will show a nice profit and that the students attending the dance will have a good time. If a dance proves to be a disappointment, it may be difficult to derive profits from future dances because students will be reluctant to attend.

Exercise 1

Using the matrix provided in figure 1.1, classify by management function the issues you should concern yourself with as chairperson of the Dance Committee.

Figure 1.1   Dance Committee Issues

	PLANNING	ORGANIZING	INFLUENCING	CONTROLLING
I S S U E S	1.	1.	1.	1.
	2.	2.	2.	2.
	3.	3.	3.	3.
	4.	4.	4.	4.
	5.	5.	5.	5.
	6.	6.	6.	6.

Exercise 2

Compare all of the issues you listed under the management functions in exercise 1. Does what you observe support any major tenet mentioned in the text? Explain.

Exercise 3

Explain what you have gained from this experience.

Experience 1-2   Burger Chef Versus Buster Brown

Introduction

Almost every college student has patronized a fast-food restaurant like Burger Chef and a shoe store such as Buster Brown. From this involvement, you should have a general understanding of the operation of each of these organizations. Many students, however, have only a rather vague idea of what a manager's job in these organizations entails in a typical working day. The three exercises that follow are designed to bring you face-to-face with this type of real-world manager.

Exercise 1

Interview the manager of a Burger Chef or similar fast-food restaurant and the manager of a Buster Brown or similar non-self-service shoe store. Write a description of what the manager in each organization does in a typical working day. (One approach might be to ask each manager to trace, in detail, what he or she does from time of arrival to quitting time in a typical working day. You should take complete notes or possibly even tape-record these interviews so that important aspects of each manager's job are not omitted from your description.)

Exercise 2

Compare the job description of the fast-food manager to the job description of the shoe store manager. Classify the similarities and differences you find between their jobs into the categories that follow.

a. Similarities in specialized knowledge   b. Differences in specialized knowledge

c. Similarities in working environment   d. Differences in working environment

e. Similarities in technology   f. Differences in technology

g. Similarities in management functions or activities   h. Differences in management functions or activities

Exercise 3

Briefly summarize what you found from categorizing the similarities and differences between managers' jobs in Exercise 2. Then relate what you learned in Exercise 2 to the universality of management concept (management as a universal process).

Experience 1-3   The Effectiveness and Efficiency of Your Study Habits

Introduction

In this experience, you apply the concepts of effectiveness and efficiency to managing your own study habits. This self-analysis of study habits should improve your effectiveness and efficiency in mastering the materials and concepts of future chapters. This experience has five exercises.

Exercise 1

Answer the questions that follow about the effectiveness of your study habits.

a.   Were the study habits you used in mastering the material in Chapter 1 effective or ineffective? How do you know they were effective or ineffective?

b.   How might you increase your effectiveness in mastering the important aspects of the modern management system found in future chapters?

Exercise 2

Answer the questions that follow about the efficiency of your study habits.

a.   Was the approach you used in mastering the material in chapter 1 efficient or inefficient? Explain why you feel the approach was efficient of inefficient.

b.   How might you increase your efficiency in mastering the material found in future chapters?

Exercise 3

Explain how the concepts of effectiveness and efficiency can be related to the seven-step process for mastering the management system (Figure 2) found in the "To the Student" section at the beginning of this workbook.

Exercise 4

Write a short essay on the following statement: Managers must be concerned about their own efficiency and effectiveness before they can hope to increase the efficiency and effectiveness of the unit they manage.

Exercise 5

Develop a list of the ways in which managers can be (a) more efficient and (b) more effective in utilizing the human resources they manage.

Efficient Uses of Human Resources	Effective Uses of Human Resources

Experience 1-4   Planning for Career Success: Is Where You Are Going Where You Really Want To Be?**

Introduction

It is not uncommon for college students to give little real thought to job and career objectives until the realization hits them about the beginning of their senior year that they will soon have to find a job. This experience gives you the opportunity to assess a year or so earlier whether "where you are going" (the job and career you are preparing yourself for) is "where you really want to be" (what you are really working to accomplish). It will give you the opportunity to reevaluate job and career plans while there is still time to refocus your education and experience.

Figure 1.2 represents a comprehensive, step-by-step individual career planning model. As you will soon discover, it will help you judge the accuracy of your present job/career perceptions, systematically evaluate how well your present job/career objectives mesh with your personal characteristics, and develop short-term plans and long-term strategies for career success. The model provides the framework for the three exercises that follow.

**This exercise, coauthored by Lee A. Graf and Masoud Hemmasi, was presented at and appeared in the proceedings of the 1989 Conference of the Association for Business Simulation and Experiential Learning, Orlando, Florida, March 1-3, 1989.

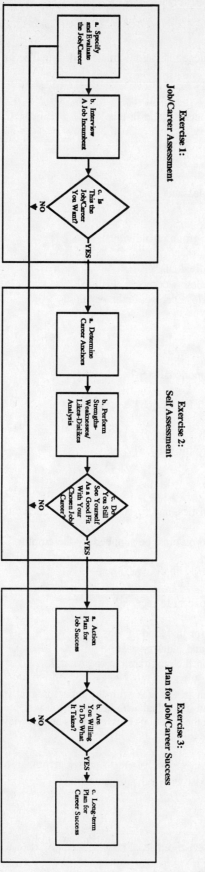

FIGURE 1.2 PLANNING FOR CAREER SUCCESS

Exercise 1:
Job/Career Assessment

a. Specify
and Evaluate
the Job/Career

b. Interview
A Job Incumbent

c. Is
This the
Job/Career
You Want?

NO

YES

Exercise 2:
Self Assessment

a. Determine
Career Anchors

b. Perform
Strengths-
Weaknesses/
Likes-Dislikes
Analysis

c. Do
You Still
See Yourself
As a Good Fit
With Your
Chosen Job/
Career?

NO

YES

Exercise 3:
Plan for Job/Career Success

a. Action
Plan for
Job Success

b. Are
You Willing
To Do What
It Takes?

NO

YES

c. Long-term
Plan for
Career Success

Exercise 1: Job/Career Assessment

a. Identify the job you hope to secure after completing college. Using the framework provided in Figure 1.2,*** jot down your perceptions of what that job would be like.

1) Nature of the Work:
   - Describe the kinds of things you would be expected to do in this job.
2) Conditions of Work:
   - What kinds of hours would you be expected to work?
   - Does the job offer security?
   - What is the work environment like?
   - Are there elements of the job that may be unpleasant?
3) Worker Qualifications:
   - Is previous experience required?
   - Is there any preference given to any particular group of individuals?
4) Worker Relationships:
   - Would you be working alone or with other individuals?
   - Would there be a lot of competition among fellow workers in this job?
   - Are there opportunities in the job to develop close personal relationships?
5) Pay, Training, and Promotion:
   - What would the expected pay be for this job?
   - What would be the normal promotional steps?
   - How long would these promotional steps take?
   - How would the pay be affected with each promotional step?
6) Physical Qualifications:
   - What physical qualifications would be required for the job?
7) Work Experience:
   - What experience would be required for the job you seek?
   - What special skills must you possess to qualify for the job?
8) Educational Requirements:
   - What level of education would be required?
9) Psychological Qualifications:
   - What aptitudes, abilities, personality characteristics, and so on would be conducive to success in this job?
10) Equipment Requirements:
   - What items such as tools, clothing, car, and so on must be supplied by the employee?
11) Performance Evaluation:
   - How would you be evaluated on this job?
   - Who would evaluate you on this job?
   - When and what kind of feedback would you expect to receive?
12) Employment Opportunities:
   - To what extent are workers in demand today for this kind of job?
   - Where is the greatest demand geographically and industry-wise?
   - What is the employment outlook for this job in the next three to five years?

b. Contact (either in person or by phone) an organization in the area with the types of jobs you hope to secure after completing college. Identify within the organization an individual who holds the job you seek and who can provide answers to questions regarding this job and career. Use the questions that follow as an interview guide. Record his/her responses for later evaluation.

1) Nature of the work
   - Does the job or career you are interested in exist within this organization?
   - Is it an entry-level job or above?

***Adapted from Edmond Billingsley, *Career Planning and Job Hunting for Today's Students* (Santa Monica, CA: Goodyear, 1978), 33-34.

- Ask for a brief description of the kinds of things an employee is expected to do.

2) Conditions of work
   - What kinds of hours are you expected to work? (Question whether overtime, night work, regular hours, irregular hours, weekends, etc. are required.) Are you paid for overtime?
   - Does the job offer security? Is it seasonal or irregular? When people leave this job for another organization, what are the usual or prevalent reasons given?
   - What is the work environment like? Are there any hazards?
   - Can the job be challenging enough to hold your attention and motivate you?
   - Are there elements of the job that might be unpleasant, such as heat, noise, and so on?

3) Worker qualifications
   - Is previous experience or training required? What is the source, nature, and length of such experience and training?
   - Is there evidence of any preference given on the basis of age, sex, or race?

4) Worker relationships
   - Do you work primarily alone or with other people in this job?
   - Is there a lot of competition among fellow workers in this job, such as commissions or promotions?
   - Are the relationships between employees on the job formal or informal?
   - Given the nature of the work, are there opportunities to develop close personal relationships?

5) Pay, training, and promotion
   - What are the maximum, average, and minimum wages for this job?
   - What are the normal promotional steps for this job? How long do the steps take on the average? Does a formal career planning program exist? How does pay change with each promotional step?
   - Does the organization support a mentorship program, formal or informal?

6) Physical qualifications
   - Are there any visual, height, strength, stamina, speech, or appearance requirements?

7) Work experience
   - What experience, if any, is required for entry-level and higher-level jobs?
   - What special skills must one possess to qualify for this job?
   - Are there any skill tests given for this job?

8) Educational requirements
   - Does entry into this job require a high school diploma, associate degree, bachelor's degree, master's degree, doctorate, or postgraduate work?
   - Does advancement on the job require formal education, advanced degrees, special classes, or special training?

9) Psychological qualifications
   - What aptitudes, abilities, personality characteristics, and so on are needed to be successful at getting and mastering the job?
   - Are there screening exams or psychological tests given? What is the nature of such exams?

10) Equipment requirements
    - What items, such as tools or clothing, must be supplied by the employee?
    - Is an automobile required?

11) Performance evaluation
    - When are employees evaluated on this job? Does it vary with length of service?
    - Who is expected to conduct these evaluations? Are superiors trained in formal performance appraisal methods? Does a formal evaluation system exist? When and in what form can the employee expect to receive feedback on his or her performance?
    - Are career planning and performance appraisals separate or simultaneous?

12) Employment opportunities
    - To what extent are workers in demand today in this type of job?
    - Where is the greatest demand, geographically or industry-wise?
    - Is employment likely to increase, decrease, or stay the same in the next three to five years?

c. Is this the job/career you want? Now that you have had a more realistic preview of your job/career interests (Part b above), compare it to your perceptions of what the job/career would be like (Part a). Given this comparison, are you still interested in pursuing such a career path? If so, the next logical step involves self-assessment (Exercise 2). Otherwise, from the perspective of career planning, you should now reconsider your job-career choice, specify (in the space provided below) an alternative job/career, and start over with Part a of Exercise 1.

Exercise 2: Self-Assessment

a. Determine Career Anchors.

1) Complete the following 44-item questionnaire**** by circling the number that best describes your feelings about each statement. Then follow the instructions provided to complete Part a of the exercise.

	STRONGLY DISAGREE	DISAGREE	AGREE	STRONGLY AGREE
1. I would leave my company rather than be promoted out of my area of expertise.	1	2	3	4
2. Becoming highly specialized and highly competent in some specific functional or technical area is important to me.	1	2	3	4
3. A career that is free from organization restriction is important to me.	1	2	3	4
4. I have always sought a career in which I could be of service to others.	1	2	3	4
5. A career that provides a maximum variety of types of assignments and work projects is important to me.	1	2	3	4
6. To rise to a position in general management is important to me.	1	2	3	4
7. I like to be identified with a particular organization and the prestige that accompanies that organization.	1	2	3	4
8. Remaining in my present geographical location rather than moving because of a promotion is important to me.	1	2	3	4
9. The use of my skills in building a new business enterprise is important to me.	1	2	3	4
10. I would like to reach a level of responsibility in an organization where my decisions really make a difference.	1	2	3	4
11. I see myself more as a generalist as opposed to being committed to one specific area of expertise.	1	2	3	4
12. An endless variety of challenges in my career is important to me.	1	2	3	4
13. Being identified with a powerful or prestigious employer is important to me.	1	2	3	4
14. The excitement of participating in many areas of work has been the underlying motivation behind my career.	1	2	3	4
15. The process of supervising, influencing, leading, and controlling people at all levels is important to me.	1	2	3	4
16. I am willing to sacrifice some of my autonomy to stabilize my total life situation.	1	2	3	4
17. An organization that will provide security through guaranteed work, benefits, a good retirement, and so forth, is important to me.	1	2	3	4
18. During my career I will be mainly concerned with my own sense of freedom and autonomy.	1	2	3	4
19. I will be motivated throughout my career by the number of products that I have been directly involved in creating.	1	2	3	4

****Adapted, by permission of the publisher, from "Reexamining the Career Anchor Model," by T.J. Delong, *Personnel,* May-June, 1982, pp. 56-57. © 1982 AMACOM, a division of American Management Association, New York. All rights reserved.

		STRONGLY DISAGREE	DISAGREE	AGREE	STRONGLY AGREE
20.	I want others to identify me by my organization and job	1	2	3	4
21.	Being able to use my skills and talents in the service of an important cause is important to me.	1	2	3	4
22.	To be recognized by my title and status is important to me.	1	2	3	4
23.	A career that permits a maximum of freedom and autonomy to choose my own work, hours, and so forth, is important to me.	1	2	3	4
24.	A career that gives me a great deal of flexibility is important to me.	1	2	3	4
25.	To be in a position in general management is important to me.	1	2	3	4
26.	It is important for me to be identified by my occupation.	1	2	3	4
27.	I will accept a management position only if it is in my area of expertise.	1	2	3	4
28.	It is important for me to remain in my present geographical location rather than move because of a promotion or a new job assignment.	1	2	3	4
29.	I would like to accumulate a personal fortune to prove to myself and others that I am competent.	1	2	3	4
30.	I want to achieve a position that gives me the opportunity to combine analytical competence with supervision of people.	1	2	3	4
31.	I have been motivated throughout my career by using my talents in a variety of different areas of work.	1	2	3	4
32.	An endless variety of challenges is what I really want from my career.	1	2	3	4
33.	An organization that will give me long-run stability is important to me.	1	2	3	4
34.	To be able to create or build something that is entirely my own product or idea is important to me.	1	2	3	4
35.	Remaining in my specialized area, as opposed to being promoted out of my area of expertise, is important to me.	1	2	3	4
36.	I do not want to be constrained by either an organization or the business world.	1	2	3	4
37.	Seeing others change because of my efforts is important to me.	1	2	3	4
38.	My main concern in life is to be competent in my area of expertise.	1	2	3	4
39.	The chance to pursue my own life-style and not be constrained by the rules of an organization is important to me.	1	2	3	4
40.	I find most organizations to be restrictive and intrusive.	1	2	3	4
41.	Remaining in my area of expertise, rather than being promoted into general management, is important to me.	1	2	3	4
42.	I want a career that allows me to meet my basic needs through helping others.	1	2	3	4
43.	The use of my interpersonal and helping skills in the service of others is important to me.	1	2	3	4
44.	I like to see others change because of my efforts.	1	2	3	4

2) Now, compute your mean response for each of the following career anchors using the item numbers listed below the respective lines (for example, for "Technical Competence" sum your responses to statements 1, 2, 27, 35, 38, and 41). Then divide each anchor total by the number of items for that anchor to obtain your subscale score for the eight career anchors. After your instructor has provided you with an explanation of the meaning of career anchors and how the subscale scores are interpreted, continue on to Part b of this exercise.

Technical Competence	_____	÷	6	=	_____
	#1, 2, 27, 35, 38, 41				

Autonomy	_____	÷	6	=	_____
	#3, 18, 23, 36, 39, 40				

Service	_____	÷	6	=	_____
	#4, 21, 37, 42, 43, 44				

Identity	_____	÷	5	=	_____
	#7, 13, 20, 22, 26				

Variety	_____	÷	6	=	_____
	#5, 12, 14, 24, 31, 32				

Managerial Competence	_____	÷	6	=	_____
	#6, 10, 11, 15, 25, 30				

Security	_____	÷	5	=	_____
	#8, 16, 17, 28, 33				

Creativity	_____	÷	4	=	_____
	#9, 19, 29, 34				

b) Perform strengths-weaknesses/likes-dislikes analysis. In light of the information gleaned from Exercise 1 pertaining to your job/career goals, list your perceived strengths, weaknesses, likes, and dislikes (SWLD) in the appropriate sections below. Strengths are one's attributes, skills, talents, and characteristics (physical and/or psychological) that contribute to one's effectiveness in a job. Weaknesses, on the other hand, are those same elements that detract from one's effectiveness. Likes are things that a person discovers enjoyable; dislikes are self-imposed restrictions. Try to be totally honest with yourself to obtain the most objective understanding of the factors that may significantly affect the outcome of your career path decision.

Strengths:	Weaknesses:
Likes:	Dislikes:

c)   Are you a "fit" with your chosen career?

1)   Given the outcome of the self-assessment exercise (Parts a and b above), do you still see yourself as a good fit with your chosen job/career? Explain.

2)   Can you think of other job/career alternatives that are consistent with your self-assessment profile (Parts a and b above)? Explain.

Exercise 3: Planning for Job/Career Success

a.   In Part b of Exercise 2, you identified your strengths, weaknesses, likes, and dislikes (SWLD) as they relate to your chosen job/career.

1)   Explain what you specifically can do to capitalize upon your strengths in preparation for that job/career.

2)   How do you intend to overcome your deficiencies in preparation for that job/career? Explain.

3)   How do you intend to cope with what you dislike about that job/career? Explain.

4) Meet with a group (preferably 3-5 other individuals with similar job/career objectives) to brainstorm other ways of addressing the above issues.

b. Now that you are aware of what it will take to be a better "fit" with your chosen job/career, do you think you have the ability and willingness to do what is necessary to build on your strengths, cope with your dislikes, and overcome your weaknesses? If your answer is NO, from the perspective of career planning, you should now reconsider your job/career choice, specify (in the space below) an alternative job/career, and start over with Part a of Exercise 1.

c. Will you obtain long-term career success?

1) Based upon the experience and the knowledge you have gained from the preceding exercises and information provided in your text, meet again in your discussion group to develop a list of "guidelines" that, if adhered to, should lead to long-term career success.

2) Explain what you have gained from Experience 1-4.

2 THE HISTORY OF MANAGEMENT

Chapter Summary

This chapter discussed five approaches to management: (1) the classical approach, (2) the behavioral approach, (3) the management science approach, (4) the contingency approach, and (5) the system approach.

Learning Objective 1   *An understanding of the classical approach to management*

The classical approach to management resulted from the first significant, concentrated effort to develop a body of management thought. The classical approach stresses efficiency and recommends that managers continually strive to increase organizational efficiency to increase production. The classical approach to management splits into two distinct areas. The first area--lower-level management analysis--consists primarily of the work of Frederick W. Taylor, Frank and Lillian Gilbreth, and Henry L. Gantt. These individuals mainly studied the jobs of workers at lower levels of the organization. The second area--a comprehensive analysis of management--concentrates more on studying the management function as a whole. The primary contributor to this category is Henry Fayol.

Although the fundamentals of the classical approach to management were developed some time ago, modern managers are just as concerned about finding the "one best way" to get the job done as were their predecessors. One example of this concern is the present-day trend of incorporating <u>robots</u> into the workplace.

Learning Objective 2   *An appreciation for the work of Frederick W. Taylor, Frank and Lillian Gilbreth, Henry L. Gantt, and Henry Fayol*

Lower-level management analysis concentrates primarily on how to structure a task situation to get the highest production from workers. The process of finding this "one best way" has become known as **scientific management.**

Because of the significance of his contributions, Frederick W. Taylor commonly is called the "father of scientific management." Taylor's primary goal was to increase worker efficiency by scientifically designing jobs. How he modified the job of employees whose sole responsibility was shoveling materials at the Bethlehem Steel Company illustrates Taylor's scientific method. Taylor made the assumption that any worker's job could be reduced to a science. Through observation and experimentation, he determined the best weight of a shovel load, which shovels work best with which materials, the time it takes to load a shovel, and the time required to throw a load a given distance and height. Three years after Taylor's shoveling efficiency plan was in operation, records in Bethlehem Steel indicated that the total number of shovelers needed was reduced from about 600 to 140, the average number of tons shoveled per worker per day rose from sixteen to fifty-nine, the average earnings per worker per day rose from $1.15 to $1.88, and the average cost of handling a tone of 2,240 pounds dropped form $0.072 to $0.033.

Frank and Lillian Gilbreth were also significant contributors to scientific management movement. The primary investigative tool in their research was **motion study,** which consisted of reducing each job to the most basic movement possible. **Motion analysis** was and still is used today to establish job performance standards. Each movement or motion that is used to do a job is studied in terms of how much time the movement takes and how necessary it actually is in performing the job. Inefficient or unnecessary motions are pinpointed and eliminated in doing the job. Frank Gilbreth discovered that bricklayers could increase their output significantly by concentrating on some motions and eliminating other motions. Using motion analysis, the Gilbreths were able to reduce twelve motions per brick to two motions per brick. The total effect of this bricklaying motion study was a 70 percent reduction in the motions necessary to lay a brick and a tripling of bricklaying production.

Henry L. Gantt also was interested in increasing worker efficiency. Gantt attributed unsatisfactory or ineffective tasks and piece rates to the fact that they were set on what had been done in the past or on someone's *opinion* of what could be done. Gantt felt that exact scientific knowledge of what could be done should be substituted for opinion. His philosophy was that the manner in which tasks are scheduled and the manner in which their performance is rewarded directly affect production efficiency. This primary scheduling device that Gantt developed is still cited as the scheduling tool that is most commonly and widely used by modern managers. His scheduling tool (now called the **"Gantt Chart"**) provides managers with an easily understood summary of what work was scheduled for specific time periods, how much of this work was completed, and by whom. While Taylor had developed a system that allowed for all workers to be paid at the same rate,

Gantt, in an effort to encourage people to higher levels of production, developed a system wherein workers could earn a bonus in addition to the piece rate if they went beyond their daily production quota.

While scientific managers approach the study of management primarily in terms of job design, managers who embrace the comprehensive view are concerned with the entire range of managerial performance. Henry Fayol is perhaps the best-known contributor to this comprehensive view. Because of his writings on the elements and general principles of management, Fayol usually is regarded as the pioneer of administrative theory. The elements of management he outlined-- planning, organizing, command, coordination, and control--and the fourteen general principles of management he suggested in 1916 still are considered by most managers to be useful in contemporary management practice. Fayol's general principles of management stress three themes: (1) organizational efficiency, (2) the handling of people, and (3) appropriate management action.

While the classical approach yielded significant improvements in productivity, it is generally agreed that the human variable of the organization and critical interpersonal areas, such as conflict, communication, leadership, and motivation, were not emphasized enough.

Learning Objectives 3 and 4   *An understanding of the behavioral approach to management*
An understanding of the studies at the Hawthorne Works of the Western Electric Company

The **behavioral approach to management** emphasizes striving to increase production through an understanding of people. The behavioral approach usually is described as beginning with a series of studies conducted between 1924 and 1932 at the Hawthorne Works of the Western Electric Company. The purpose of the relay assembly test room experiments was to determine the relationship between intensity of lighting and efficiency of workers as measured by worker output. However, no matter what illumination condition employees were exposed to, production increased. An extensive interviewing campaign with the experiment subjects determined that production increased because the subjects liked to work in the test room, were allowed to work freely without fear, realized that they were taking part in an important study, and became friendly as a group. The experimenters concluded that human factors within organizations could significantly influence production.

The bank wiring observation room experiment at the Hawthorne Works analyzed in more detail the social relationships in a work group. More specifically, the study focused on the effect of group piecework incentives on a group of men who assembled terminal banks for use in telephone exchanges. The experimenters believed that the study would find that members of the work group would pressure one another to work harder so that each group member would receive more pay. To the surprise of the researchers, the work group pressured the faster workers, not the slower ones. Evidently, the men were more interested in preserving the work group than in making more money.

The series of studies at the Hawthorne plant gave management thinkers a new direction for research. The human variable in the organization needed much more analysis since it could either increase or decrease production drastically.

Learning Objective 5   *An understanding of the management science approach to management*

The **management science approach** (or operations research approach) is an application of the scientific methods to problems arising in the operation of a system, and the solving of these problems by finding a solution to mathematical equations representing the system.

Learning Objective 6   *An understanding of how the management science approach has evolved*

The management science or operations research (OR) approach can be traced to World War II. During this era, scientists were organized into teams that tried to solve operational problems in the military. These OR groups typically used what is called the **scientific method**. The scientific method involves observation of the system, construction of a generalized framework (a model), use of the model to deduce how the system would behave, and finally, testing of the model to see if predicted changes actually occur.

The success of OR groups was so obvious in the military that managers were anxious to try management science techniques in an industrial environment. By 1955, the management science approach to solving industrial problems had proven very effective. Management science techniques were being applied to diverse management problems, such as production scheduling, finding a new plant location, and product packaging. In the 1980's, surveys of firms using management science techniques indicate that these techniques are used extensively in very large, complex organizations. Finding new and beneficial ways of applying management science techniques to smaller organizations is undoubtedly a worthwhile challenge facing managers in the 1990's and beyond.

Four primary characteristics usually are present in situations in which management science techniques are applied. First, application of management science techniques usually increases the effectiveness of decision making related to complex management situations. Second, a management science application generally uses economic implications as guidelines for making a particular decision. Third, the use of mathematical models to investigate the decision situation is typical in management science applications. The fourth characteristic of a management science application is the use of a computer.

Learning Objective 7   *An understanding of the system approach to management*

The system approach to management is based upon general system theory. Ludwig von Bertalanffy is recognized as the founder of general system theory. The main premise of general system theory is that to understand fully the operation of an entity, it must be viewed as a system. A **system** is defined as a number of interdependent parts functioning as a whole for some purpose.

There are two basic types of systems: closed systems and open systems. **Closed systems** are not influenced by and do not interact with their environment. A clock is an example of a closed system. **Open systems** constantly interact with their environment. A plant is an example of an open system.

The concept of "wholeness" is very important in general system analysis. A thorough knowledge of how each part functions and the interrelationships among the parts must be present before modifications of the parts can be made for the overall benefit of the system. Since the system approach to management is based upon general system theory, analysis of the management situation as a system is stressed.

As with all systems, the **management system** is composed of a number of parts that function on an interdependent basis to achieve a purpose. The main parts of the management system are organizational input, organizational process, and organizational output. These parts consist of organizational resources, the production process, and finished goods, respectively. The parts represent a combination that exists to achieve organizational objectives, whatever they may be. The management system is an open system, one that interacts with its environment. Environmental factors with which the management system interacts include the government, suppliers, customers, and competitors. Each of these factors could significantly change the future of a management system. The critical importance of managers knowing and understanding various components of the environments of their organizations is perhaps best illustrated by the constant struggle of supermarket managers to know and understand their customers. Supermarket managers fight for the business of a national population that is growing by less than 1% per year. Survival requires that supermarket managers know their customers better than the competition. Many food retailers are conducting and using market research to uncover customer attitudes about different kinds of foods and stores to hopefully win business from competitors who are not benefitting from insights gained though such research.

Learning Objective 8   *An understanding of how triangular management and the contingency approach to management are related*

The **contingency approach to management** emphasizes the viewpoint that what managers do in practice depends on, or is contingent upon, a given set of circumstances the situation. In essence, this approach emphasizes "if-then" relationships. "If" this situational variable exists, "then" this is the action a manager probably should take. In general, the contingency approach attempts to outline the conditions or situations in which various management methods have the best chance of being successful. This approach is based on the premise that, although there is probably no one best way to solve a management problem in all organizations, there probably is one best way to solve any given management problem in any one organization. Perhaps the main challenges of using the contingency approach are perceiving organizational situations as they actually exist, choosing management tactics best suited to those situations, and competently implementing those tactics.

Although the notion of a contingency approach to management is not new, the use of the term itself is relatively new. The general consensus of management writers appears to indicate that, if managers are to apply management concepts, principles, and techniques successfully, they must consider the realities of the specific organizational circumstances they face.

Information from any discipline can increase the understanding of management system operations and thereby enhance the success of the system. The information used to discuss the management system comes from three primary sources: (1) the classical approach to management, (2) the behavioral approach to management, and (3) the management science approach to management. Using these three sources of information to analyze the management system is referred to as **triangular management**. These three bodies of management-related information plus an understanding of the contingency approach are very valuable to managers analyzing the management system.

Knowing You Know

Matching   *Directions: Match items 1-15 with items a-o. There is only one correct answer for each item.*

____ 1. Frank and Lillian Gilbreth
____ 2. Behavioral approach
____ 3. Management science approach
____ 4. Triangular management
____ 5. Open system
____ 6. Frederick W. Taylor
____ 7. Henry Gantt
____ 8. Classical approach
____ 9. System approach
____10. Henri Fayol
____11. Contingency approach
____12. Gantt chart
____13. Authority
____14. Bethlehem Steel
____15. Hawthorne Works

a. Used motion study
b. The right to give orders and the power to exact obedience
c. Characterized by "if-then" relationships
d. Where the relationships between intensity of lighting and efficiency of workers as measured by worker output was tested
e. "Father of scientific management"
f. Outlined the elements of management: planning, organizing, command, coordination, and control
g. Increasing production through an understanding of people
h. Summary of what work was scheduled for specific time periods, how much of this work was completed, and by whom
i. Interacts with its environment
j. Using the classical, behavioral, and management science sources of information to analyze the management system
k. Wanted to substitute exact scientific knowledge for opinion
l. Uses the scientific method and mathematical models to solve operational problems
m. Stresses efficiency to increase production
n. To understand the operation of an entity, it must be viewed as a number of interdependent parts functioning as a whole for some purpose
o. Where scientific management was impressively applied to the task of shoveling

Multiple Choice   *Directions: Circle the letter of the word or phrase that best completes each statement.*

16. Which of the following could *not* be said of the work of Taylor, the Gilbreths, and Gantt?
    a. They were concerned with the management function as a whole.
    b. They were looking for the "one best way" to perform a task.
    c. They were concerned with how to structure a task situation to get the highest production from workers.
    d. They studied jobs being performed by workers at lower levels of the organization.
    e. *a* and *d*

17. Three years after Taylor's shoveling efficiency plan was in operation
    a. the number of shovelers was reduced significantly
    b. the average number of tons shoveled per workers per day rose significantly
    c. the average earnings per workers per day rose significantly
    d. the average cost of handling a ton of material dropped significantly
    e. all of these are true statements

18. In the relay assembly test room experiments, it was discovered that
    a. no matter what illumination conditions employees were exposed to, production increased
    b. members of the work group would pressure one another to work harder so that each member would receive more pay
    c. workers pressured faster workers, not slower ones
    d. problems of human groups could be solved by solving the equations representing the system
    e. all of these statements are true of the relay assembly test room experiments

19. The management science approach
    a. had its beginning during World War II
    b. utilizes the scientific method
    c. is also called operations research
    d. has been used to solve such industrial problems as production scheduling and new plant location
    e. all of these are true statements

20. Which of the following is *not* a primary characteristic present when management science techniques are applied?
    a. Management science techniques usually are applied to increase the effectiveness of management decision making.
    b. Computers are used in management science applications.
    c. A management science application is based on general system theory.
    d. The use of mathematical models to investigate the decision situation is typical in management science applications.
    e. A management science application generally uses economic implications as guidelines for making a particular decision.

21. According to the text, there are several approaches to analyzing management situations to solve organizational problems. Which of the following is *not* one of those approaches?
    a. the system approach
    b. the behavioral approach
    c. the management simulation approach
    d. the classical approach
    e. all of these are approaches identified in the chapter

22. Henry Gantt
    a. added a bonus plan to the purely piece-rate system of Taylor
    b. identified fourteen general principles of management
    c. was an apprentice bricklayer
    d. developed a shoveling efficiency plan
    e. none of these is a true statement about Gantt

23. Fayol's general principles of management seem to stress three general themes. Which of the following is *not* one of those themes?
    a. organizational efficiency
    b. conflict, communication, leadership, and motivation
    c. the handling of people
    d. appropriate management action
    e. Fayol did not stress any of the above

24. The concept of "wholeness" is very important in general system analysis. Which of the following is an *incorrect* statement about system "wholeness"?
    a. The parts should be the main focus of analysis.
    b. Integration is the key variable in wholeness analysis.
    c. Possible modifications in each part should be weighed in relation to possible effects on every other part.
    d. Each part has some role to perform in order that the whole can accomplish its purpose.
    e. All of these are correct statements.

25. The management system
    a. is a closed system
    b. is composed of a number of independent parts
    c. is composed of organizational resources (inputs), the production process (process), and finished goods (outputs)
    d. can be modified by using information from only one primary source--the management science view
    e. none of the above

Applying What You Know

Experience 2-1   Analyzing a Baseball Swing

Introduction

Frank and Lillian Gilbreth spent most of their lives searching for the "one best way" to perform numerous work activities. In one experiment, the Gilbreths reduced the number of motions normally needed to lay a brick from twelve to two and thus tripled bricklayers' productivity. In this experience, you apply the Gilbreths' concept of motion study to two baseball swing sequences.

Exercise 1

Figure 2.1 shows the baseball swing sequence of an inexperienced baseball player; figure 2.2 shows the baseball swing sequence of an accomplished baseball player. Compare the baseball swing of the inexperienced player to that of the accomplished batter to identify ways of increasing the batting effectiveness of the inexperienced player. Assume that the objective of a baseball swing is to hit the ball with power. Now identify the motions that could be eliminated from the swing sequence in figure 2.1 without reducing the effectiveness of the swing. Keep the power objective in mind when completing the exercise.

Source of Experience 2-1: This adapted material and the photographs of the accomplished baseball player are courtesy of Daniel Litwhiler.

Figure 2.1   Baseball swing sequence 1.

Figure 2.2   Baseball swing sequence 2.

Exercise 2

Now identify the motions that could be added to the swing sequence in figure 2.1 to increase the effectiveness of the swing. Again, keep the power objective in mind when completing the exercise.

Exercise 3

Is it the responsibility of a manager to eliminate wasted motions from jobs that person manages? Explain.

Exercise 4

Think about the job you hope to obtain after completing college or the job you presently hold. What ideas from experience 2-1 do you feel you can apply to the job? Explain.

Experience 2-2   Applying the Triangular Management Model**

Introduction

To develop an understanding of the many and varied situations encountered daily in the modern management system, managers should analyze each situation using any pertinent **classically based, behaviorally based, and management science based information**. Managers never really get a complete picture of any situation if one or more of these bases of information are omitted in the analysis of the situation. Using all three sources of information to analyze the management system is referred to as **triangular management.**

In this experience, you analyze a situation in which the triangular management model has not been fully utilized. Read the incident and analyze the data provided; then complete the exercises as directed.

Incident

Landham Glass Company presently produces glass panes to be used in the windows and doors of homes and other buildings. It also makes heavier glass sheets to be used for such things as glass coffee and end tables and desk-top protectors. The company president and board of directors, however, jointly have agreed that the production of a more diverse line of glass products would smooth out the somewhat seasonal sales patterns that now exist at Landham. (The greatest demand for Landham's glass products is in the summer months, when home construction reaches its peak and most window and door installation takes place.)

To smooth out seasonal variations in demand, the company has decided to establish a jar-manufacturing department in a vacant wing of the company's main factory. In this department, glass jars will be produced from molten glass. The glass parts will be produced on bottle-making machinery that, in effect, blows the molten glass into a mold. Immediately after the molding operation is completed and while the glass is still very hot, holes are punched into the parts by a mechanized apparatus called a punch. As the glass components revolve, a gas flame melts the glass in the desired area and blows a

---

**Source of Experience 2-2: Adapted from Certo, Samuel C. and Lee A. Graf, "Integrating Schools of Management Thought: A Principles of Management Experiential Exercise," in *Journal of Experiential Learning and Simulation* 1 January 1979; pp. 44-47. Used with the permission of Elsevier-North Holland, Inc.

smooth hole in the component. Next, the parts must be annealed by an air-cooling process. The parts are then inspected for defects and packaged in cartons (cartons are stored under the conveyors and must be folded together by packers before they can be filled). Finally, the cardboard cartons are sealed and placed in temporary storage.

The newly organized management science (OR) group at Landham has been provided with what the company president considers relevant data (see "Relevant Data" that follows) and assigned the job of designing a floor plan for the jar-manufacturing department. In addition, the OR group must design the cardboard carton in which to pack the manufactured jars. After considerable thought and effort, the OR group sent the floor plan and storage box design shown in figures 2.3 and 2.4 to the president.

Figure 2.3 OR group's floor plan for jar-manufacturing department

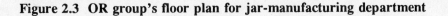

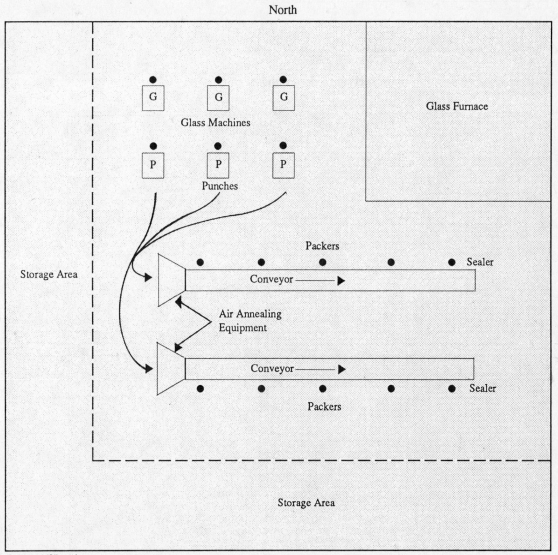

Scale: 1/8" = 1'

Figure 2.4   OR group's proposed box design

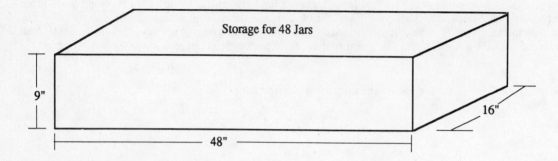

Note: Each jar will occupy an approximate 4" x 4" x 9" space

Figure 2.5   Dimensions of new jar-manufacturing department.

North

Scale: 1/8" = 1'

Relevant Data for Landham's Proposed Jar-Manufacturing Department

1. Sixteen employees will be hired for the jar-manufacturing department: three employees will operate glass molding machines, three will be punch operators, eight will inspect and pack annealed jars as they travel along two 28-1/2-foot annealer/conveyor systems, and two will seal the filled boxes and transport them to storage.
2. After removing the jars from the punches, the punch operators place the parts on the annealer/conveyor systems.
3. Packers inspect the jars and fill the boxes as the jars come down the conveyor; filled boxes are placed back on the conveyor to be transported to the sealer.
4. Sealers use hand trucks to transport all sealed boxes to storage.
5. At least 688 square feet of departmental storage must be maintained at all times; only one level of storage is possible due to low ceiling. Boxes must be stored at least eight feet from the glass furnace to comply with state and federal fire regulations.
6. The 16' x 16' glass furnace must be located in the Northeast corner of the department due to the already existing chimney.
7. The temperature in the areas within eight feet of the glass furnace frequently reaches 100°F.
8. Interaction between employees is not possible if employee work stations are located more than five feet apart because of the noise made by the glass machines, punches, and air annealing equipment.
9. The speed of already purchased annealer/conveyor systems cannot be adjusted. Also, conveyor systems are of a straight-line design (must be set up in a straight line). At least six feet *must* separate employees along the conveyor to allow adequate time to perform assigned tasks and enough space to work.
10. To eliminate significant cooling of molten glass as it is forced through overhead tubes, glass machines cannot be located more than thirty feet from the glass furnace.

Exercise 1

The OR group's floor plan and storage box design (figures 2.3 and 2.4) satisfactorily complete the assignment given the OR group by Landham's president. However, the OR group utilized only management science based information to complete its designs. From your knowledge of the three information bases of the triangular management model, what deficiencies do you see in the OR group's floor plan and storage box design? Categorize these deficiencies as resulting from lack of application of classically based information or of behaviorally based information.

Exercise 2

Now that you have identified the deficiencies in the OR group's floor plan and storage box design from a classical and behavioral perspective, redesign the floor plan and the storage box to alleviate these deficiencies. The outside dimensions of the floor area of the new jar-manufacturing department are diagrammed in figure 2.5. Cut out the glass machines (G), the punches (P), the annealer/conveyor systems, and the required storage area in figure 2.6 and properly reposition them on the floor area in figure 2.5 to improve the floor plan design. (The storage area can, of course, be segmented in any way that appears most effective.) In addition, position the people around the equipment (*use dots to represent people*). Once you feel you have machines and people properly positioned, secure everything in place with tape.

You need not construct your redesigned storage box (if you feel a new design is called for); simply indicate its new dimensions in the space below and explain why the new design is an improvement over the original.

Figure 2.6   Equipment and storage area for jar-manufacturing department.

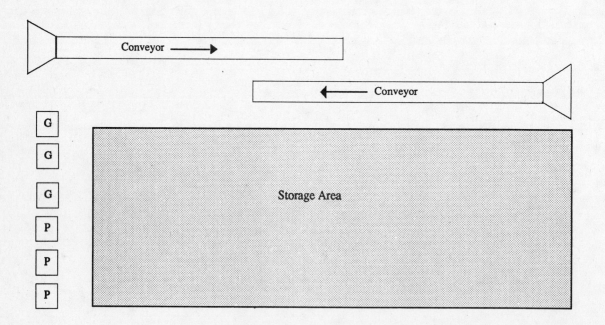

Exercise 3

What have you learned from this experience? Be specific.

Experience 2-3 The Interrelatedness of Parts in a System

Introduction

A system is defined as a number of interdependent parts functioning as a whole for some purpose. To understand completely how a system operates, it is not enough to know only the parts of the system; it is also critical to understand how each part affects and, in turn, is affected by every other part. For example, an apprentice watchmaker can be trained in a short time to identify all the parts of a wristwatch (a system). However, this information probably would not enable the apprentice to repair a broken watch. To repair the watch, the apprentice also would need to know how each part of that wristwatch relates to every other part of the watch--for example, which gear is supposed to mesh with which other gear, and so forth. Once these interrelationships are understood, the malfunction in the watch can be identified, and the system can once again be made to perform its designated time-keeping purpose. This experience is designed to increase your understanding of systems through an application of the system concept.

Exercise 1

A human being (human system) often is described as being composed of six major subsystems: the nervous system, the digestive system, the circulatory system, the respiratory system, the skeletal system, and the muscular system. Now, picture in your mind a human being having to walk from point A to point B in a remote wooded area (a distance of some one hundred miles) to obtain medical assistance for an injured fellow camper. In this situation, the hiker's *immediate objective* or purpose is the one-hundred-mile trek to obtain help for the injured person. What, if any, contribution does each of the major subsystems listed make to the attainment of that objective?

a. Contribution of the nervous system to objective attainment

b. Contribution of the digestive system to objective attainment

c. Contribution of the circulatory system to objective attainment

d. Contribution of the respiratory system to objective attainment

e. Contribution of the skeletal system to objective attainment

f. Contribution of the muscular system to objective attainment

Exercise 2

Do you feel that there are any significant interrelationships among the major subsystems of the human organism that permit it to make the one-hundred-mile trek? Describe those interrelationships.

3 CORPORATE SOCIAL RESPONSIBILITY AND BUSINESS ETHICS

Chapter Summary

This chapter presents the topic of social responsibility as a major area of concern for the manager of the future. Specifically, this chapter discusses fundamentals of social responsibility, social responsiveness, social responsibility activities and management functions, how society can help meet social obligations, and ethics and social responsibility.

Learning Objective 1   *An understanding of the term social responsibility*

The term *social responsibility* means different things to different people. For purposes of this chapter, however, **corporate social responsibility** is defined as the managerial obligation to take action that protects and improves the welfare of society as a whole and also organizational interests. The amount of attention given to the area of social responsibility by both management and society has increased in recent years and probably will continue to increase in the future.

A generally accepted model of corporate social responsibility was developed by Keith Davis. Stated simply, **Davis's model** is a list of five propositions that describe why and how business should adhere to the obligation to take action that protects and improves the welfare of society and the organization. Proposition 1 states that *social responsibility arises from social power*. This proposition is built on the premise that business has a significant amount of influence or power over such critical social issues as minority employment and environmental pollution. In essence, the collective action of all business in the country mainly determines the proportion of minorities employed and the prevailing condition of the environment in which all citizens must live. Building on this premise, Davis reasons that since business has this power over society, society can and must hold business responsible for social conditions that result from exercising this power. Davis explains that society's legal system does not expect more of business than it does of each individual citizen exercising his or her personal power.

Proposition 2 states that *business shall operate as a two-way open system with open receipt of inputs from society and open disclosure of its operation to the public*. According to this proposition, business must be willing to listen to societal representatives on what must be done to sustain or improve societal welfare. In turn, society must be willing to listen to the reports of business on what it is doing to meet its social responsibilities. Davis suggests that continuing, honest, and open communications between business and societal representatives must exist if the overall welfare of society is to be maintained or improved.

Proposition 3 states that *both social costs and benefits of an activity, product, or service shall be thoroughly calculated and considered to decide whether or not to proceed with it*. This proposition stresses that technical feasibility and economic profitability are not the only factors that should influence business decision making. Business also should consider both the long- and short-run societal consequences of all business activities before such activities are undertaken.

Proposition 4 states that *social costs related to each activity, product, or service shall be passed on to the consumer*. This proposition states that business cannot be expected to finance completely activities that may be economically disadvantageous but socially advantageous. The cost of maintaining socially desirable activities within business should be passed on to consumers through higher prices for the good or services related to those socially desirable activities.

Finally, proposition 5 states that *business institutions, as citizens, have the responsibility to become involved in certain social problems that are outside of their normal areas of operation*. This last proposition makes the point that, if a business possesses the expertise to solve a social problem with which it may not be directly associated, it should be held responsible for helping society to solve that problem. Davis reasons that, since business eventually will share increased profit from a generally improved society, business should share in the responsibility of all citizenry to generally improve that society.

Social responsibility is the obligation of a business manager to take action that protects and improves the welfare of society along with the interests of the organization. The areas in which business can become involved to protect and improve the welfare of society are numerous and diversified. Perhaps the most publicized of these areas are urban affairs, consumer affairs, environmental affairs, and fairness in employment practices.

Learning Objective 2   *An appreciation for the arguments both for and against business assuming social responsibilities*

Although numerous businesses are and will continue to perform social responsibility activities, much controversy persists about whether or not it is necessary or appropriate for them to do so. The best-known **argument against business performing social responsibility activities is advanced by Milton Friedman**, one of America's most distinguished economists. Friedman argues that to make business managers simultaneously responsible to business owners for reaching profit objectives and to society for enhancing societal welfare represents a conflict of interest that has the potential to cause the demise of business as it is known today. According to Friedman, this demise almost certainly will occur if business continually is forced to perform socially responsible behavior that is in direct conflict with private organizational objectives. Friedman also argues that to require business managers to pursue socially responsible objectives may in fact be unethical since it requires managers to spend money that really belongs to other individuals.

The best-known **argument supporting the performance of social responsibility activities** is that business as a whole is a subset of society as a whole and exerts a significant impact on the way in which society exists. The argument continues that, since business is such an influential member of society, it has the responsibility to help maintain and improve the overall welfare of society. After all, the argument goes, since society asks no more or no less of any of its members, why should business be exempt from such responsibility? In addition, some make the argument that business should perform social responsibility activities because profitability and growth go hand in hand with responsible treatment of employees, customers, and the community. In essence, this argument implies that performing social responsibility activities is a means of earning greater organizational profit. However, later empirical studies have not demonstrated any clear relationship between social responsibility and profitability.

Regardless of which argument or combination of arguments particular managers might support, they generally should make a concentrated effort to (1) perform all legally required social responsibility activities, (2) consider the possibility of voluntarily performing social responsibility activities beyond those legally required, and (3) inform all relevant individuals of the extent to which their organization will become involved in performing social responsibility activities.

Federal legislation requires that businesses perform certain social responsibility activities. In fact, several government agencies have been established and are maintained to develop such business-related legislation and to make sure that such legislation is followed. Examples of specific legislation that require the performance of social responsibility activities are: (1) the Equal Pay Act of 1963, (2) the Equal Employment Opportunity Act of 1972, (3) the Highway Safety Act of 1978, and (4) the Clean Air Act Amendments of 1990.

Adherence to legislated social responsibilities represents the minimum standards of social responsibility performance that business managers must achieve. Managers must ask themselves, however, how far beyond these minimum standards, if at all, they should attempt to go. The process entails managers assessing both positive and negative outcomes of performing social responsibility activities over both the short and long runs and then performing only those social responsibility activities that maximize management system success while making some desirable contribution to maintaining or improving the welfare of society. While the results of numerous studies can be of some help to managers attempting to assess the positive and negative outcomes of performing social responsibility activities, managers can determine the appropriate level of social responsibility involvement for a specific organization only be examining and reacting to specific factors related to that organization.

Determining the extent to which a business should perform social responsibility activities beyond legal requirements is an extremely subjective process. Despite this subjectivity, however, managers should have a well-defined opinion in this vital management area, and should inform all organization members of this position. Taking these steps will ensure that managers and organization members behave consistently to support this position and that societal expectations of what a particular organization will achieve in this area will be realistic.

Learning Objective 3   *Useful strategies for increasing the social responsiveness of an organization*

Social responsiveness is the degree of effectiveness and efficiency an organization displays in pursuing its social responsibilities. The greater the degree of effectiveness and efficiency an organization displays while pursuing its social responsibilities, the more socially responsive the organization is said to be. The socially responsive organization that is both effective and efficient meets its social responsibilities and does not waste organizational resources in the process.

Deciding exactly which social responsibilities an organization should pursue and then how to accomplish activities necessary to meet those responsibilities are perhaps the two most critical decision-making aspects of maintaining a high level of social responsiveness within an organization. For managers to achieve and maintain a high level of social responsiveness within an organization, they must pursue only those social responsibilities that their organization actually possesses and has a right to undertake. Furthermore, once managers decide to meet a specific social responsibility, they must decide the best way in which activities related to meeting this obligation should be undertaken; that is, managers must decide if their organization should undertake the activities on its own or acquire the help of outside individuals with more expertise in the area. (See text figure 3.1 for a flowchart that managers can use as a general guideline for making social responsibility decisions.)

There are various **approaches that managers can use to meet social obligations.** For example, **Harry A. Lipson** suggests that the organization incorporate social goals into the annual planning process; seek comparative industry norms for social programs; present reports to organization members, the board of directors, and stockholders on social responsibility progress; experiment with different approaches for measuring social performance; and attempt to measure the cost of social programs as well as the return on social program investments.

S. Prakash Sethi presents three management approaches to meeting social obligations: (1) the social obligation approach, (2) the social responsibility approach, and (3) the social responsiveness approach. The *social obligation approach* reflects an attitude that considers business as having primarily economic purposes and confines social responsibility activity mainly to conformance to existing legislation. The *social responsibility approach* is characterized by an attitude that sees business as having both economic and societal goals. The third approach, the *social responsiveness approach*, reflects an attitude that considers business as having both societal and economic goals as well as the obligation to anticipate upcoming social problems and to work actively toward preventing their appearance. Organizations characterized by attitudes and behavior consistent with the social responsiveness approach generally are more socially responsive than organizations characterized by attitudes and behaviors consistent with either the social responsibility approach or the social obligation approach. As one moves from the social obligation approach to the social responsiveness approach, management becomes more proactive. Such proactive managers do what is prudent from a business viewpoint to reduce liabilities whether an action is required by law or not.

Learning Objective 4   *Insights on the planning, organizing, influencing, and controlling of social responsibility activities*

Social responsibility activities should be subjected to the same management techniques used to perform other major organizational activities, such as production, personnel, finance, and marketing. Managers have known for some time that desirable results in these areas are not achieved if managers are not effective in planning, organizing, influencing, and controlling. Achieving social responsibility results is not any different.

Planning is the process of determining how the organization will achieve its objectives or get where it wants to go. *Planning social responsibility activities,* therefore, involves determining how the organization will achieve its social responsibility objectives or get where it wants to go in the area of social responsibility. Social responsibility activities can be handled as part of the overall planning process of the organization. First, social trends should be forecast within the organizational environment along with the more typically performed economic, political, and technological trends forecasts. Examples of such social trends would be prevailing and future societal attitudes toward water pollution or safe working conditions and improving the national educational system. In turn, each of the forecasts would influence the development of the long run plans or plans for the more distant future and short run plans or plans for the relatively near future. Second, managers should establish organizational policies in the social responsibility area just as they do in some of the more generally accepted areas, such as hirings, promotions, and absenteeism. To be effective, however, such social responsibility policies must be converted into appropriate action. Conversion of social responsibility policy into action involves three distinct and generally sequential phases. Phase 1 consists of top management recognizing that its organization possesses some social obligation and, as a result, formulating and communicating some policy to all organization members about its acceptance of this obligation. In phase 2, top management gathers information related to actually meeting the social obligation accepted in phase 1. Staff personnel generally are involved at this point to give advice on technical matters related to meeting the accepted social obligation. Finally, in phase 3, top management, staff personnel, and division management strive to obtain the commitment of organization members to live up to the accepted social obligation and attempt to create realistic expectations about the effects of such a commitment on organizational productivity.

Organizing is the process of establishing orderly uses for all resources within the organization. These uses, of course, emphasize the attainment of management system objectives and flow naturally from management system plans. Correspondingly, *organizing for social responsibility activities* entails establishing for all organizational resources logical uses that emphasize the attainment of the organization's social objectives and also are consistent with social responsibility plans. The vice-president for Law and Public Affairs at Standard Oil Company of Indiana holds the primary responsibility in the area of societal affairs and is responsible for overseeing the related activities of numerous individuals who report directly to this person. (See text figure 3.4.) While this figure is a useful illustration of how a company might include its social responsibility area on its organization chart, the specifics of how any single company organizes in this area always should be tailored to the unique needs of that company.

Influencing is the management process of guiding the activities of organization members in directions that enhance the attainment of organizational objectives. *As applied to the social responsibility area, influencing is* simply the process of guiding the activities of organization members in directions that will enhance the attainment of the organization's social responsibility objectives. More specifically, to influence appropriately in this area, managers must lead, communicate, motivate, and work with groups in ways that result in the attainment of existing social responsibility objectives.

Controlling is making things happen as they were planned to happen. To control, managers assess or measure what is occurring in the organization and, if necessary, change these occurrences in some way to make them conform to plans. *Controlling in the area of social responsibility* entails these same two major tasks.

All companies probably should take social **responsibility measurements in at least four major areas.** A measurement should be made of whether or not the organization is performing such activities as producing goods and services that people need, creating jobs for society, paying fair wages, and ensuring worker safety. This measurement gives some indication of the economic contribution the organization is making to society. A measurement also should focus on determining if the organization is improving or degrading the general quality of life in society. Producing high-quality goods, dealing fairly with employees and customers, and making an effort to preserve the natural environment all could be indicators that the organization is upholding or improving the general quality of life within society. A measurement also should be made of the degree to which the organization is investing both money and human resources to solve community social problems. Here, the organization could be involved in assisting community organizations related to education, charities, and the arts. Finally, a measurement should focus on the degree to which the organization deals with social problems as opposed to symptoms of these problems. Such activities as participating in long-range community planning and conducting studies to pinpoint social problems generally could be considered dealing with social problems as opposed to symptoms of those social problems.

A **social audit** is the process of actually taking social responsibility measurements such as those discussed in the preceding paragraph to assess organizational performance in the social responsibility area. The basic steps taken to conduct a social audit are monitoring, measuring, and appraising all aspects of an organization's social responsibility performance. Although companies like General Electric that pioneered concepts of social reporting are still continuing their efforts, few new companies are joining their ranks.

Learning Objective 5   *A practical plan for how society can help business to meet its social obligations*

Although the point previously was made that there must be an open and honest involvement of both business and society for business to meet desirable social obligations, the bulk of this discussion has focused on what business should do in the area of social responsibility. There are, however, numerous actions society should take to assist business in living up to its social responsibilities. Jerry McAfee, chairman of the board and chief executive officer of Gulf Oil Corporation, indicates that society has the responsibilities to business of (1) setting rules that are clear and consistent (society must spell out clearly what it wants corporations to do); (2) keeping the rules technically feasible (environmental standards have on occasion exceeded those of Mother Nature); (3) making sure that the rules are economically feasible (society cannot impose a rule that society is not prepared to pay for because, ultimately, society must pay, either through higher prices, higher taxes, or both); (4) making the rules prospective, not retroactive (it is counterproductive to make today's rules apply retroactively to yesterday's ball game); and (5) making the rules goal-setting, not procedure-prescribing (society should set the atmosphere but not tell business how to do it, should tell business what it wants made but not how to make it, should tell business the destination it is seeking but not how to get there).

Learning Objective 6   *An understanding of the definition and importance of business ethics*

The study of ethics can be approached from many different viewpoints. Perhaps the most practical approach is to view ethics as a catalyst which causes managers to take socially responsible actions in organizations. According to Dr. Albert Schweitzer, **ethics** is "our concern for good behavior. We feel an obligation to consider not only our own personal well-being, but also that of other human beings." Overall, ethics is similar to the following golden rule: Do unto others as you would have them do unto you.

In business, ethics can be defined as the capacity to reflect on values in the corporate decision-making process, to determine how these values and decisions affect the various stakeholder groups, and to establish how managers can use these obvservations in day-to-day company management. Ethical managers strive for success within the confines of sound management practices that are characterized by fairness and justice.

Learning Objectice 7   *An understanding of how ethics can be incorporated into management practice*

John F. Akers, chairman of the board of IBM, recently said that it makes good business sense for managers to be ethical. Without being ethical, he feels, companies cannot be competitive at either the national or international levels. While ethical management practices may not necessarily be linked to specific indicators of financial profitability, there is no inevitable conflict between ethical practices and a firm's emphasis on making a profit.

The employment of ethical business practices can enhance overall corporate health in three important areas. The first area is productivity. The employees of a corporation are stakeholders who are affected by management practices. When management employs a consideration of ethics in its actions toward stakeholders, employees can be positively affected. Secondly, ethical management practices can enhance corporate health by positively affecting "outside" stakeholders, such as suppliers and customers. A positive public image can attract customers who view such an image as desirable. The third area in which ethical management practices can enhance corporate health is in minimizing regulation from government agencies. Where companies are believed to be acting unethically, the public is more likely to put pressure on legislators and other government officials to regulate those businesses or to enforce existing regulations.

A **code of ethics** is a formal statement that acts as a guide for how people within a particular organization should act and make decisions in an ethical fashion. Ninety percent of the Fortune 500 firms and almost half of all other firms have ethical codes. Codes of ethics commonly address issues like conflict of interest, competitors, privacy of information, gift giving, and giving and receiving political contributions or business. There is no way that all ethical and unethical conduct within an organization can be written into one code. Codes of ethics must continually be monitored to see if they are not only comprehensive but also usable guidelines for making ethical business decisions. Managers should view codes of ethics as tools that must continually be evaluated and refined in order to more efficiently and effectively encourage ethical practices within organizations.

Managers in most organizations commonly strive to encourage ethical practices not only to be morally correct, but to gain whatever business advantage there may be in having potential consumers as well as employees view their companies as being ethical. **Steps managers can take to create ethical workplaces** are: (1) creating, distributing, and continually improving a company's code of ethics, (2) creating a special office or department with the responsibility of ensuring ethical practices within the organization, and (3) furnishing organization members with appropriate training. General Dynamics, McDonnell Douglas, Chemical Bank, and Americal Can Company are examples of corporations that conduct training programs aimed at encouraging ethical practices within their organizations. Such programs do not attempt to teach managers what is moral or ethical but rather give managers criteria they can use to help determine how ethical a certain action might be. Managers can feel confident that a potential action will be considered ethical by the general public if it is consistent with one or more of the following standards:

1. *The Golden Rule*--act in a way you would expect others to act toward you.

2. *The Utilitarian Principle*--act in a way that results in the greatest good for the greatest number.

3. *Kant's Categorical Imperative*--act in such a way that the action taken under the circumstances could be a universal law or rule of behavior.

4. *The Professional Ethic*--take actions which would be viewed as proper by a disinterested panel of professional peers.

5. *The TV Test*--a manager should always ask: "Would I feel comfortable explaining to a national TV audience why I took this action?"

6. *The Legal Test*--is the proposed action or decision legal? Established laws are generally considered minimum standards for ethics.

7. *The Four-Way Test*--managers can feel confident that a decision is ethical if they can answer "yes" to the following questions as they relate to the decision:

   --Is the decision truthful?
   --Is it fair to all concerned?
   --Will it build goodwill and better friendships?
   --Will it be beneficial to all concerned?

One additional step a manager can take to create ethical workplaces is taking responsibility for creating and sustaining conditions in which people are likely to behave ethically, and for minimizing conditions in which they may be tempted to behave unethically. It is often advisable to minimize unethical behavior in organizations by minimizing the conditions that seem to induce it. Two conditions that commonly induce unethical behavior in organizations are: giving unusually high rewards for good performances, giving unusually severe punishments for poor performances. By eliminating such conditions in organizations, managers can eliminate much of the pressure that people feel to perform unethically in organizations.

Knowing You Know

Fill-in-the-Blank   *Directions: Fill in each blank with the appropriate word or phrase.*

1. _____ is the degree of effectiveness and efficiency an organization displays in pursuing its social responsibilities.

2. A _____ is the process of taking social responsibility measurements to assess organizational performance in the social responsibility area.

3. The term _____ is defined as the managerial obligation to take action that protects and improves the welfare of society as a whole and also organizational interests.

4. The _____ reflects an attitude that considers business as having primarily economic purposes and confines social responsibility activity mainly to conformance to existing legislation.

5. Perhaps the most publicized areas in which business can become involved to protect and improve the welfare of society are the areas of _____ , _____ , _____ , and _____ .

6. The _____ formulates and enforces environmental standards in such areas as water, air, and noise pollution.

7. The _____ states that managers should act in a way that results in the greater good for the greatest number.

8. All companies probably should take social responsibility measurements in the following four areas: the economic function area, the _____ area, the _____ area, and the problem-solving area.

9. The _____ reflects an attitude that considers business as having both societal and economic goals as well as the obligation to anticipate upcoming social problems and to work actively toward preventing their appearance.

10. _____ states that social costs related to each activity, product, or service shall be passed on to the consumer.

True/False   *Directions: On the lines provided, place a "T" for true and an "F" for false for each of the statements that follow.*

____11. Milton Friedman argues that, to make business managers simultaneously responsible to business owners for reaching profit objectives and to society for enhancing societal welfare represents a conflict of interest that has the potential to cause the demise of business as it is known today.

____12. McAfee suggests that society has a responsibility to business to set rules that are economically feasible.

____13. Federal legislation requires that businesses perform certain social responsibility activities.

____14. Although numerous businesses are and will continue to perform social responsibility activities, much controversy persists about whether or not it is necessary or appropriate for them to do so.

____15. The process of determining how far beyond minimal standards of social responsibility a manager should attempt to go is relatively easy to describe and implement.

____16. Social responsibility activities can be handled as part of the overall planning process of the organization. First, strategic and tactical plans are developed; then social trends are forecast.

____17. Measurement in the social investment area focuses on determining if the organization is improving or degrading the general quality of life in society.

____18. There is really only one accepted approach that mangers can use to meet social responsibility obligations.

____19. The employment of ethical business practices can enhance overall corporate health in three areas: 1) productivity, 2) positively affecting "outside" stakeholders, 3) minimizing regulation from government agencies.

_____20. As applied to the social responsibility area, influencing is simply the process of guiding the activities of organization members in directions that enhance the attainment of the organization's social responsibility objectives.

_____21. In Sandra Holmes's study of executives' perceptions of corporate social responsibility, the overwhelming negative outcome has decreased short-run profitability.

_____22. The attention given to social responsibility by business and society has been increasing in recent years. However, experts do not expect it to be given that same level of attention in the future.

_____23. There is no way that all ethical and unethical conduct within an organization can be written into one code.

_____24. A social audit requires monitoring, measuring, and appraising all aspects of an organization's social responsibility performance.

_____25. The minimum standards of social responsibility performance are set by business ethics.

Applying What You Know

Experience 3-1   Who is Responsible?***

Introduction

Social responsibility is the managerial obligation to take action that protects and improves the welfare of society and the organization. While the social responsibility of business has more or less become a household term in recent years, universal agreement on whether or not business should perform social responsibility activities has not been reached. The incident that follows reflects the widely varying perspectives on the issue of social responsibility. Read the incident, and then complete the exercises as directed.

Incident

Fred Daniels, personnel supervisor for American Auto Works, had just returned to his office from a recent business conference where one of the major sessions on the agenda had dealt with the social responsibilities of the firm. Social responsibility, as he had discovered, was "the firm's obligation to assess the impact of its decisions on the whole social system. It is a concern for the ethical consequences of the firm's actions as they affect the interests of others."

During the conference proceedings, two major and simultaneous themes by two widely known authorities on business matters had been quoted consistently.

One authority, a prominent economist and author, had concluded that the doctrine of social responsibility was a fundamentally subversive doctrine in a free society. According to him, there was one and only one social responsibility of business--to use business resources to engage in activities designed to increase business profits--as long as business operated and engaged in open and free competition without deception and fraud. Furthermore, this authority had claimed that social responsibilities referred to actions taken by executives that resulted in the expenditure of money in a different way than stockholders, customers, or employees would want to spend that money. Essentially, he had said, social matters should be the concern of the government, and the private sector should merely cooperate with government programs.

The other authority, a professor at a leading western university, had stated that there had been a decided shift in thinking about the concept of the corporation. She had said that, thirty years ago, most business executives visualized the corporation solely as an economic organization, since its concepts and values were primarily economic. However, she had felt that, in more recent times, the feeling had become that modern business was more than an economic institution, that it was a social institution and a community institution as well and needed to be managed as such. She also had claimed that vigorous programs and activities to meet the crucial social and environmental problems of our society were not compatible with the long-run profit goals of business. According to her, by responding to social problems, the business sector could reinforce societal confidence in the preservation of the free enterprise system.

Exercise 1

Your instructor will divide the class into groups of four to six members and will ask each group to either prepare a list of arguments supporting business performing social responsibility activities or a list of arguments against business performing social responsibility activities. After all of the groups have had fifteen minutes to prepare their arguments, two groups with

***Source of Experience 3-1: Reprinted with permission from Bernard A. Deitzer and Karl Shiliff, *Contemporary Management Incidents*, Grid, Inc., Columbus, Ohio, 1977. Pages 173-175.

opposing perspectives will be selected to debate the issue. After the debate, your instructor may ask for comments from other groups.

Exercise 2

Meet again with members of your group from exercise 1 and answer the questions that follow.

a. What do you believe the professor meant when she stated that modern business was a social as well as an economic institution?

b. With what authority--the economist or the professor--do you agree? Discuss the reasons for your support.

Exercise 3

Explain what you have gained from this experience.

Experience 3-2 Mishap at Three Mile Island

Introduction

The Davis model of social responsibility is a list of five propositions that describe why and how business should adhere to the obligation to take action that protects and improves the welfare of society and the organization. Use the logic of Davis's social responsibility model to evaluate the circumstances surrounding the nuclear mishap that occurred at Three Mile Island near Harrisburg, Pennsylvania, on March 28, 1979. Read the incident that follows, and then complete the exercises as directed.

Incident

Thursday, March 29, 1979 Yesterday, a cooling system malfunction caused by human error and equipment failure at Metropolitan Edison's Three Mile Island Nuclear Generator Plant near Harrisburg, Pennsylvania, brought about the worst nuclear accident at a commercial reactor in U.S. history. While the accident began around 4 A.M., federal and state officials reportedly were not notified until a few hours after that. The Nuclear Regulatory Commission (NRC), for example, indicated its regional office was not notified of the accident until about 7:45 A.M.[1]

Monday, April 2, 1979 Executives of Metropolitan Edison Company, the General Public Utilities Corporation (GPU) unit that operates the 880,000 kilowatt plant at Three Mile Island, reported that they suspected part of the dilemma they were facing at the nuclear generating facility was created by a hydrogen explosion in the reactor containment building on Thursday afternoon. Nuclear Regulatory Commission (NRC) officials, however, say the explosion occurred Wednesday afternoon, though it claims the company did not inform them about it until Friday.[2]

Wednesday, April 18, 1979 A spokesman for General Public Utilities Corporation has indicated that the company believes that the cost associated with the accident should be shared by the company's customers, shareholders, and employees; and that the company intends to seek a rate increase to cover the estimated $800,000 per day extra expenses that GPU is paying to secure the alternate power needed because of the Three Mile Island generating station.[3]

Thursday, April 26, 1979 Directors of the General Public Utilities Corporation reduced the company's dividend and suspended the employee stock option plan in an apparent effort to convince regulators that it is sharing the financial burden brought about by the Three Mile Island nuclear plant accident with shareholders and employees as well as with customers. The company cut its quarterly dividends to twenty-five cents a share from forty-five cents, payable May 25 to stock of record on May 11. It also suspended the dividend reinvestment and stock purchase plan.[4]

Friday, May 4, 1979 Sources close to the Nuclear Regulatory Commission (NRC) have indicated that the accident at Three Mile Island involved a greater degree of radioactive contamination than did any other incident at a commercial reactor in U.S. history. Staff members in the Department of Health, Education, and Welfare estimate that two million people received an average of 1.7 millirems of radiation between March 28 and April 7 and expect the total dose to increase even more as time goes by. Some scientists have estimated that, as a result of the accident, there could be up to twenty additional cancer cases, half of them fatal, among area residents.[5]

Monday, May 7, 1979 General Public Utilities Corporation (GPU) announced that its Jersey Central Power and Light Company subsidiary is asking New Jersey regulators for permission to raise rates the equivalent of $113 million annually to help defray some of the costs of the Three Mile Island nuclear power plant accident. A GPU spokesperson indicated that the higher rates would cover Jersey Central's share of the increased cost of supplying replacement electricity for the crippled Three Mile Island facility.[6]

In Washington, an estimated seventy thousand people met behind the White House, marched up Pennsylvania Avenue, and assembled on the Capitol steps to protest the nation's growing dependence on nuclear power. It was the first major antinuclear protest in Washington since the occurrence of the Three Mile Island reactor accident.[7]

Exercise 1

Answer the questions that follow, using the propositions of the Davis model of social responsibility.

a. Do you feel that the General Public Utilities Corporation (GPU) and its Metropolitan Edison subsidiary were acting in a socially responsible manner? Explain.

b.   Was GPU acting in a socially responsible way when it asked for a rate increase to partially offset some of the costs of the Three Mile Island accident? Explain.

c.   If GPU had not elected to cut dividends and suspend dividend reinvestments and stock purchase plans, would you have reacted differently to question *b*? Explain.

d.   Which of the Davis propositions would provide at least a partial explanation for the seventy thousand demonstrators protesting the nation's growing dependence on nuclear power? Explain.

Exercise 2

Edward Radford, a committee member of the National Academy of Science and a member of the University of Pittsburgh's School of Public Health, contends that the current federal standard for occupational exposure to radiation should be dropped from five thousand millirems annually to five hundred millirems. Radford estimates that a worker exposed to five thousand millirems annually for thirty years runs twice the risk of contracting cancer as a person not exposed.[8] Assume that the federal standard for occupational exposure to radiation is changed today and that within the next thirty years numerous lawsuits are filed by technicians against GPU and other firms for exposing them to more than five hundred millirems of radiation. If the courts find in favor of the technicians, has society helped business meet its social obligation? Explain.

Exercise 3

Explain what you have gained from this experience.

Footnotes

1. "Cooling System Malfunction at Nuclear Power Plant Leads to Release of Radioactivity, Closing of Reactor," *Wall Street Journal* (Eastern ed.), 29 March 1979.
2. John R. Emshwiller, "Experts Converge at Reactor in Pennsylvania in Delicate, Risky Effort to Avert Catastrophe," *Wall Street Journal* (Eastern ed.), 2 April 1979.
3. John R. Emshwiller, "Danger at Three Mile Island Could Last for Weeks, As Cooling Down Continues," *Wall Street Journal* (Eastern ed.), 18 April 1979.
4. "GPU Cuts Dividends, Apparently to Show It's Sharing Financial Burden of Mishap," *Wall Street Journal* (Eastern ed.), 27 April 1979.
5. "HEW Raises Estimate of Radiation Exposure at Three Mile Island," *Wall Street Journal* (Midwest ed.), 4 May 1979.
6. "GPU Unit Seeks Annual Rate Rise of $113 Million," Wall Street Journal (Midwest ed.), 7 May 1979.
7. "An Antinuclear Rally in Washington Attracted an Estimated 70,000 People," *Wall Street Journal* (Midwest ed.), 7 May 1979.
8. Gail Bronson, "Nuclear Accident Seen Adding to Row Over Danger of Low Radiation Doses," *Wall Street Journal* (Eastern ed.), 2 April 1979.

Experience 3-3   The Ethics of Various Business Practices ****

Listed on the next page are 17 hypothetical situations. Each of these situations describes an action or behavior that most business persons will more than likely either personally encounter or at least be exposed to at one time or another during their management careers. Glance over this list of situations, then follow the directions provided below to complete the experience.

Exercise 1

Certain human behaviors in organizational settings such as bribery, price fixing, and stock manipulation have been judged to be unethical. At the other extreme, one can find behaviors that almost everyone--businessmen and the general public alike-- would consider perfectly acceptable. Between these two extremes are a vast array of practices that may or may not be considered acceptable. Under the column labeled "Impact" in Figure 3.1, indicate what you feel to be the magnitude of the impact if the following actions or behaviors were being practiced in a business organization you worked for. Use 1 for "no impact," 2 for "minor impact," 3 for "moderate but not particularly serious impact," 4 for "rather serious impact," or 5 for "extremely serious impact."

Figure 3.1
IMPACT OF BEHAVIORS ON THE BUSINESS ORGANIZATION*****

BEHAVIOR	IMPACT
1. Passing blame for errors to an innocent co-worker	_____
2. Divulging confidential information	_____
3. Falsifying time/quality/quantity reports	_____
4. Claiming credit for someone else's work	_____
5. Padding an expense account over 10 percent	_____
6. Pilfering company materials and supplies	_____
7. Accepting gifts/favors in exchange for preferential treatment	_____
8. Giving gifts/favors in exchange for preferential treatment	_____
9. Padding an expense up to 10 percent	_____
10. Authorizing a subordinate to violate company rules	_____
11. Calling in sick to take a day off	_____
12. Concealing one's errors	_____
13. Taking longer than necessary to do a job	_____
14. Using company services for personal use	_____
15. Doing personal business on company time	_____
16. Taking extra personal time (lunch hour, breaks)	_____
17. Not reporting others' violations of company policies or rules	_____

****Experience developed from materials presented in John W. Newstrom and William A. Ruch, "The Ethics of Management and The Management of Ethics," *MSU Business Topics*, Winter 1975, pp. 29-37.

*****The list of questionable behaviors were originally enumerated in John W. Newstrom and William A. Ruch, "The Ethics of Management and The Management of Ethics," *MSU Business Topics*, Winter 1975, pp. 29-37.

Exercise 2

Now that you have assessed the impact of each of the above behaviors for the hypothetical organization in which you work, indicate in the appropriate column in Figure 3.2:

1. The extent to which YOU believe each action to be ethical or unethical.
2. The extent to which you feel your PEERS (co-workers) would consider the 17 behaviors to be unethical.
3. The extent to which you feel TOP MANAGEMENT in your organization would consider the 17 behaviors to be unethical.

Use 1 for "very unethical," 2 for "basically unethical," 3 for "somewhat unethical," 4 for "not particularly unethical," or 5 for "not at all unethical."

Figure 3.2

YOUR BELIEFS AND YOUR PERCEPTIONS OF PEERS' AND TOP MANAGEMENT'S BELIEFS

BEHAVIOR	YOU	PEERS	TOP MGT.
1. Passing blame for errors to an innocent co-worker	_____	_____	_____
2. Divulging confidential information	_____	_____	_____
3. Falsifying time/quality/quantity reports	_____	_____	_____
4. Claiming credit for someone else's work	_____	_____	_____
5. Padding an expense account over 10 percent	_____	_____	_____
6. Pilfering company materials and supplies	_____	_____	_____
7. Accepting gifts/favors in exchange for preferential treatment	_____	_____	_____
8. Giving gifts/favors in exchange for preferential treatment	_____	_____	_____
9. Padding an expense account up to 10 percent	_____	_____	_____
10. Authorizing a subordinate to violate company rules	_____	_____	_____
11. Calling in sick to take a day off	_____	_____	_____
12. Concealing one's errors	_____	_____	_____
13. Taking longer than necessary to do a job	_____	_____	_____
14. Using company services for personal time	_____	_____	_____
15. Doing personal business on company time	_____	_____	_____
16. Taking extra personal time (lunch hour, breaks)	_____	_____	_____
17. Not reporting others' violations of company policies or rules	_____	_____	_____

Exercise 3

Now that you have rated the ethicality of the 17 questionable behaviors and have recorded your perceptions of how peers and top management would rate these behaviors, indicate in Figure 3.3:

1. How frequently YOU WOULD ENGAGE in each behavior.
2. How frequently you believe your PEERS (CO-WORKERS) WOULD ENGAGE in such behaviors.

Use **1** for "never," **2** for "seldom," **3** for "about half the time," **4** for "often," or **5** for "at almost every opportunity."

Figure 3.3

FREQUENCY OF YOUR ENGAGING AND YOUR PERCEPTION OF FREQUENCY OF PEERS' ENGAGING IN SPECIFIED BEHAVIORS

BEHAVIOR	YOU	PEERS
1. Passing blame for errors to an innocent co-worker	_____	_____
2. Divulging confidential information	_____	_____
3. Falsifying time/quality/quantity reports	_____	_____
4. Claiming credit for someone else's work	_____	_____
5. Padding an expense account over 10 percent	_____	_____
6. Pilfering company materials and supplies	_____	_____
7. Accepting gifts/favors in exchange for preferential treatment	_____	_____
8. Giving gifts/favors in exchange for preferential treatment	_____	_____
9. Padding an expense account up to 10 percent	_____	_____
10. Authorizing a subordinate to violate company rules	_____	_____
11. Calling in sick to take a day off	_____	_____
12. Concealing one's errors	_____	_____
13. Taking longer than necessary to do a job	_____	_____
14. Using company services for personal use	_____	_____
15. Doing personal business on company time	_____	_____
16. Taking extra personal time (lunch hour, breaks)	_____	_____
17. Not reporting others' violations of company policies or rules	_____	_____

Exercise 4

Answer the following questions from the data you have compiled in Figures 3.1, 3.2, and 3.3:

a.   Calculate the arithmetic average (mean) of the numbers recorded in each of the six columns in Figures 3.1 through 3.3. Record these average or mean scores in the spaces provided below. Then use these statistics to answer the questions in parts "b" and "c."

      1) IMPACT (mean) _____

      2) Your beliefs about yourself ["YOU" column] (mean) _____

      3) Your beliefs about your PEERS (mean) _____

      4) Your beliefs about TOP MANAGEMENT (mean) _____

      5) The FREQUENCY with which YOU would engage in the 17 behaviors (mean) _____

      6) The FREQUENCY with which you believe YOUR PEERS would engage in the 17 behaviors (mean) _____

b.   Do you see your beliefs being more closely aligned with those of top management or your peers? How can this be explained?

c. Was it your belief that you or your peers more frequently engage in these types of behaviors (compare the mean figures for parts 5 and 6 in part "a" above)? How can this discrepancy be explained?

d. If you had to put a price tag on the cost of such unethical practices to an organization employing 1,000 people, what would this figure be? Explain.

e. What can be done to diminish unethical acts (such as the 17 mentioned above) from occurring in the business organization in which you currently work (or the business organization for which you hope to work after finishing your college education)?

Exercise 5

Your instructor will conduct a general class discussion of your reactions to the issues raised in Exercise 4. Come prepared to discuss your observations. Use the space below to note the especially pertinent points that are raised in the discussion that you may have overlooked.

Exercise 6

Your instructor will share the responses of a sample of 121 managers (Newstrom and Ruch Study) who were asked to react to the same issues you were asked to respond to in Figures 3.1, 3.2, and 3.3. In general, the respondents were male, married, ranging in age from thirty to fifty years, were earning a yearly salary between $11,000 and $25,000 in 1975 (salaries approximately equal to $22,000 and $50,000 in 1993), and worked in business, government, or public utilities. After perusing these statistics, with which mean figure reflecting beliefs (manager, managers' peers, or top management) do you most closely compare? With which mean figure for frequency (manager or managers' peers) do you most closely compare? Explain. Now that you have compared your responses with those of the managerial group, what additional generalizations can you make?

Exercise 7

What have you personally gained from this experience?

Experience 3-4   Assessing Your Ethicality******

Introduction

Many situations encountered in day-to-day business activity are not simply right or wrong, black or white. Rather, they often fall into that gray area that makes deciding what to do a difficult task. Of all the decisions that challenge managers today, decisions involving ethical issues may be some of the toughest to reach. In fact, there may be some ethical issues that you have yet to experience that should be confronted before you can argue that you are fully prepared to face such situations in the real-world. The experience that follows was designed to help you identify those issues so that you will be better prepared to deal with them should they occur.

Exercise 1

Complete the ethics self-assessment test below to identify the areas that you must further ponder as you continue your preparation for that (current/first/next) real-world job.

******Questionnaire Source: Lowell G. Rein, "Is Your (Ethical) Slippage Showing?" *Personnel Journal* (September 1980):743. Used with permission.

ETHICS SELF-ASSESSMENT TEST

Instructions: Based upon your degree of agreement/disagreement with each of the following statements, check one of the following response categories.

Strongly Agree = SA   Disagree = D
Agree = A   Strongly Disagree = SD

	SA	A	D	SD
1. Employees should not be expected to inform on their peers for wrongdoings.	—	—	—	—
2. There are times when a manager must overlook contract and safety violations in order to get on with the job.	—	—	—	—
3. It is not always possible to keep accurate expense account records; therefore, it is sometimes necessary to give approximate figures.	—	—	—	—
4. There are times when it is necessary to withhold embarrassing information from one's superior.	—	—	—	—
5. We should do what our managers suggest, though we may have doubts about its being the right thing to do.	—	—	—	—
6. It is sometimes necessary to conduct personal business on company time.	—	—	—	—
7. Sometimes it is good psychology to set goals somewhat above normal if it will help to obtain a greater effort from the sales force.	—	—	—	—
8. I would quote a "hopeful" shipping date in order to get the order.	—	—	—	—
9. It is proper to use the company WATS line for personal calls as long as it's not in company use.	—	—	—	—
10. Management must be goal oriented; therefore, the end usually justifies the means.	—	—	—	—
11. If it takes heavy entertainment and twisting a bit of company policy to win a large contract, I would authorize it.	—	—	—	—
12. Exceptions to company policy and procedures are a way of life.	—	—	—	—
13. Inventory controls should be designed to report "underages" rather than "overages" in goods received. (The ethical issue here is the same as that faced by someone who receives too much change from a store cashier.)	—	—	—	—
14. Occasional use of the company's copier for personal or community activities is acceptable.	—	—	—	—
15. Taking home company property (pencils, paper, tape, and so on) for personal use is an accepted fringe benefit.	—	—	—	—

Exercise 2

After your instructor has provided you with the "Ethics Self-Assessment Test Scoring Key," reexamine the situations with which you "strongly agreed" or "agreed." Use the space below to explain the reasoning that underlay each of these favorable responses.

Exercise 3

Compare your logic (for the strongly agrees/agrees) in Exercise 2 above to any two of the following seven ethical standards. Do you still believe your justification(s) to be acceptable reasoning for these favorable responses? Explain in the space provided below.

Ethical Standards:
1. The golden rule
2. The utilitarian principle
3. Kant's categorical imperative
4. The professional ethic
5. The TV test
6. The legal test
7. The four-way test

Exercise 4

As you now know, agreeing with any of the 15 situations presented in the "Ethics Self-Assessment Test" would put you in conflict with most if not all of the ethical standards and generally reflects questionable business practices from an ethical perspective. Use the space below to explain what you have learned about yourself.

4 ORGANIZATIONAL OBJECTIVES

Chapter Summary

This chapter can help prospective managers gain a broad appreciation of how managers can use objectives to appropriately guide organizations to success. It discusses the general nature of organizational objectives, different types of organizational objectives, various areas in which organizational objectives should be set, how managers actually work with organizational objectives, and management by objectives (MBO).

Learning Objective 1   *An understanding of organizational objectives*

Organizational objectives are the targets toward which the open management system is directed. Organizational input, process, and output exist to reach organizational objectives. If properly developed, organizational objectives reflect organizational purpose--what the organization exists to do.

Organizations exist for various purposes and thus have various types of organizational objectives. In a classic article, John F. Mee has suggested that organizational objectives for businesses can be summarized as follows: (1) profit is the motivating force for managers; (2) service to customers justifies the existence of the business; and (3) social responsibilities exist for managers in accordance with ethical and moral codes established by the society in which the industry resides.

One of the most important actions managers take is deciding upon the objectives for an organization. Unrealistically high objectives are frustrating for employees while objectives that are too low do not push employees to maximize their potential. Managers should establish performance objectives that they know from experience are within reach for employees, but not within easy reach.

Learning Objective 2   *An appreciation for the importance of organizational objectives*

The clear identification of organizational objectives gives managers and all other organization members important guidelines for action in such areas as decision making, organizational efficiency, organizational consistency, and performance evaluation.

Once managers have a clear understanding of organizational objectives, they know the direction in which the organization must move. It then becomes their responsibility to make decisions that move the organization toward the achievement of organizational objectives.

Clearly identified organizational objectives also can increase organizational efficiency. Efficiency is defined in terms of the total amount of human effort and resources an organization uses to achieve organizational goals. Therefore, before organizational efficiency can improve, managers must have a clear understanding of organizational goals.

Organizational objectives also can establish consistency. If organizational objectives are the basis for work-related directives, the objectives serve as a guide to consistently encourage such things a productive activity, quality decision making, and effective planning.

Finally, organizational goals are the guidelines or criteria that should be the basis for performance evaluations of all organization members. Specific recommendations on increasing productivity should be comprised of suggestions about what individuals can do to better help the organization move toward goal attainment.

Learning Objective 3   *An ability to tell the difference between organizational objectives and individual objectives*

Objectives can be separated into two categories: organizational objectives and individual objectives. **Organizational objectives** are the formal targets of the organization and are set to help the organization accomplish its purpose. They concern such areas as organizational efficiency, high productivity, and profit maximization. **Individual objectives** are the personal goals each organization member would like to reach as a result of his or her activity within the organization. These objectives might include high salary, personal growth and development, peer recognition, and societal recognition.

A management problem arises when organizational objectives and individual objectives are not compatible. When this occurs, one alternative available to managers is structuring the organization so that individuals have the opportunity to accomplish individual objectives while contributing to organizational goal attainment.

Barrett's **goal integration model** can assist managers trying to understand and solve problems related to conflict between organizational and individual objectives. Barrett's model consists of two circles: one circle represents organizational objectives and the other circle represents individual objectives. The overlap (interface) of the two circles represents the extent of compatibility (extent of goal integration) that exists between individual and organizational goals. The individual in this model will tend to work for organizational goals in the overlapping area without much management encouragement because the attainment of these goals will result in some type of reward that individual considers valuable. However, this individual usually will not work for other organizational goals without some significant type of management encouragement because the attainment of these goals holds little promise of reward the individual considers valuable. Barrett suggests that "significant types of management encouragement" could be modifications to existing pay schedules, considerate treatment from superiors, and additional opportunities to engage in informal social relationships with peers.

Learning Objective 4   *A knowledge of the areas in which managers should set organizational objectives*

Peter F. Drucker, a very influential management writer, indicates that the very survival of an organization may be endangered if managers emphasize only a profit objective. In practice, managers should strive to develop and attain a variety of objectives. Drucker advises managers to set organizational objectives in the following areas: (1) market standing, (2) innovation, (3) productivity, (4) physical and financial resources, (5) profitability, (6) managerial performance and development, (7) worker performance and attitude, and (8) public responsibility. Drucker feels that, since the first five goal areas relate to tangible, impersonal characteristics of organizational operation, most managers would not dispute the designation of these as key areas. Designation of the last three as key areas could arouse some managerial opposition, however, since these areas are more personal and subjective.

Learning Objective 5   *An understanding of the development of organizational objectives*

Appropriate objectives are fundamental to the success of any organization. Therefore, any manager should approach the development, use, and modification of organizational objectives with utmost seriousness. In general, an organization should have **short-tun objectives** (targets to be achieved within from one year or less), **intermediate-run objectives** (targets to be achieved within from one to five years), and **long-run objectives** (targets to be achieved within from five to seven years). The necessity of predetermining appropriate organizational objectives has led to the development of what is called the **principle of the objective**. This principle recommends that, before managers initiate any action, organizational objectives should be clearly determined, understood, and stated. Setting objectives is increasingly becoming a required and important part of a manager's job. Managers are commonly being asked to establish objectives for themselves, their departments, and their employees.

Managers must take three main steps to develop a set of working organizational objectives. First, managers must determine the existence of any environmental trends that could significantly influence the operation of the organization. They should list the major trends that have existed in the organizational environment over the past five years and determine if these trends have had a noticeable impact on organizational success. Managers should then decide which present trends and which new trends are likely to affect organizational success over the next five years. The trends could include such factors as changing customer needs, marketing innovations of competitors or governmental controls.

The second step in developing a set of working organizational objectives is that managers should develop objectives that reflect the analysis of environmental trends for the organization as a whole. For example, if analysis shows that a major competitor has been continually improving its products over the past five years and, as a result, has gained an increasingly larger share of the market, management probably should set a product improvement objective in an effort to keep up with competitors.

Financial, product-market mix, and functional objectives are common objectives developed for most organizations. In many organizations, the setting of **financial objectives** (organizational targets relating to monetary issues) is influenced mainly by return on investment and a financial comparison of an organization with its competitors. Return on investment (ROI) is the amount of money an organization earns in relation to the amount of money invested to keep the organization in operation. If the calculated return on investment is too low, managers can set an overall objective to improve the organization's rate of return. In addition, comparing company figures with Dun and Bradstreet's *Ratios for Selected Industries* should tell managers in which areas new financial objectives probably should be set or ways in which existing objectives should be modified. **Product-market mix objectives** outline which products--and the relative number or mix of these products--the organization will attempt to sell. Granger suggests the following five steps for formulating product-market mix objectives: (1) examination of key trends in the business environments of the product-market areas; (2) examination of growth trends and profit trends in the individual product mix areas; (3) separation of product-market areas into those that are going to pull ahead and those that are going to drag; (4) consideration of the need or desirability of adding new products or market areas to the mix; and (5) derivation of an optimum yet realistic product-market mix profile based on the conclusions reached in steps 1-4.

Functional objectives are targets relating to key organizational functions, such as marketing, accounting, production, and personnel. Functional objectives that are consistent with the financial and product-market mix objectives should be developed for these areas.

The third step in developing a set of working organizational objectives is that each objective must be broken down into subobjectives so that individuals in different levels and sections of the organization know what they must do to help reach the overall organizational objective. The overall organizational objective and the subobjectives assigned to the various people or units of the organization are referred to as a **hierarchy of objectives**. Basic to the hierarchy of objectives concept is the idea that objectives for an entire organization are reached through the accomplishment of subobjectives. **Suboptimization** exists when subobjectives are conflicting or not directly aimed at accomplishing the overall organizational objective. For example, suboptimization would exist if supervisors needed new equipment to maintain their production, but the finance and accounting department could not approve the loan because it would result in company borrowing surpassing 50 percent of company assets. In this situation, a manager would have to choose which subobjective would best contribute to obtaining overall objectives and should therefore take precedence. Managers can attempt to minimize suboptimization by developing a thorough understanding of how various parts of the organization relate to one another and then making sure that subobjectives properly reflect these relationships.

Learning Objective 6   *Some facility in writing good objectives*

Managers can increase the quality of their objectives by following some **general guidelines**. Managers should: (1) allow the people responsible for attaining the objectives to have a voice in setting them; (2) state objectives as specifically as possible; (3) relate objectives to specific actions; (4) pinpoint expected results; (5) set goals high enough, but not so high that employees give up trying to reach them; (6) identify deadlines by which goals are to be achieved; (7) set objectives only in relation to other organizational objectives; and (8) state objectives clearly and simply.

Objectives must be stated in operational terms to be useful. If an organization has operational objectives, managers should be able to tell if the objectives are being attained by comparing the actual results with goal statements. For example, a physical education instructor might state that students should strive to develop a sense of balance or should work on becoming powerful. These objectives are not operational because the activities or operations a student must perform to attain the objectives are not specified. An operational objective for power could be: Each student will strive to develop the power to do standing broad jumps the distance of his or her height plus one foot.

Learning Objective 7   *An awareness of how managers use organizational objectives and help others to attain the objectives*

Attainment of organizational objectives is the obvious goal of all conscientious managers. Mangers quickly discover, however, that moving the organization toward goal attainment requires taking appropriate means or actions within the organization to reach the desired ends. This process is called **means-ends analysis** and entails starting with the general goal to be achieved, discovering a set of means for accomplishing this goal, and then taking each of these means as a new subgoal and discovering a more detailed means for achieving it. Effective managers are aware of the importance of not only setting organizational objectives, but clearly outlining the means by which these objectives can be attained.

Organizational objectives flow naturally from organizational purpose and reflect the organization's environment. If, however, the organizational purpose or the organizational environment changes, new organizational objectives must be developed. Objectives are not unchangeable directives. In fact, a significant managerial responsibility is to help the organization change objectives when necessary.

Learning Objective 8   *An appreciation for the potential of a management by objectives (MBO) program*

Some managers believe that organizational objectives are such an important part of management that they use a management approach based exclusively on organizational objectives. This approach, called **management by objectives (MBO)**, has three main parts: (1) all individuals within an organization have a specific set of objectives they try to reach during an operating period (these objectives are mutually set and agreed upon by individuals and their managers); (2) periodic performance reviews are conducted to determine how well individuals are attaining their objectives; and (3) organization members are rewarded on how well they were able to reach their goals. The MBO process contains five steps: (1) reviewing organizational objectives, (2) setting worker objectives, (3) monitoring progress, (4) evaluating performance, and (5) giving rewards.

Certain key factors are necessary for an MBO program to be successful. First, top management must be comitted to the MBO process and set appropriate objectives for the overall organization. If overall objectives are inappropriate, individual MBO objectives also are inappropriate, and the related individual work activity is nonproductive. Second, managers and subordinates together must develop and agree on each individual's goals. Both parties must feel that the individual objectives are just and appropriate if the objectives are to be effective guides for action. Third, employee performance should be conscientiously evaluated against established objectives. Finally, after a comparison of employee performance with the established objectives, employee performance should be rewarded accordingly. If employees are to continue to strive to reach their MBO objectives, management must reward those employees who reach or surpass their objectives more than those who perform well below their objectives. Management must be careful, however, not to always conclude that employees have produced at an acceptable level simply because they have reached their objectives. The objectives that were set for the employees may have been set too low in the first place and management failed to recognize it at the time.

MBO programs have advantages and disadvantages. Experienced MBO managers say that one advantage of MBO is that it continually emphasizes what should be done in an organization to achieve organizational goals. MBO also tends to secure employee commitment to attaining organizational goals. Because managers and subordinates have developed objectives together, both parties are more interested in working together to reach those goals. One disadvantage, however, is that the process of jointly developing objectives is time consuming and frequently generates a large volume of paperwork. Even so, most managers think that MBO's advantages outweigh its disadvantages.

Knowing You Know

True/False   *Directions: On the lines provided, place a "T" for true or an "F" for false for each of the statements that follow.*

_____ 1.   Objectives give managers and all other organization members important guidelines for action.
_____ 2.   While organizational objectives serve as guidelines in such areas as decision making, organizational efficiency, and organizational consistency, they are too general to be used for performance evaluation.
_____ 3.   Managers appreciate situations where there is compatibility between individual and organizational objectives.
_____ 4.   The survival of an organization may be endangered if managers emphasize only a profit objective.
_____ 5.   Short-run objectives are targets to be achieved within from one year or less; long-run objectives are targets to be achieved within from one to five years.
_____ 6.   The three steps that managers must take to develop a set of working objectives for their organization are: (1) determine the existence of any environmental trends that could influence the organization's operation, (2) develop a set of objectives for the organization as a whole, and (3) develop a hierarchy of organizational objectives.
_____ 7.   If a company earned $100,000 and invested $200,000, the ROI would be 5 percent.
_____ 8.   One important guideline for establishing quality objectives is that managers should state objectives in general terms so that employees can use their own discretion in meeting the objectives.
_____ 9.   Attainment of organizational objectives is the obvious desired goal of all conscientious managers.
_____ 10.   Management should consider organizational objectives as unchangeable directives to guide action.
_____ 11.   A comparison of Dun and Bradstreet's *Ratios for Selected Industries* with company figures would tell management in which areas new financial objectives probably should be set or ways in which existing objectives should be modified.
_____ 12.   One disadvantage of MBO is that it infrequently results in employee commitment to attainment of organizational goals.
_____ 13.   The first step in setting organizational objectives is to list major trends that have existed in the organizational environment over the past five years and determine if these trends have had a noticeable impact on organizational success.

Matching

Directions: Match items 14-25 with items a-l. There is only one correct answer for each item.

_____ 14. Hierarchy of objectives
_____ 15. Organizational objectives
_____ 16. Management by objectives
_____ 17. Suboptimization
_____ 18. Operational objectives
_____ 19. Functional objectives
_____ 20. Primary business objective
_____ 21. Goal integration model
_____ 22. Individual objectives
_____ 23. Financial objectives
_____ 24. Objectives are guidelines for
_____ 25. Guideline for establishing quality objectives

a. When subobjectives are conflicting or not directly aimed at accomplishing the overall organizational objectives

b. Influenced by return on investment and a comparison of an organization with its competitors activities that take place within the organization

c. Specify the activities or operations needed to attain them

d. Targets toward which the open management system is directed

e. Objectives developed for key areas, such as marketing, accounting, and personnel

f. Goals each organization member would like to accomplish as a result of his or her activity within the organization

g. Making a profit

h. Can assist managers in understanding and solving problems related to conflict between organizational and individual objectives

i. The overall organizational objective and sub-objectives assigned to various segments of the organization

j. Objectives are mutually set and agreed upon by individuals and their managers

k. Performance evaluation, decision making, organizational consistency, and organizational efficiency

l. Managers should specify when goals are expected to be achieved

Applying What You Know

Experience 4-1   Establishing and Operationalizing Objectives

Introduction

Organizational objectives are the targets toward which an open management system is directed. However, vague or poorly worded objectives provide neither managers nor employees with much insight or direction. This experience is designed to develop your ability to establish quality objectives and to operationalize those objectives.

Exercise 1

For each of the three objectives that follow, identify the major guidelines for establishing quality objectives that have been overlooked and then rewrite the objective to eliminate the deficiencies you identified.

a. "An objective of the production department is to increase per capital output per hour."

   1. Overlooked guidelines:

   2. Rewritten objective statement:

b. "It is our corporate objective to reduce overtime by 5 percent."

   1. Overlooked guidelines:

   2. Rewritten objective statement:

c. "An objective of the maintenance department is to keep production equipment functioning properly with minimum interruptions to production scheduling."

    1. Overlooked guidelines:

    2. Rewritten objective statement:

Exercise 2

Explain what must be done to operationalize the rewritten objective in exercise 1.

Exercise 3

Re-examine objective statements b and c in exercise 1. Would you expect any conflict if these were objective statements in the same, large corporation? How could this situation have been avoided? Refer to the guidelines for establishing quality objectives in your text. Use appropriate terminology in your explanation.

Experience 4-2 Reevaluating Organizational Objectives

Introduction

As the text indicates, financial objectives, product-market mix objectives, and functional objectives are developed for most organizations as a whole. In this experience, you utilize your knowledge of objectives in these areas. Read the incident and then complete the exercises as directed.

Incident

Rodney Fargo, president of Strong-Arm Cork Company, has just learned that company earnings are down from earnings last year. While Fargo feels that this turn of events is cause for reevaluation of the company's major objectives, his schedule does not permit him to personally perform the analysis. Fargo's assistant, Dean Dau, therefore, has been assigned the task. After considerable research, Dau isolates some areas where objective reevaluation may be merited. He, however, wants your advice. Figure 4.1 shows the information that Dau feels may be important.

Figure 4.1   Dau's data

FROM THE DESK OF DEAN DAU		
Strong-Arm Cork Co.	1994	1993
Earnings after taxes	*$43,150	$44,160
Total investments	$575,335	$537,121
Percent increase in net sales	13.8%	12.8%
Sales by Product Class		
Floor coverings	$431,200	$293,600
Ceilings	132,610	108,050
Furniture	8,363	99,110
Total interior furnishings	572,173	500,760
Industrial and other products and services	74,183	67,111
Net Sales	$646,356	$567,871
Advertising Expenses by Product Class		
Floor coverings	$5,116	$5,312
Ceilings	3,161	3,111
Furniture	2,115	867
Total advertising expenses (interiors)	10,392	9,290
Industrial and other products and services	692	678
Net Advertising Expense	$11,084	$9,968
Industry Information		
ROI (industry average)	8.9%	8.3%
Percent increase in net sales (industry average)	16.7%	12.7%

*(000)

Exercise 1

Analyze Dau's notations. Make any calculations or jot down any information that you feel supports a reevaluation of company objectives.

Exercise 2

Write a formal memo to Dau, identifying the area or areas in which you feel organizational objectives should be reevaluated. Support your advice whenever possible.

Memorandum

To:

From:

Subject: Reevaluation of objectives

Experience 4-3   The Objective-Setting Interview (MBO)

Introduction

This experience is designed to increase your understanding of an important aspect of management by objectives: the objective-setting interview. From reading your text, you know that objectives are mutually set and agreed upon by individual subordinates and their immediate supervisors. But you probably have not given much thought to what subordinates or supervisors do **before, during, or after the objective-setting interview.** Since managers can be a subordinate in an MBO interview (for example, a supervisor in an objective-setting interview with a middle-level manager) and a supervisor in an

MBO interview (for example, a supervisor in an objective-setting interview with a line employee), knowledge of both roles is very important. Read the Carbox Company incident and then complete the exercises as directed.

Incident

The Carbox Company makes pasteboard after-shave and cologne boxes for three of the major companies producing men's grooming aids. Most of the two hundred employees of Carbox operate one of a variety of mechanized folding, cutting, or pasting machines. However, within the past week, Carbox has accepted a special contract from one of its customers. This new contract calls for the manual folding of 8-1/2-by-11-inch posters of celebrities into 4-1/4-by-5-1/2-inch lids for men's cologne boxes. The customer predicts that, if the folding operation can be performed so that posters can be unfolded by consumers without being damaged, the customer's cologne sales will increase dramatically. Carbox Company has decided to make the lids using the origami method outlined in figure 4.2 because no cutting or pasting is required. Six employees will be hired to perform the poster-folding operation. The management by objectives approach is used throughout the organization.

Figure 4.2   Origami instruction sheet.[*]

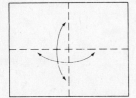

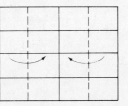

1. Begin with a sheet of paper
    8½" x 11" and make creases
    for vertical and horizontal
    center lines.

2. Fold the narrow sides up to
    the center line. Then unfold.

3. Now fold the wide sides to the vertical
    center line and unfold again. (Fold
    the first sides narrower than the second
    if you are using a square sheet.)

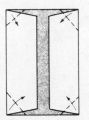
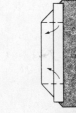
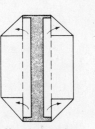
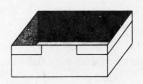

4. Using the valley fold, diagonal-
    fold corners from the folded
    edges to crease lines.

5. Now the raw edges
    may be folded over
    the folded corners.

6. Open up the sides
    and, as shown,
    reverse the folds.

7. The finished box.

Exercise 1

Assume that you are one of the six employees hired to perform the poster-folding operation. Explain what you should do to prepare for the objective-setting interview with your supervisor, what you should do during the interview, and what you should do after the interview.

[*]From *The Practical Encyclopedia of Crafts* by Maria DiValentin/Louis DiVanentin, © 1970, published by Sterline Publishing Co., Inc., New York.

Exercise 2

Assume that you are the supervisor of the six employees hired to perform the poster-folding operation. Explain what you should do to prepare for the objective-setting interview with each of your six immediate subordinates, what you should do during the interview, and what you should do after the interview.

Exercise 3

Explain what you have gained from this experience.

Experience 4-4 Balancing Multiple Objectives[**]

Introduction

This experience demonstrates the practical problems faced by managers who must attempt to balance a system in which there are multiple objectives and conflicting demands. Form a small group with three or four other class members and familiarize yourselves with the incident that follows; then complete the exercises as directed.

Incident

You are managers of a relatively small manufacturing firm with sales of about $25 million per year. In recent years, your sales have increased somewhat, but rising costs have resulted in two successive years of operating in the red. Last year (the worst), you lost approximately $150,000. Altogether you employ about 800 people, including 130 supervisory, technical, and professional people. Turnover is fairly high, employee morale is declining, customer complaints are increasing, and much of your equipment is getting old. Competition from several major competitors is increasing. The market for the industry looks good in the long run.

Exercise 1

a. Your company is faced with the five problems that follow. Individually, review each problem and decide what you think should be done. Then note your decision in box 1 on the summary sheet in figure 4.3.
b. Arrive at a group decision regarding what to do about each problem, again noting the group decision in box 1 on the summary sheet in figure 4.3.

Balancing Multiple Objectives: Company Problems

1. Your market research staff has projected a strong increase in demand for products like yours over the next five years. Several competitors have been carrying out active research and development programs on product design, and your research and development expenditures are below the industry average. You have been operating the plant at close to a capacity level.
   Choice a: Increase the research and development budget by $80,000 next year and invest a minimum of $800,000 to increase production capacity. (These are the minimum amounts that will do any good.)
   Choice b: Take no action now.
   Choice c: Other_____

2. Although your safety record is better than average, there still is a 40 percent probability of at least one serious injury or death a year due to physical hazards outside of employee control. Your safety director estimates that spending $130,000 will reduce the probabilities of such a serious accident to about 10 percent.
   Choice a: Spend $130,000.
   Choice b: Take no action now.
   Choice c: Other_____

3. One of your new products has sold very well. However, last year the number of units returned by customers for repairs under the warranty was relatively high, and service costs were a serious problem. Improved quality control, at a cost of $280,000 (for inspections and for modification of certain problem components), could reduce the warranty expense to a reasonable level within two years.
   Choice a: Spend $280,000 now on the quality control problem.
   Choice b: Take no action now.
   Choice c: Other_____

[**]Source of Experience 4-4: Adapted from Vaughan, James A., and Samuel D. Deep, *Program of Exercises for Management and Organizational Behavior.* © 1975 Glencoe Press, Encino, CA. Reprinted by permission of the authors.

4. Certain of your plant operations create problems in the surrounding community, partly because of noise but mostly because of smoke and air pollution. You meet current legal standards for air pollution control. However, you could further reduce the pollution problem by purchasing $300,000 worth of special filtration equipment. Use of such equipment probably would pacify the very active local Environmental Protection Citizens Committee.

   Choice a: Spend the $300,000.

   Choice b: Take no action now.

   Choice c: Other_____

5. Turnover of supervisory and professional employees is proving extremely costly. A reputable consultant has recommended instituting a comprehensive personnel selection and training program and also revising the pay system for salaried employees. This would cost over $200,000 per year, mostly in increased salary expenses. You hope it would improve morale, the quality of supervisory performance, etc.

   Choice a: Spend the $200,000.

   Choice b: Take no action now.

   Choice c: Other_____

Figure 4.3   Summary sheet.

	Problems				
	1–Invest.	2–Safety	3–Q.C.	4–Pollut.	5–Pers.
Your decisions					
Group decisions					

Objectives	Your ranking	Impact of Objectives on Decisions, in %					Average %
		Problem 1	Problem 2	Problem 3	Problem 4	Problem 5	
Profit							
Maintain or increase market share							
Smooth, efficient internal operations							
High quality products							
Good public reputation							
Good employee morale and welfare							
		100%	100%	100%	100%	100%	100%

Name _____

Exercise 2

a.   Refer to box 2 on the summary sheet in figure 4.3, which gives a list of six possible objectives for your company. Individually, rank order those objectives and record your rankings on the summary sheet.

b.   Within your group, compare individual rankings of the six objectives. If appropriate, revise your personal rankings after group discussion.

Exercise 3

As a group, discuss the impact your views on objectives may have had on your decisions about how to deal with the five problems.

a.   Taking the problems one at a time, consider the decision of your group and estimate the relative impact of each of the objectives on that decision. For example, in problem 1 on research and development and investment decisions, how much weight did the profit objective have? Assign a percentage to each of the six objectives so that the sum of the percentages is 100 percent. Do this for each of the five problems and record the group decision (consensus) in box 3 on the summary sheet in figure 4.3.

b.   To assess the relative weight of each objective as you dealt with the total set of problems, calculate the average percent assigned to each objective and record the percent in the far right-hand column in box 3 on the summary sheet in figure 4.3.

Exercise 4

Discuss the implications of this experience. Compare the views of different groups in the class to the questions that follow, among others. Use the space provided to write your reactions to these questions.

a.   Do decisions about solving problems adequately reflect personal objectives? Why or why not?

b.   To what extent can decisions about investment, safety, social responsibility, product quality, customer satisfaction, efficiency, etc. be made with only one objective in mind?

c.   How does the time perspective--short or long run--affect problem solving?

d.   What does the experience suggest about the relationship between objectives, planning, and decision making?

e.   What does the experience suggest about the key tasks of managers?

f.   Does having specific dollar figures or probability estimates help in making decisions? Should statements of objectives include specific figures?

Exercise 5

Answer the questions that follow about this experience.

a.   In your opinion, how should managers make decisions on allocating resources when their organizations have several (possibly competing) objectives?

b.   What did you observe about yourself or others as you participated in this experience?

c.   What are the implications of this experience to you personally? (Did you learn anything new? Get new insights? Have old ideas reinforced? Identify things you want to learn more about? Change your approaches? etc.)

5 FUNDAMENTALS OF PLANNING

Chapter Summary

This chapter (1) outlines the general characteristics of planning; (2) discusses steps in the planning process; (3) describes the planning subsystem; (4) elaborates upon the relationship between planning and the chief executive; (5) summarizes the qualifications and duties of planners and how planners are evaluated; and (6) explains how to maximize the effectiveness of the planning process.

Learning Objective 1   *A definition of planning and an understanding of the purposes of planning*

Planning is the process of determining how the organization can reach its goals and what exactly the organization will do to accomplish its objectives. Jones defines planning as "the systematic development of action programs aimed at reaching agreed business objectives by the process of analyzing, evaluating, and selecting among the opportunities which are foreseen."

Planning is a critical management activity regardless of the type of organization being managed. Modern managers face the challenge of sound planning in small and relatively simple organizations as well as large, more complex organizations. In addition, challenges of planning face managers of nonprofit organizations as well as for-profit organizations.

Over the years, management writers have presented several different purposes of planning. C. W. Roney indicates that organizational planning has two purposes: protective and affirmative. The **protective purpose of planning** is to minimize risk by reducing the uncertainties surrounding business conditions and clarifying the consequences of related management action. The **affirmative purpose of planning** is to increase the degree of organizational success. Another purpose of planning is to establish a coordinated effort within the organization. The *fundamental* purpose of planning, however, is to help the organization reach its objectives. All other purposes of planning are simply spin-offs of this fundamental purpose.

Learning Objective 2   *A knowledge of the advantages and potential disadvantages of planning*

One advantage to planning is that it helps managers to be future oriented. They are forced to look beyond their normal everyday problems to project what may face them in the future. Decision coordination is a second advantage of a sound planning program. A decision should not be made today without some idea of how it will affect a decision that will have to be made tomorrow. The planning function assists managers in coordinating decisions. A third advantage to planning is that it emphasizes organizational objectives, which are the starting points for planning. Overall, planning is very advantageous to an organization. According to a recent survey, as many as 65% of all newly started businesses are not around to celebrate a 5th anniversary. This high failure rate seems primarily due to inadequate planning within the new businesses. Successful businesses have an established plan, a formal statement that outlines the objectives the organization is attempting to achieve. Planning does not eliminate risk, but it can help managers to identify and eliminate organizational problems before they arise.

If, however, the planning function is not well executed within the organization, planning can have several disadvantages. For example, an overemphasized planning program can take up too much managerial time. Managers must strike an appropriate balance between time spent on planning and time spent on organizing, influencing, and controlling.

Planning is the **primary** management function--the function that precedes and is the foundation for the organizing, influencing, and controlling functions of managers. Only after managers have developed their plans can they determine how they want to structure their organization, place their people, and establish organizational controls.

Learning Objective 3   *Insights on how the major steps of the planning process are related*

The **planning process has six major steps**: (1) stating organizational objectives, (2) listing alternative ways of reaching organizational objectives, (3) developing premises upon which each alternative is based, (4) choosing the best alternative for reaching objectives, (5) developing plans to pursue the chosen alternative, and (6) putting the plans into action. A clear statement of organizational objectives is necessary for planning to begin because planning focuses on how the management system will reach those objectives. Once organizational objectives have been clearly stated, a manager should list as many available alternatives as possible for reaching those objectives. The feasibility of using any one alternative to reach organizational objectives is largely determined by the premises, or assumptions, upon which the alternative is based. For example, one alternative that could be used to attain an organizational objective of increased profits might be increasing the sales of products presently being produced. This alternative would be based on the premise or assumption that the organization could get a larger share of an existing market. An evaluation of alternatives must include an evaluation of the premises upon which the alternatives are based. A manager usually finds that the premises upon which some alternatives are based are unreasonable, and he or she can therefore exclude those alternatives from further consideration. After an alternative has been chosen, a manager begins to develop strategic (long-range) and tactical (short-range) plans. Once plans have been developed, they are ready to be put into action. The plans should furnish the organization with both long-range and short-range direction for activity.

Learning Objective 4　　*An understanding of the planning subsystem*

Even though managers might be experts on facts related to planning and the planning process, if they cannot transform this understanding into appropriate action, they are not able to generate useful organizational plans. One way of approaching this implementation is to view planning activities as an organizational subsystem. A subsystem is a system created as part of the process of the overall management system. The purpose of the planing subsystem is to increase the effectiveness of the overall management system through more effective planning. Obviously, only a portion of organizational resources are used as input in the planning subsystem. This input is allocated to the planning subsystem and transformed into output by following the steps of the planning process.

Planning subsystems in the industrial world can be formal or informal. At Quaker Oats Company, speculations about the future are conducted, for the most part, on an informal basis. To help anticipate particular future social changes, the company has opened communication lines with various groups believed to be the harbingers of change. To spearhead this activity, a company "noncommittee" listens to what is going on--monitors social changes--and thus augments the company's understanding of social change. There are many companies throughout the world like Quaker Oats that plan on somewhat of an informal basis.

At Sun Oil Company, however, several groups are engaged in formal business planning and forecasting. Operational planning with a five-year horizon is done annually. A centralized planning group, reporting to the vice-president of development and planning, is responsible for assisting top management in setting the company's long-term objectives, developing plans to achieve these objectives, and identifying likely consumer needs and market developments of the future that might indicate business areas for diversification. Current efforts are focused on discussing a series of long-range issues with the executive committee, a planning process designed to generate a restatement of long-term objectives.

Learning Objective 5　　*A knowledge of how the chief executive relates to the planning process*

According to Mintzberg, top managers or chief executives of organizations have many different **roles to perform**. As organizational *figureheads*, they must represent their organizations in a variety of social, legal, and ceremonial matters. As *leaders*, they must ensure that organization members are properly guided in relation to organizational goals. As *liaisons*, they must establish themselves as links between their organizations and factors outside their organizations. As *monitors*, they must assess organizational progress. As *disturbance handlers*, they must settle disputes between organization members. And as *resource allocators*, they must determine where resources will be placed to benefit their organizations best.

In addition, chief executives have the final responsibility for organizational planning. As planners, chief executives determine the direction in which the organization should be going, the direction in which the organization is presently going, whether changes in direction are appropriate, and whether the organization is continuing in an appropriate direction. Information about social, political, and scientific trends is of utmost importance to chief executives in these determinations. Given both the importance of top management participation in organizational planning and the importance of top management performing other time-consuming roles, more and more top managers obtain planning assistance by establishing a position for an organization planner.

Learning Objective 6　　*An understanding of the qualifications and duties of planners and how planners are evaluated*

Perhaps the most important input in the planning subsystem is the planner. This individual combines all other input and influences subsystem process so that effective organizational plans become subsystem output. The planner is responsible not only for the plans that are developed but also for advising management about what action should be taken in relation to those plans.

One of the major **qualifications of the organization planner** is that the individual has considerable practical experience within the organization. Preferably, the planner should have been an executive in one or more of the organization's major departments. This experience should help the planner to develop plans that are practical and tailor-made for the organization. In addition, the planner should be able to replace any narrow view of the organization (probably acquired while holding other organizational positions) with an understanding of the organization as a whole. The planner must know how all parts of the organization function and interrelate. In other words, he or she must possess an abundance of conceptual skills. Third, the planner should have some knowledge of and interest in the social, political, technical, and economic trends that could affect the future of the organization. The planner must have the skill to define these trends and the expertise to determine how the organization should react to them to maximize success. The fourth and last qualification is that the planner should be able to work well with others. He or she inevitably will work closely with several key members of the organization and should possess personal characteristics that are helpful in collaborating and advising effectively. One of the most important of these characteristics is the ability to communicate clearly.

The organization planner has at least **three general duties to perform**. First, the planner must see that planning gets done. To this end, the planner establishes rules, guidelines, and planning objectives that apply to the planner and others involved in the planning process. In essence, the planner must develop a plan for planning, a listing of all of the steps that must be taken to plan for an organization. The second general duty of the planner is to evaluate plans that have been developed. The planner must decide if plans are sufficiently challenging for the organization, if plans are complete, and if plans are consistent with organizational objectives. If the developed plans do not fulfill these three requirements, they should be modified appropriately. The third general duty of the planner is to gather information that will help solve planning problems. Sometimes, the planner may find it necessary to conduct special studies within the organization to obtain this information. The planner then can recommend actions to deal with these problems. For example, a planner may observe that production objectives set by the organization are not being met. This is a symptom of a planning problem. The problem causing this symptom might be that objectives are unrealistically high or that plans developed to achieve production objectives are inappropriate. The planner must gather information pertinent to the problem and suggest to management how the organization can solve its problem and become more successful. Other symptoms that could indicate the existence of planning problems are weakness in dealing with competition, declining sales volume, inventory levels that are either too high or too low, high operating expenses, and too much being invested in equipment.

The main focus of the planner's activities is to advise management on what should be done in the future. He or she assists management not only in determining appropriate future action but also in ensuring that the timing of that action is appropriate. In the end, the possibility always exists that the manager may not accept the planner's recommendations. As with all other organization members, it is very important that the performance of planners is evaluated against the contribution they make toward helping the organization achieve its objectives. The quality and appropriateness of the system for planning and the plans that the planner develops for the organization should be primary considerations in this evaluation. Because the organizing, influencing, and controlling functions of the manager are based on the fundamental planning function, the evaluation of the planner becomes critically important. Although assessment of the planner is somewhat subjective, a number of objective indicators do exist. For example, use of appropriate techniques is one objective indicator. If the planner is using appropriate techniques, the probability increases that she or he is doing an acceptable job. The degree of objectivity displayed by the planner is another objective indicator. To a great extent, the planner's advice should be based on a rational analysis of appropriate information. This is not to say that subjectivity and judgment should be excluded by the planner. This subjectivity and judgment, however, typically should be based on specific and appropriate information.

Malik suggests that **objective evidence that the planner is doing a reputable job exists if**: (1) organizational plans are in writing; (2) the plan is the result of all elements of the management team working together; (3) the plan defines present and possible future businesses of the organization; (4) the plan specifically mentions organizational objectives; (5) the plan includes future opportunities and suggestions on how to take advantage of them; (6) the plan emphasizes both internal and external environments; (7) the plan describes the attainment of objectives in operational terms when possible; and (8) the plan includes both long- and short-run recommendations. More subjective considerations in evaluating a planner's performance include how well the planner gets along with key members of the organization, the amount of organizational loyalty the planner displays, and the planner's perceived potential.

Learning Objective 7   *Guidelines on how to get the greatest return from the planning* process

Success in implementing a planning subsystem is not easily attainable. As the size of the organization increases, the planning task becomes more complicated, requiring more people, more information, and more complicated decisions. Several safeguards, however, can **ensure the success of an organizational planning effort**. First, top management must support the planning effort, or other organization members may not take the planning effort seriously. Whenever possible, top management should actively help to guide and participate in planning activities. Furnishing the planner with whatever resources are needed to structure the planning organization, encouraging planning as a continuing process and not as a once-a-year activity, and preparing people for changes usually resulting from planning are clear signs that top management is solidly behind the planning effort. The chief executive must give continual and obvious attention to the planning process if it is to be successful.

Second, the planner must take the time to design an efficient and effective planning organization. A well-designed planning organization is the primary vehicle by which planning is accomplished. The planning organization should use established management systems within the company; be simple, yet complex enough to ensure a coordinated effort of all planning participants; and be flexible and adaptable to changing conditions.

Third, because the end result of the planning process is some type of action that will help achieve stated organizational objectives, planning should be aimed at implementation. Plans should be developed and scrutinized after looking ahead to when they are to be implemented. Ease of implementation should be built in whenever possible. The marketing plan of the Edsel automobile is an example of how a sound plan can become unsuccessful simply because of ineffective implementation. The rationale behind the Edsel was complete, logical, and defensible. In fact, three consumer trends at that time solidly justified the introduction of that automobile. But two factors in the implementation of the plan turned the entire Edsel situation into a financial disaster. First, the network of controllers, dealers, marketing managers, and industrial relations managers created within Ford to get the Edsel to the consumer became very complicated and inefficient. Second, because Ford pushed as many Edsels as possible on the road immediately after introduction, the quality of the Edsel suffered, and many consumers bought poorly manufactured products. Although the plan to make and market the Edsel was completely defensible, the long-run influence of the organization, and the manufacturing processes created to implement the plan doomed it to failure.

Fourth, planning must include the right people. Whenever possible, the planner should obtain input from the managers of the functional areas for which he or she is planning. These managers are close to the everyday activity in their segments of the organization and can provide the planner with invaluable information. These managers probably also will be involved in implementing whatever plan develops and, therefore, can furnish the planner with feedback on how easily various plans are being implemented. In general, managers who will be involved in implementing plans should also be involved in developing the plans. Input from individuals who will be directly affected by the plans also can help the planner to determine how various alternative plans will influence work flow. But it is extremely important that the planner involve the right organization members. The kinds of decisions and types of data needed should dictate the choice of who is involved in what aspects of organizational planning.

Knowing You Know

True/False   *Directions: On the lines provided, place a "T" for true or an "F" for false for each of the statements that follow:*

_____   1.   In the industrial world, effective planning subsystems are formal.
_____   2.   One of the most important duties of the organization planner is to develop a plan for planning.
_____   3.   Implementation is the key to a successful planning process; if a planner cannot transform understanding into appropriate action, she or he is not able to generate useful organizational plans.
_____   4.   The final responsibility for organizational planning clearly rests with the organization planner.
_____   5.   While organization planners must possess an abundance of conceptual skills, have considerable practical experience within the organization, and possess some knowledge of and interest in the social, political, technical, and economic trends that could affect the organization, research indicates that many organization planners have little ability to work well with others.
_____   6.   The marketing plan of the Edsel automobile is an example of how a poorly developed and unsound plan can frequently spell disaster for a company.
_____   7.   The organization planner is usually an individual who is not the chief executive of the organization.
_____   8.   Evaluation of the organization planner usually is deemphasized since only a few objective indicators are available with which to evaluate his or her performance.
_____   9.   To maximize the effectiveness of the planning process, all organization members must be involved in one way or another.
_____ 10.   A well-designed planning organization is the primary vehicle by which planning is accomplished.
_____ 11.   Because the organizing, influencing, and controlling functions of the manager are based on the fundamental planning function, the evaluation of the planner becomes critically important.
_____ 12.   The primary management function that precedes all other functions is organizing.
_____ 13.   Malik suggests that an objective evaluation of planning is possible and indicates several ways to evaluate planner performance.
_____ 14.   The planner should not solicit input from individuals who will be affected by the plans being developed.
_____ 15.   Ease of implementation is a positive feature of a plan that should be built in whenever possible.

Multiple Choice   *Directions: Circle the letter or the word or phrase that best completes each statement.*

16. Which of the following is *not* a step in the planning process?
    a. choosing the best alternative
    b. putting the plans into action
    c. developing decisional strategies
    d. stating organizational objectives
    e. all of these are steps in the planning process

17. Which of the following is *not* cited in the text as an advantage of planning?
    a. a concentrated planning effort reduces the amount of time managers must spend performing the organizing, influencing, and controlling functions.
    b. Planning forces managers to look beyond everyday problems and into the more distant future.
    c. Planning ensures that the decisions made by managers over a period of time will be coordinated.
    d. Planning emphasizes organizational objectives, since objectives are the starting points for planning.
    e. All of these are advantages of planning.

18. The step in the planning process that immediately follows "stating organizational objectives" is
    a. developing premises upon which each alternative is based
    b. choosing the best alternative for reaching objectives
    c. putting plans into action
    d. listing alternative ways of reaching objectives
    e. none of these is the step that follows "stating organizational objectives"

19. The fundamental purpose of planning is to
    a. minimize risk by reducing the uncertainties surrounding business conditions and clarifying the consequences of related management action
    b. increase the degree of organizational success
    c. help the organization reach its objectives
    d. establish a coordinated effort within the organization
    e. none of the above

20. Three purposes for planning defined in the text are
    a. protective, affirmative, and supplemental
    b. affirmative, supplemental, and organizational
    c. coordination, protective, and affirmative
    d. supplemental, organizational, and coordination
    e. none of the above

21. Which management function precedes all others?
    a. organizing
    b. influencing
    c. planning
    d. controlling
    e. none of the above; they all occur simultaneously

22. The effectiveness of the planning subsystem depends on
    a. the qualifications of the planner
    b. the duties of the planner
    c. the evaluation of the planner
    d. all of the above are important to the effectiveness of the planning subsystem
    e. none of the above is important to the effectiveness of the planning subsystem

23. The qualifications of a planner include
    a. having minimal experience with the organization
    b. a narrow or specialized background in the organization
    c. an ability to work well with others
    d. knowledge of social, political, technical, and economic trends that could affect the future of the organization
    e. *c* and *d*

24. Several safeguards ensure the success of a planning effort. Which of the following is *not* a safeguard?
    a. top management support
    b. an effective and efficient planning organization
    c. inclusion of the right people
    d. an "end justifies the means" planning orientation
    e. none of the above are safeguards

25. Chief executives, as planners, should seek answers to which of the following questions?
    a. In what direction should the organization be going?
    b. In what direction is the organization currently going?
    c. Should something be done to change the current direction?
    d. Is the organization continuing in an appropriate direction?
    e. All of the above are correct

Applying What You Know

Experience 5-1   Planning for a Weekend Trip

Introduction

While planning is an integral part of the managing process, it is not unique to management. In fact, one generally plans (consciously or unconsciously) in every situation. This exercise gives you firsthand experience in planning a hypothetical weekend trip to a city about one hundred miles from your campus.

Exercise 1

Assume that you want to make a trip to a city about one hundred miles from campus this weekend and that you need to plan how to get to that city. Your last class ends at 3:00 p.m. on Friday, and you want to get to your destination as early as possible Friday evening. You can afford to spend up to twenty-five dollars to get there (although you would prefer to spend as little as possible). Keeping these constraints in mind, follow the steps in the planning process and establish a plan for getting to your destination. As you plan, write your thoughts under the appropriate headings in the planning process model that follows.

The Planning Process

Step 1: **Statement of the objective**

To get from campus to a city one hundred miles away as soon after 3:00 p.m. on Friday as possible and spend no more than twenty-five dollars in reaching that destination.

Step 2: **Alternative ways of reaching objective**

Step 3: Premises upon which each alternative is based

Step 4: Selected alternative for best reaching objective

Step 5: Plan to pursue chosen objective

Exercise 2

Your instructor will provide you with information about **three basic approaches to planning**: the *maximizing approach*, the *adapting approach*, and the *high probability approach*. Now that you have planned your trip, explain which of the three approaches to planning you feel best describes your planning behavior.

Exercise 3

Now that you have identified the planning approach that most closely matches your planning behavior in exercise 1, do you feel another approach would have been more effective? Explain.

Exercise 4

Explain what you personally have learned about planning and planning approaches from participating in this exercise.

Experience 5-2   Developing Planning Premises

Introduction

Premises are assumptions upon which alternatives are based; in other words, premises make up the environment of plans in operation. Planners must be proficient at premising because the selection of a course of action is to a large extent determined by the premises (assumptions) established. The development of premises is probably the most confusing and most misunderstood step of the planning process. This experience is designed to provide you with greater insight into this very important aspect of planning. Read the incident that follows and complete each exercise as directed

Incident

Mike's Furniture Mart is a relatively large furniture store in the downtown district of a large American city. The store carries a wide line of furniture and appliance items and caters primarily to middle-class families with annual incomes ranging from $20,000 to $30,000. Because of declining sales and profits in recent years (see figure 5.1 below), the company is now evaluating the following alternatives to improve its position:

1. Entering the interior decorating business--a move designed to secure more business from higher-income groups
2. Adding a line of cheaper furniture and appliances--a move to increase sales by attracting customers with lower incomes

Exercise 1

Explain what you feel are the major planning premises the company should consider and analyze in view of the two identified alternatives.

Figure 5.1 Sales and profits of Mike's Furniture Mart (1989-1993).

Year	Total Sales	Net Profit
1993	$1,399,000	$46,000
1992	1,411,000	75,000
1991	1,419,000	99,000
1990	1,441,000	109,500
1989	1,380,000	86,000

Exercise 2

Premises frequently are classified as either internal or external. External premises are assumptions for business planning that lie outside the firm (for example, the general business environment, the product market, etc.); internal premises are assumptions for planning that relate to the firm itself and items in the firm (for example, the sales forecast, capital investments made or planned for, etc.). Categorize as either internal or external the premises you developed in relation to each alternative in exercise 1. (You may discover that in exercise 1 you considered only things external to the firm or only internal to the firm and that you may want to add to your list of premises.)

Exercise 3

Identify some premises (internal and/or external) that probably would cause the company to reject alternative 2.

Exercise 4

Give concrete examples of some of the derivative plans the company should establish if it decides to adopt alternative 1.

Experience 5-3   The Problem with Planning at Eastern Electric[*]

Introduction

This experience permits you to evaluate the effectiveness of planning implementation and the individuals with important planning responsibilities. In the role of a consultant, you apply your knowledge of planning to increase the chances of more effective planning implementation at Eastern Electric in the future. Read the incident that follows and then complete the exercises as directed.

Incident

Margaret Quinn, president of Eastern Electric Corporation, one of the large electric utilities operating in the eastern United States, had long been convinced that effective planning in the company was absolutely essential to success. For more than ten years, she had tried, without much success, to get a company planning program installed. Over this time, she consecutively had appointed three vice-presidents in charge of planning (each had previously been a successful corporate planner in another organization), and although each had seemed to work hard at the job, she had noticed that individual department heads kept going their own ways. They made decisions on problems as they came up, and they prided themselves on doing an effective job of "fighting fires."

But the company seemed to be drifting, and individual decisions of department heads did not ways jibe. The executive in charge of regulatory matters was always pressing state commissions to allow higher electric rates, but the commissions felt that costs, although rising, were not justified. The head of public relations was constantly appealing to the public to understand the problems of electric utilities, but electric users in the various communities felt that the utility was making enough money and that the company should solve its problems without raising rates. The vice-president in charge of operations, pressed by many communities to expand electric lines, to put all lines underground to get rid of unsightly poles and lines, and to give customers better service, felt that costs were secondary to keeping customers off his back.

When a consultant, called in at the request of Quinn, looked over the situation, he found that the company was not planning very well. The vice-president for planning and his staff were working diligently at making studies and forecasts, but all the department heads considered the forecasts impractical "long-hair stuff" that had no importance for day-to-day operations.

Exercise 1

Assume that you are the consultant called in by Margaret Quinn to evaluate the situation at Eastern Electric. What would you identify as the major reasons for the ineffective planning organization at Eastern Electric? Explain.

---

[*]Source of Experience 5-3: Adapted from Koontz, Harold and Cyril O'Donnell, *Essentials of Management*. © 1978 McGraw-Hill, Inc. Reprinted by permissioni of McGraw-Hill Book Company.

Exercise 2

Explain how well the key planning personnel identified below shouldered their planning responsibilities.

    a. The president, Margaret Quinn

    b. All vice-presidents of planning

Exercise 3

From the somewhat scant information in the incident, is there any objective evidence that the vice-presidents of planning were doing a reputable job? Explain.

Exercise 4

Assume that you have discovered, through your evaluation of key planning personnel, that the current vice-president of planning does not know how far into the future he should extend his analysis (in other words, how far into the future he should plan). What would your advice be? Explain.

6 MAKING DECISIONS

Chapter Summary

This chapter discusses the fundamentals of decisions, the elements of the decision situation, the decision-making process, various decision-making conditions, and decision-making tools.

Learning Objective 1   *A fundamental understanding of the term decision*

A **decision** is a choice made between two or more available alternatives. Although decision making is covered in the planning section of the test, managers also must make decisions when performing the other three managerial functions: organizing, controlling, and influencing.

A practicing manager quickly realizes that all decisions are not equal in significance to the organization. Some affect a large number of organization members, cost a large sum of money to carry out, and/or have a long-run effect on the organization. These significant decisions can have a major impact on the management system itself and also on the career of the manager. Other decisions are fairly insignificant and affect only a small number of organization members, cost very little to carry out, and have only a short-run effect on the organization.

Decisions can be categorized by how much time a manager must spend in making them, what proportion of the organization must be involved in making them, and the organizational functions on which they focus. Probably the most generally accepted method of categorizing decisions is based on computer technology language and divides decisions into two basic types: programmed and nonprogrammed. **Programmed decisions** are routine and repetitive, and the organization typically develops specific ways to handle them. A programmed decision might involve determining how products will be arranged on the shelves of a grocery store. **Nonprogrammed decisions**, on the other hand, typically are one-shot occurrences and are usually less structured than programmed decisions. One example of a nonprogrammed decision that many managers have had to make in recent years is whether or not to close a plant. Another example would be a decision focusing on whether or not a grocery store should carry an additional type of bread. The grocery store manager must consider whether the new bread will stabilize bread sales by competing with existing bread carried in the store or increase bread sales by offering a choice of bread to the customer who has never before bought bread in the store.

Many different kinds of decisions must be made within an organization, such as how to manufacture a product, how to maintain machines, how to ensure product quality, and how to establish advantageous relationships with customers. One rationale for deciding who has the responsibility for making organizational decisions is based primarily on two factors: (1) the scope of the decision to be made and (2) levels of management. The **scope of the decision** refers to the proportion of the total management system that the decision will affect. The greater this proportion, the broader the scope of the decision is said to be. **Levels of management** simply refers to lower-level management, middle-level management, and upper-level management,. The broader the scope of a decision, the higher the level of the manager responsible for making that decision. E. I. DuPont de Nemours and Company follows this decision-making rationale in handling decisions related to the research and development function. This organization has relatively narrow-scope research and development decisions, such as "which markets to test," made by lower-level managers, and relatively broad-scope research and development decisions, such as "authorize full-scale plant construction," made by upper-level managers.

Even though a manager may have the responsibility for making a particular decision, he or she can ask the advice of other managers and/or subordinates. In fact, some managers advise having groups make certain decisions. **Consensus** is one method a manager can use in getting a group to arrive at a particular decision. Consensus is agreement on a decision by all individuals involved in making the decision. Consensus usually occurs after lengthy deliberation and discussion by members of the decision group, who may be either all managers or a mixture of managers and subordinates. Although asking individuals to arrive at a concensus decision is an option available to a manager, the manager must keep in mind that some individuals simply may not be able to arrive at such a decision. Perhaps lack of technical skill or poor interpersonal relations within a group are barriers to arriving at a concensus decision. Among the advantages of making decisions by consensus are that managers can focus "several heads" on making a decision and that individuals in the decision group are more likely to be committed to implementing a decision if they helped to make it. The main disadvantage to decisions through consensus is that discussions relating to the decisions tend to be quite lengthy and, therefore, very costly.

Wilson and Alexis have indicated that there are **six basic parts or elements to the decision situation.** The *state of nature* is the element that refers to those aspects of the decision maker's environment that can affect his or her choice. Duncan attempted to identify environmental characteristics that influenced decision makers. He grouped the characteristics into two categories: the internal environment and the external environment. For example, included in the internal environment is the organizational personnel component and included in the external environment are customer and supplier components.

The *decision maker element* in the decision situation consists of the individuals or groups who actually make the choice between the alternatives. Dale suggests that weak decision makers can have four different orientations: (1) the receptive orientation, (2) the exploitation orientation, (3) the hoarding orientation, and (4) the marketing orientation. Receptive decision makers feel that the source of all good is outside themselves, and, therefore, they rely heavily on suggestions from other organization members. Basically, they like others to make their decisions for them. Exploitation decision makers also believe that good is outside themselves, and they are willing to take ethical or unethical steps to steal ideas necessary to make good decisions. They build their organization on the ideas of others and typically extend little or no credit for the ideas to anyone but themselves. Hoarding decisions makers preserve the status quo as much as possible. They accept little outside help, isolate themselves from others, and are extremely self-reliant. They emphasize maintaining their present existence. Marketing-oriented decision makers consider themselves commodities that are only as valuable as the decisions they make. They try to make decisions that will enhance their value and are therefore conscious of what others think of their decisions. The ideal decision-making orientation is one that emphasizes trying to realize the potential of the organization as well as of the decision maker. Ideal decision makers try to use all of their talents and are influenced mainly by reason and sound judgment. They do not possess the qualities of the four undesirable decision-making orientations just described.

The third element in the decision situation consists of the *goals* that decision makers seek to attain. In the case of managers, these goals should most often be organizational objectives.

The fourth element in the decision situation involves *relevant alternatives*. A relevant alternative is one that is considered feasible for implementation and also for solving an existing problem. Irrelevant alternatives should be excluded from the decision-making situation.

The fifth element in the decision situation is the *ordering of alternatives*. The decision situation must have a process or mechanism that ranks alternatives from most desirable to least desirable. The process can be subjective (for example, based on past experience), objective (for example, rate of output per machine), or some combination of the two.

The last element in the decision situation is an actual *choice between available alternatives*. Typically, managers choose the alternative that maximizes long-run return for the organization.

Learning Objective 3   *An ability to use the decision-making process*

The decision-making process is defined as the **five steps the decision maker takes** to actually choose an alternative. The process that a manager uses to make decisions has a significant impact on the quality of decisions made. If managers use an organized and systematic process the probability that their decisions will be sound is higher than if the process is more disorganized and unsystematic. Decision making is essentially a problem-solving process that involves eliminating barriers to organizational goal attainment. Naturally, the first step in this elimination process is *identifying exactly what these problems or barriers are*. Only after the barriers have been adequately identified can management take steps to eliminate them. Barnard suggests that organizational problems be brought to the attention of managers mainly through orders issued by managers' supervisors, situations relayed to managers by their subordinates, and/or the normal activity of the managers themselves.

Once a problem has been identified, the next step in the decision-making process is to *list the various alternative problem solutions*. Very few organizational problems can only be solved in one way. Managers must search out the many alternative solutions that exist for most organizational problems. Managers, however, must be aware of five limitations on the number of problem-solving alternatives available: (1) authority factors (for example, a manager's superior may have told the manager that the alternative was feasible); (2) biological factors (for example, human factors within the organization may be inappropriate to implement the alternatives); (3) physical factors (for example, physical facilities of the organization may be inappropriate for certain alternatives to be seriously considered); (4) technological factors (for example, the level of organizational technology may be inadequate for certain alternatives); and (5) economic factors (for example, certain alternatives may be too costly for the organization). The feasible alternatives available to managers sometimes are designated as the managers' "discretionary area." Additional factors that limit this "discretionary area" are legal restrictions, moral and ethical norms, formal policies and rules, and unofficial social norms.

Decision makers can select the most beneficial alternative only after they have *evaluated each alternative very carefully*. This evaluation should consist of three steps. First, decision makers should list, as accurately as possible, the potential effects of each alternative, as if the alternative had already been chosen and implemented. Second, a probability factor should be assigned to each of these potential effects. This would indicate how probable the occurrence of the effect would be if the alternative was implemented. Third, keeping organizational goals in mind, decision makers should compare each alternative's expected effects with its respective probabilities. The alternative that seems to be most advantageous to the organization should be chosen for implementation. The next step is to actually *put the chosen alternative into action*.

Even after the chosen alternative has been implemented, decision makers must *gather feedback to determine the effect of the implemented alternative on the identified problem*. If the identified problem is not being solved, managers need to search out and implement some other alternative.

This model of the decision-making process is based on three primary assumptions. First, the model assumes that humans are economic beings with the objective of maximizing satisfaction or return. Second, the model is based on the assumption that, within the decision-making situation, all alternative solutions, as well as the possible consequence of each alternative, are known. Third, this model assumes that decision makers have some priority system that allows them to rank the desirability of each alternative. In reality, one or more of these assumptions usually are not met, and related decisions, therefore, are usually something less than the best possible for the organization.

Learning Objective 4   *An appreciation for the various situations in which decisions are made*

It is usually impossible for decision makers to be sure of exactly what the future consequences of an implemented alternative actually will be. Because organizations and their environments are constantly changing, future consequences of implemented decisions are not perfectly predictable. In general, there are three different conditions under which decisions are made. These conditions are based on the degree to which the future outcome of a decision alternative is predictable.

The **complete certainty condition** exists when decision makers know exactly what the results of an implemented alternative will be. In this instance, managers have complete knowledge about a decision. Decision makers simply list outcomes for alternatives and then pick the outcome with the highest payoff for the organization. For example, the outcome of an investment alternative based on buying government bonds is, for all practical purposes, completely predictable due to established government interest rates. Unfortunately, most organizational decisions are made outside of the complete certainty situation.

The **complete uncertainty condition** exists when decision makers have absolutely no idea what the results of an implemented alternative will be. This condition would exist, for example, if there was no historical data upon which to base a decision. Not knowing what happened in the past makes it difficult to predict what will happen in the future. In this situation, decision makers find that sound decisions are a matter of chance. Fortunately, few organizational decisions are made in the complete uncertainty situation.

The **risk condition** exists when decision makers have only enough information about the outcome of each alternative to estimate how probable the outcome will be if the alternative is implemented. Obviously, the risk condition is somewhere between the complete certainty situation and the complete uncertainty situation. For example, the manager who hires two extra salespeople to increase annual organizational sales is deciding in a risk situation. He or she may feel that the probability is high that these two new salespeople will increase total sales, but it is impossible to know for sure. In reality, degrees of risk can be associated with decisions made in the risk situation. The lower the quality of information related to the outcome of an alternative, the closer the situation is to the complete uncertainty situation and the higher the risk associated with choosing the alternative. Most decisions made in organizations normally have some amount of risk associated with them.

Learning Objective 5   *An understanding of probability theory and decision trees as decision-making tools*

Most managers develop intuition about what decisions to make. This intuition is a mostly subjective feeling, developed from years of experience in a particular organization or industry, that gives managers insights about making a decision. Although intuition can be an important part of making a decision, most managers tend to use more objective decision-making tools, such as linear programming, queuing or waiting-line methods, and game theory. However, probability theory and decision trees are perhaps the two most widely used of these more objective decision-making tools.

Probability theory is a decision-making tool used in risk situations--situations wherein decision makers are not completely sure of the outcome of an implemented alternative. Probability refers to the likelihood that an event or outcome will actually occur and allows decision makers to calculate an expected value for each alternative. The **expected value** (EV) for an alternative is the income (I) the alternative would produce multiplied by its probability of making that income (P). In formula form: $EV = I \times P$. Decision makers generally choose and implement the alternative with the highest expected value. For example, if the manager of a store that specializes in renting surfboards considers three location alternatives (A, B, and C); projects earnings of $90,000 in Location A, $75,000 in Location B, and $60,000 in Location C; and determines that there is a .1, a .4, and a .8 probability, respectively, of ideal conditions in these locations; then the decision maker should open his or her store in Location C because it is the alternative with the highest expected value.

Probability theory is applicable to relatively simple decision situations. Some decisions, however, are more complicated and involve a series of steps. These steps are interdependent; that is, each step is influenced by the step that precedes it. A **decision tree** is a graphic decision-making tool typically used to evaluate decisions containing a series of steps.

John F. Magee has developed a classic illustration that outlines how decision trees can be applied to a production decision. In his illustration, the Stygian Chemical Company must decide whether to build a small or a large plant to manufacture a new product with an expected life of ten years.

Whether to build a small plant or a large one is Decision Point 1. If the choice is to build a large plant, the company could face product demands of high or low average demand, or high initial and then low demand. If, on the other hand, the choice is to build a small plant, the company could face initially high or initially low product demand. If the small plant is built, however, and high product demand exists during an initial two-year period, management could then choose whether or not to expand its plant (Decision Point 2). In either case, management could then face either high or low product demand.

With the various possible alternatives related to this decision outlined, the financial consequences of each different course of action must be compared. To adequately compare these consequences, management must: (1) study estimates of investment amounts necessary for building a large plant, for building a small plant, and for expanding a small plant; (2) weigh probabilities of facing different product demand levels for various decision alternatives; and (3) consider projected income yields per decision alternative. Analysis of the expected values and net expected gain for each decision alternative helps management to decide on an appropriate choice. Net expected gain is defined in this situation as the expected value of an alternative minus investment cost. For example, if in Magee's example, building a large plant yields the highest net expected gain, Stygian management should decide to build the large plant.

Knowing You Know

True/False   *Directions: On the lines provided, place a "T" for true or an "F" for false for each of the statements that follow:*

_____ 1. Nonprogrammed decisions are typically one-shot occurrences and usually more structured than programmed decisions.

_____ 2. A relevant alternative is one that is considered feasible for implementation and also for solving an existing problem.

_____ 3. A last step in the decision-making process is selecting the most beneficial alternative to solve the problem.

_____ 4. Complete certainty exists when decision makers can determine in advance exactly what the results of an implemented alternative will be.

_____ 5. The ideal decision-making orientation emphasizes trying to realize the potential of the organization as well as of the decision maker.

_____ 6. Linear programming, queuing or waiting-line methods, and game theory are subjective decision-making tools used by modern managers.

_____ 7. The last element of the decision situation is an actual choice between available alternatives.

_____ 8. Decision trees can be applied to relatively simple decision situations, while probability theory is more useful to evaluate decisions containing a series of steps.

_____ 9. Managers make many decisions when performing the planning function and only a few decisions when organizing, influencing, and controlling.

_____10. The first step in the decision-making process is identifying the existing problems or barriers.

_____11. The significance of a decision to the organization is mainly a function of what the decision will cost to carry out, the number of organization members affected, and whether the effect on the organization will be long run or short run.

_____12. The rationale for designating who makes which decision is: The broader the scope of a decision, the lower the level of the manager responsible for making that decision.

_____13. The decisions made by John Cunin at Bearings, Inc, are classic examples of decision making under conditions of complete certainty.

_____14. Most managers develop intuition about what decisions to make.

_____15. In the Stygian Chemical Company illustration, if building a large plant would yield the largest net expected gain, Stygian management should decide to build the large plant.

Directions: *Match items 16-25 with items a-j. There is only one correct answer for each item.*

_____16. Programmed decisions
_____17. Hoarding-oriented decision maker
_____18. Scope of the decision and levels of management
_____19. Objective decision-making tool
_____20. Consensus
_____21. Risk condition
_____22. Exploitation-oriented decision maker
_____23. Uncertainty condition
_____24. Legal restrictions, moral and ethical norms, formal policies and rules, and unofficial social norms
_____25. Decision

a. Decision trees
b. Choice made between two or more available alternatives
c. One method managers can use to have a group arrive at a particular decision
d. Decision maker who accepts little outside help and is extremely self-reliant
e. These are routine and repetitive, and the organization typically develops specific ways to handle them
f. Rationale for determining decision-making responsibility
g. Decision makers have no idea what the results of an implemented alternative will be
h. Decision makers can estimate how probable the outcome will be if the alternative is implemented
i. Factors limiting the "discretionary area"
j. Decision maker who is willing to take ethical or unethical steps to steal ideas necessary to make good decisions.

Applying What You Know

Experience 6-1   Desert Survival: Individual Versus Group (Consensus) Decision Making*

Introduction

Should a manager responsible for a decision make that decision alone, or should the manager make the decision with the assistance of other organization members? In this experience, you become involved in individual and group (consensus) decision-making situations to gain further insight into these different decision circumstances. Read the incident that follows and then complete the exercises as directed.

Incident

It is approximately 10 a.m. in mid-August, and you have just crash-landed in the Sonora Desert in the southwestern United States. The light twin-engine plane, containing the bodies of the pilot and co-pilot, has completely burned. Only the air frame remains. None of the rest of you has been injured.

The pilot was unable to notify anyone of your position before the crash. However, he had indicated before impact that you were seventy miles south-southwest from a mining camp that is the nearest known habitation and that you were approximately sixty-five miles off the course that was filed in your VFR flight plan.

The immediate area is quite flat and, except for occasional barrel and saguaro cacti, appears to be rather barren. The last weather report indicated that the temperature would reach 110 degrees that day, which means that the temperature at ground level will be 130 degrees. You are dressed in light clothing--short-sleeved shirts or blouses, pants, and street shoes. Everyone has a handkerchief. Collectively, your pockets contain $2.83 in change, $85.00 in bills, a pack of cigarettes, and a ballpoint pen. Before the plane caught fire, your group was able to salvage the fifteen items shown in figure 6.1

---

*Source of Experience 6-1: "The Desert Survival Situation," *Human Synergistics.* © 1974 Experiential Learning Methods.

Exercise 1

Rank the fifteen items in figure 6.1 in terms of their importance for survival. Number one should be the most important item, number two the second most important, and so on through number fifteen, the least important. Place your rankings in the "Individual Ranking" column on the form in figure 6.1. In addition, note the time before you start ranking these items and again after you have completed your ranking. Then record the number of minutes that it took to complete your ranking in the space provided at the bottom of the "Individual Ranking" column.

Exercise 2

Your instructor will assign you to a group to complete this exercise. Your group will use a consensus decision-making approach to determine which items are critical for survival. The term consensus means that the ranking of each of the fifteen survival items must be agreed upon by each group member before it becomes a part of the group decision. Therefore, consensus is difficult to reach. Not every ranking will meet with everyone's complete approval. Even so, try, as a group, to make each ranking one with which all group members can at least partially agree. Five guidelines to use in reaching consensus follow. Place consensus rankings in the "Group Ranking" column in figure 6.1. Again, keep track of the number of minutes it took for your group to reach a decision on the ranking of items. Then write this time in the space provided at the bottom of the "Group Ranking" column. Finally, you may assume the following: (1) the number of survivors is the same as the number on your team; (2) you are the actual people in the situation; (3) the team has agreed to stick together; and (4) all items are in good condition.

Guidelines to Use in Achieving Consensus

1. Avoid arguing for your own rankings. Present your position as lucidly and logically as possible, but listen to the other members' reactions and consider them carefully before your press your point.
2. Do not assume that someone must win and someone must lose when discussion reaches a stalemate. Instead, look for the next most acceptable alternative for all parties.
3. Do not change your mind simply to avoid conflict and to reach agreement and harmony. When agreement seems to come too quickly and easily, be suspicious. Explore the reasons and be sure everyone accepts the solution for basically similar or complimentary reasons. Yield only to positions that have objective and logically sound foundations.
4. Avoid conflict-reducing techniques, such as majority votes, averages, coin-flips, and bargaining. When a dissenting member finally agrees, don't feel that this person must be rewarded by having his or her own way on some later point.
5. Differences of opinion are natural and expected. Seek them out and try to involve everyone in the decision process. Disagreements can help the decision of the group because, with a wide range of information and opinions, there is a greater chance that the group will hit upon more adequate solutions.

Figure 6.1 Evaluation of individual and group decision making

Items	Individual Ranking	Error Points	Group Ranking	Error Points	Survival Experts' Ranking
Flashlight (four-battery size)					
Jackknife					
Sectional air map of the area					
Plastic raincoat (large size)					
Magnetic compass					
Compress kit with gauze					
.45 caliber pistol (loaded)					
Parachute (red and white)					
Bottle of salt tablets (1,000 tablets)					
One quart of water per person					
A book entitled *Edible Animals of the Desert*					
A pair of sunglasses per person					
Two quarts of 180-proof vodka					
One topcoat per person					
A cosmetic mirror					
Total Error Points					
Number of minutes spent ranking items					

Exercise 3

Now that you have ranked the fifteen items on both an individual and group basis, your instructor will provide you with the answers given by experts in desert survival and tell you how to determine your total individual and total group error points.

Exercise 4

Use what you have learned about individual and group decision making in this experience to answer the questions that follow.

a. Based on the experience you have just been involved in, what generalizations can you make about individual and group decision making? Explain.

b. If each individual's time was worth ten dollars per minute, what would your individual decision cost? What would the group's decision cost?

c.   From your involvement in this experience, what do you perceive to be the major considerations in determining whether to use individual or group decision making? Explain.

Experience 6-2   The Missing Keys: Evaluating a Decision-Making Process**

Introduction

The decision-making process--the actions decision makers take to actually choose an alternative--involves five steps: (1) identifying a problem, (2) listing possible alternatives to solve this problem, (3) selecting the most beneficial alternative to solve the problem, (4) implementing that alternative, and (5) gathering feedback to determine if the implemented alternative is alleviating the identified problem. Ineffectiveness at any step in this process an cause decision makers to fail in solving the problem.

In this experience, you evaluate the decision-making process employed by an administrator in what appears to be a critical decision situation. Familiarize yourself with the incident that follows and then complete the exercises as directed.

Incident

The administrator of the state mental hospital learned that keys to security wards had been lost or stolen when he received an early morning telephone call the first of May from the night administrator of the hospital. Since duplicate keys were available in the hospital safe, the administrator, James Jackson, knew that the loss of the keys would not interfere with the routine functioning of the hospital. But he decided to call a general staff meeting for later that morning to consider the problem of the missing keys.

At the meeting, Jackson explained the problem of the missing keys and asked for suggestions on what to do. The assistant administrator suggested that the matter be kept confidential among the staff since public knowledge could lead to damaging publicity and possibly to an investigation by higher officials in the Department of Health and Rehabilitative Services.

The head of security for the hospital reported that only two keys were missing and that, although he could not yet determine if the keys had been stolen or lost, he thought they probably had been stolen. He emphasized that the missing keys were "master keys" that could open all individual cells as well as the doors to all the security wards, where the most dangerous criminals (convicted first-degree murderers and sexual psychopaths, among others) were housed. In his opinion, replacement of the locks on all individual cell doors was required.

The director of accounting estimated the cost of replacing all the locks at over $5,000. She reminded the meeting participants that the operating costs of the hospital already had exceeded the operating budget by about 10 percent due to unexpected inflation and other unforeseen expenses and that an emergency request for a supplemental budget appropriation to cover the deficit had been sent to the Department of Health and Rehabilitative Services the previous week. In sum, she concluded, no funds were available in the budget for replacing the locks, and an additional request for $5,000 might jeopardize the request for supplementary operating funds already submitted. Besides, she added, since it was early May, the hospital

---

** Source of Experience 6-2: John M. Champion and John H. James, *Critical Incidents in Management* (Homewood, IL: Richard D. Irwin, 1975), pp. 130-31. © 1975 by Richard D. Irwin, Inc.

would begin operating under the budget for the next fiscal year in approximately sixty days. The locks could then be replaced and the costs charged against the new budget. Another staff member reasoned aloud that, if the keys had been lost, any person finding them would not likely know of their purpose, and that if the keys had been stolen, they probably would never be used in any unauthorized way.

Jackson thanked the staff members for their contributions, ended the meeting, and faced the decision. He recalled his impeccable fifteen-year record as an efficient and effective hospital administrator. After briefly considering all of the suggestions made by his staff, Jackson decided to submit an additional request for $5,000 to cover the cost of lock replacement. Jackson directed his secretary to begin filling out the vast amount of paperwork needed to support his decision.

Exercise 1

Evaluate the decision-making process employed by James Jackson. Where (in what step or steps) did he go wrong? Explain.

Exercise 2

Outline the decision-making process you would employ if you were in Jackson's shoes and had received the early morning phone call about the missing keys

Exercise 3

Explain what you have learned about decision making and the decision-making process from this experience.

Experience 6-3 A New Plant or Plant Expansion?

Introduction

Of all the skills that managers must possess, the decision-making skill may well be the most critical. But how does one develop this skill? Many experienced managers have found that they can increase their effectiveness in this critical skill area by using appropriate decision-making tools. This experience was designed to increase your understanding of one such tool-- the decision tree. Both probability theory and decision trees employ the concept of expected value. The **decision tree method**, however, typically is used to evaluate the more complicated decision circumstance involving a series of steps. Read the incident that follows and complete the exercises as directed.

Incident

A company that produces wood- and coal-burning stoves is trying to decide whether it should expand its old building or build a new plant to increase its production capacity. If the old building is expanded at a cost of $2 million, it is estimated that the present value of resulting operating profits (without allowing for increased costs) will be $4 million.

Management, however, is somewhat uncertain about the future demand for this type of heating system. While it would seem that the energy crunch should increase consumer demand for alternate heating methods, the wood- and coal-burning stove is in direct competition with solar and other alternate heating systems. However, with the promotional effort to be undertaken with the new plant, the marketing research department predicts a 0.4 chance of a significant increase in demand for these stoves and a 0.6 chance of a moderate increase in demand. If a new plant is built to manufacture these stoves, the cost will be $16 million. The estimated present value of resulting operating profits (without allowing for increased costs) is $21 million if there is a significant increase in demand and $17 million if there is a moderate increase in demand for wood- and coal-burning stoves. Increased profits result partly from operating efficiencies in a new plant.

Exercise 1

Construct the decision tree for this problem.

Exercise 2

Use the information in the decision tree you constructed in exercise 1 to answer the questions that follow.

a.   Use your decision tree to determine the expected value of each alternative (show your calculations).

b.   Which alternative (build new plant or expand old building) should the company select?

Experience 6-4   Personnel Promotion Decision

Introduction

All managers have to make decisions affecting their subordinates--paying, promoting, transferring, disciplining, firing. These are difficult decisions to make, because they often influence both organizational effectiveness and the lives of the individuals involved. Sometimes, the decision is positive for both the organization and the individual, but sometimes the organizational needs do not fit the individual's personal needs. Frequently, feelings and emotional reactions enter into decision making.

In making decisions, managers need to be aware of the criteria that are being used to evaluate alternatives. Sometimes, these criteria are objective and fairly tangible--the result of a conscious planning and goal-setting process. Sometimes, these criteria--often very important ones--are less clearly articulated. They may reflect a manager's personal biases and values. For example, some managers place great value on dependability and length of service, while other managers feel that seniority should be given only secondary consideration in personnel decisions.

Some decision criteria are primarily organizational in nature--efficiency, profitability, dollar costs, ability of two or more departments to be cooperative, and so on. Other criteria are much more personal to the decision-maker--the impact of a particular decision on the decision maker's career, how easy or difficult the decision will make the decision-maker's job, the difficulty in communicating unpleasant messages to others, and how that makes the decision-maker feel. Most of the time, both organizational and personal criteria are likely to influence the decision maker.

Familiarize yourself with the incident that follows; then complete the exercises as directed.

Incident

You are Fred Donner, the personnel manager in the home office of a large insurance company. Your department serves several thousand people who work in the home office. You report to the vice-president of personnel for the company, as do the managers of a personnel research department, a staff training department, and a corporate publications department. The various regional offices have their own personnel departments, which are relatively small. Your department is responsible for wage and salary administration, employment, training, insurance and benefits, employee services (including cafeteria, parking, recreation), and safety and security.

Because of the death of the personnel manager in a regional office, a vacancy has arisen. No one presently in the regional office is experienced enough to fill the vacancy, but two of the supervisors who work for you appear to be good possibilities. You have to make a recommendation soon, and while you are pleased that it will be possible to promote one of your people, you wonder what effect his or her leaving will have on your own department.

Cindy presently is supervisor of hourly employment in your department. She came to the company five years ago after earning her master's degree in personnel administration from the state university. She has done an outstanding job and has accepted responsibilities usually reserved for individuals somewhat older. Her experience includes one year as an assistant in the wage and salary section, one year as an employment interviewer, and three years as a supervisor. She has clearly demonstrated her competency. She has fine ability to get people to work with her and for her. Her interpersonal skills have enabled her to handle a number of sensitive situations, and she is well organized and an effective planner. Her personality and attractiveness may have helped to open doors for her, and she has been able to get people to accept some innovations in employment standards and procedures. She is single and says she is very career oriented and will keep working even if she does get married. You believe that she has excellent potential for a highly successful managerial career.

The other possible candidate for the job--Bob--has been outstanding for the past five years as supervisor of wage and salary administration. He has worked for the company for seventeen years, mostly in personnel. He has an undergraduate degree in psychology, is in his early forties, and is married with three children. He works hard and diligently and probably has as much knowledge of company personnel policies as anyone. Bob has played an important role in the updating and development of the wage and salary programs of the company. A few people find him a bit impatient and abrupt, perhaps in part because he has high expectations both for himself and his employees. The overall output of his section has been excellent. Recently, he has indicated that he feels he has spent enough time in his present job and would welcome a chance for additional responsibilities.

The vacant position in the regional office reports to the regional manager, with only advisory contacts with the home office. There are several hundred employees in the regional office, and the personnel department has about half a dozen employees. The job will encompass broader, more general responsibilities than do the more specialized supervisory jobs in the home office. There appears to be a considerable need to improve the personnel program in the regional office, and some of the older line managers there may be somewhat resistant to change.

You have to decide which person--Cindy or Bob--to promote to the vacant position. In making your decision, you are aware that you must consider as many of the relevant criteria as possible. Some of the factors you know you must consider include:

1. Effects on the organization. What would be the impact on morale if a long-service employee like Bob is bypassed for a younger person? On the other hand, is Bob, in fact, the best suited for the new job? Who would make the greatest contribution to the new job?

2. Effects on your home office department. You stand to lose an excellent employee. How will your people feel about the decision?

3. Effects on Bob and Cindy.

4. Effects on you personally. What will be the impact of the decision on your reputation? On your ability to continue doing your job? What additional work will you create for yourself?

5. What will you tell the individual who is not promoted?

Exercise 1

Working individually, develop two lists of criteria that could be used in making the decision. One list should be "Organizational Criteria for Promotion"; the other list should be "Personal Criteria for Promotion." Each list should include at least four or five criteria.

Organizational Criteria for Promotion   Personal Criteria for Promotion

Exercise 2

a. Form into groups of four or five people to discuss the criteria you developed in exercise 1; then develop a group list of the criteria ranked by priority.

b. Use the criteria your group has prioritized and arrive at a decision based on these criteria. Identify the person the group selected, and be prepared to explain why you selected the person you did.

Exercise 3

Explain to the class who your group promoted and why that person was chosen. Summarize the results for the class by tallying the number of groups selecting each candidate and then writing each group's major rationale for making that choice.

a. Tally of groups selecting Cindy

Major rationales for making this choice

b. Tally of groups selecting Bob

Major rationales for making this choice.

Exercise 4

Your instructor will choose two people from those groups that selected Bob to participate in role play 1 and two people from those groups that selected Cindy to participate in role play 2. After each role play, discuss "Fred's" effectiveness in communicating his decision. Then, in the space provided, write what you have learned about communicating such decisions from participating in, observing, or discussing these role plays.

Exercise 5

Answer the questions that follow about the experience you have just been involved in.

a.   Which promotion criteria should receive the highest priority? Explain.

b.   Could this nonprogrammed decision problem in fact have been handled through a more programmed approach? Explain.

c.   What does this experience suggest about decision making?

7 STRATEGIC PLANNING

Chapter Summary

The material in this chapter explains how developing a competitive strategy fits into strategic planning and discusses the strategic planning process as a whole. Major topics included in this chapter are: (1) strategic planning, (2) tactical planning, (3) comparing and coordinating strategic and tactical planning, (4) and planning and levels of management.

Learning Objective 1   *Definitions of both strategic planning and strategy*

Strategic planning is long-range planning that focuses on the organization as a whole. Long range usually is defined as a period of time extending about three to five years into the future. Hence, managers are trying to determine what their organization should do to be successful at some point three to five years in the future. The most successful managers tend to be those that are able to encourage innovative strategic thinking within their organizations.

Managers may have a problem trying to decide exactly how far into the future they should extend their strategic planning. As a general rule, they should follow the **commitment principle**, which states that managers should commit funds for planning only if they can anticipate, in the foreseeable future, a return on planning expenses as a result of the long-range planning analysis. Realistically, planning costs are an investment and, therefore, should not be incurred unless a reasonable return on that investment is anticipated.

Strategy is defined as a broad and general plan developed to reach long-range organizational objectives. Actually, strategy is the end result of strategic planning. Every organization should have a strategy of some sort. For a strategy to be worthwhile, however, it must be consistent with organizational objectives, which, in turn, must be consistent with organizational purpose.

Learning Objective 2   *An understanding of the strategy management process*

Strategy management is the process of ensuring that an organization possesses and benefits from the use of an appropriate organizational strategy. An appropriate strategy, therefore, is a strategy best suited to the needs of an organization at a particular time. The strategy management process is generally thought to consist of five sequential and continuing steps: (1) environmental analysis, (2) establishing organizational direction, (3) strategy formulation, (4) strategy implementation, and (5) strategic control.

Learning Objective 3   *A knowledge of the impact of environmental analysis on strategy formulation*

The first step of the strategy management process is environmental analysis. Chapter 2 presented an organization as an open management system, a system which is constantly interacting with its environment. An organization can only be successful if it is appropriately matched to its environment. Environmental analysis is the study of the environment in which an organization exists to pinpoint environmental factors that can significantly influence organizational operations.

For purposes of environmental analysis, the environment is generally divided into three distinct levels: the general environment, the operating environment, and the internal environment. Overall, managers must be aware of these three environmental levels, understand how each level impacts organizational performance, and then formulate organizational strategies in response to this understanding.

The general environment is defined as that level of an organization's external environment which contains components normally having broad and little immediate implication for managing an organization. Factors normally considered to be components of the general environment are defined and discussed below:

- **The economic component** is that part of the general environment which indicates how resources are being distributed and used within the environment. This component is based on economics, a science that focuses on understanding how people of a particular community or nation produce, distribute, and use various goods and services. Important issues considered in an economic analysis of an environment generally include the wages paid to labor, inflation, the taxes paid by labor and businesses, the cost of materials used during the production process, and the prices at which produced goods and services are sold to customers. Economic issues such as these can significantly influence the environment in which a company operates and the ease or difficulty the organization experiences in attempting to reach its objectives. Organizational strategy should reflect the specific economic issues within the organization's environment.

- The **social component** describes characteristics of the society in which the organization exists. Two important features of a society commonly studied during environmental analysis are demographics and social values.
- **Demographics** are the statistical characteristics of a population. Demographic characteristics like increases in population and changes in income distribution among various population segments can influence the reception of organizational goods and services within the organization's environment and thus should be reflected in organizational strategy.
- **Social values** are the relative degrees of worth that society places upon the manner in which it exists and functions. Over time, social values can change dramatically, causing obvious changes in the way people live.
- The **political component** is that part of the general environment which contains those elements related to government affairs. Types of government in existence and lobbying efforts by interest groups are examples.
- The **legal component** is that part of the general environment which contains passed legislation. Simply stated, this component contains rules or laws which society members must follow; examples are the Clean Air Act of 1963 (most recently amended in 1990) that focuses on minimizing air pollution, the Occupational Safety and Health Act of 1970 (most recently amended in 1984) that aims at maintaining a safe workplace, the Comprehensive Environmental Response, Compensation and Liability Act of 1980 (most recently amended in 1988) that emphasizes controlling hazardous waste sites, and the Consumer Products Safety Act of 1972 (most recently amended in 1988) that upholds the notion that businesses must provide safe products for consumers. Over time new laws will be enacted and old ones will be eliminated.
- The **technology component** includes new approaches to producing goods and services--from new procedures to the introduction of new equipment. Contemporary trends toward exploiting robots to improve productivity is an example of the technology component in the general environment being tracked by many modern managers.

The **operating environment** is that level of the organization's external environment which contains components normally having relatively specific and more immediate implications for managing the organization. The major components in this environmental level are generally thought to include customers, competition, labor, suppliers, and international issues.

- The **customer component** is comprised of factors relating to those who buy goods and services provided by the organization. Developing profiles, or describing in detail those who buy organizational products, helps management to generate ideas for improving customer acceptance of organizational goods and services.
- The **competition component** is comprised of those with whom an organization must battle in order to obtain resources. Overall, strategy involves the search for a plan of action that will give one organization an advantage over its competitors. Basically, the purpose of competitive analysis is to help management understand strengths, weaknesses, capabilities, and possible likely strategies of existing and potential competitors.
- The **labor component** is comprised of factors influencing the supply of workers available to perform needed organizational tasks. Issues such as skill levels, trainability, desired wage rates, average age of potential workers, and the desirability of working within a particular company are important to the operation of the organization.
- The **supplier component** entails all variables related to those individuals or agencies that provide organizations with resources needed to produce goods or services. Such agencies or individuals are called suppliers. Issues like how many suppliers offer specified resources for sale, the relative quality of materials offered by the suppliers, the reliability of the suppliers' deliveries, and credit terms offered by suppliers all become important in managing an organization effectively and efficiently.
- The **international component** is comprised of all factors relating to international operations. Significant factors within this component include foreign environment laws, politics, culture, and economics.

The **internal environment** is that level of the organization's environment which exists inside the organization and normally has immediate and specific implications for managing the organization. Unlike components of the general and operating environments which exist outside the organization, components of the internal environment exist within the organization. In broad terms, the internal environment includes organizational aspects regarding marketing, financing, and accounting. From a more specific management viewpoint, the internal environment includes aspects regarding planning, organizing, influencing, and controlling within an organization.

Establishing organizational direction is the second step of the strategy management process. Through an interpretation of information gathered during environmental analysis, managers can determine the direction in which an organization should move. Two important ingredients of organizational direction are organizational mission and organizational objectives. **Organizational mission** is the purpose for which, or reason why, an organization exists. A **mission statement** is a written document developed by management, normally based upon input by managers as well as nonmanagers, that describes and explains the actual mission of an organization. An organizational mission is normally very important to an organizartion because it usually helps management to increase the probability that an organization will be successful. This probability is increased for several reasons. First, the existence of an organizational mission helps management to focus human effort in a common direction. Second, it serves as a sound rationale for allocating resources. Third, it pinpoints broad but important job areas within an organization. The purpose of an organization is contained in its mission statement. As a result, useful **organizational objectives** must reflect and flow naturally from an organizational mission which, in turn, was designed to reflect and flow naturally from the results of an environmental analysis.

Strategy formulation, which is the third step of the strategy management process, is the process of determining appropriate courses of action for achieving organizational objectives and thereby accomplishing organizational purpose. Critical question analysis, SWOT analysis, and business portfolio analysis are three tools available to managers to assist in strategy formulation.

Learning Objective 4   *Insights on how to use Critical Question Analysis and SWOT analysis to formulate strategy*

Formulating appropriate organizational strategy is a process of **critical question analysis**, which consists of answering the following four basic questions:

1. What are the purpose(s) and objective(s) of the organization? The answer to this question tells where the organization wants to go. Appropriate strategy reflects organizational purpose and objectives. By answering this question during strategy formulation, managers are likely to remember this important point and thereby minimize inconsistencies among purposes, objectives, and strategies.
2. Where is the organization presently going? The answer to this question can tell managers if an organization is achieving organization goals and, if so, whether or not the level of such progress is satisfactory. Whereas the first question focuses on where the organization wants to go, this one focuses on where the organization is actually going.
3. In what kind of environment does the organization now exist? Both internal and external environments are covered in this question. Naturally, appropriate strategy must reflect such factors.
4. What can be done to better achieve organizational objectives in the future? The answer to this question actually results in the strategy of the organization. This question should only be answered after managers have had adequate opportunity to reflect on the answers to the previous three questions. Managers can develop appropriate organizational strategy only if they have a clear understanding of where the organization wants to go, where the organization is going, and the environment in which the organization exists.

Developing organizational strategy by answering the preceding four questions is a relatively simple, straightforward strategy development technique.

Another strategy development technique that uses somewhat different procedures is SWOT analysis. **SWOT analysis** is a strategic planning tool that matches internal organizational strengths and weaknesses with external opportunities and threats. SWOT is an acronym for a firm's Strengths and Weaknesses and its environmental Opportunities and Threats. If managers carefully review such strengths, weaknesses, opportunities, and threats, a useful strategy for ensuring organizational success in the future will become evident.

Learning Objective 5   *An understanding of how to use business portfolio analysis and industry analysis to formulate strategy*

Business portfolio analysis is another strategy development tool that has gained wide acceptance. Business portfolio analysis is an organizational strategy formulation technique that is based on the philosophy that organizations should develop strategy much as they handle investment portfolios. Just as sound financial investments should be supported and unsound ones should be discarded, sound organizational activities should be emphasized and unsound ones deemphasized. Two business portfolio tools are the BCG Growth-Share Matrix and GE's Multifactor Portfolio Matrix.

The **BCG (Boston Consulting Group) Growth-Share Matrix** approach to business portfolio analysis involves development of business-related strategy based primarily on the market share of businesses and the growth of markets in which businesses exist. The first step in using the BCG approach is identifying strategic business unit (SBUs) that exist within the organization. A **strategic business unit** is defined as a significant organizational segment that is analyzed to develop organizational strategy aimed at generating future "business" or revenue.

After SBUs have been identified for a particular organization, the next step in using the BCG Matrix is to categorize the SBUs as being within one of the four matrix quadrants. SBUs can be categorized as "stars," "cash cows," "question marks," or "dogs." SBUs that are "stars" have a high share of a high-growth market. These SBUs typically need large amounts of cash to support their rapid and significant growth. SBUs that are "cash cows" have a large share of a market that is growing only slightly. These SBUs provide the organization with larger amounts of cash. Since the market is not growing significantly, however, this cash generally is used to meet financial demands of the organization in other areas. SBUs that are "question marks" have a small share of a high-growth market. These SBUs are called "question marks" because it is uncertain whether management should invest more cash in them to get a larger share of the market, or whether management should deemphasize or eliminate them because such an investment would be ineffective. SBUs that are "dogs" have a relatively small share of a low-growth market. These SBUs may barely support themselves, or they may even drain cash resources that other SBUs have generated.

Companies like Westinghouse and Shell Oil have used the BCG Matrix in their strategy management process. There are, however, some possible pitfalls managers should avoid in using this technique. For example, the matrix does not consider such factors as: (1) various types of risk associated with product development; (2) threats that inflation and other economic conditions can create in the future; and (3) social, political, and ecological pressures. Managers must remember to weigh such factors carefully when designing organizational strategy based upon the BCG matrix.

The General Electric Company has also developed a popular portfolio analysis tool. This tool, called the **GE Portfolio Matrix**, helps managers develop organizational strategy that is based primarily upon market attractiveness and business strengths. The GE Portfolio Matrix was designed to be more complete than the BCG Portfolio Matrix. First, each of the organization's businesses or SBUs is plotted in a matrix on two dimensions, industry attractiveness and business strengths. Each of these two dimensions is actually a composite of a variety of factors that each firm must determine for itself given its own unique situation. When plotted in the matrix, each circle represents a company line of business or SBU, circle size indicates the relative market size, and the shaded portion; the porportion of the total SBU market the company has captured. Specific strategies for a company are implied by where their businesses (circles) fall on the matrix. Businesses falling in the cells that form a diagonal from lower left to upper right are medium strength businesses that should be invested in only selectively, those to the left of this diagonal are the strongest and should be invested in and helped to grow, and those to the right of the diagonal are low in over all strength and are serious candidates for divesting. Portfolio models provide graphic frameworks for analyzing relationships among the businesses of an organization and can provide useful strategy recommendations. However, no such model yet devised provides a universally accepted approach for dealing with these issues.

Perhaps the most well known tool for formulating strategy is a model developed by Michael E. Porter. **Porter's Model for industry analysis** outlines the primary forces that determine competitiveness within an industry and illustrates how the forces are related. Understanding the forces that determine competitiveness within an industy should help managers to develop strategies that will help them to make individual companies within the industry more competitive. Porter has developed three generic strategies to illustrate the kinds of strategies managers might utilize to make organizations more competitive. These are: (1) **differentiation**--a strategy that focuses on making an organization more competitive by developing a product that customers perceive as being different from products offered by competitors, (2) **cost leadership**--a strategy that focuses on making an organization more competitive by producing its products more cheaply than competitors, and (3) **focus**--a strategy that emphasizes making an organization more competitive by targeting a particular customer.

Organizational strategies that can evolve as a result of using one or more of the strategy tools are: (1) growth, (2) stability, (3) retrenchment, and (4) divestiture. **Growth** is a strategy adopted by management to increase the amount of business that an SBU is currently generating. The growth strategy is generally applied to "star" SBUs or to "question mark" SBUs that hold the potential of becoming "stars." **Stability** is a strategy adopted by management to maintain or slightly improve the amount of business that an SBU is generating. This strategy is generally applied to "cash cows" since these SBUs are already in an advantageous position. Through **retrenchment** strategy, management attempts to strengthen or protect the amount of business an SBU is generating. The retrenchment strategy generally is applied to "cash cows" or "stars" that begin to lose market share. **Divestiture** is a strategy generally adopted to eliminate an SBU that is not generating a satisfactory amount of business and has little hope of doing so in the near future. The organization sells or closes down the SBU in question. This strategy generally is applied to SBUs that are "dogs" or that are "question marks" that have failed to increase market share but still require significant amounts of cash.

Strategy implementation, the fourth step of the strategy management process, is putting formulated strategies into action. Without success in strategy implementation, valuable and worthwhile strategies that managers have developed are virtually worthless. The successful implementation of strategy requires four basic skills. These are: **interacting skill**--the ability to manage people during implementation, **allocating skill**--the ability to provide organizational resources necessary to implement a strategy, **monitoring skill**--the ability to use information to determine if a problem has arisen that is blocking implementation, and **organizing skill**--the ability to create a network of people throughout the organization that can help to solve implementation problems when they occur. Overall, the successful implementation of a strategy requires all four of the above mentioned skills, but perhaps the most important requirement is knowing and being able to involve people who can solve specific implementation problems when those problems arise.

Strategic control, the last step of the strategy management process, is monitoring and evaluating the strategy management process as a whole in order to make sure that it is operating properly. Strategic control focuses on improving, if necessary, activities involved in environmental analysis, establishing organizational direction, strategy formulation, strategy implementation, and strategic control itself. Overall, strategic control focuses on ensuring that all steps of the strategy management process are appropriate, compatible, and functioning properly.

Learning Objective 6   *Insights on what tactical planning is, and on how strategic and tactical planning should be coordinated*

   Tactical planning is short-range planning that emphasizes current operations of various parts of the organization. Short range is defined as a period of time extending only about one year or less into the future. Managers use tactical planning to outline what the various parts of the organization must do for the organization to be successful at some point one year or less into the future. Managers need both tactical and strategic planning programs, and these programs must be highly related to be successful. Tactical planning should focus on what to do in the short run to help the organization achieve the long-run objectives determined by strategic planning.

   Managers must remember, however, several basic differences between strategic planning and tactical planning. First, it is usually advisable to have strategic plans mainly developed by upper-level management and tactical plans mainly developed by lower-level management. Second, facts upon which to base strategic plans are usually more difficult to gather than facts upon which to base tactical plans. Third, strategic plans generally are less detailed than tactical plans. Fourth, strategic plans cover a relatively long period of time, while tactical plans cover a relatively short period of time.

Knowing You Know

Matching   *Directions: Match items 1--15 with items a-o. There is only one correct answer for each item.*

_____ 1.   Strategy management
_____ 2.   Internal environment
_____ 3.   BCG approach to business portfolio analysis
_____ 4.   Strategic Business Unit
_____ 5.   Strategic planning
_____ 6.   SWOT analysis
_____ 7.   "Stars"
_____ 8.   Retrenchment strategy
_____ 9.   Tactical planning
_____10.   Operating environmen
_____11.   "Cash cows"
_____12.   Growth
_____13.   Middle managers
_____14.   Commitment principl
_____15.   Environmental analysis

a.   Long-range planning that focuses on the organization as a whole
b.   Level of an organization's external environment which contains components normally having relatively immediate and specific implications for managing the organization
c.   Level of organization's environment which exists inside the organization and normally has immediate and specific implications for managing the organization
d.   Have a high share of a high-growth market
e.   Used to strengthen or protect the amount of business that an SBU is generating
f.   Development of business-related strategy that is based primarily on market share of businesses and growth of markets in which businesses exist
g.   Have a large share of a market that is growing only slight
h.   A strategy used to increase the amount of business
i.   A significant organizational segment that is analyzed to develop organizational strategy aimed at generating future "business" or revenue
j.   They usually plan neither for the short term nor the long term
k.   Study of the environment that affects the organization
l.   The process of ensuring that an organization possesses and benefits from the use of an appropriate strategy
m.   Use of funds for planning only if there is a foreseeable return
n.   Short-range planning
o.   Strategic planning tool

16. The strategy management process consists of five sequential and continuing steps. What is the correct order of these steps?
    a.   implementation, control, formulation, establishing organizational direction, and environmental analysis
    b.   establishing organizational direction, environmental analysis, formulation, implementation, and control
    c.   environmental analysis, establishing organizational direction, formulation, inplementation, and control
    d.   control, formulation, implementation, establishing organizational direction, and environmental analysis
    e.   none of the above reflect the proper sequence

17. Which of the following is *not* a component of the general environment?
    a. economic
    b. competitive
    c. legal
    d. technology
    e. all are components of the general environment

18. What strategy development tool requires the answering of four basic questions?
    a. SWOT analysis
    b. environmental analysis
    c. business portfolio analysis
    d. critical question analysis
    e. all of the above

19. SBUs that have a small share of a high-growth market are called
    a. "dogs"
    b. "question marks"
    c. "cash cows"
    d. "stars"
    e. unmanageable

20. Divestiture is
    a. a strategy adopted to increase the amount of business
    b. a strategy used to maintain or slightly improve a business
    c. a strategy used to improve a shrinking market
    d. a strategy adopted to eliminate an SBU
    e. none of the above

21. Short-range planning that emphasizes current operations is called
    a. strategic planning
    b. tactical planning
    c. obsolete planning
    d. incomplete planning
    e. none of the above

22. Upper-level managers primarily plan for the
    a. short term
    b. intermediate term
    c. long term
    d. all of the above
    e. none of the above

23. A strategy is defined as
    a. a broad, general plan developed to reach long-range organizational objectives
    b. the end result of objective setting
    c. the process of determining the objectives of the organization
    d. assumptions upon which management alternatives are based
    e. none of these are acceptable definitions of a strategy

24. Which of the following is *not* a step in the process of strategy management?
    a. strategy results measurement
    b. strategy evaluation
    c. strategy modification
    d. strategy formulation
    e. all of these are steps in the process of strategy management

25. The commitment principle states
    a. that managers are committed to shoulder job responsibilities once they accept the job
    b. that managers should commit funds for planing only if they can anticipate a return on planning expenses as a result of the long-range planning analysis
    c. that any manager is committed to work toward reaching the superordinate organizational objective
    d. all of these pertain to the commitment principle
    e. none of these pertain to the commitment principle

Applying What You Know

Experience 7-1   Identifying Environmental Threats and Opportunities*

Introduction

The external environment in which an organization operates provides both threats and opportunities. Threats are trends or occurrences that can cause the firm to lose sales volume, customers, or profits. Opportunities are trends that, if identified quickly, can provide the organization with new product ideas, markets, or customer groups.

A major portion of strategy management consists of environmental analysis. External environmental analysis is done so that the organization can identify potential threats and opportunities and develop plans, rather than react to changes. In order to perform an environmental analysis efficiently and effectively, a manager must thoroughly understand how organizational environments are structured. The environment of an organization is often divided into three distinct levels for analysis purposes. These are titled the general and the operating environment, which are considered external environments, and the internal environment. The **general environment** had broad long-term management implications: it includes economic, social, political, legal, and technological components. The level of an organization's external environment that contains components normally having relatively specific and more immediate implications for managing the organization is the operating environment. The **operating environment** includes customers, competitors, labor, suppliers, and international issues. The internal environment includes specific issues with immediate implications. In broad terms, the **internal environment** includes factors related to organizational, marketing, financial, personnel, and production issues. However, from a management perspective, issues related to planning, organizing, influencing, and controlling provide the analytical framework.

Opportunities and threats are usually seen as coming from outside the organization (external) while strengths and weaknesses are identified from internal analysis. The purpose of this experience is to provide you with the opportunity to conduct an external environmental analysis of an actual company and develop a threat and opportunity profile from that analysis. Your instructor will provide you with further instructions and assign you a specific company.

---

*Experience 7-1 was developed by C. E. Kellogg, the University of Mississippi, and updated by L. A. Graf, Illinois State University. Used with permission of the author.

Exercise 1

Find copies of three articles that indicate environmental occurrences that are either threats or opportunities for the company that you and/or your group have been assigned. Provide a brief description in the space provided of the relationship between the environmental force and your assigned firm. You should be prepared to fully discuss with the class the information that you assimilate.

EXTERNAL ENVIRONMENTAL ANALYSIS FOR (FIRM NAME):_____

a.   General Environment:

Economic

1. _____

2. _____

3. _____

Social

1. _____

2. _____

3. _____

Political

1. _____

2. _____

3. _____

Legal

1. _____

2. _____

3. _____

Technological

1. _____

2. _____

3. _____

b. Operating Environment:

Customers

1. _____

2. _____

3. _____

Competitors

1. _____

2. _____

3. _____

Labor

1. _____

2. _____

3. _____

Suppliers

1. _____

2. _____

3. _____

International

1. _____

2. _____

3. _____

Exercise 2

a. For each environmental area, assess whether the information provided by you and/or your group members indicates that the area provides an opportunity or a threat. Explain in the space provided.

General Environment:

Economic

Social

Political

Legal

Technological

Operating Environment:

Customers

Competitors

Labor

Suppliers

International

b.   As a group, identify the area that provides the greatest opportunities and the area that poses the greatest threats for your firm.

c.   Do you think that the same areas you identified in part b will be important for the companies that other class groups are examining? Explain.

Exercise 3

a.   As a group, develop some potential strategies for how your firm should prepare for the threats and opportunities identified.

b.   Should other firms in the same industry use similar strategies since they face a similar environment? Explain.

Exercise 4

Explain what you have gained from this experience.

Experience 7-2   Identifying Grand Strategies by Type

Introduction

A grand strategy is a term meaning the overall general plan of an enterprise. Your text identifies four such grand organizational strategies: growth, stability, retrenchment, and divestiture. In the exercises that follow, you have the opportunity to test your skill at identifying the type of underlying grand strategy by ten well-known business organizations.

Exercise 1

Read the descriptions that follow of the strategies being used by ten well-known business organizations. Then write the grand strategy or strategies (growth, stability, retrenchment, or divestiture) being followed by each firm in the blank to the left of the company description.

Type of Strategy(s)   **Company**

a._____   *Union Pacific Railroad*[1] In the late 1960s, the Union Pacific Railroad made an important strategic decision: to move into the energy field. This decision led to the purchase of the Champlin Petroleum Company, which is engaged in the exploration, projection, manufacturing, transportation and marketing of petroleum products; the Rocky Mountain Energy Company, which conducts extensive mining operations and owns 25 percent of all U.S. coal reserves; and the Upland Industries Corporation, a land development/land management subsidiary. The company's strategic plan has basically two parts: to maintain the railroad (keep it in the best possible physical condition) and to aggressively develop its natural resources.

b._____   *Mary Kay Cosmetics, Inc.*[2] Richard R. Rogers, president of Mary Kay Cosmetics and son of founder Mary Kay Ash, is looking beyond direct sales to a new strategy. Elements of this new strategy include doing a better job of screening new employees and evaluating employee performance, increasing television advertising of the firm's products, expanding the product line into hair care and lotion products, and establishing Mary Kay products in foreign markets.

c._____   *Bethlehem Steel Corporation*[3]   Despite a depressed market for its major product, Bethlehem Steel will continue to place available dollars into the steel business for at least the next couple of years. Management at Bethlehem believes that the company's efforts to become "the lowest cost" steel maker in the industry will pay off when the demand picks up.

d._____   *Philip Morris*[4] In 1969, Philip Morris paid $130 million for controlling interest in Miller Brewing Company. Shortly after the transaction was finalized, Miller offered its "Lite" beer to the market, pursuing a very creative and aggressive advertising campaign. This effort moved Miller from seventh to second in the highly competitive brewing industry.

e. _____ *International Telephone and Telegraph (ITT)*[5] During the 1970s, International Telephone and Telegraph expanded vigorously, buying firms in many different areas, including heating and cooling systems, food, cosmetics, wire products, and electrical parts distribution. By decade's end, the company knew that the returns on investment from many of these acquisitions were too low to justify keeping them. As a result, within a twenty-four-month time period, ITT sold more than thirty businesses, which together accounted for total revenues of $1.2 billion.

f. _____ *Firestone Tire and Rubber Company*[6] After suffering a negative cash flow of $391.5 million in three years and accumulating debt of more than $1 billion, Firestone hired Zenith Corporation's John J. Nevin to become chairman and CEO. His first action was to nullify Firestone's decade-old strategy of trying to be the market leader in all lines of tires. To implement this strategy, Nevin initiated action to sell operations in five foreign countries, reduced ownership to a minority position in other foreign subsidiaries, shut down seventeen U.S. and Canadian tire plants, and reduced the variety of tires produced from 7,300 to 2,600.

g. _____ *Pan American World Airways*[7] In 1982, faced with increased competition and an economic downswing, C. Edward Acker, Pan Am's CEO, initiated a change in strategy. Pan Am's plan was to reduce its work force from thirty thousand to twenty-five thousand, to cut flight miles by 8 percent and expenses by 4 percent, and to attempt to keep average fares unchanged.

h. _____ *Motorola*[8] Mention the name Motorola, and many people still think of televisions. Actually, by the early 1980s, Motorola had been out of television production for years, having sold its profitless Quasar line to Mitsushita Electric Industrial Company of Japan in 1974. In the 1970s, Motorola began an acquisition strategy designed to add computers to its base in electronics. The company purchased the Codex Corporation, a supplier of computer equipment, and Four-Phase Systems, Inc., a manufacturer of computer terminals and a software supplier. It also began to look into mobile communications that would permit managers to communicate with a home-based computer when out of the office. By 1981, the company dominated the U.S. mobile communications market and was fast closing in on Texas Instruments, the world leader in semiconductor chip production. As a result of these and other developments, Motorola's sales jumped from $800 million in 1970 to $3.75 billion in 1982. Sales are forecasted to reach $15 billion by the early 1990s.

i. _____ *Ralston Purina Company*[9] William P. Stiritz, recently named president of Ralston Purina, made it clear in his first interview that improving profit margins will be a priority. Stiritz indicated that the end is not just selling foods; rather, it is to earn an adequate return.

j. _____ *Apple Computer, Inc.*[10] Apple has more than 150 competitors, the most threatening of which at the moment is IBM. Apple is preparing for battle armed with what John Sculley, Apple's CEO, says is focus, discipline, and a defined marketing strategy. He also is trying to open up internal communications and improve relations with dealers by keeping them better informed.

Exercise 2

Reexamine parts *a* and *f* in exercise 1. Do you notice anything about the strategies of these two companies that is different from the strategies of the other eight companies? Explain.

Exercise 3

After discussing exercises 1 and 2, explain what you have gained from this experience.

Footnotes

1. From "Back to Railroading for a New Era," *Business Week*, 14 July 1980, 64-70.
2. From "Mary Kay Cosmetics: Looking Beyond Direct Sales to Keep the Party Going," *Business Week*, 28 March 1983, 130.
3. From Amal Nag, "Bethlehem's Near-Term Tactic Is to Stay with Steel While Competitors Diversity," *Wall Street Journal*, 15 January 1982, 10.
4. From Information on Miller Brewing Company found in *Fortune*, 29 June 1981, 62-63; *Time*, 26 April 1982, 50; and *Business Week*, 15 February 1982, 39.
5. From "ITT: Groping for a New Strategy," *Business Week*, 15 December 1980, 66-69.
6. From "Survival in the Basic Industries: How Four Companies Hope to Avoid Disaster," *Business Week*, 26 April 1982, 74-76.
7. From John D. Williams, "Pan Am Hopes That a Smaller Work Force and Fewer Flights Will Bring Back Profits," *Wall Street Journal*, 26 October 1982, 31.
8. From "Motorola's New Strategy," *Business Week*, 29 March 1982, 129.
9. From David P. Garino, "New Ralston Chief Says He'll Sacrifice Sales to Keep Company's Profit Margins High," *Wall Street Journal*, 2 July 1981, 19.
10. From Erik Larson and Carrie Dolan, "Growing Pains: Once All Alone in the Field, Apple Computer Girds for Industrial Shakeout," *Wall Street Journal*, 4 October 1983, 1, 16.

Experience 7-3 Operational Planning

Introduction

The purpose of this experience is to help you gain additional insights into operational planning. Although there are a number of ways to describe operational planning, the description of operational planning that follows should be very helpful. A key factor in successful operational planning is attention to detail. Read the section "Operational Planning"; then complete the exercises as directed.

Operational Planning

Within a framework of broad objectives, strategies, and policies, managers make operational plans for carrying out the activities necessary to achieve the objectives. Procedures, budgets, and schedules represent planned commitments to methods, money, and time. Generally, a procedure is established for handling repetitive problems or programmed decision situations. Budgets and schedules are more likely to be for one-time use, nonprogrammed situations.

The operational planning process involves a number of steps that require highly specific thinking and careful attention to detail. One way to describe the steps in operational planning is as follows:

1. Describe *where you stand today*. (Take stock of resources; evaluate current strengths and weaknesses.)
2. Develop *planning premises*. (A premise is a statement of a condition that is likely to exist in the future.)
3. Establish *goals*. (A well-stated goal should be specific and capable of being verified. To be verifiable, the objective should be observable and stated in measurable terms.)
4. Identify and evaluate specific *activities* that must be carried out to achieve the goal(s). (Since planning involves *deciding* about what will be done in the future, alternative courses of action-that is, sets of activities-will need to be considered and evaluated.) Note that activities will require resources of time, money, energy, etc., and thus the planning process involves deciding how best to use the available resources.
5. Consider the *sequence* in which activities should be carried out. Network planing techniques place special attention on the logical flow of activities. In most problem situations, a number of activities can be carried out simultaneously, and not all activities are dependent on the completion of every other activity. (For example, in building a house, once the walls are constructed, it is possible for both plumbers and electricians to work simultaneously since their activities are relatively independent of each other.)
6. Estimate the *time* required to perform each activity. Time estimates are of two types: estimates of specific work-hours required (for example, thirty-seven work-hours are required to complete activity X) and estimates of time duration (for example, the activities will begin July 1 and must be completed by September 30). In laying out a schedule of activities, a useful approach is to identify the completion date and work backward through the activities, determine the latest date at which any given activity can begin.
7. Identify the *resources* (money, people, equipment, supplies, facilities) needed for each activity.

The outcome of the operational planning process should be a time-phased schedule of activities, with an interrelated resource allocation *budget* phases in.

Exercise 1

Your group is to work step-by-step through the operational planning process on a problem you will be assigned in class. Work quickly to come up with examples of what to do in each step of the process, and be prepared to evaluate the strengths and weaknesses of the operational planning process.

Your group assignment is _____

Step 1   *Describe where you stand today.* List four current resources, strengths, weaknesses, etc. that are relevant to your task.
1.

2.

3.

4.

Step 2   *Develop planning premises.* Planning premises are statements of conditions that will be assumed to exist and that will be used in making the plan. Premises, thus, are the planning assumptions-the expected environment in which plans will operate. State two planning premises relevant to your planning task.
1.

2.

Step 3   *Establish goals.* State two possible goals in terms that are both observable and measurable.
1.

2.

(NOTE: To show steps 4, 5, 6, and 7, fill in the worksheet that follows. State at least eight to ten activities, sequence them, indicate probable time interval requirements for each activity or task, and indicate the resources needed for each activity.)

Step 4   *Identify the activities* that might be conducted to achieve goals. (Note that there may be many possible activities; later on you will have to decide which activities are the best alternatives.)

Step 5   *Arrange the activities* in a reasonable sequence.

Step 6   *Estimate the time* requirements for each activity.

Step 7   *Identify the resources* needed for each activity.

Important Note: The process of planning is likely to involve "iteration"--working through the steps, going back and changing what was done in an earlier step, working through more steps, and making final revisions.

Worksheet

Activity	Starting time or date	Ending time or date	Resource needs

Exercise 2

a.   What are the strengths and weaknesses of the operational planning process described in this experience?

b. What are the pros and cons of the argument that goals should be stated in terms that allow for observation and measurement?

c. Is operational planning more similar to strategic planning or tactical planning? Explain.

d. Discuss the implications of this experience for you personally.

8 PLANS AND PLANNING TOOLS

Chapter Summary

This chapter emphasizes several fundamental issues about plans that should be useful to managers. Basically, this chapter describes what plans are and discusses several valuable tools that can be used in actually developing plans.

Learning Objective 1   *A complete definition of a plan*

A **plan** is a specific action proposed to help the organization achieve its objectives. A critical part of the management of any organization is developing logical plans and then taking necessary steps to put the plans into action.

Learning Objective 2   *Insights regarding various dimensions of plans*

According to Kast and Rosenzweig, a plan has four major dimensions: (1) repetitiveness, (2) time, (3) scope, and (4) level. Each of these dimensions should be considered carefully during plan development. The **repetitiveness** dimension describes the extent to which a plan is used time after time. Some plans are specially designed for one certain situation that is relatively short run in nature. However, some plans are designed to be used time after time for situations that exist continually over the long run. These plans are basically repetitive in nature.

The **time dimension** is the length of the time period the plan covers. In chapter 7, strategic planning was defined as being long run in nature, and tactical planning was defined as short run. Strategic and tactical plans, then, reflect the time dimension of planning.

The **scope dimension** describes the portion of the total management system at which the plan is aimed. Some plans are designed to cover the entire open management system: the organizational environment, inputs, process, and outputs. A plan for the management system as a whole is often referred to as a master plan. Some plans, however, are developed to cover only a portion of the management system. An example would be a plan developed to cover the recruitment of new workers--a portion of the organizational input segment of the management system. The greater the portion of the management system that a plan covers, the broader the scope of the plan is said to be.

Finally, the **level dimension** of a plan indicates the level of the organization at which the plan is aimed. Top-level plans are those designed for the top management level of the organization, while middle-level and lower-level plans are designed for middle-level and lower-level management, respectively. Because of the very nature of the management system, however, plans for any level of the organization have some effect on all other levels. All parts of the management system are interdependent, and no single part can be affected without some effect on all other parts.

Learning Objective 3   *An understanding of various types of plans*

Organizational plans usually are divided into two types: standing plans and single-use plans. Standing plans are used over and over again because they focus on organizational situations that occur repeatedly, while single-use plans are used only once or several times because they focus on dealing with relatively unique situations within the organization. Standing plans can be subdivided into policies, procedures, and rules, while single-use plans can be subdivided into programs and budgets.

A **policy** is a standing plan that furnishes broad, general guidelines for channeling management thinking toward taking action consistent with reaching organizational objectives. For example, an organizational policy relating to personnel might be worded as follows: "Our organization will strive to recruit only the most talented employees." This policy statement is very broad and only gives managers a general idea of what to do in the area of personnel employment.

A **procedure** is a standing plan that outlines a series of related actions that must be taken to accomplish a particular task. In general, procedures outline more specific action than do policies. An example of a procedure would be the series of steps recruiters take to interview prospective personnel in a company.

A **rule** is a standing plan that designates specific required action. A rule indicates what an organization member should or should not do and allows no room for interpretation. An example of a rule that many companies are now establishing is "No Smoking." Although policies, procedures, and rules are all standing plans, they are all defined differently and have different purposes within the organization. For them to be effective, however, policies, procedures, and rules must be consistent and mutually supportive.

A **program** is a single use plan designed to carry out special projects within an organization. The program itself typically is not intended to be in existence over the entire life of the organization. However, it exists to achieve some purpose that, if accomplished, will contribute to the organization's long-run success. A common example of a program is the management development program found in many organizations. This program exists to raise managers' skill level. Increasing the skill level of these managers, however, is not an end in itself. The purpose of the program is to produce competent managers who are equipped to help the organization be successful over the long run. Once managerial skills have been raised to a desired level, the management development program can be deemphasized. Areas upon which modern management development programs commonly focus include understanding and using the computer as a management tool, handling international competition, and planning for a major labor shortage by the year 2000.

A **budget** is a single-use financial plan that covers a specified length of time. A firm's budget is a plan detailing how funds will be spent on labor, raw materials, capital goods, and so on, as well as how the funds for these expenditures will be obtained. Although budgets are planning devices, they are also strategies for organizational control.

Learning Objective 4   *Insights on why plans fail*

Not all plans are successful. However, if managers know why plans fail, they can take steps to eliminate the factors that cause failure and thereby increase the probability that their plans will be successful. Ringbakk indicates that plans fail when: (1) corporate planning is not integrated into the total management system; (2) there is a lack of understanding of the different steps of the planing process; (3) management at different levels in the organization has not properly engaged in or contributed to planning activities; (4) responsibility for planning is wrongly vested solely in the planning department; (5) management expects that plans developed will be realized with little effort; (6) in starting formal planning, too much is attempted at once; (7) management fails to operate by the plan; (8) financial projections are confused with planning; (9) inadequate inputs are used in planning; and (10) management fails to see the overall planning process.

Learning Objective 5   *A knowledge of various planning areas within an organization*

Organizational inputs, process, outputs, and environment are major factors in determining how successful a management system will be, and a comprehensive organizational plan should focus on each of these factors. Plant facilities planning and human resource planning normally are considered input planning-the development of proposed action that will furnish sufficient and appropriate organizational resources for reaching established organizational objectives.

Plant facilities planning involves determining the type of buildings and equipment an organization needs to reach its objectives. One important aspect of plant facilities planning its site selection, determining where a plant facility should be located. Several major areas to be considered when selecting a plant site include market location and competition (profit); suppliers, utilities, wages, and taxes (operating costs); land and development of site (investment costs); and other factors such as transportation, laws, labor, unionization, living conditions, and community relations.

One factor that can significantly influence site selection is whether a site is being selected in a foreign country. In a foreign country, management may face issues like foreign governments taking different amounts of time to approve site purchases and political pressures slowing down or preventing purchase of a site. As an example of criteria that managers might use to select sites in other countries, Japanese investors tend to locate businesses in the United states in those states which have low unionization rates, low employment rates, relatively impoverished populations, and high educational levels. Japanese managers feel that such dimensions help ensure the future success of Japanese business at a site.

Many organizations use a weighting process to compare site differences among foreign countries. Basically, this weighting process involves (1) deciding on a set of variables that are critical to obtaining an appropriate site, (2) assigning each of these variables a weight or rank of relative importance, and (3) ranking alternative sites, depending upon how they reflect these different variables.

Human resources are another concern for the input planner. Organizational objectives cannot be attained without appropriate **personnel**. Future needs for human resources mainly are influenced by employee turnover, the nature of the present work force, and the organization's rate of growth. Personnel planners should try to answer such questions as: (1) What types of people does the organization need to reach its objectives? (2) How many of each type are needed? (3) What steps for the recruitment and selection of these people should the organization take? (4) Can present employees be further trained to fill future needed positions? (5) At what rate are employees lost to other organizations? These are not the only questions personnel planners should ask, but they are representative. Coleman feels that effective human resource planning involves reflecting on organizational objectives to determine overall human resource needs, comparing these needs to the existing human resource inventory to determine net human resource needs, and, finally, seeking appropriate organization members to meet the net human resource needs.

Learning Objective 6 *A definition of forecasting*

Planning tools are techniques managers can use to help develop plans. One important planning tool is **forecasting**, the process of predicting future environmental happenings that will influence the operation of the organization. The importance of forecasting lies in its ability to help managers better understand the future makeup of the organizational environment, which, in turn, helps them to formulate more effective plans. While forecasting for the organization as a whole can provide managers with a good overall understanding of planning, other more specialized types of forecasting frequently are used, such as economic forecasts, technological forecasts, social trends forecasts, and sales forecasts. Although a complete organizational forecasting process can and usually should include all of these types of forecasting, sales forecasting typically is cited as the "key" organizational forecast. A sales forecast is a prediction of how high or how low sales will be over the period of time under consideration. It is the "key" forecast because it serves as the fundamental guideline for planning within the organization. Once the sales forecast has been completed, managers can decide, for example, if more salespeople should be hired, if more money for plant expansion must be borrowed, or if layoffs are upcoming and cutbacks in certain areas are necessary.

Learning Objective 7 *An ability to see the advantages and disadvantages of various methods of sales forecasting*

The **jury of executive opinion method** of sales forecasting is very straightforward. A group of managers within the organization assemble to discuss their opinions on what will happen to sales in the future. Since these discussion sessions usually revolve around the hunches or experienced guesses of each of the managers, the resulting forecast is a blending of expressed opinions.

A more recently developed forecasting method similar to the jury of executive opinion method is called the **delphi method**. This method also gathers, evaluates, and summarizes expert opinions as the basis for a forecast. In the basic delphi method, various experts are asked to answer independently, in writing, a series of questions about the future of sales or whatever other area is being forecasted. A summary of all answers then is prepared. No expert knows how any other expert answered the questions. Copies of the summary are given to the individual experts with the request that they modify their original answers if they think they should. Then another summary is made of these modifications, and again it is distributed to the experts. This time, however, expert opinions that deviate significantly from the norm must be justified in writing. These opinions and justifications are again summarized and distributed to the experts. Justification for all answers is now required in writing. Finally, the forecast is generated from all of the opinions and justifications that arise from the preceding step.

The **sales force estimation method** is a sales forecasting technique that predicts future sales by analyzing the opinions of salespeople. Salespeople interact with customers and use this interaction as the basis for predicting future sales. As with the jury of executive opinion method, the resulting forecast normally is a blend of the views of the salespeople as a group. The sales force estimation method is generally considered a very valuable management tool and is commonly used in business and industry throughout the world.

The **time series analysis method** predicts future sales by analyzing the historical relationships between sales and time. Information showing the relationships between sales and time typically is presented on a graph. This presentation clearly displays past trends, which can be used to predict future sales. The actual number of years included in a time series analysis will vary from company to company. As a general rule, managers should include as many years as necessary to make sure that important sales trends do not go undetected.

Managers using the time series analysis method must take a product's life cycle into account to avoid overly optimistic projections. A **product life cycle** is the five stages through which most new products and services pass. These five stages are introduction, growth, maturity, saturation, and decline. In the introduction stage, a product is brand-new, and sales are just beginning to build. In the growth stage, because the product has been in the marketplace for some time and is now becoming more accepted, product sales continue to climb. During the maturity stage, competitors enter the market, and while sales are still climbing, they normally climb at a slower rate than in the growth stage. After the maturity stage comes the saturation stage, when nearly everyone who wants the product already has it. Sales during the saturation stage typically are due to replacing a worn-out product or to population growth. The last product life cycle stage-decline-finds the product being replaced by a competing product. Managers may be able to keep products out of the decline stage through improvements in product quality or innovations. On the other hand. a product such as scissors may never reach this last stage due to the lack of competing products.

In practice, managers find that each sales forecasting method has both advantages and disadvantages (see Table 8.5 in the text). Before deciding to use a particular sales forecasting method, a manager must carefully weigh the advantages and disadvantages as they relate to his or her particular organization. A manager may decide to use a combination of these methods rather than just one.

Learning Objective 8   *A definition of scheduling*

Scheduling is the process of formulating a detailed listing of activities that must be accomplished to attain an objective. Two scheduling techniques are Gantt charts and the program evaluation and review technique (PERT).

Learning Objective 9   *An understanding of Gantt charts and PERT*

The **Gantt chart** is essentially a bar graph with time on the horizontal axis and the resource to be scheduled on the vertical axis. Possible resources to be scheduled include management system inputs, such as human resources and machines. Managers can use the chart as a summary overview of how organizational resources are being used. From this summary, managers can detect such facts as which resources are consistently contributing to productivity. Managers also can use the Gantt chart to help coordinate organizational resources. The Gantt chart can show which resources are not being used during specific periods and, therefore, can be scheduled to work on other production efforts. In addition, the Gantt chart can be used to establish realistic worker output standards. For example, if workers are completing scheduled work too quickly output standards may need to be raised so that workers are scheduled for more work per time period.

The main weakness of the Gantt chart is that it does not contain any information about the interrelationship of tasks to be performed. All tasks to be performed are listed on the chart, but there is no way of telling if one task must be performed before another can be completed. The **program evaluation and review technique (PERT)**, a technique that evolved partially from the Gantt chart, is a scheduling tool designed to emphasize the interrelationships of tasks. PERT is a network of project activities showing both estimates of time necessary to complete each activity within the project and the sequential relationship between activities that must be observed to complete the project. PERT was developed in 1958 for use in designing the Polaris submarine weapon system.

The PERT network contains two primary elements: activities and events. **Activities** are specified sets of behavior within a project, while **events** are the completions of major project tasks. Within the PERT network, each event is assigned corresponding activities that must be performed before the event can materialize. A sample PERT network designed for the building of a house is presented in text figure 8.8. In this figure, events are symbolized by boxes, and activities are symbolized by arrows. To illustrate, figure 8.8 indicates that after the event "Foundation Complete" (represented by a box) has materialized, certain activities (represented by arrows) must be performed before the event of "Frame Complete" (represented by another box) can materialize.

Two other features of a PERT network also should be emphasized. First, the left-to-right presentation of events shows how events interrelate or the sequence in which they should be performed. Second, the numbers in parentheses above each arrow indicate the units of time necessary to complete each activity. These two features help managers to ensure that only necessary work is being done on a project and that no project activities are taking too long.

Close attention should be paid to the critical path of a PERT network. The **critical path** is the sequence of events and activities requiring the longest period of time to complete. This path is called the critical path because a delay in the time necessary to complete this sequence results in a delay for the completion of the entire project. Managers try to control a project by keeping it within the time designated by the critical path. The critical path can help managers to predict which features of a schedule will become unrealistic and to provide insights concerning how the issues might be eliminated.

When designing a PERT network, managers should follow four primary steps: (1) list all activities/events that must be accomplished for a project and the sequence in which these activities/events should be performed; (2) determine how much time will be needed to complete each activity/event; (3) design a PERT network that reflects all of the information contained in steps 1 and 2; and (4) identify the critical path.

Knowing You Know

True/False   *Directions: On the lines provided, place a "T" for true and an "F" for false for each of the statements that follow.*

_____ 1.   A rule allows room for interpretation and generally outlines desired action.
_____ 2.   Two important planning tools are forecasts and schedules.
_____ 3.   The Gantt chart can be used to schedule human resources or machines.
_____ 4.   A plan is specific action proposed to help the organization achieve its objectives.
_____ 5.   Examples of standing plans are programs and budgets.
_____ 6.   If managers know why plans fail, they can take steps to eliminate the factors that cause failure and thereby increase the probability that their plans will be successful.
_____ 7.   An example of a budget commonly found in organizations is a management development program.

_____ 8. Output planning is the development of proposed action that will furnish sufficient and appropriate organizational resources for reaching established organizational objectives.

_____ 9. Events in a PERT network are defined as specified sets of behavior within a project.

_____10. Before deciding to use a particular sales forecasting method, a manager should carefully weigh the advantages and disadvantages as they relate to his or her particular organization.

_____11. Site selection is not an important task for firms such as McDonald's.

_____12. The statistical correlation method and the computer simulation method are not approaches that can be used for sales forecasting.

_____13. A product life cycle is defined as five stages through which most new products and services pass.

Multiple Choice *Directions: Circle the letter of the word or phrase that best completes each statement.*

14. According to Kast and Rosenzweig, which of the following is not a major dimension of a plan?
    a. repetitiveness
    b. level
    c. time
    d. space
    e. all of these are major dimensions of plans

15. According to your text, the forecasting method most similar to the jury of executive opinion method is the
    a. delphi method
    b. sales force estimation method
    c. time series analysis method
    d. statistical correlation method
    e. computer simulation method

16. Policies
    a. are single-use plans
    b. are a series of related actions that must be taken to accomplish a particular task
    c. are standing plans that furnish broad guidelines for channeling management thinking toward taking action consistent with reaching organizational objectives
    d. designate specific, required action
    e. are also called rules

17. Which of the following is not a correct relationship?
    a. event-represented by a circle
    b. critical path-requires longest period of time to complete
    c. activity-represented by an arrow
    d. PERT-program evaluation and resource transfer
    e. all of these are correct relationships

18. The scope dimension of a plan describes
    a. the portion of the total management system at which the plan is aimed
    b. the length of the time period the plan covers
    c. the extent to which a plan is used time after time
    d. the level in the organization at which the plan is aimed
    e. all of these describe the scope dimension of a plan

19. Plant facilities planning involves determining the type of buildings and equipment an organization needs to reach its objectives. An important aspect of plant facilities planning discussed in the text is
    a. human resource planning
    b. layout patterns
    c. inventory control
    d. site selection
    e. warehousing

20. In the PERT network, the critical path
    a. is the path deserving of the most attention
    b. requires the longest time to complete
    c. is the path in which delays can occur if the project is to be completed at the earliest possible time
    d. is that path in which those with critical project skills can be found
    e. a and b

21. Which of the following is an incorrect statement?
    a. The Gantt Chart can be used as a summary overview of how organizational resources are being used.
    b. The Gantt Chart can help managers to coordinate organizational resources.
    c. The Gantt Chart does not contain any information about the interrelationships of tasks to be performed.
    d. The Gantt Chart can be used to establish realistic worker output standards.
    e. All of these are correct statements.

22. The "key" organizational forecast is
    a. the economic forecast
    b. the sales forecast
    c. the social trends forecast
    d. the technological forecast
    e. none of these is considered to be a "key" organizational forecast

23. Forecasting
    a. is the process of formulating a detailed listing of activities that must be accomplished to attain an objective
    b. is the process that details how funds will be spent on labor, raw materials, and capital goods, as well as how the funds for these expenditures will be obtained
    c. outlines a series of related actions that must be taken to accomplish a particular task
    d. is the process of predicting future environmental happenings that will influence the operation of the organization
    e. all of these statements about forecasting are true

24. The time series analysis method
    a. predicts future sales by analyzing the historical relationship between sales and time
    b. is essentially a bar graph with time on the horizontal axis and the resource to be scheduled on the vertical axis
    c. was the forerunner to modern network techniques
    d. was developed in 1958 for use in designing the Polaris submarine weapon system
    e. none of these statement is true of the time series analysis method

25: The process of formulating a detailed listing of activities that must be accomplished to attain an objective is
    a. forecasting
    b. planning
    c. scheduling
    d. routing
    e. none of the above

Applying What You Know

Experience 8-1   Effective Scheduling: The Gantt Chart

Introduction

From reading the text, you undoubtedly know for what the Gantt Chart is used. However, knowing how to use it for planning and scheduling may be something quite different. In this experience, you use the Gantt Chart to plan and then schedule work in a hypothetical situation.

Exercise 1

Assume that your instructor has just picked you and two of your classmates to be involved in a special assignment. While the three of you are expected to work together, you have been asked to coordinate the activities of the group. The job of the group is to read and be ready to discuss ninety pages in your management textbook by class time this coming Thursday morning. (Today is the first Monday of the month.) Seventy-two additional textbook pages are to be read by the group by class time one week from today (the second Monday of the month). Plan for and then schedule these reading activities for the group using the Gantt Chart in figure 8.1.

Figure 8.1   Gantt Chart for scheduling activities of the group.

Human Resources	First Week							Monday
	Monday	Tuesday	Wednesday	Thursday	Friday	Saturday	Sunday	
You	( )	( )	( )	( )	( )	( )	( )	( )
Classmate I	( )	( )	( )	( )	( )	( )	( )	( )
Classmate II	( )	( )	( )	( )	( )	( )	( )	( )
	( )	( )	( )	( )	( )	( )	( )	( )

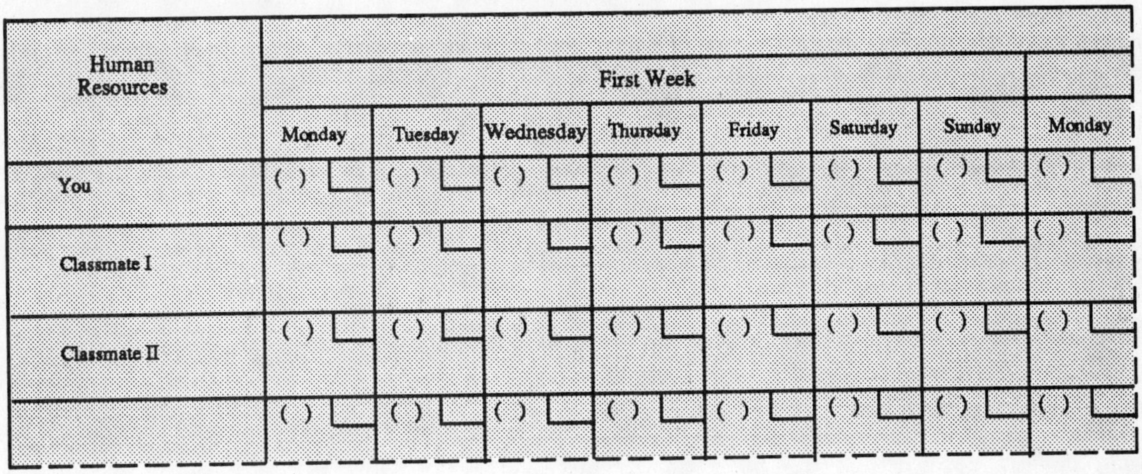

( ) Planned production for the period

▨ Actual production for the period

Γ When work is to begin

⌐ Planned time of completion

—— Percentage of work actually completed during a time period

▬▬ Cumulative actual production for a number of periods

Exercise 2

You obtain the following progress report from the other group members very late on Tuesday evening (first Tuesday of the month): classmate 1 reports that he read nineteen pages on Monday and eleven pages on Tuesday; classmate 2 indicates that she could not find the time to do any reading on Monday but read six pages on Tuesday. You realize at this time that you also are a little behind schedule; you read ten pages on Monday but only seven pages on Tuesday. Using this information, update the partially completed Gantt chart in figure 8.1 to reflect actual production (reading) through Tuesday for the group.

Exercise 3

Since you are to coordinate the efforts of the group, what *actions* would you suggest, after updating the Gantt chart, to get the group project back on schedule?

Exercise 4

How did having the information presented in the form of a Gantt chart improve your perspective of the situation on the first Tuesday evening of the month? Explain.

Experience 8-2   Changing a Flat Tire: PERT

Introduction

While the Gantt Chart is a very useful planning and scheduling tool, it has one major weakness: there is no way of telling if one task must be performed before another can be completed. The program evaluation and review technique (PERT), a technique that evolved partially from the Gantt chart, is a scheduling tool designed to emphasize the interrelationship of tasks. To increase your understanding of this planning and scheduling tool, you are asked in this experience to examine in some detail a PERT network for the changing of a flat tire. Read the incident that follows and then complete the exercises as directed.

Incident

In two days, the Midwestern Management Society (MMS) will meet in a city ninety miles from campus. You and three other class members want to attend this conference because the subject of one of the presentations is also the topic for the term project of your group. While you recognize the importance of attending the MMS conference, you are not sure whether the group should pay the thirty-dollar registration fee. The problem is transportation. The only transportation available is your father's 1946 delivery truck, and it will not be available until 10:50 A.M. on the day of the conference. The conference begins at 1:00 P.M. If you leave at 10:50 A.M. and average fifty miles per hour, you calculate that you will have twenty-two minutes remaining to get into your seat before the doors are closed and the conference begins. This, of course, is assuming that no problems are encountered on the ninety-mile trip.

After consulting with your father about the condition of the delivery truck, you discover that there is only one real area for concern: the right rear tire on the truck could go flat at any time. While a spare tire is available in the rear of the delivery truck, the truck is scheduled for deliveries until 10:50 A.M. on the day of the conference, allowing no opportunity to change the tire. In light of these circumstances, the group members decide that they would still be willing to send in the thirty-dollar registration fee if they would have at least five minutes to get into the conference room when they reach their destination. In an effort to determine how long it would take to change a flat tire, you obtain a PERT network for changing a flat tire from one of your professors (see figure 8.2).

Figure 8.2 PERT network for changing a flat tire.

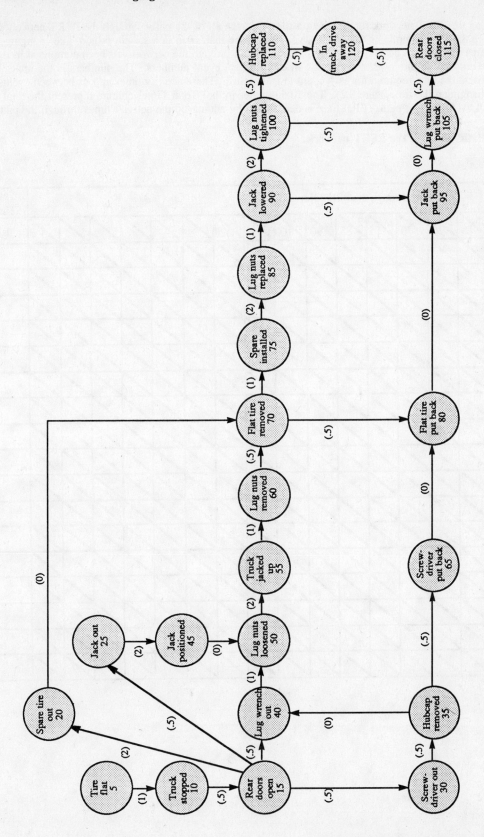

Exercise 1

After examining the PERT network for changing a flat tire, trace all of the paths through the PERT network and fill in the matrix in figure 8.3. By completing this matrix, you should see that, even in a simple project like changing a flat tire, the interrelationships of tasks can be somewhat complex. One path through the network has been completed in figure 8.3 as an example. The numbers in the lower right section of each cell are event numbers. The numbers in the upper left section of each cell represent the time required for each event to materialize. These activity times appear between events in the PERT network for changing a flat tire (figure 8.2). The 10.5 minutes in the "Total Time" column represent the total time required to complete all events in that path. Total time is determined by adding up the activity times through the path.

Figure 8.3 Paths through the PERT network.

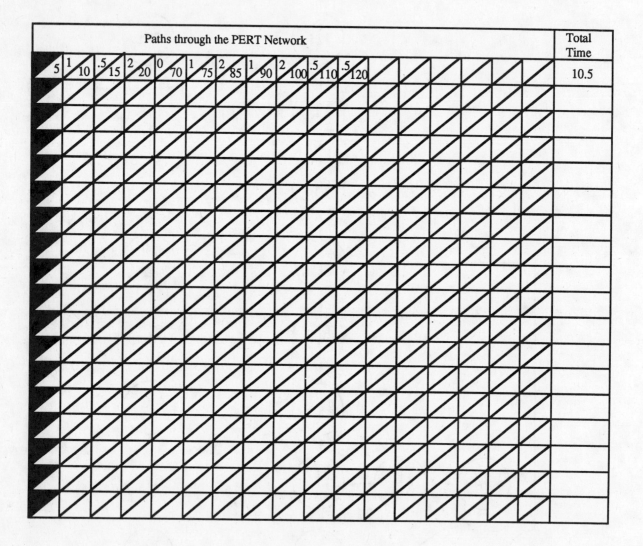

Exercise 2

Once you have filled in the matrix in figure 8.2, answer the questions that follow.

a.   How many paths through the PERT network did you identify?

b.   What is the critical path? (List the event numbers in the critical path.)

c.   What is the shortest possible time needed to change a flat tire?

d.   From the PERT network in figure 8.2, how many people would have to be simultaneously involved to change a tire in the shortest possible time? Explain.

e.   How can the PERT network for changing a flat tire be used to plan and schedule your proposed trip to the Midwestern Management Society conference? Explain.

f.   From the information obtained by completing the paths through the PERT network matrix, should your group send in the thirty-dollar registration fee and plan to attend the Midwestern Management Society conference? Explain.

Experience 8-3　Selecting a Plant Site:　An Application of the Planning Process*

Introduction

Plant site location is, in many respects, a typical application of the planning process. Read the incident that follows and then complete the exercises as directed.

Incident

The Bojo Corporation is an established manufacturer located in a small town in southwestern New York. The company was founded about ninety years ago and initially served both the railroad industry and the oil fields of northern Pennsylvania. At the present time, a large part of Bojo's business is associated with the oil industry. In recent years, however, it has branched into other fields and has been able to develop applications of products originally used in the oil fields to other areas. The Bojo Corporation is a subsidiary company of a large national firm that has headquarters in St. Louis. The national headquarters controls all capital expenditures, reviews operating budgets developed by the subsidiary corporations, follows up to ensure the meeting of budgetary goals, and also exerts strong influence in the labor relations area. All labor contracts and labor policies are determined by the headquarters staff.

In recent years, the Bojo Corporation has developed a new type of pipe coupling that is used to join two pieces of pipe without having to thread the ends of the pipes being joined or cut them to an exact length. The coupling saves time and money, and the company has experienced a remarkable sales volume from municipalities, since the coupling is used primarily to replace existing water and gas lines. There is every reason to believe that the market will expand and that the Bojo Corporation will receive a large share of the increase. Since the coupling is particularly useful in the replacement market, the greatest potential market for the immediate future is on the eastern seaboard, where the water and gas system is the oldest in the country.

The present coupling manufacturing facility, a department in the main plant, is now running at capacity, and new facilities are needed to meet the anticipated increase in demand. Since the present plant location does not permit expansion, it has been decided that a new plant should be built to house the present coupling department and to provide for future increases in volume. A member of the St. Louis controller's staff, Jack Johnson, has been assigned the task of conducting a plant location survey and submitting subsequent recommendations to the president of the Bojo Corporation and the officials of the parent company.

In preparing for his assignment, Johnson has contacted several executives, among them the executive vice-president responsible for the Bojo Corporation and other subsidiaries in Pennsylvania, New York, and Massachusetts. It is the executive vice-president's wish that the plant be located on a direct route between Pittsburgh, Pennsylvania, and its present location; or between Buffalo, New York, and its present location. Having the plant in these areas would make it convenient for him as a company executive to fly into either the Buffalo or Pittsburgh airport, rent a car, and drive directly to the plant.

A conversation with the home office vice-president for industrial relations has revealed that the company, as a matter of policy, wishes to have a different international union in the plant rather than to have the employees represented by the same union that organized the Bojo New York plant. The reason for the policy is that having a different union in each plant lessens the possibility of all plants closing as the result of a strike, since no one international union would represent more than one plant. The vice-president has indicated that it would be necessary to locate at least one hundred miles from the present plant to be assured of a different union. She also has recommended analyzing the labor rates of any community proposed as a location for the new plant so that maximum savings might be realized from low initial labor costs. She has stated further that, by starting operations with labor rates as low as possible, the company would be in a better position to increase rates in the future.

Johnson has found that the president of Bojo Corporation has a few ideas of his own to add to the picture. The president has indicated that it is mandatory that the new location have complete rail facilities, since raw materials are received most economically by rail and many of the finished product shipments could be made by rail. He wants the plant located east of the present facility to minimize transportation costs to the East Coast markets. This means a direct flow of materials from the present plant, through the new location, to the major markets between Boston and New York City on the eastern seaboard. The president is also insistent, as operating head of the company, that the new plant be located in an area with a well-defined, stable tax structure. He feels that tax stability is necessary to predict long-range profits with some degree of accuracy. Another requirement is that the site chosen be large enough to permit future expansion of the proposed plant to twice its initial size with twice the personnel. (When the plant opens, it will employ about one thousand employees.) The president of Bojo has not placed exact limitations on construction costs, provided they are in line with typical costs for the area selected.

---

*Source of Experience 8-3: Adapted from Sisk, Henry L., *Management and Organization*. © 1973 South-Western Publishing Co., Cincinnati, OH. Reprinted by permission.

Exercise 1

Assume that you are Jack Johnson. Prepare an initial determination of the relative significance of the factors considered to be important by:

a.   The executive vice-president from the home office

b.   The vice-president for industrial relations from the home office

c.   The president of the subsidiary Bojo Corporation

Exercise 2

Now that you have evaluated the plant site location factors mentioned by executives in this incident and have identified those factors that you feel should have a significant bearing on the new plant location decision, indicate on the map in figure 8.4 the area in the northeastern United States that would remain an acceptable plant site location territory after taking the significant geographical concerns of the executives into consideration.

Figure 8.4   Map of the northeastern United States

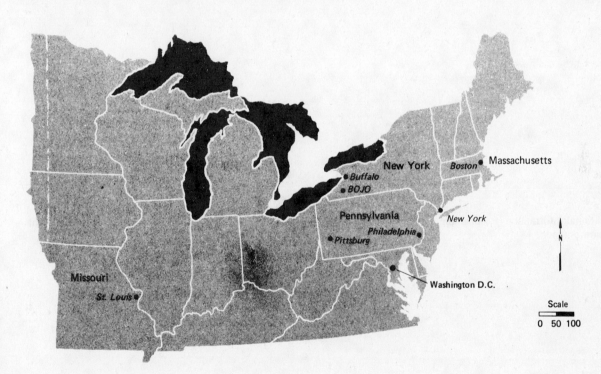

Exercise 3

Now that you have indicated the area on the map in figure 8.4 that does not violate the significant geographical considerations of executives in this incident, show in detail the steps that you would follow in conducting a study to evaluate alternate sites for the new plant in this area. Make sure you include in your discussion all factors identified by executives that you consider to be significant to the new plant location decision.

Exercise 4

Assume that it is your job to obtain information about the significant factors identified in exercise 3. What information is needed, and where could you get this information? For example, where could you obtain information about the volatility of taxes at a particular site? Conduct research at the library or consult with available resource people to obtain this information.

Exercise 5

What additional information (for example, environmental considerations) do you feel should be obtained before a final plant site decision is made?

Experience 8-4   Policy, Procedure, or Rule?

Introduction

Policies, procedures, and rules are standing plans that have different purposes within the organization. Policies are general guidelines for channeling management thinking toward taking action consistent with reaching organizational objectives; procedures outline the sequential steps that must be taken to accomplish a task; and rules are required courses of action allowing no room for interpretation. In this experience, you are given the opportunity to learn more about these important standing plans.

Exercise 1

Identify in the space after each statement whether the statement is a policy, a procedure, or a rule. (Refer back to the text if you have trouble making this distinction.)

a.   Before employees can pick up their paychecks, they must first punch out for the day, then turn in their tools to the toolroom supervisor, and finally change into street clothes. _____

b.   Employees who smoke in designated "No Smoking" areas are subject to discharge. _____

c.   It is improper for any employee to work for any company customer, for any competitor, or for any vendors or suppliers of goods or services to the company. Outside employment is further discouraged if it results in a division of loyalty to the company or a conflict of interest, or if it interferes with or adversely affects the employee's work or opportunity for advancement in the company. _____

d.   When a bill of sale is written up, the first copy must go to the credit department for approval, the second copy to production scheduling for an estimated completion date, the third copy to accounting where the sale will be recorded, and the fourth copy to shipping. _____

c.   Each manager must notify the personnel department of an employee absence by 10:00 A.M. on the day of the absence. The personnel department will then call the employee's home to determine the reason for the absence. If the absence extends to a third day, a nurse will visit the employee's home. Management will pay for sick days (over two days absent) only if the nurse certifies that an actual illness exists. _____

f.   This company strives to reward effective performance. Managers should endeavor to reward their more effective employees with training and transfer opportunities. _____

g.   Employees who smoke in designated "No Smoking" areas will be automatically discharged. _____

h.   No officer or employee shall accept favors or entertainment from an outside organization or agency that are substantial enough to cause undue influence in his or her selection of goods or services for the company. _____

i.   Except for token gifts of purely nominal or advertising value, no employees shall accept gifts or gratuities from suppliers. _____

j.   We encourage promotion from within. _____

k.   We shall have several sources of supply so as not to be totally reliant on only one source. _____

l.   Only graduates of business or engineering schools will be hired for any management position above supervisor. _____

m. All potential managers will have a full-day site visit, will be interviewed by the immediate supervisor over the vacant position, and will meet with three middle-level managers before final selection is made. _____

n. Wages shall be established and maintained on a level favorable to that found for similar positions within our industry and the community. _____

Exercise 2

Now that you have categorized the statements in exercise 1 as policies, procedures, or rules, reexamine statements a and e. From a closer examination, do you note any peculiarities that might cause you to reconsider how you categorized these statements? Explain.

Exercise 3

Reexamine statements b and g in exercise 1. You should have identified statement b as a policy (general guide to thinking) and statement g as a rule (required course of action). Why is it important that a manger be able to distinguish between rules and policies, especially when the line is often such a fine one?

9 FUNDAMENTALS OF ORGANIZING

Chapter Summary

A primary focus of organizing includes determining both what individuals will do in an organization, and how their individual efforts should best be combined to contribute to the attainment of organizational objectives.

Learning Objective 1   *An understanding of the organizing function*

Organizing is the process of establishing orderly uses for all resources within the management system. These orderly uses emphasize the attainment of management system objectives and assist managers not only in making objectives apparent but also in clarifying which resources will be used to attain them. In essence, each organizational resource represents an investment from which the management system must get a return. Appropriate organization of these resources increases the efficiency and effectiveness of their use.

The organizing function is extremely important to the management system because it is the primary mechanism with which managers activate plans. Organizing creates and maintains relationships among all organizational resources by indicating which resources are to be used for specific activities, and when, where, and how the resources are to be used. Some management theorists consider the organizing function so important that they advocate the creation and use of an organizing department within the management system. Typical responsibilities of this department would include developing reorganization plans that make the management system more effective and efficient, developing plans to improve managerial skills to fit current management system needs, and attempting to develop an advantageous organizational climate within the management system.

The **organizing process** is composed of five main steps: (1) reflecting on plans and objectives, (2) establishing major tasks, (3) dividing major tasks into subtasks, (4) allocating resources and directives for subtasks, and (5) evaluating the results of implemented organizing strategy. As managers repeat these steps, they obtain feedback that helps them to improve the existing organization. (Refer back to your text for an illustration of how the organizing process might work in the restaurant industry.)

The organizing function, like the planning function, can be visualized as a subsystem of the overall management system. The primary purpose of the organizing subsystem is to enhance the goal attainment of the general management system by providing a rational approach for using organizational resources. The specific ingredients of the organizing subsystem are input, process, and output. Input is comprised of a portion of the total resources of the organization, process is made up of the steps of the organizing process, and output is organization.

Classical organizing theory is the cumulative insights of early management writers on how organizational resources can best be used to enhance goal attainment. According to the classicist Max Weber, the main components of an organizing effort include detailed procedures and rules, a clearly outlined organizational hierarchy, and mainly impersonal relationships among organization members. Weber used the term bureaucracy to label the management system that contains these components. He felt that a bureaucracy is not an end in itself but a means to the end of management system goal attainment. The main criticism of Weber's bureaucracy, as well as the concepts of other classical organizing theorists, is the obvious lack of concern for the human variable within the organization.

Learning Objective 2   *An appreciation for the complications of determining appropriate organizational structure*

A primary consideration from classical organizing theory that all managers should include in their organizing efforts is organizational structure. **Structure** refers to designated relationships among resources of the management system. The purpose of structure is to facilitate the use of each resource, both individually and collectively, as the management system attempts to attain its objectives. Organizational structure is represented primarily by means of a graphic illustration called an **organization chart.** Traditionally, an organization chart is constructed in pyramid form, with individuals toward the top of the pyramid having more authority and responsibility than individuals toward the bottom. The relative positioning of individuals within boxes on the chart indicates broad working relationships, while lines between boxes designate formal lines of communication between individuals. These traditional pyramidal organization structures were probably modeled on the structure of military command. In the western world, the structure of organized religion has also been hierarchical, with authority derived from the top. Some researchers have found that women are not comfortable with this type of hierarchical structure. As more and more women enter the management field, a new model may need to be created. Women create networks or "webs" of authority, and their leadership styles are relational rather than hierarchical and authoritarian. In the

1990s, these styles will be inherently better suited to new kinds of organizational structures required for a competitive global environment, which will feature team work and participative management.

In reality, two basis types of structure exist within management systems: formal structure and informal structure. **Formal structure** is defined as relationships between organizational resources as outlined by management. Formal structure is represented primarily by the organization chart. **Informal structure,** on the other hand, is defined as patterns of relationships that develop because of the informal existence of organization members. Informal structure evolves naturally and tends to be molded by individual norms, values, and/or social relationships. In essence, informal structure is a system or network of interpersonal relationships that exists within but is not usually identical to an organization's formal structure.

The most common method of establishing formal relationships between resources is by establishing departments. Basically, a **department** is a unique group of resources established by management to perform some organizational task. The process of establishing departments within the management system is called **departmentalization**. The creation of these departments typically is continent upon such factors as the work functions being performed, the product being assembled, the territory being covered, the target customer, and the process designed to manufacture the product. Perhaps the most widely used base for establishing departments within the formal structure is the type of *functions* (activities) being performed within the management system. The major categories into which functions typically are divided include marketing, production, and finance. Structure based on function departmentalizes workers and other resources according to the types of activities being performed. Organization structure based primarily on *product* departmentalizes resources according to the product(s) being manufactured. As the management system manufactures more and more products, it becomes increasingly difficult to coordinate activities across products. Organizing according to product allows managers to logically group resources necessary to produce each product. Structure based primarily on *territory* departmentalizes according to the place where the work is being done or the geographic market area on which the management system is focusing. As market areas and work locations expand, physical distance between various places can make the management task extremely cumbersome. These distances can range from a relatively short span between two points in the same city to a relatively long span between two points in the same state, different states, or even different countries. To minimize the effects of distances, resources can be departmentalized according to territory. Structure based primarily on the *customer* establishes departments in response to major customers of the management system. This structure, of course, assumes that major customers can be identified and divided into logical categories. Finally, structure based primarily on *manufacturing process* departmentalizes according to major phases of the process used to manufacture products. In the case of a furniture company, major phases of the manufacturing process might be woodcutting, sanding, gluing, and painting. While resources are grouped or departmentalized in organizations on any one of the five bases mentioned, it is not uncommon to find organizations that departmentalize on more than one base (see figure 9.10 in your text).

The formal structure of a management system is not actually fixed over time but is continually evolving. Shetty and Carlisle indicate that **four primary forces influence this evolution:** (1) forces in the manager, (2) forces in the task, (3) forces in the environment, and (4) forces in the subordinates. The evolution of a particular organization is actually the result of a complex and dynamic interaction between these forces. Forces in the manager are comprised of the unique way in which a manager perceives organizational problems. Such factors as background, knowledge, experience, and values influence the manager's perception of how formal structure should exist or be changed. Forces in the task include the degree of technology involved in the task and the complexity of the task. As task activities change, a force is created to change the organization that exists. Forces in the environment include the customers and suppliers of the management system, along with the existing political and social structures. Forces in the subordinates include the needs and skill levels of subordinates. Obviously, as the environment and subordinates vary, forces are created simultaneously to change the organization.

Learning Objective 3 *Insights on the advantages and disadvantages of division of labor*

Another primary consideration from classical organizing theory that all managers should include in their organizing efforts is division of labor. The **division of labor** concept is the assignment of various portions of a particular task among a number of organization members. Rather than one individual doing the entire job, several individuals perform different parts of the total activity. Several generally accepted reasons have been offered for why division of labor should be employed within organizing strategy. First, since workers specialize in a particular task, their skill for performing that task tends to increase. Second, workers do not lose valuable time in moving from one task to another; time is not lost changing tools or locations. Third, because workers concentrate on performing only one job, they naturally tend to try to make their job easier and more efficient. Lastly, division of labor creates a situation in which workers only need to know how to perform their part of the work task. Therefore, the task of understanding their work does not become too much of a burden.

Some arguments also have been presented, however, that seem to discourage the use of extreme division of labor or specialization. Overall, these arguments stress that the advantages of division of labor focus solely on efficiency and economic benefit and overlook the human variable. Work that is extremely specialized tends to be very boring and therefore usually causes production rates to go down. Clearly, some type of balance is needed between specialization and human motivation.

Learning Objective 4   *A working knowledge of the relationship between division of labor and coordination*

In a division of labor situation with different individuals doing portions of a task, the importance of effective coordination within the organization becomes obvious. **Coordination** involves encouraging the completion of individual portions of a task in a synchronized order that is appropriate for the overall task. Groups cannot maintain their productivity without coordination. For example, part of the synchronized order for assembling an automobile entails installing seats only after the floor has been installed. Adhering to this order of installation is coordination. Establishing and maintaining coordination may, but does not always, involve close supervision of employees. Managers can also establish and maintain coordination through bargaining, formulating common purpose, and or improving upon specific problem solutions. Managers should try to break away from the idea that coordination is only achieved through close employee supervision.

Mary Parker Follett has furnished concerned managers with valuable advice on how to establish and maintain coordination within the organization. First, Follett indicates that coordination can be attained with the least difficulty through direct horizontal relationships and personal communications. When a coordination problem arises, speaking with peer workers may be the best way to solve it. Second, Follett suggests that coordination be a discussion topic throughout the planning process. In essence, managers should plan for coordination. Third, maintaining coordination is a continuing process and should be treated as such. Managers cannot assume that because their management system shows coordination today that it will show coordination tomorrow. Follett also says that managers should not leave the existence of coordination up to chance. Coordination can be achieved only through purposeful managerial action. Lastly, according to Follett, the importance of the human element and the communication process should be considered when attempting to encourage coordination. Employee skill levels and motivation levels are primary considerations, as is the effectiveness of the human communication process used during coordination activities.

Learning Objective 5   *An understanding of span of management and the factors that influence its appropriateness*

A third primary consideration from classical organizing theory that all managers should include in their organizing efforts is span of management. **Span of management** refers to the number of individuals a manager supervises. The more individuals a manager supervises, the greater the span of management. The span of management has a significant impact on how well managers can carry out their responsibilities. Span of management is also called span of control, span of authority, span of supervision, and span of responsibility. The central concern of span of management is a determination of how many individuals a manager can effectively supervise. To use human resources efficiently, managers should supervise as many individuals as they can best guide toward production quotas. If they are supervising too few individuals, they are wasting a portion of their production capacity. On the other hand, if they are supervising too many individuals, they necessarily lose part of their effectiveness.

Harold Koontz suggests that the five situational factors that influence the appropriateness of an individual's span of management include (1) similarity of functions, (2) geographic contiguity, (3) complexity of functions, (4) coordination, and (5) planning. Similarity of functions is the degree to which activities performed by supervised individuals are similar or dissimilar. As the similarity of subordinates' activities increases, the span of management appropriate for the situation becomes wider. The converse is also generally true. **Geographic contiguity** is the degree to which subordinates are physically separated. In general, the closer subordinates are physically, the more individuals managers can supervise effectively. Complexity of functions refers to the degree to which activities are difficult and involved. The more difficult and involved these activities are, the more difficult it is to manage a large number of individuals effectively. Coordination refers to the amount of time managers must spend to synchronize the activities of their subordinates with the activities of other works. The greater the amount of time managers must spend on coordination, the smaller their span of management should be. Planning is the final important consideration, according to Koontz, and is the amount of time managers must spend developing management system objectives and plans and integrating them with the activities of their subordinates. The more time they must spend on planning activities, the fewer individuals they can manage effectively.

Perhaps the best-known contribution to span of management literature was made by V. A. Graicunas. **Graicunas's formula** was developed to determine the number of *possible* relationships between a manager and his or her subordinates when the number of subordinates is known. Graicunas observed that, as the number of subordinates increases arithmetically, the number of possible relationships between the manager and those subordinates increases geometrically. While a number of criticisms have been leveled at Graicunas's work, his research did successfully point out that span of management is an important consideration that can have far-reaching organizational impact.

A definite relationship exists between span of management and the height of an organization chart. Normally, the greater the height of the organization chart, the smaller the span of management within that organization. It also follows that the lower the height of the organization chart, the greater the span of management. Organization charts with little height are usually referred to as **flat**, while organization charts with much height are usually referred to as **tall**.

An organization's structure should be built from top to bottom to ensure that appropriate spans of management are achieved at all levels. Increasing spans of management simply to eliminate certain management positions and thereby reduce salary expenses may be very shortsighted. Increasing spans of management for objectives such as increasing the speed of organizational decision making or building a more flexible organization seem more appropriate for helping the organization achieve success in the longer run. But competition (especially international competition) has caused many large U.S. organizations to review their structure and cut out layers of management to become flatter. This can reduce expense, but more importantly can and usually does increase the speed of decision-making. This is especially valuable in new product development.

Learning Objective 6   *An understanding of scalar relationships*

A fourth primary consideration from classical organizing theory that all managers should include in their organizing efforts is scalar relationships. **Scalar relationships** refer to a chain of command. Organization is built upon the premise that the individual at the top possesses the most authority and that other individuals' authority is scaled downward according to their relative position on the organization chart. The lower an individual's position on the organization chart, the less authority he or she possesses.

The scalar relationship concept, or chain of command, is related to the unity of command concept. The **unity of command** concept recommends that an individual should have only one boss. If too many bosses give orders, the most probable result is confusion, contradictory orders, and frustrated workers, a situation that usually results in ineffectiveness and inefficiency. Although the unity of command principle first appeared in more modern management literature well over 75 years ago, it is still discussed today as a critical ingredient of successful, contemporary organizations.

However, Fayol indicates that always adhering to the chain of command is not advisable. For example, if individual A in one department needs information from individual B in another department, A cannot go directly to B if the organization requires close adherence to the chain of command. A must, at the very least, go through his or her boss who, in turn, must communicate to B's superior who, in turn, must communication to B. B's superior must then pass the needed information back to A's superior, who passes it along to A. This long and involved process can be very expensive for the organization in terms of time spent getting the information. To decrease this expense, Fayol recommends that in some situations a bridge or "gangplank" should be used to allow A to go directly to B for information (see figure 9.14 in your text for a graphic illustration of the **"gangplank"** concept). Managers should use these organizational bridges with great care, however, because although A might get the information from B more quickly and cheaply, individuals in the chain of command are left out of the communication channel. This lack of information caused by using Fayol's bridge might be more costly in the long run than going through the established chain of command. If managers do use an organizational bridge, they must be extremely careful to inform all other appropriate individuals within the organization of the information they received.

Knowing You Know

Matching   *Directions: Match items 1-10 with items a-j. There is only one correct answer for each item.*

_____ 1.   Organizational chart

_____ 2.   Synchronization

_____ 3.   Span of management

_____ 4.   A step in the organizing process

_____ 5.   Organizing

_____ 6.   Scalar relationships

_____ 7.   Departmentalization by function

_____ 8.   Unity of Command

_____ 9.   Specialization

_____ 10.   Department

a.   A unique group of resources established by management to perform some organizational task

b.   Establishing major tasks

c.   Another word for coordination

d.   A representation of organizational structure

e.   Major categories include marketing, production, and finance

f.   Chain of command

g.   An individual should have only one boss for a task

h.   Often the result of division of labor

i.   The number of individuals a manager is supervising

j.   The process of establishing orderly uses for all resources within the management system.

Multiple Choice   *Directions: Circle the letter of the word or phrase that best completes each statement.*

11. The classicist Max Weber
    a. showed great concern for improving personal relationships among organization members
    b. felt that a bureaucracy was an end in itself
    c. placed considerable emphasis on a clearly outlined organizational hierarchy
    d. showed considerable concern for the human variable within the organization
    e. all of these are true statements

12. The organization chart
    a. shows informal lines of communication among individuals
    b. shows a hierarchy of authority and responsibility
    c. indicates broad working relationships by showing the relative positions of individuals within boxes on the chart
    d. is often constructed in reverse pyramidal form
    e. *b* and *c*

13. The most widely used base for establishing departments is
    a. product
    b. territory
    c. customer
    d. manufacturing process
    e. function

14. According to Shetty and Carlisle, four primary forces influence the evolution of formal structure. Which of the following is *not* one of those primary forces?
    a. forces in the manager
    b. forces in the technology
    c. forces in the environment
    d. forces in the subordinates
    e. forces in the task

15. Which of the following is *not* a correct statement about division of labor?
    a. With greater and greater division of labor and specialization, the job generally becomes more challenging and exciting.
    b. As workers specialize in a particular task, their skill for performing that task tends to increase.
    c. Specialized workers do not lose valuable time in moving from one task to another.
    d. As workers concentrate on performing only one job, they naturally tend to try to make that job easier and more efficient.
    e. All of these are correct statements.

16. Which of the following is a correct statement about the span of management concept?
    a. Another name for span of management is span of accountability.
    b. The central concern of span of management is a determination of the ideal number of supervisory personnel at the first managerial level.
    c. The ideal span of management is determined by production quotas.
    d. The span of management for any supervisor should not exceed his or her unity of command.
    e. None of these is a correct statement.

17. Which of the following is *not* an important factor in influencing the appropriateness of an individual's span of management?
    a. similarity of functions
    b. complexity of functions
    c. coordination
    d. chain of command
    e. planning

18. V. A. Graicunas
    a. suggested that, as the number of subordinates increases geometrically, the number of possible relationships between the manager and those subordinates increases arithmetically
    b. was mainly concerned with communication flows between manager and subordinates
    c. pointed out that the span of management concept can have far-reaching organizational impact
    d. all of these are true statements
    e. none of these is a true statement

19. The chain of command
    a. is also referred to as unity of command
    b. or scalar relationships concept is the idea that the individual at the top of the organization chart possesses the most authority and that other individuals' authority is scaled downward according to their relative position on the organization chart
    c. should always be followed to maintain an efficient and effective operation
    d. and Fayol's "gangplank" are terms almost synonymous in meaning
    e. none of these statements is correct

20. The taller the organization
    a. the shorter the chain of command
    b. the wider the span of management
    c. the narrower the span of management
    d. the higher the probability that the organization will be functionally departmentalized
    e. none of these statements is correct

21. Which of the following is *not* a true statement about the organizing function of management?
    a. It outlines the allocation of resources to tasks.
    b. It is the primary mechanism for activating plans.
    c. It can be viewed as a subsystem of the management system.
    d. It is the primary function of management.
    e. It establishes relationships between all organizational resources.

22. An appropriate span of management is dependent upon
    a. coordination
    b. geographic contiguity
    c. task complexity
    d. planning
    e. all of the above

23. From the perspective of classical organizing theory, which of the following is *not* one of the four main considerations that managers should include in an organizing effort?
    a. structure
    b. scalar relationships
    c. division of labor
    d. span of management
    e. monetary resources

24. Which of the following is *not* an input to the organizing subsystem?
    a. machines
    b. money
    c. raw materials
    d. plans
    e. people

25. Which of the following is *not* one of the advantages of division of labor?
    a. less time wasted moving workers from task to task
    b. less burden upon workers to understand their tasks
    c. increased attention to human characteristics of the worker
    d. an increase in worker efficiency
    e. an increase in worker skill level

Applying What You Know

Experience 9-1   Diagnosing Organizational Problems from the Organization Chart

Introduction

Professional consultants frequently are hired by business organizations to analyze how efficiently and effectively organizational resources are being utilized. While consultants must look into many areas to assess the well-being of the organization, it is not uncommon for these organization analysts to begin their examination with a close look at the firm's formal organization chart. While such an examination generally is intended to provide consultants with an understanding of some of the more important formal organizational relationships, analysts often identify variations from the traditional organizational structure that can lead to less than effective use of organizational resources. This nontraditional structuring of relationships then becomes the point of departure for further questioning and analysis.

In this experience, you use your knowledge of organizational structure to isolate variations from traditional organizational structure that could cause an organization to operate ineffectively.

Exercise 1

Figures 9.1 through 9.6 show six organization charts. Assume that you are a consultant hired to isolate ways to more efficiently and effectively utilize the resources of each of the organizations depicted in the figures. Carefully examine each figure and determine if there are any departures or variations from traditional organizational structure that could result in less than effective use of organizational resources. (These might be described as *potential problem areas*.) Then describe the nature of the potential problem (for example, overspecialization, break in the scalar chain, etc.). **Be sure you use appropriate management terminology.** Once you have identified the potential problem areas, explain *why* these nontraditional organizational structures should be of concern to management.

Figure 9.1   Organization chart for company A.

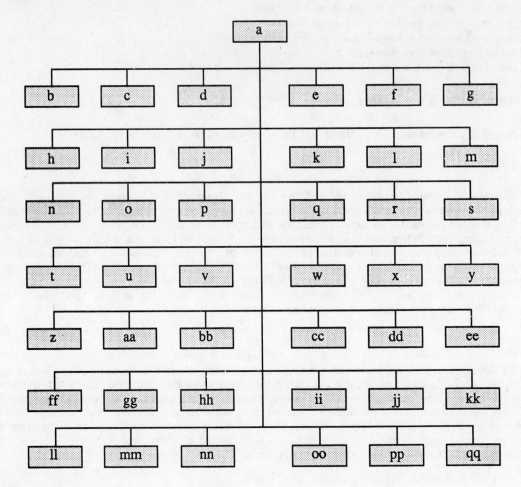

Potential problems?

Why?

Figure 9.2   Organization chart for company B.

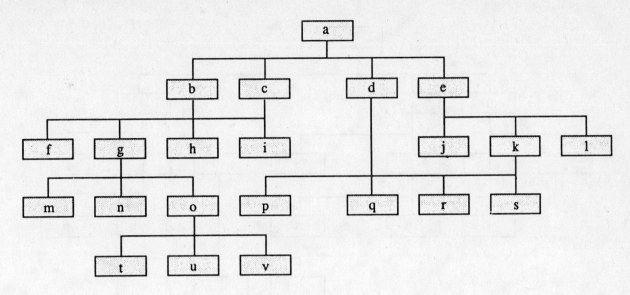

Potential problems?

Why?

Figure 9.3   Organization chart for company C.

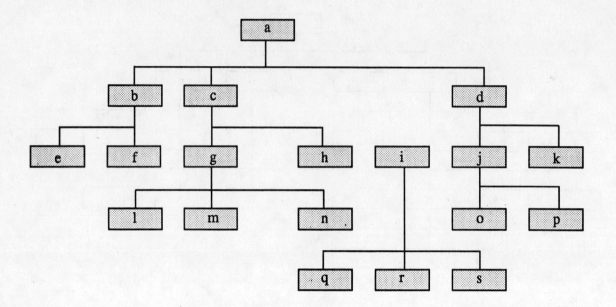

Potential problems?

Why?

Figure 9.4 Organization chart for company D.

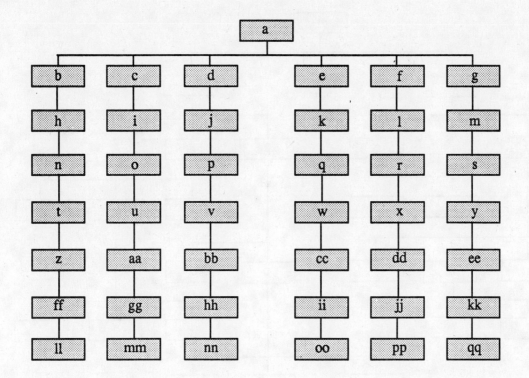

Potential problems?

Why?

Figure 9.5   Organization charge for company E.

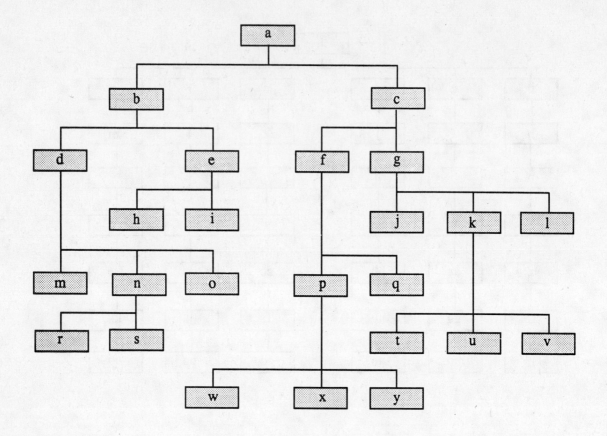

Potential problems?

Why?

Figure 9.6   Organization chart for company F.

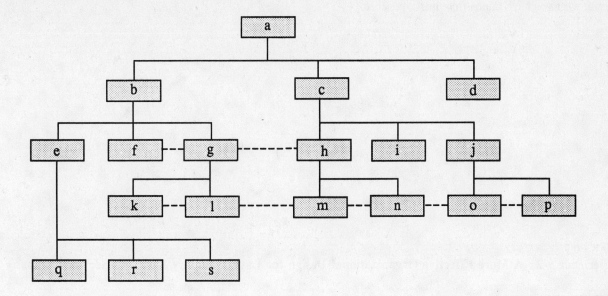

Potential problems?

Why?

Exercise 2

Explain what you have gained from this experience.

Experience 9-2   A More Effective Organizational Design for Lavern County Farmer's Service Company

Introduction

Now that you have read chapter 9, you are fairly knowledgeable about the organizing process and traditional or classical perspectives on organization. However, you have not yet had much opportunity to integrate and apply this new knowledge base. In this experience, you use what you know about organizing to solve an organizational design problem for Lavern County Farmer's Service Company. In completing the experience, make sure that you use all of the knowledge about organizing you have gained from chapter 9 of your text. Read the incident that follows and then complete the exercises as directed.

Incident

The Lavern County Farmer's Service Company is a farmer-owned service organization that was formed ten years ago in an attempt to diminish farmers' unit cost on fertilizers, seed corn, feed products, and chemicals (herbicides and pesticides). Ted Halim, a moving force in the establishment of the company and a local farmer, was hired as general manager five years ago when Halim's son took over his local farming operation and Halim retired from farming. Since that time, a second facility has been opened in the northern part of the county in an attempt to better serve the farming community. The northern facility is the smaller of the two and is located thirteen miles from the original (southern) facility. Both locations carry the same product lines (fertilizer, seed corn, etc.); however, only a limited number of chemicals are stocked at the northern facility. Sales representatives at each facility sell mainly to farmers that visit the facility or phone in their orders. Only on rare occasions do sales representatives leave the facility to talk with customers.

Much of the growth of the organization must be directly attributed to Halim's "personal touch." He just seems to have the knack to make positive things happen for the organization. However, since the northern facility was opened two years ago, Halim has been too busy to call on some of the major accounts (a function he had performed since becoming general manager), and business has tapered off. This led Halim to believe that his sales representatives are just not highly motivated, even though they are remunerated on a part-commission basis.

While Ted Halim is an outstanding salesperson, he admits having little understanding of management and organization. Two weeks ago, Halim hired you as personnel manager to help him reorganize the company. He indicated that you are the ideal person for the job because you have a farm background, have worked for the company for the past two summers (this summer as a sales representative at the southern facility and last summer as a fertilizer mixer at the northern facility), basically know the personalities at both facilities, and are a management major at Midwest College. While your primary charge is to improve the company's present organizational setup, Halim also has asked you to develop job descriptions for all positions in the company. In addition, he wants you to develop a personnel selection procedure for the company. Figure 9.7 shows the present organizational setup of Lavern County Farmer's Service Company.

Figure 9.7 Present structure of Lavern County Farmer's Service Company.

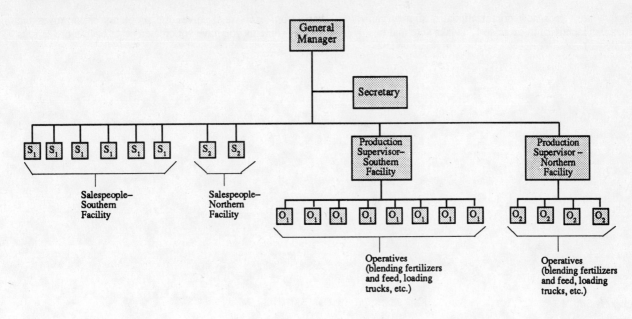

Exercise 1

Determine which of Ted Halim's concerns can be completely or partially dealt with by redesigning the organization (a new organization chart). Which of Halim's concerns cannot be eliminated with a new organizational design?

Exercise 2

Now that you have identified the problems that can be solved or situations that can be improved with a new organizational design, draw and label the organization chart you would recommend to Ted Halim.

Exercise 3

Explain how your new organizational design (organization chart) from exercise 2 solves the problems or improves the situations identified in exercise 1. (Make sure that in solving Halim's problems you have not created other even more serious problems.)

Exercise 4

After you have discussed in class the problems at Lavern County Farmer's Service Company, drawn an organization chart to solve those problems, discussed proposed organizational designs (charts) of other individuals or groups in the class and benefited from your instructor's perspectives on the case, identify the organizing concepts and issues presented in your text that you did not seriously consider or that you completely omitted from your analysis that would have helped you to come up with a better organizational design.

Experience 9-3   Organization Chart Analysis--Wee-Fold-Up Company*

Introduction

Figure 9.8 is an organization chart of the Wee-Fold-Up (W-F-U) Company, a manufacturer of baby furniture, such as playpens and high chairs. Over the years, the organization has grown without careful planning. Review the structure of the W-F-U Company; then complete the exercises as directed.

---

*Source of Experience 9-3: This exercise was developed by Peter D. Couch, Professor of Management, Illinois State University. Used with the permission of the author.

Figure 9.8 Wee-Fold-Up Company, Inc.

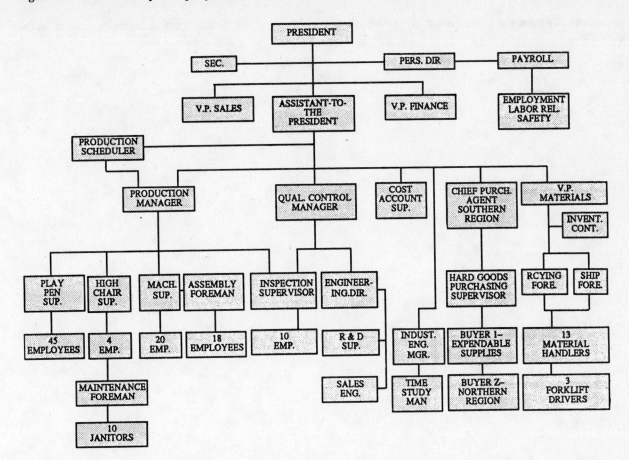

Exercise 1

There are at least fifteen questionable features in the W-F-U Company organization chart. Identify as many as you can. (Some problems are with the organization itself; others are simply weaknesses in the way the chart is drawn.)

Exercise 2

What specifically have you learned about organizational structure that you did not know before involving yourself in this experience?

10 RESPONSIBILITY, AUTHORITY, AND DELEGATION

Chapter Summary

An effective organizing effort includes not only a rationale for the orderly use of management system resources but also three other elements of organizing that specifically channel the activities of organization members. These three elements are responsibility, authority, and delegation.

Learning Objective 1 *An understanding of the relationship between responsibility, authority, and delegation*

Responsibility is perhaps the most fundamental method of channeling the activity of individuals within an organization. Responsibility is the obligation to perform assigned activity. It is a person's self-assumed commitment to handle a job to the best of his or her ability. The source of this responsibility lies within the individual. If a person accepts a job, he or she agrees to carry out a series of duties or activities, or to see that someone else carries them out. The act of accepting the job means that the person is obligated to a superior to see that the job activities are successfully completed. Hence, the person has accepted responsibility for those activities (the job).

Since responsibility is an obligation that a person *accepts*, there is no way it can be delegated or passed on to a subordinate. Yet, a great deal of misunderstanding exists in management literature about delegation of responsibility. Some of the confusion is a matter of semantics, since responsibility is often loosely defined as a duty of some kind, and duties can be delegated. Over many years, the assigning of duties and activities and the accepting of responsibility for those activities have been linked together as one act rather than two separate acts; hence, the popular term *delegation of responsibility*. When the term *delegation of responsibility* is used in the text, it means that activities are assigned or delegated; true responsibility is accepted and **cannot be delegated.**

A summary of an individual's job activities within an organization is usually in a formal statement called a job description. A **job description** is simply a listing of specific activities that must be performed by whoever holds the position. When properly designed, job descriptions communicate job content to employees, establish performance levels that employees must maintain, and act as a guide that employees can follow to help the organization reach its objectives. Job activities are delegated by management to enhance the accomplishment of management system objectives. Management analyzes its objectives and assigns individuals specific duties that will lead to reaching those objectives. A sound organizing strategy includes specific job activities for each individual within the organization. As objectives and other conditions within the management system change, however, individual job activities within the organization may have to be changed.

Individuals are delegated job activities to channel their behavior appropriately. Once they have been delegated these activities, however, they also must be delegated a commensurate amount of authority to perform the obligations. Authority is the right to perform or command. Authority allows its holder to act in certain designated ways and to directly influence the actions of others through orders that he or she issues. The following example illustrates the relationship between job activities and authority. Two primary tasks for which a service station manager is responsible are pumping gasoline and repairing automobiles. In this example, the manager has the complete authority necessary to perform either of these tasks. If this manager chooses, however, he or she can delegate the activity of automobile repair to the assistant manager. Along with this activity of repairing, however, the assistant also should be delegated the authority to order parts, to command certain attendants to help, and to do anything else necessary to perform the obligated repair jobs. Without this authority, the assistant manager may find it impossible to complete the delegated job activities.

The positioning of individuals on an organizational chart indicates the relative amount of authority delegated to each individual. Individuals toward the top of the chart possess more authority than individuals toward the bottom. Chester Barnard writes, however, that, in reality, the source of authority is not determined by decree from the formal organization but by whether or not authority is accepted by those existing under the authority. According to Barnard, authority exists and will exact obedience only if it is accepted. Barnard indicates that authority will be accepted only if (1) an individual can understand the order being communicated; (2) an individual believes that the order is consistent with the purpose of the organization; (3) an individual sees the order as compatible with his or her personal interests; and (4) an individual is mentally and physically able to comply with the order. The fewer of these four conditions that exist, the smaller the probability that authority will be accepted and that obedience will be exacted.

Barnard also offers some guidance on what action managers can take to raise the odds that their commands will be accepted and obeyed. According to Barnard, more and more of a manager's commands will be accepted over the long run if formal channels of communication are used by the manager and are familiar to all organization members, if each organization member has an assigned formal communication channel through which he or she receives orders, if the line of communication between manager and subordinate is as direct as possible, if the complete chain of command is used to issue orders, if a manager possesses adequate communication skills, if a manager uses formal communication lines only for organizational business, and if a command is authenticated as coming from a manager.

Learning Objective 2 — *Information on how to divide and clarify job activities of individuals within an organization*

Since, typically, many individuals work within a given management system, organizing necessarily involves dividing job activities among a number of people. One individual cannot perform all activities within an organization. Some method of distributing job activities and thereby channeling the activities of several individuals is needed. The phrase functional similarity refers to what many management theorists believe to be the most basic method of dividing job activities. Stated simply, the **functional similarity method** suggests that, to divide job activities, management should: (1) examine management system objectives, (2) designate appropriate activities that must be performed to reach those objectives, (3) design specific jobs by grouping similar activities, and (4) stimulate specific individuals to accept responsibility for performing those activities.

Thierauf, Klekamp, and Geeding have indicated that at least three additional guides can be used to supplement the functional similarity method. The first of these supplemental guides suggests that overlapping responsibility should be avoided when making job activity divisions. **Responsibility overlap** exists when more than one individual is responsible for the same activity. When two or more employees are unclear about who should do a job because of overlapping responsibility, it usually leads to conflict and poor working relationships among the employees. Often neither employee will do the job, assuming the other will do it. The second supplemental guide is to avoid responsibility gaps. A **responsibility gap** exists when certain tasks are not included in the responsibility area of any individual. In essence, a responsibility gap creates a situation in which nobody within the organization is obligated to perform certain necessary activities. The third supplemental guide is that creating job activities for accomplishing tasks that do not enhance goal attainment should be avoided. Organization members should be obligated to perform only those activities that lead to goal attainment.

Clarification of the job activities of managers is as important, if not more important, than dividing the job activities of nonmanagers since managers affect greater portions of resources within the management system. One process used to clarify management job activities enables each manager to actively participate with his or her superiors, peers, and subordinates in systematically describing the managerial job to be done and then clarifying the role each manager plays in relationship to his or her work group and to the organization. Although this process typically has been used to clarify the responsibilities of managers, it may also be effective in clarifying the responsibilities of nonmanagers. A specific tool developed to implement this interaction process is a management responsibility guide. The management responsibility guide assists organization members in describing the various responsibility relationships that exist in their organization and summarizing how the responsibilities of various managers within their organization relate to one another.

The seven main organizational responsibility relationships described by a management responsibility guide are: (1) general responsibility, (2) operating responsibility, (3) specific responsibility, (4) "must be consulted" responsibility, (5) "may be consulted" responsibility, (6) "must be notified" responsibility, and (7) "must approve" responsibility. Once organization members have decided which of these management responsibility relationships exist within their organization, they then define the relationships between these responsibilities on a management responsibility guide (see figure 10.2 in your text for a sample management responsibility guide).

Managers can be described as responsible if they perform the activities they are obligated to perform. Responsible management behavior is highly valued by top executives because the responsible manager guides many other individuals within the organization in performing their duties appropriately. The degree of responsibility that managers possess can be determined by analyzing their attitude toward and conduct with subordinates, their behavior with upper management, their behavior with other groups, and their personal attitudes and values (see table 10.2 in your text for a summary of each of these dimensions).

Learning Objective 3 — *Knowledge of the differences between line authority, staff authority, and functional authority*

Authority (or managerial authority) is the right to perform or command. It allows its holders to act in certain designated ways and to directly influence the actions of others through orders. It also allows its holder to allocate the organization's resources in order to achieve the objectives of the organization.

Three main types of authority can exist within an organization: (1) line authority, (2) staff authority, and (3) functional authority. **Line authority** is the right to make decisions and to give orders concerning the production, sales, or finance-related behavior of subordinates. Overall, line authority pertains to matters directly involving management system production, sales, and finance, and, as a result, the attainment of objectives. Individuals directly responsible for these areas within the organization are delegated line authority to assist them in performing their obligated activities.

Staff authority is the right to advise or assist those who possess line authority and other staff personnel. Staff authority exists to enable those responsible for improving the effectiveness of line personnel to perform their required tasks. Examples of organization members with staff authority are members of accounting and human resource departments. Obviously, line and staff personnel must work closely together to improve the efficiency and effectiveness of the organization. To help ensure that line and staff personnel work together productively, a manager must be sure that both groups understand the organizational mission, have specific objectives to strive for, and understand how they act as partners to help the organization reach its objectives.

The size of a business organization is perhaps the most significant factor in determining whether or not staff personnel will be used within an organization. Generally, the larger the organization, the greater the need and ability to pay for staff expertise. As an organization grows, management generally finds a greater need for more expertise in more diversified areas. Although the small organization may also need this expertise, hiring part-time consultants when a need arises may be more practical than hiring a full-time staff individual who may not always be kept busy. (See figure 10.3 in your text for an example of how some important line-staff relationships can be presented on an organization chart.)

Harold Stieglitz has pinpointed three main roles that staff personnel typically perform to assist in personnel. One role of staff personnel is that of advisor or counselor. In this role, staff personnel are seen as internal consultants, with the relationship between line and staff being similar to that between a professional and a client. An example of this role might be the staff quality control manager who advises the line production manager on possible technical modifications to the production process that would help to maintain the quality of products produced.

Staff personnel also have a service role to play. Staff personnel provide services that can more efficiently and effectively be provided by a single centralized staff group than many individuals within the organization attempting to provide these services themselves. This role can probably best be understood by viewing staff personnel as suppliers and line personnel as customers. For example, members of a personnel department recruit, employ, and train workers for all organizational departments. In essence, they are the suppliers of workers, and the various organizational departments needing workers are their customers. Stieglitz also sees a control role for staff personnel. In this role, staff personnel help to establish a mechanism for evaluating the effectiveness of organizational plans. Staff personnel exercising this role are seen as representatives or agents of top management.

Functional authority is the right to give orders within a segment of the organization in which this right is normally nonexistent. This authority usually is assigned to individuals to complement the line or staff authority already possessed. Functional authority generally covers only specific task areas and is operational only for designated amounts of time. It typically is possessed by individuals who, in order to meet their responsibilities, must be able to exercise some control over organization members in other areas.

The vice-president for finance in an organization could be an example of someone with functional authority. Among her basic responsibilities is the obligation to monitor the financial situation within the management system. To accomplish this monitoring, however, she must have appropriate financial information continually flowing to her from various segments of the organization. The vice-president for finance usually is delegated the functional authority to order various departments to furnish her with the kinds and amounts of information she needs to perform her analysis. In reality, the functional authority this vice-president possesses allows her to give orders to personnel within departments in which she normally cannot give orders.

From the previous discussion on line authority, staff authority, and functional authority, it is reasonable to conclude that, although authority can exist within an organization in various forms, these forms should be used in a combination that will best enable individuals to carry out their assigned responsibilities and thereby best help the management system to accomplish its objectives. (For an example of how these authority combinations are used in one organization, see figure 10.3 in your text.)

Learning Objective 4   *An appreciation for the issues that can cause conflict in line and staff relationships*

Most management practitioners readily admit that a noticeable amount of conflict usually centers around line-staff relationships. From the viewpoint of line personnel, conflict is created between line and staff personnel because staff personnel tend to assume line authority, do not give sound advice, steal credit for success, do not keep line personnel informed, and do not see the whole picture. From the viewpoint of staff personnel, conflict is created between line and staff personnel because line personnel do not make proper use of staff personnel, resist new ideas, and do not give staff personnel enough authority.

To overcome these potential conflicts, staff personnel must strive to emphasize the objectives of the organization as a whole, encourage and educate line personnel in the appropriate use of staff personnel, obtain needed skill if it is not already possessed, and deal with resistance to change rather than view this resistance as an immovable barrier. Line personnel's effort in minimizing line-staff conflict should include using staff personnel wherever possible, making proper use of the abilities of staff personnel, and keeping staff personnel appropriately informed.

Learning Objective 5   *Insights on the value of accountability to the organization*

An analysis of activities necessary to accomplish management system objectives results in specific individuals accepting responsibility for performing those activities. The individuals obligated to perform these activities are correspondingly delegated the authority necessary to do their jobs. **Accountability** is a management philosophy whereby individuals are held liable or accountable for how well they use their authority and live up to their responsibility of performing predetermined activities. The concept of accountability implies that, if predetermined activities are not performed, some type of penalty or punishment is justifiably forthcoming. Also implied within the accountability concept, however, is the notion that some kind of reward will follow if predetermined activities are performed well.

Learning Objective 6   *An understanding of how to delegate*

Delegation is the actual process of assigning job activities and corresponding authority to specific individuals within the organization. According to Newman and Warren, there are three steps in the delegation process, any of which may be either observable or implied. The first of the three steps is assigning specific duties to the individual. In all cases, the manager must be sure that the subordinate has a clear understanding of what these duties entail. Whenever possible, the activities should be stated in operational terms so that a subordinate knows exactly what action must be taken to perform the assigned duties. The second step of the delegation process involves granting appropriate authority to the subordinate. The subordinate must be given the right and power within the organization to accomplish the duties assigned. The last step of the delegation process involves creating the obligation for the subordinate to perform the duties assigned. The subordinate must be aware of the responsibility to complete the duties assigned and his or her acceptance of that responsibility.

Learning Objective 7   *A strategy for eliminating various barriers to delegation*

Numerous "obstacles" can make delegation within an organization difficult or even impossible. One supervisor-related obstacle to delegation is that some supervisors resist delegating their authority to subordinates because they may find using their authority very satisfying. In addition, supervisors may be afraid that their subordinates will not do a job well or that surrendering some of their authority may be seen by others as a sign of a weak manager. Also, if supervisors are insecure in their job or see specific activities as being extremely important to their personal success, they may find it difficult to put the performance of these activities into the hands of others.

Even if supervisors wish to delegate to subordinates, they may encounter several subordinate-related roadblocks. First, subordinates may be reluctant to accept delegated authority for fear of failure, lack of self-confidence or because of a feeling that the supervisor doesn't have confidence in him or her. Other obstacles include the feeling that the supervisor will not be available for guidance once the delegation is made or that being a recipient of additional authority may complicate comfortable working relationships that presently exist.

Characteristics of the organization itself also may make delegation difficult. For example, a very small organization may present the supervisor with only a minimal number of activities to be delegated. In addition, if very few job activities and little authority have been delegated over the history of the organization, attempting to initiate the delegation process could make individuals very reluctant and apprehensive.

Eliminating obstacles to delegation is important to managers because delegation usually results in several organizational advantages, such as improved subordinate involvement and interest, more free time for the supervisor to accomplish tasks, and, as the organization gets larger, assistance from subordinates in completing tasks the manager simply wouldn't have time for otherwise.

Although delegation also has potential disadvantages, such as the possibility of the manager losing track of the progress of a task once it has been delegated, the potential advantages of some degree of delegation generally outweigh the potential disadvantages. To minimize the effect of obstacles to delegation, managers must continually strive to uncover obstacles to delegation that exist in their organization. Next, they should approach specific action to minimize the effect of these obstacles with the understanding that the obstacles may be deeply ingrained in the situation and, therefore, require long-run time and effort to overcome. Specific managerial actions usually necessary to overcome obstacles include building subordinate confidence in the use of delegated authority, minimizing the impact of delegated authority on established working relationships, and helping the delegatee with any problems whenever necessary.

In addition, Koontz and O'Donnell imply that, for managers to overcome obstacles to delegation, they must possess certain critical characteristics. These characteristics include the willingness to consider seriously the ideas of others, the insight to allow subordinates the free rein necessary to carry out their responsibilities, trust in the abilities of subordinates, and the ability to allow people to learn from their mistakes without suffering unreasonable penalties for making them.

Noticeable differences exist in the relative number of job activities and the relative amount of authority delegated to subordinates from organization to organization. In practice, it is not a case of delegation either existing or not existing within an organization. Delegation exists in most organizations but in varying degrees. The terms **centralization** and **decentralization** describe the general degree to which delegation exists within an organization. These terms can be visualized at opposite ends of a delegation continuum. Centralization implies that a minimal number of job activities and a minimal amount of authority have been delegated to subordinates by management, while decentralization implies the opposite. The problems usually facing practicing managers are determining whether to further decentralize an organization and deciding how to decentralize if that course of action is advisable.

The degree of decentralization managers should employ is contingent upon their own unique organizational situation. One question to determine the amount of decentralization appropriate for a situation is, "What is the present size of the organization?" The larger the organization, the greater the likelihood that decentralization would be advantageous. Another question is, "Where are the organization's customers located?" The more physically separated the organization's customers, the more viable the situation for a significant amount of decentralization. A third question is, "How homogeneous is the product line of the organization?" As the product line becomes more heterogeneous or diversified, the appropriateness of decentralization generally increases. Yet another question is, "Where are organizational suppliers?" The location of raw materials from which organization products are manufactured is another important consideration. Time loss and perhaps even transportation costs associated with shipping raw materials over great distances form suppliers to manufacturer could support the need for decentralization of certain functions. A fifth question is, "Is there a need for quick decisions in the organization?" If there is a need for speedy decision making within the organization, a considerable amount of decentralization probably is in order. The sixth question is, "Is creativity a desirable feature of the organization?" If the answer to this question is yes, then some decentralization probably is advisable. Decentralization allows delegates the freedom to find better ways of doing things. The mere existence of this freedom can encourage the incorporation of new and more creative techniques within the task process.

Positive decentralization is decentralization that is advantageous for the organization in which it is being implemented, while negative decentralization is the opposite. Perhaps the best way to ascertain how an organization should be decentralized is to study the efforts of an organization with positive decentralization: Massey-Ferguson.

Massey-Ferguson is a worldwide farm equipment manufacturer that has enjoyed noticeable success with decentralization over the past several years. At Massey-Ferguson, the following three guidelines determine the degree of decentralization of decision making appropriate for a situation: (1) the competence to make decisions must be possessed by the person to whom authority is delegated (a derivative of this is that the superior must have confidence in the subordinate to whom authority is delegated); (2) adequate and reliable information pertinent to the decision is required by the person making the decision (decision-making authority, therefore, cannot be pushed below the point at which all information bearing on the decision is available); and (3) if a decision affects more than one unit of the enterprise, the authority to make the decision must rest with the manager accountable for the most units affected by the decision. Massey-Ferguson also encourages a definite attitude toward decentralization. The organization manual of Massey-Ferguson indicates that delegation is not delegation in name only but is a frame of mind that includes both what a supervisor says to subordinates and the way he or she acts toward them. Managers at Massey-Ferguson are encouraged to allow subordinates to make a reasonable number of mistakes and to help subordinates learn from these mistakes. Another feature of the positive decentralization at Massey-Ferguson is that decentralization is complemented with centralization. Massey-Ferguson management recognizes that decentralization is not necessarily an either/or decision and uses the strengths of both centralization and decentralization to its advantage. Not all activities at Massey-Ferguson, however, are eligible for decentralization consideration. Only management can follow through on some responsibilities. For example, management cannot delegate the task of determining organizational objectives. Nor can it delegate the responsibility for formulating the policies that guide the enterprise.

Knowing You Know

Matching

Directions: Match items 1-10 with items a-j. There is only one correct answer for each item.

_____1. Responsibility
_____2. Staff authority
_____3. Accountability
_____4. Authority
_____5. Delegation
_____6. Centralization
_____7. Functional authority
_____8. Line authority
_____9. Roles of staff personnel
_____10. Chester Barnard

a. The right to perform or command
b. Authority exists and will exact obedience only if it is accepted
c. Advise, service, control
d. Generally covers specific task areas and is frequently operational only for designated amounts of time
e. The obligation of the subordinate to his or her superior to perform assigned activity
f. The right to make decisions and to give orders concerning the production, sales, or fiance-related behavior of subordinates
g. When a minimal number of job activities and a minimal amount of authority have been delegated to subordinates by management
h. The process of assigning job activities and corresponding authority to specific individuals within the organization
i. Liability for not shouldering accepted responsibility
j. The right to advise or assist those who possess line authority

True/False

Directions: On the lines provided, place a "T" for true or an "F" for false for each of the statements that follow.

_____11. The smaller the organization, the greater the likelihood that decentralization be advantageous.

_____12. If creativity is a desirable feature of the organization, some decentralization probably is advisable.

_____13. One of the guidelines used at Massey-Ferguson to determine the degree of decentralization of decision making appropriate for a situation is that the competence to make decisions must be possessed by the person to whom authority is delegated.

_____14. In the truest sense, responsibility *cannot* be delegated.

_____15. Generally speaking, only one individual should be responsible for completing any one activity.

_____16. The purpose of functional similarity is to assist organization members in describing the various responsibility relationships that exist in their organization and summarizing how the responsibilities of various managers within their organization relate to one another.

_____17. Authority allows its holder to act in certain designated ways and to directly influence the actions of others through orders that he or she issues.

_____18. According to Barnard, more of a manager's commands will be accepted over the long run if the manager uses formal communication lines only for organizational business.

_____19. According to the text, the age of the business organization is perhaps the most significant factor in determining whether or not staff personnel will be used within the organization.

_____20. From the viewpoint of line personnel, conflict is created between line and staff personnel because staff personnel do not make proper use of line personnel, resist new ideas, and do not give line personnel enough authority.

_____21. The philosophy of accountability takes into account punishment, but not reward.

_____22. The amount of authority delegated usually must exceed the amount of responsibility held if the person is to function effectively.

_____23. The disadvantages of delegation frequently outweigh the advantages in small organizations.

_____24. In organizations with a highly diversified product line, decentralization should be increased.

_____25. When certain tasks are not included in the responsibility area of any individual, a responsibility gap exists.

Applying What You Know

Experience 10-1   Fecke & Company: Understanding Authority Relationships

Introduction

Authority is not an easily understood organizational concept. This is partly because authority of position is unobservable; it can only be assumed from the actions of the individual in the position. For example, you can watch an operative employee in an automobile manufacturing plant tightening bolts on a cylinder head or a quality-control inspector testing that head-bolt torque; you even can observe the production supervisor giving orders to the employee tightening head-bolts. While you can observe duties or activities of a position, you cannot see authority.

Further confusion about authority stems from the fact that three types of authority are found within organizations, and it is possible for a person in one position to possess more than one type at the same time. For example, the quality-control inspector already mentioned may have the right to *advise* the employee torquing head-bolts that the foot-pounds of torque on a particular head-bolt on the last few engines inspected just barely met company standards (*staff authority*) and at the same time have the right to reject an engine or even stop the engine assembly line if performance falls below the acceptable company standard (*functional authority*).

This experience tests your understanding of the authority concept. Read the incident that follows and then complete the exercises as directed. If you have a good understanding of authority, you should have little difficulty in reasoning answers to the questions on authority relationships at Fecke & Company.

Incident

The manufacturing department at Fecke & Company was having problems with production efficiency. Cost per unit had been on the rise for over six months. To correct the situation, Art Smith, vice-president of finance, called Bob Johnson, vice-president of production, and suggested that they meet to deal with the problem.

SMITH: Bob, for the past six months, your department has been exceeding its initial estimates of cost per unit. This is affecting our financial position. We're just not getting the usual profit margin.

JOHNSON: I know there's a problem, but I'm not really sure what to do about it.

SMITH: Well, I have a suggestion that might be the solution to our problem. Let me see if I can get Calvin Martin, vice-president of accounting, to transfer one of his people to you on a full-time basis. This person can act as your cost accountant and, at the same time, perform other accounting and record-keeping activities for you. This should help you to identify how those excess costs are being generated. If you can concentrate on these critical areas, I'm sure you can solve the problem.

JOHNSON: Hey that's a great idea. Does Calvin have someone with a cost-accounting background with whom he would be willing to part?

SMITH: I think he has just the person. Sally Southern is a steady worker and extremely competent in the cost area. And he feels he's overstaffed since they got the computer.

JOHNSON: Great, when can this arrangement be finalized?

SMITH: Just give me a few days to work out all the details with Calvin.

JOHNSON: It's a deal.

With the discussion apparently over, Bob Johnson got up to leave.

SMITH: Say, Bob, before you leave, there's one other concern I'd like to discuss. Since my department has the responsibility for financial expenditures and cost problems that markedly affect such expenditures, I'd like to have the accountant take orders from me when she is working in cost-related areas.

JOHNSON: I'm not sure I understand.

SMITH: Well, I'd like her to provide me with the cost figures, so that if you start to encounter a problem, I can see it coming and be prepared to deal with it from a financial standpoint. You see, when costs per unit go up, profit margin goes down, and my department is directly affected.

JOHNSON: I see where you are coming from. I'll think it over and get back to you tomorrow.

On the way back to his office, Bob Johnson mulled the idea over in his mind. Then he called in his personal assistant, Ted Melvin, to talk over Art Smith's suggestion.

JOHNSON: You know, I'm not sure what Art's motives are, but he must have something up his sleeve. After all, Sally Southern will be working for this department, and her salary will be paid by us. No, Art's got something else in mind. Give me your gut reaction, Ted.

Exercise 1

a. If Bob Johnson agrees to Art Smith's suggestion, who would Sally Southern take orders from? Explain.

b. If Bob Johnson agrees to Art Smith's suggestion, what type of authority would Smith have over Sally Southern? Explain. What type of authority would Johnson have over Southern?

c. If Sally Southern accepts the new position, would Calvin Martin have any authority over her? Explain. What type of authority does Calvin Martin have over those below him in his own department (other accountants)? Explain.

d. Do you see this arrangement creating any serious problems for Bob Johnson? For Art Smith? For Calvin Martin? Explain.

e. Do you see this arrangement creating any serious problems for Sally Southern? Explain.

f. If Art Smith's suggestion is implemented and Sally Southern accepts the job in the manufacturing department, who could hold her accountable for ineffective performance? Explain.

g. Does functional authority take precedence over line authority? Explain.

Exercise 2

After you have discussed this incident in class, explain what you have gained from involving yourself in this experience.

Experience 10-2   Decentralization: Fact or Fiction at Dynamic Industries?[**]

Introduction

When authority is systematically delegated or pushed downward throughout an organization, the approach or practice is known as decentralized management. Yet decentralization is not an either/or proposition. The terms *centralization* and *decentralization* describe the general degree to which delegation exists within an organization. These terms can be visualized at opposite ends of a delegation continuum, with a high degree of centralization and a high degree of decentralization marking

[**]Source of Experience 10-2: Adapted from Sisk, Henry L., Management and Organization. © 1973 South-Western Publishing Co., Cincinnati, OH. Reprinted by Permission.

the limits of the continuum. In this experience, you are asked to evaluate decentralization at Dynamic Industries. Read the incident that follows, and then complete the exercises as directed.

Incident

Dynamic Industries, a diversified manufacturer of automotive replacement parts, is growing rapidly because of an aggressive policy of acquisition. Board chairman John Rafferty believes that the growth of his company is sound and that the main reason for the extremely rapid growth is that the company operates on a highly decentralized basis. Since growth is the result of acquiring companies that are going concerns, Rafferty encourages the managements of the subsidiary companies to carry on as they had prior to joining Dynamic Industries.

At present, merger discussions are being held with Central Electronics, a company that manufactures a broad line of electronic components, many of which have applications in the defense and space industries. Central Electronics is interested in Dynamic Industries because Dynamic could supply the much-needed capital to complete the final developmental stages of a high-performance transformer and to build a plant in which to manufacture the new product. However, George Owens, the founder and president of Central, realizes that the potential danger of merging with another company is that he might lose control of his firm and become only an employee for a larger corporation.

Rafferty, however, continually assures Owens that Dynamic Industries operates on a highly decentralized basis and describes their concept of decentralization as follows:

We expect you, as the president of a subsidiary company, to manage as you have in the past. You are successful with your own company, and there is no reason why you shouldn't continue to be a success operating as part of Dynamic. The major functions of sales, manufacturing, engineering, and product development are all yours to do with as you see fit. In a sense, we are sort of the banker; that is, we supply the money that you need for capital improvements and expansion. Even though the profits of each subsidiary company go into the corporate till, it is still like having your own company because your pay for the year is a combination of a guaranteed salary and a percentage of the net profits of your company.

Thus assured, Owens decided to merge with Dynamic Industries.

During the first six months, all went well, and Owens saw very little of anyone from corporate headquarters. At the beginning of the seventh month, the corporate controller paid Owens a visit and explained to him in detail the company's requirements for profit planning and requested that Owens develop a profit plan--a detailed forecast of Central's revenues and operating expenses--for the coming year. Though very pleasant, the controller made it quite plain that should the performance of the company deviate significantly from the forecast, a team of cost analysts and industrial engineers would arrive from headquarters to determine the cause of the deviation and to recommend necessary changes.

Shortly after this experience with the controller, the industrial relations vice-president of Dynamic Industries called on Owens and informed him that a member of the corporate industrial relations staff would be on hand to conduct the coming negotiations with the union representing the employees of Central. Owens protested, saying that he had been negotiating his own labor contracts for years. However, it was explained to him that, because of companywide employee benefit plans, such as pensions and insurance, and to prevent the unions from pitting one subsidiary company against another in the area of wages, centralized control over negotiations was very necessary. At the time of this visit, the provisions of the company's salary plan were outlined to Owens, and arrangements were made for the installation of the corporate clerical and supervisory salary plans by a member of the headquarters industrial relations staff.

The following month, Owens called Rafferty and asked what steps should be taken to secure capital for the new building intended for the manufacture of the high-performance transformer. Rafferty answered by saying, "I'll have someone from the treasurer's office call on you and show you how to fill out the forms used in requesting funds for capital expansion. It's quite a process, but remember you are only one of fifteen subsidiaries, and they all seem to want money at the same time. Whether or not you get it this year depends not only upon your needs but also upon the needs of the other fourteen companies."

Exercise 1

a. Has Dynamic Industries decentralized its operations as much as possible? Explain.

b. As George Owens, president of Central Electronics, would you regard the management policies of the parent organization as primarily centralized or primarily decentralized? Explain.

c. Is Dynamic Industries exerting too much control over Central Electronics? Why or why not?

d. Recommend the optimum degree of decentralization for the situation described in the incident. Explain your recommendation.

Exercise 2

Now that you have determined what you feel to be the optimum degree of decentralization at Dynamic Industries compare what you have suggested to the "positive decentralization" at Massey-Ferguson explained in chapter 10 of the text. Have you suggested decentralization of any functions that remain highly centralized in the Massey-Ferguson "positive decentralization" plan? Can these functions really be decentralized in the Dynamic Industries situation? Explain.

Experience 10-3 First Among Equals[***]

Introduction

The incident that follows depicts a classic type of problem that exists in most medium- to large-size organizations. Your role in this experience is that of organizational consultant to Peerless Machine International; your task is to evaluate the current situation that exists at Peerless and to recommend a course of action to improve organizational relationships. Familiarize yourself with the incident; then complete the exercises as directed.

[***]Source of Experience 10-3: Reprinted with permission from *Contemporary Management Incidents*, by Bernard A. Deitzer and Karl A. Shilliff, Grid Publishing Inc., Columbus, Ohio, 1977. Pages 38-39.

Incident

Betty Kelly is a supervising engineer in the Corporate Staff Engineering Department of Peerless Machine International, a large manufacturing firm located in upstate New York. About 60 percent of the company's sales consist of complex, precision-built machinery manufactured by the job shop method. The remaining 40 percent is comprised of standardized products, several of which are mass produced.

Kelly is a recent graduate in mechanical engineering and, because of her competency, was quickly promoted ahead of her male peers into management. As a supervising engineer, Kelly was responsible for the design and installation of an extremely complex and more efficient production system to be used on one of the company's standardized products. The firm's in-house newsletter heralded this achievement with a front-page photo showing Betty and her staff engineers on the production line being congratulated by the vice-president of engineering.

Not long afterward, the experienced and older production supervisors began to phone Kelly or her department manager and complain that the new system was "calibrated too fast." "The production line is all fouled up because Kelly and her bushy-tailed college kids (staff engineers) accelerated the automatic timing sequences, which consequently speeded up our runs. We're always having problems with staff engineering's work."

Kelly replied by telling her boss that "those production people just don't understand. They aren't paying attention to the system's load tolerances that staff originally established. Besides, when you go down there to tell them how to monitor the system, all they do is stand around and gape like they never saw a lady engineer before."

The production supervisors countered that everything was satisfactory with the previous sequencing on the line "before Kelly and her geniuses in white frocks and ties began to mess around with it. Now everything breaks down with the slightest overload."

"Baloney," retorted Kelly in the running battle. "It's a very complex mechanical system. Much staff work and energy went into its design specifications. The new equipment, moreover, was subjected to sensitive tests and analyses before being purchased. It's suitable for the rate and schedule of production the staff engineers established for it. Furthermore, the vice-president of engineering complimented our group at the last director's meeting."

Presently, the battle is at a stalemate. The production line still insists that the system fails because of staff's improper installation, which has caused production to lag behind schedule. The phone complaints to staff seem to have slacked off, and Kelly and her group seem to be avoiding further contact with that production group.

Exercise 1

Identify what you feel are basic problems in the line and staff relationships at Peerless Machine International.

Exercise 2

Describe a course of action that you, as organizational consultant, would follow to alleviate the present impasse between the staff engineering group and the production line.

Exercise 3

Jot down notes to answer the questions that follow. Then, playing the role of organizational consultant, use these notes to act out a solution to this problem.

a.   Describe the setting for the meeting you will have with representatives from the staff engineering group and the production line (including room and chair arrangements).

b.   Describe how you will "break the ice" at the meeting.

c.   What specifically do you want to accomplish in the meeting?

d.   How will you close the meeting? (What kind of follow-up do you intend to do?)

11 MANAGING HUMAN RESOURCES

Chapter Summary

This chapter outlines the process of managing human resources within an organization and illustrates how the hiring of the right employees fits within this process. It focuses on first defining appropriate human resources and then examining the steps to be followed in providing them.

Learning Objective 1   *An overall understanding of how appropriate human resources can be provided for the organization*

The phrase **appropriate human resources** refers to those individuals within the organization who make a valuable contribution to management system goal attainment. This contribution is a result of productivity in the positions they hold. Productivity in all organizations is determined by how human resources interact and combine to use all other management system resources. Such factors as background, age, job-related experience, and level of formal education all have some role in determining the degree of appropriateness of the individual to the organization.

To provide appropriate human resources to fill either managerial or nonmanagerial openings, managers should follow four sequential steps: (1) recruitment, (2) selection, (3) training, and (4) performance appraisal.

Learning Objective 2   *An appreciation for the relationship among recruitment efforts, an open position, sources of human resources, and the law*

Recruitment, the first step in providing appropriate human resources for the organization, is the initial attraction and screening of the total supply of prospective human resources available to fill a position. The purpose of recruitment is to narrow a large field of prospective employees to a relatively small group of individuals from which someone eventually will be hired. To be effective at recruiting, recruiters must know (1) the job they are trying to fill, (2) where potential human resources can be located, and (3) how the law influences recruiting efforts.

Recruitment activities must begin with a thorough understanding of the position to be filled so that the broad range of potential employees can be narrowed intelligently. **Job analysis** is a technique commonly used to gain an understanding of a position. Basically, job analysis is a research procedure aimed at determining a job description--the activities a job entails-- and a **job specification**--the characteristics of the individual who should be hired for the job.

Besides a thorough knowledge of the position the organization is trying to fill, recruiters must be able to pinpoint sources of human resources. A barrier to this pinpointing is the fact that the supply of individuals from which to choose in the labor market is continually changing; there are times when finding appropriate human resources is much harder than other times.

Overall, sources of human resources available to fill a position can be categorized in two ways: (1) sources inside the organization and (2) sources outside the organization. The existing pool of employees presently within an organization is one source of human resources. Individuals already within an organization may be excellently qualified for an open position. Promotion from within typically has the advantages of building morale, encouraging employees to work harder in hopes of being promoted, and making individuals inclined to stay with a particular organization because of possible future promotions.

Some type of **human resources inventory** usually is helpful to a company to keep current with the possibilities for filling a position from within. The inventory should indicate which individuals within an organization would be appropriate for filling a position if it became available. Walter S. Wikstrom has suggested three types of records that can be combined to maintain a useful human resources inventory within an organization. The first of Wikstrom's three record-keeping forms for a human resources inventory is a **management inventory card**. This card indicates the employee's age, year of employment, present position and length of time held, performance ratings, strengths and weaknesses, the positions to which the employee might move, when the employee would be ready to assume these positions, and additional training the employee would need to fill these positions. In short, this card is both an organizational history of the employee and an explanation of how the employee might be used in the future.

Wikstrom's second human resources inventory form is the **position replacement form**. This form focuses on maintaining position-centered information, rather than the people-centered information on the management inventory card. This particular form, therefore, indicates very little about the employee as a person but very much about individuals who could replace the employee. The position replacement form is helpful in determining what would happen to an employee's present position if the employee were selected to be moved within the organization or left the organization altogether.

Wikstrom's third human resources inventory form is called a **management manpower replacement chart**. This chart presents a composite view of those individuals management considers significant for human resources planning. The performance rating and promotion potential of the employee easily can be compared with that of other human resources when trying to determine which individual would most appropriately fill a particular position.

While the management inventory card, the position replacement form, and the management manpower replacement chart are three separate record-keeping devices for a human resources inventory, managers should consider all inventory information collectively to ensure the success of hiring-from-within decisions. Computer software is available to help managers keep track of complex human resource inventories and resultingly to make better decisions about how people should be best deployed and developed.

If for some reason a position cannot be filled by someone presently within the organization, numerous sources of prospective human resources are available outside the organization. One commonly tapped external source of human resources is competing organizations. Since there are several advantages to luring human resources away from competitors, this type of piracy has become a common practice. Among the advantages are: (1) the individual knows the business, (2) the competitor will have paid for the individual's training up to the time of hire; (3) the competing organization probably will be weakened somewhat by the loss of the individual; and (4) once hired, the individual becomes a valuable source of information regarding how to best compete with his or her former organization.

An employment agency is an outside source that specializes in matching individuals with organizations. These agencies help people to find jobs and organizations to find people. Employment agencies can be either public or private. Public employment agencies do not charge fees, while private employment agencies collect a fee from either the person hired or the organization once a hiring has been finalized.

Perhaps the most widely addressed source of potential human resources is the readership of certain publications. To tap this source, recruiters simply place an advertisement in a suitable publication. The objective is to advertise in a publication whose readers are likely to be interested in filling the position. An opening for a top-level executive might be advertised in the *Wall Street Journal*, whereas an educational opening might be advertised in the *Chronicle of Higher Education*.

Several recruiters go directly to educational institutions (liberal arts schools, business schools, engineering schools, junior colleges, and community colleges) to interview students close to graduation. Recruiting efforts should focus on those schools with the highest probability of providing human resources appropriate for the open position.

Modern legislation has a major impact on organizational recruitment practices, and a recruitment effort must reflect the laws that govern it. In part, the Civil Rights Act passed in 1964 and amended in 1972 created the **Equal Employment Opportunity Commission (EEOC)** to enforce the laws established to prohibit discrimination on the basis of race, color, religion, sex, or national origin in recruitment, hiring, firing, layoffs, and all other employment practices. Equal opportunity legislation protects the rights of a citizen to work and to get a fair wage rate based primarily on merit and performance. The EEOC seeks to maintain the existence of these rights by holding labor unions, private employers, educational institutions, and governmental bodies responsible for their continuance.

In response to equal opportunity legislation, many organizations have begun **affirmative action programs**. Hodges says that, in the area of equal employment opportunity, positive movement or affirmative action eliminates barriers and increases opportunities for using underutilized and/or disadvantages individuals. The organization can judge how well it is eliminating these barriers by (1) determining how many minority and disadvantages individuals it presently employs, (2) determining how many minority and disadvantaged individuals it should employ according to EEOC guidelines, and (3) comparing the numbers obtained in steps 1 and 2. If the two numbers are equivalent, employment practices within the organization probably should be maintained; if the two numbers are not equivalent, employment practices should be modified accordingly.

Modern management writers recommend that managers follow the guidelines of affirmative action, not because they are mandated by law, but primarily because of the characteristics of today's labor supply. According to these writers, more than 1/2 of the U.S. workforce now consists of minorities, immigrants, and women. Because the overall workforce of today is diverse in its makeup, employees in today's organizations will tend to be more diverse groups. Modern managers are faced with the challenge of developing a productive workforce from an increasingly diverse labor pool. This task is more formidable than simply complying with affirmative action laws.

Learning Objective 3   *Insights on the use of tests and assessment centers in employee selection*

After recruitment, the second major step involved in managing human resources for the organization is **selection.** Selection is choosing an individual to hire from all those who have been recruited. The selection process typically is represented as a series of stages through which prospective employees must pass to be hired. This process involved preliminary screening of candidates, a preliminary interview, intelligence tests, aptitude tests, personality tests, performance references, a diagnostic interview, a physical exam, and finally, personal judgment as to which employee will be selected to fill the position. Each successive stage reduces the total group of prospective employees until, finally, one individual is hired.

Two tools often used in the selection process are testing and assessment centers. **Testing** can be defined as examining human resources for qualities relevant to performing available jobs. Tests generally can be divided into four categories: aptitude tests, achievement tests, vocational interest tests, and personality tests.

Apptitude tests measure the potential of an individual to perform some task. Aptitude tests are diversified in that some measure general intelligence, while others measure special abilities, such as mechanical, clerical, or visual. Achievement tests measure the level of skill or knowledge an individual possesses in a certain area. Vocational interest tests attempt to measure an individual's interest in performing various kinds of activities and are administered on the assumption that certain people perform jobs well because the job activities are interesting to them. The basic purpose of this type of test is to help select those individuals who find certain aspects of an open position interesting. Personality tests attempt to describe an individual's personality dimensions, such as emotional maturity, subjectivity, honesty, and objectivity. Personality tests can be used advantageously if the personality characteristics needed to do well in a particular job are well defined and if individuals possessing those characteristics can be pinpointed and selected.

Several guidelines should be observed when using tests as part of the selection process. First, care should be taken to ensure that the test being used is both valid and reliable. A test is valid if it measures what it is designed to measure and reliable if it measure similarly time after time. Second, test results should not be used as the sole source of information to determine whether or not someone is hired. People change over time, and someone who does not score well on a particular test still might be developed into a productive future employee. Finally, care should be taken to determine that tests used are nondiscriminatory in nature. Many tests contain language or cultural biases that may discriminate against minorities. This third guideline is especially important in that the EEOC has the authority to prosecute discriminatory testing practices within organizations.

Another tool often used to help increase the success of employee selection is the assessment center. **An assessment center** is a program (not a place) in which participants engage in a number of individual and group exercises constructed to simulate important activities at the levels to which participants aspire. These exercises might include such activities as participating in leaderless discussion, giving some type of oral presentation, or leading a group in solving some assigned problem. Individuals performing these activities are observed by managers or trained observers who evaluate both their ability and potential. Participants are assessed on a number of bases, such as leadership, organizing and planning, decision making, and use of delegation.

Learning Objective 4   *An understanding of how the training process actually operates*

After recruitment and selection, the next step in providing appropriate human resources for the organization is training. **Training** is the process of developing qualities in human resources that ultimately will enable them to be more productive and, thus, contribute more to organizational goal attainment.

The training of individuals is essentially a **four-step process**. The first step of the training process is *determining the organization's training needs*. Training needs are the information or skill areas of an individual or group that require further development to increase the organizational productivity of that individual or group. Training of organization members is typically a continuing activity. Even individuals who have been with an organization for some time and who have undergone initial orientation and skills training need continued training to improve skills.

Several methods of determining which skills to focus on for more established human resources are available. One method is to look for deficiencies in existing levels of production-related expertise. Another method for determining training needs is direct feedback from organization members on what they feel are the organization's training needs. A third way of determining training needs involves looking into the future. If the manufacture of new products or the use of newly purchased equipment is foreseen, some type of corresponding training almost certainly will be needed.

Once training needs have been determined, a *training program aimed at meeting those needs must be designed*--the second step of the training process. Basically, designing a program entails assembling various types of facts and activities that will meet the established training needs.

The third step of the training process is *administering the training program, or actually training the individuals*. Various techniques exist for both transmitting necessary information and developing needed skills in training programs. Two techniques for transmitting information in training programs are lectures and programmed learning. The **lecture** is perhaps the most widely used technique for transmitting information in training programs. The lecture is primarily a one-way communication situation in which an instructor presents information to a group of listeners. Trainees participate primarily by listening and note taking. The lecture allows the instructor to expose trainees to a maximum amount of information within a given time period. The lecture also has numerous disadvantages. For example, little or no opportunity exists to clarify or to check on whether trainees really understand the lecture material. Also, there is little or no opportunity for practice, reinforcement, knowledge of results, or overlearning. In addition, all the evidence available indicates that the nature of the lecture situation makes it of minimal value in promoting attitudinal or behavioral change.

Another commonly used technique for transmitting information in training programs is called programmed learning. **Programmed learning** is a technique for instructing without the presence or intervention of a human instructor. Small parts of information that necessitate related responses are presented to individual trainees. Trainees can determine from the accuracy of their responses whether their understanding of the obtained information is accurate. The types of responses required of trainees vary from situation to situation but usually are multiple-choice, true-false, or fill-in-the-blank. (In effect, the self-test in the "Knowing You Know" section that follows is a programmed learning mechanism.) As with the lecture method, programmed learning has both advantages and disadvantages. Among the advantages are that it can be computerized and students can learn at their own pace, they know immediately if they are right or wrong, and they participate actively. The primary disadvantage of this method is that there is nobody to answer a question for the learner should a question arise. (This is partially resolved in the "Knowing You Know" section by citing the text page where more information can be obtained.)

Techniques for developing skills in training programs can be divided into two broad categories: on-the-job techniques and classroom techniques. Techniques for developing skills on the job usually are referred to as **on-the-job-training**. These techniques reflect a blend of job-related knowledge and experience and include coaching, position rotation, and special project committees. Coaching is direct critiquing of how well an individual is performing a job, while position rotation involves moving an individual from job to job to obtain an understanding of the organization as a whole. Special project committees involve assigning a particular task to an individual to furnish the individual with experience in a designated area.

Classroom techniques for developing skills also reflect a blend of both job-related knowledge and experience. The skills addressed via these techniques can range from technical skills, such as computer programming to interpersonal skills, such as leadership. Specific classroom techniques aimed at developing skills include various types of management games and a diversity of role-playing activities. The most common format for management games requires small groups of trainees to make and then evaluate various management decisions. The role-playing format typically involves acting out and then reflecting upon some people-oriented problem that must be solved in the organization. Contrary to the typical one-way communication role in the lecture situation, the skills instructor in the classroom encourages high levels of discussion and interaction among trainees, develops a climate in which trainees learn new behavior from carrying out various activities, acts as a resource person in clarifying related information, and facilitates learning via job-related knowledge and experience in applying that knowledge.

After the training program has been completed, management should evaluate its effectiveness, the fourth step of the training process. Because training programs represent a cost investment, management should obtain some reasonable return. Basically, the training program must be evaluated to determine if it meets the needs for which it was designed. Answers to such questions as the following help to determine training program effectiveness: (1) Has the excessive reject rate declined? (2) Are deadlines being met more regularly? (3) Are labor costs per unit produced decreasing? If the answer to questions such as these is yes, the training program is at least somewhat successful, but perhaps its effectiveness could be enhanced through certain selective changes. If, on the other hand, the answer is no, some significant modification to the training program is warranted.

In a recent survey of business people, 50% of the respondents felt that there would be no change in their sales per year if training programs for experienced salespeople were halted. Based upon the results of this survey, the training will probably be changed significantly to make it valuable to experienced sales people. This survey illustrates the importance of gathering feedback aimed at making training more effective and efficient.

Learning Objective 5   *A concept of what performance appraisals actually are and how they best can be conducted*

Even after individuals have been recruited, selected, and trained, the task of making them productive individuals within the organization is not finished. The fourth step in the process of providing appropriate human resources for the organization is performance appraisal. **Performance appraisal** is the process of reviewing individuals' past productive activity to evaluate the contribution they have made toward attaining management system objectives. As with training, performance appraisal is a continuing activity and focuses on the relatively new as well as the more established human resources within the organization. Performance appraisal also has been called performance review or performance evaluation. The fact that most U.S. firms use some type of performance appraisal system is some indication of the high importance that most managers place on performance appraisal.

One of the main purposes of performance appraisals is to furnish feedback to the organization members regarding how they can become more productive and help the organization in its quest for quality. Performance appraisals also provide systematic judgments to support salary increases, promotions, transfers, and sometimes demotions or terminations; are a means of telling a subordinate how he or she is doing and of suggesting needed changes in behavior, attitudes, skills, or job knowledge (they let the subordinate know where he or she stands with the boss); and are being used increasingly as a basis for the coaching and counseling of the individual by the supervisor.

If performance appraisals are not handled well, their benefit to the organization is minimal. Several guidelines can assist in increasing the appropriateness with which performance appraisals are conducted. First, performance appraisals should stress both performance within the position the individual holds and the success with which the individual is attaining objectives. Second, appraisals should emphasize the individual in the job and not the evaluator's impression of observed work habits. Third, the appraisal should be acceptable to both the evaluator and the evaluatee; both individuals should agree that the appraisal can be of some benefit both to the organization and the worker. Finally, performance appraisals should be used as the basis for improving individual's productivity within the organization by making them better equipped to produce.

If performance appraisals are to be of maximum value to the organization, supervisors and employees must view the performance appraisal process as an opportunity to increase the worth of the individual through constructive feedback, not as a means of rewarding or punishing individuals through positive or negative comments. In addition, paperwork should be seen only as an aid in providing this feedback and not as an end in itself. Finally, care should be taken to make appraisal feedback as tactful and objective as possible to help minimize any negative reactions of the evaluatee.

Knowing You Know

True/False   *Directions: On the lines provided, place a "T" for true or an "F" for false for each of the statements that follow.*

_____ 1. Appropriate human resources are effective in their jobs.

_____ 2. The position replacement form focuses on maintaining people-centered human resources inventory information.

_____ 3. Modern legislation has a major impact on organizational recruitment practices.

_____ 4. In response to affirmative action programs, many companies have set up EEOC groups.

_____ 5. Selection is the process of developing qualities in human resources that ultimately will enable them to be more productive and, thus, contribute more to organizational goal attainment.

_____ 6. Many tests contain language or cultural biases that may discriminate against minorities.

_____ 7. An assessment center is the place where an activity, such as participation in leaderless discussion, is evaluated.

_____ 8. The last step in the training of individuals is administering the training program (actually conducting the training).

_____ 9. Management games usually follow the format of acting out and then reflecting on some people-oriented problems that must be solved in the organization.

_____ 10. Performance appraisal should stress both performance within the position the individual holds and how successfully the individual is attaining objectives.

_____ 11. A job description contains such items as the job title, the job location, the duties that must be performed, the machines, tools, and equipment that the job incumbent must be able to operate, and the working conditions associated with the job.

_____ 12. One advantage of hiring employees from competitors is that the employees are already trained.

Multiple Choice   *Directions: Circle the letter of the word or phrase that best completes each statement.*

13. Which of the following sequence of steps in providing appropriate human resources is correct?
    a. recruitment, training, performance appraisal, selection
    b. performance appraisal, recruitment, training, selection
    c. recruitment, selection, training, performance appraisal
    d. performance appraisal, recruitment, selection, training

14. Job specification
    a. identifies the activities a job entails
    b. is basically a research procedure aimed at determining the activities of the job and the type of individual to hire to perform the job
    c. identifies the necessary characteristics the individual must possess to be hired for the job
    d. is the first step in providing appropriate human resources for the organization
    e. is the initial screening of the total supply of prospective human resources available

15. Which of the following is perhaps the most widely addressed outside source of potential human resources?
    a. the readers of certain publications
    b. new graduates
    c. competition
    d. private and public employment agencies
    e. "walk-ins" looking for work

16. An aptitude test measures
    a. such things as an individual's emotional maturity, subjectivity, or objectivity
    b. the potential of an individual to perform some task
    c. the level of skill or knowledge an individual possesses in a certain area
    d. an individual's interest in performing various kinds of activities
    e. none of these describes an aptitude test

17. Which of the following is *not* a guideline that should be employed when using tests as part of the selection process?
    a. Those involved in selection should use more than test results to determine whether or not someone is hired
    b. Tests should be administered in an assessment center context.
    c. Care should be taken to ensure that tests being used are both valid and reliable.
    d. Care should be taken to ensure that tests are nondiscriminatory in nature.
    e. All of these are test guidelines.

18. According to your text, which of the following is *not* an advantage of promotion from within?
    a. encourages individuals to stay with a particular organization because of possible future promotions
    b. reduces probability of unionization
    c. builds morale
    d. encourages employees to work harder in hopes of being promoted
    e. all of these are advantages of promotion from within

19. According to your text, the most widely used technique for transmitting information in training programs is
    a. programmed learning
    b. management games
    c. position rotation
    d. the lecture
    e. role playing

20. One of the *main* purposes of performance appraisal is
    a. to furnish feedback to organization members regarding how they can become more productive and help the organization in its quest for quality
    b. to reward or punish individuals through positive or negative comments; this should indicate appropriate future behavior
    c. to create paperwork to support promotions, transfers, demotions, or terminations
    d. to provide a foundation for coaching and counseling the supervisor
    e. to give supervisors an opportunity to record their impression of observed work habits

21. Which of the following is *not* an advantage of the programmed learning method?
    a. Students can learn at their own pace.
    b. Students know immediately if they are right or wrong.
    c. Students must participate actively in the learning experience.
    d. Students are forced to work things out on their own if a question arises.
    e. All of these are advantages of programmed learning.

22. Which of the following is *not* a stage in a typical selection process?
    a. performance references
    b. physical exam
    c. intelligence test
    d. preliminary interview
    e. all of these are stages in a typical selection process

23. The management manpower replacement chart
    a. provides performance ratings and promotion potential of employees and can be utilized to determine which individual would most appropriately fill a particular position.
    b. indicates age, year of employment, present position and length of time it has been held, performance ratings, strengths and weaknesses, the positions to which a person might move, when he or she would be ready to assume these positions, and additional training he or she would need to fill the positions.
    c. focuses on maintaining position-centered information regarding who could fill a position should it open.
    d. none of the above reflect the totality of information that can be gleaned from a management manpower replacement chart.

24. The degree to which an individual is appropriate to the organization depends on which of the following factors?
    a. age
    b. job-related experience
    c. background
    d. level of formal education
    e. all of these factors are correct

25. A management inventory card
    a. indicates such things as performance rating, strengths and weaknesses, and length of time at present position
    b. is also called the management manpower replacement chart
    c. is an excellent outside source of prospective human resources
    d. is the most frequently utilized form to maintain a useful human resources inventory
    e. all of these describe a management inventory card.

Applying What You Know

Experience 11-1   Recruitment*

Introduction

Recruitment activities are designed to attract potential employees to fill job vacancies. They can be as simple as having recruits walk in off the street, or as complex and expensive as hiring full-time professional recruiters to search for potential employees. Usually recruiting efforts intensify as the importance of the vacancy to be filled increases.

Exercise 1

Assume that you have been assigned the task of recruiting potential employees who you feel will turn out to be cooperative and productive work group members. List six to eight sources of recruits and the advantages and disadvantages associated with recruiting from each source.

---

*Source of Experience 11-1: Reproduced by permission from *Personnel Management in Action: Skill Building Experiences* by Whatley & Kelley, Copyright © 1977, West Publishing Company. All rights reserved.

EXAMPLE

Source: Private employment agency
Advantages: Some prescreening is done by the agency.
Disadvantages: The organization is charged a fee for the agency's services.

Exercise 2

Certain personal information about recruits is needed before it is possible to select individuals who will be cooperative and productive employees. For example, the trait of achievement motivation may be assessed through a paper-and-pencil test. Figure 11.1 lists some of the kinds of information you may want to know about a recruit. Decide which of the sources shown are appropriate means of assessing or obtaining the information desired. Indicate your choices with a check.

Figure 11.1 Information required about a recruit.

Information Required: Desirable Characteristics	References	Application Blank	Interview	Test	Other (Specify)
1. Work experience					
2. Educational attainment					
3. Medical history					
4. Ability to get along with others					
5. Intelligence					
6. Career plans					
7. Reasons for applying for the job					
8. Dependability					

Exercise 3

a. In exercise 1, did you identify at least one source of minority recruits? Does this type of recruiting pose any special problems for management?

b. References are often used to obtain certain information about a recruit. What are some of the weaknesses in using references for this purpose?

c. If you were recruiting to fill the job vacancy of an electrician, which (if any) types of information listed in exercise 2 would not be of value? Why?

Experience 11-2 Loaded or Blank?**

Introduction

Anyone currently involved or that expects to be involved in the interviewing process at some point in the future must have at least a basic knowledge of the Equal Employment Opportunity Commission's Uniform Guidelines on Employee Selection Procedures. The 1964 Civil Rights Act and the Age Discrimination in Employment Act of 1967 as amended in 1978 basically prohibit discrimination on the basis of race, color, religion, sex, national original, or age in employment practices. The guidelines specifically emphasize that use of any employee selection device that results in the exclusion of a disproportionate number of women or minority applicants may be unlawful unless it can be shown that the device is a valid measure of on-the-job performance. In other words, all questions have to be job related, or they cannot be asked. In this experience, you become familiar with one such selection device: the employment application blank.

Exercise 1

Your instructor will divide the class into groups, and each group will be assigned a different job title. Write your group's job title in the space that follows.
(Job title)_____

Before meeting with your group, individually examine the employment application blank in figure 11.2. Then, using your "gut feelings" and common sense, determine the lawfulness (L) or unlawfulness (U) of each item with regard to your job. Use the space below each item on the application blank to jot down your thoughts.

Figure 11.2 Employment application blank.

Application for Employment
(You must fill out this application
to be considered for employment
in this company.)

1. Name: Mr. Miss. Mrs. Ms._____

Have you worked for this company under a different name? Yes_____No_____

2. Marital status: a. Currently married_____   Currently unmarried_____

b. Are you currently pregnant? Yes_____No_____

3. If hired, can you submit proof of age? Yes_____No_____

4. a. Are you handicapped? Yes_____No_____

b. If yes, what is the nature of your handicap? _____

5. a. Height: feet _____ inches _____   b. Weight: _____lbs.

c. Color of hair: _____   d. Type of hair: _____

6. Address: _____

7. Birthplace of parents: _____

8. If employed, can you supply a birth certificate? Yes _____No _____

PHOTO
Applicants: Your
Photograph should be
submitted only after the
interview has been
conducted.

**Source of Experience 11-2: This exercise was developed by A. Magid Mazen, Suffolk University. Used with the permission of the author.

9. a. Do you observe any particular religious customs? Yes _____ No _____

    b. If yes, what customs? _____

10. a. What type of military experience do you have?

    _____

    b. What was the type of discharge you received?

    Honorable _____   Dishonorable _____ Why (explain briefly):

    _____

11. a. Are you a citizen of the United States: Yes _____ No _____

    b. If not, of what country are you a citizen? _____

12. a. What languages do you speak fluently? _____

    b. What is your native language? _____

13. a. What is the highest degree you have earned? _____

    b. What school did you attend for your highest degree? _____

14. a. Work experiences: (1) _____

                           (2) _____

                           (3) _____

    b. Explain why you left each of your previous employers.

15. Have you ever been arrested?   Yes _____ No _____

16. Have you ever been convicted? Yes _____ No _____

17. a. Do any of your relatives work for this company? Yes _____ No _____

    b. If no, provide a name and address of a relative to be notified in case of an accident or emergency:

    Name _____

    Address _____

    c. If no relatives exist, provide the name and address of a person to be notified in case of an accident or emergency:

        Name _____

        Address _____

18. List all organizations, clubs, societies, and lodges to which you belong.

    _____

19. Can you supply a recommendation from your pastor after the interview?

   Yes _____   No _____

20. Who referred you for this position? _____

I understand that any misstatements or omissions of material facts in this application may be cause for dismissal.

Signature _____

Date _____

Exercise 2

Meet with your group and discuss your individual decisions and their rationale. Reach a consensus decision on the lawfulness of each item based again on the group's "gut feelings" and common sense. Make changes in your earlier individual thoughts on the application blank in figure 11.2 where appropriate.

Exercise 3

Meet as a class and discuss group decisions and rationale. Again, make changes/comments on the application blank in figure 11.2 where appropriate.

Exercise 4

As directed by your instructor, compare your "gut feelings" and common sense reactions to the *Uniform Guidelines on Employee Selection Procedures*. What are the differences between your logic and that of the *Uniform Guidelines*?

Experience 11-3 Role Playing: An Analysis of the Appraisal Interview***

Introduction

When supervisors conduct performance evaluation interviews with their subordinates, the result is often the creation of ill feelings and misunderstanding, rather than improved relations and employee development. Frequently, subordinates feel that there is undue emphasis on deficiencies. To protect their interests, they become defensive. When supervisors, as a result, feel compelled to justify their points of view, their behavior similarly becomes defensive. The result is that the interview situation frequently becomes one in which conflict and new problems are produced, rather than one in which solutions to existing problems are found.

A common cause of the difficulties encountered is the different frames of reference of supervisors and subordinates with respect to overall performance. Supervisors' frame of reference tends to make them sensitive to deficiencies in job outcomes because these deficiencies create problems for the supervisors. They are likely to take adequate performance more or less for granted. Subordinates, on the other hand, are aware of the little extras they do and are likely to attribute poor results to inadequate assignments, poor training, or someone else's failure to cooperate. Thus, the evaluation interview situation tends to be one in which the divergent views are highlighted in such a manner that understanding is hindered, rather than promoted.

Because difficulties are encountered in interviews of this kind, supervisors are reluctant to let employees know where they stand. When a company program requires periodic evaluations, a marked tendency exists for supervisors to suppress the unfavorable evaluations. In this instance, the purpose of the evaluation is defeated. The success or failure of an employee developmental program largely depends on the skill with which employees are interviewed by their supervisors.

This experience uses a role-playing procedure to help you to develop sensitivity to the communication problems in performance evaluation interviews. Read the incident that follows and then complete the exercises as directed.

Incident

George Stanley is the electrical section head in the engineering department of American Construction Company. Work in the engineering department includes designing, drafting, estimating costs, keeping maps up-to-date, checking standards and building codes, making field inspections, conducting follow-ups, etc. Eight first-line supervisors report to George Stanley. The duties of the supervisors are partly technical and partly supervisory. The organization chart for Stanley's section is shown in figure 11.3.

Company policy requires that all section heads interview each of their supervisors once a year, the purpose being: (1) to evaluate the supervisor's performance during the year, (2) to give recognition for jobs well done, and (3) to correct weaknesses.

The company believes that employees should know where they stand and that everything should be done to develop management personnel. The evaluation interviews were introduced to serve this purpose.

Tom Burke is one of the supervisors reporting to Stanley. Burke has a college degree in electrical engineering, and in addition to his technical duties, which often take him into the field, he supervises the work of one junior designer (J.D.), six draftspeople, and two clerks. He is highly paid, as are all of the supervisors in this department, because of the high requirements in technical knowledge. Burke has been with the company for twelve years and has been a supervisor for two years. He is married and has two children. He owns his home and is active in the civic affairs of the community in which he lives.

You will witness an evaluation interview conducted by George Stanley with Tom Burke. Two of your class members already have been selected to play these roles; one will play the role of the supervisor who conducts the evaluation interview, and the other will play the employee interviewed. You will be asked to participate as an observer. Please read the "Instructions for Observers" that follow; this list of questions will help you to be a more effective observer.

***Source of Experience 11-3: Reprinted from : N.R.F. Maier, A.R. Solem, and A.A. Maier, *The Role Play Technique*, San Diego, CA: University Associates, Inc., 1975. Used with permission.

Figure 11.3 Organization chart for engineering department.

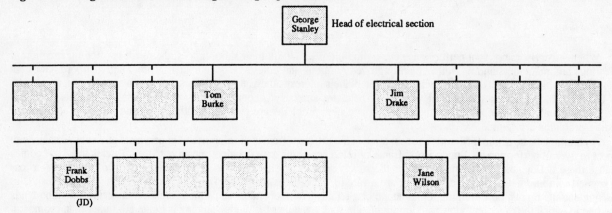

Instructions for Observers

1. Observe the manner in which the interviewer began the interview.
   a. What did the interviewer do, if anything, to create a permissive atmosphere?
   b. Did the interviewer state the purpose of the interview early in the session?
   c. Was the purpose of the interview stated clearly and concisely?

2. Observe how the interview was conducted.
   a. To what extent did the interviewer learn how the employee felt about the job in general?
   b. Did the interviewer use broad, general questions at the outset?
   c. Did the interviewer criticize the employee?
   d. Was the interviewer acceptant of the employee's feelings and ideas?
   e. Who talked the most?
   f. What things did the interviewer learn?
   g. Did the interviewer praise the employee?

3. Observe and evaluate the outcome of the interview.
   a. To what extent did the interviewer arrive at a fairer and more accurate evaluation of the employee as a result of the interview?
   b. What things did the interviewer do, if any, to motivate the employee to improve?
   c. Were relations better or worse after the interview? If worse, why did this occur?
   d. In what ways might the interviewer have done a better job?

Exercise 1

When role playing has ended, evaluate the interview by answering the questions that follow.

a. Was mutual understanding increased or decreased as a result of the interview? Explain.

b.   Did Burke go up or down in Stanley's estimation as a result of the interview? Explain.

c.   Is Burke's opinion of Stanley better or worse as a result of the interview? Explain.

d.   Will Stanley alter his judgment about the performance rating of Burke as a result of the interview? Explain.

e.   Who talked the most, Stanley or Burke?

f. Will the interview have favorable or unfavorable effects on Burke's future motivation? Explain.

g. In what ways was Burke's motivation influenced (helped or hindered) by the interview? Explain.

h. Could you have avoided all of the pitfalls present in this type of situation? How?

Exercise 2

Now that you have generally appraised the interview, reflect on Stanley's interview method and answer the questions that follow.

a. How did Stanley begin the interview?

b. What opportunities were there for Stanley to be more permissive and acceptance of Burke's feelings and ideas?

c. What did Stanley learn and not learn from Burke? (Examine Burke's role instructions in Appendix G.)

d. Did Stanley use leading questions to explore Burke's views and feelings, or did he explore mostly for facts?

e. To what extent was each of the company's three stated purposes of the interview accomplished?

f. What were the things you liked about the way the interview was handled, and how would you do things differently?

Exercise 3

Now that you have examined Stanley's interview method, answer the questions that follow about developing an improved interview plan.

a. How should an interview of this kind be started?

b. In what areas could Stanley have given Burke recognition or praise?

c. What are the best ways for getting Burke to talk freely about problems or things that give him trouble?

d. How can supervisors in such interviews make it clear that they want to be helpful?

e. How can supervisors ask questions without seeming to cross-examine and question an employee's ability?

f. How accurately can employees evaluate their own performance?

g. What type of interview situation makes people feel most free to discuss their shortcomings?

h. What conclusions about evaluation interviewing can be drawn from this experience?

12 ORGANIZATIONAL CHANGE AND STRESS

Chapter Summary

This chapter discusses the fundamentals of changing an organization, the factors to consider when changing an organization, and organizational change and stress.

Learning Objective 1   *A working definition of "changing an organization"*

"**Changing an organization**" is the process of modifying an existing organization. The purpose of organizational modifications is to increase organizational effectiveness; that is, the extent to which an organization accomplishes it objectives. These modifications can involve virtually any organizational segment and typically include changing the lines of organizational authority, the levels of responsibility held by various organization members, and the established lines of organizational communication. Most managers agree that, if an organization is to be successful, it must change continually in response to significant developments, such as changes in customer needs, technological breakthroughs, and new government regulations.

The study of organizational change is extremely important because all managers at all organizational levels are faced throughout their careers with the task of changing their organization. Because change is such a fundamental and necessary part of organizational existence, managers who can successfully implement change are very important to organizations of all kinds. Many managers consider change to be so critical to the success of the organization that they encourage employees to continually search for areas in which beneficial organizational change can be made. Within the General Motors Corporation, for example, employees are provided with a "think list" to encourage them to develop ideas for organizational change and to remind them that change is extremely important to the continued success of GM.

The major factors that managers should consider when changing an organization are: (1) the change agent, (2) determination of what should be changed, (3) the type of change to make, (4) individuals affected by the change, and (5) evaluation of change. The collective influence of these factors ultimately determines the success of a change.

Perhaps the most important factor to be considered by managers when changing an organization is determining who will be the change agent. The term **change agent** refers to anyone inside or outside the organization who tries to effect change. The change agent might be a self-designated manager within the organization or possibly an outside consultant hired because of a special expertise he or she possesses in a particular area. The terms *change agent* and *manager* are used synonymously in this section.

Several special skills are necessary to be a successful change agent, including the abilities to determine how a change should be made, solve change-related problems, and use behavioral science tools to influence people appropriately during the change. Perhaps the most overlooked skill necessary to be a successful change agent is deciding how much change organization members can withstand. Overall, managers should choose change agents who possess the most expertise in areas suggested by the special skills already mentioned so that the most beneficial changes for the organization can be realized.

Learning Objective 2   *An understanding of the relative importance of change and stability to an organization*

In addition to organizational change, some degree of stability is a prerequisite for long-run organizational success. Hellriegel and Slocum developed a model that shows the relative importance of change and stability to organizational survival. This model stresses that the greatest probability of organizational survival and growth exists when both stability and adaption are high within the organization. The organization without stability to complement or supplement change has a declining probability of organizational survival and growth. Change after change without stability typically results in confusion and employee stress.

Another major factor managers should consider when changing an organization is what should be changed within the organization. In general, managers should make changes that increase organizational effectiveness. It has been generally accepted for many years that organizational effectiveness is primarily the result of organizational activities centering around three main classes of factors: (1) people, (2) structure, and (3) technology. **People factors** are defined as attitudes, leadership skills, communication skills, and all other characteristics of the human resources within the organization. Organizational controls, such as policies and procedures, constitute **structural factors,** while **technological factors** are any types of equipment or processes that assist organization members in the performance of their jobs. For an organization to maximize effectiveness, appropriate people must be matched with appropriate technology and appropriate structure. Thus, people factors, technological factors, and structural factors are not independent determinants of organizational effectiveness. Instead, organizational effectiveness is determined by the relationship among these three factors.

Learning Objective 3 — *Some ability to know what type of change should be made within an organization*

The type of change to make is a third major factor managers should consider when changing an organization. Most changes can be categorized as one of three types (1) people change, (2) structural change, and (3) technological change. These three types obviously correspond to the three main determinants of organizational effectiveness. For example, **technological change** emphasizes modifying the level of technology within a management system. In general, a manager's choice of the type of change to make within an organization should be based on the results of internal and external organizational diagnoses. For example, if information gathered by conducting organizational diagnoses suggests that organizational structure is the main cause of organizational ineffectiveness, managers should choose to emphasize structural changes within the organization. Since technological change often involves outside experts and highly technical language, structural change and people change are the two types discussed in more detail.

Structural change is aimed at increasing organizational effectiveness through modifications to existing organizational structure. These modifications can take several forms: (1) clarifying and defining jobs; (2) modifying organizational structure to fit the communication needs of the organization; and (3) decentralizing the organization to reduce the cost of coordination, increase the controllability of subunits, increase motivation, and gain greater flexibility. Although structural change must include some consideration of people and technology to be successful, its primary focus is obviously on changing organizational structure. After organizational structure has been changed, management should conduct periodic reviews to make sure that the change is accomplishing its intended purpose.

Structural change is perhaps best illustrated by describing matrix organizations. A **matrix organization** is a more traditional organization that is modified primarily for the purpose of completing some type of special project. In essence, a matrix organization is an organization design in which individuals from various functional departments are assigned to a project manager, who is responsible for accomplishing some specific task. The project itself may be either long run or short run, with employees needed to complete the project borrowed from various organizational segments. After organizational structure has been changed, management should conduct periodic reviews to make sure that the change is accomplishing its intended purpose.

John F. Mee has developed a classic example showing how a more traditional organizational can be changed into a matrix organization. Although in Mee's example the traditional organizational design might be generally useful, managers could learn through internal organizational diagnosis that this design makes it impossible for organization members to give adequate attention to three government projects of extreme importance to long-run organization. A manager would be appointed for each of the three government projects and allocated personnel with appropriate skills to complete the project. The three project managers would have authority over personnel assigned to them and be accountable for the performance of those personnel.

Several advantages and disadvantages to making structural changes such as those reflected by the matrix organization can be cited. Among the major advantages are the claims that such structural changes generally result in better control of a project, better customer relations, shorter project-development time, and lower project costs. Accompanying these advantages, however, are the claims that such structural changes also generally create more complex internal operations which commonly cause conflict, encourage inconsistency in the application of company policy, and actually result in an overall more difficult situation to manage. One point, however, is clear. For a matrix organization to be effective and efficient, organization members must be willing to learn and execute somewhat different organizational roles.

People change emphasizes increasing organizational effectiveness by changing organization members. The focus of this type of change is on such factors as modifying employees' attitudes and leadership skills. In general, managers should attempt to make this type of change when the results of organizational diagnoses indicate that human resources are the main cause of organizational ineffectiveness. The process of people change can be referred to as **organization development (OD)**. Although OD focuses mainly on changing people, these changes are based on an overview of structure, technology, and all other organizational ingredients. This overview approach generally contains both overt and covert organizational components considered during OD efforts. Overt factors are generally easily detectable, while covert factors are usually more difficult to assess.

One commonly used OD technique for changing people in organizations is called **Grid OD**. The **managerial grid** is based on the premise that various managerial styles can be described by means of two primary attitudes of the manager: concern for people and concern for production. Within this model, each attitude is placed on an axis scaled 1 through 9 and is used to generate five managerial styles. The central theme of the managerial grid is that 9,9 Management is the ideal managerial style. Managers using this style have both high concern for people and high concern for production. Managers using any other style have lesser degrees of concern for people or production and are thought to reduce organizational success accordingly.

The Grid OD program has six main training phases conducted for all managers within the organization. The first two of these phases focus on acquainting managers with the managerial grid concept and assisting them in determining which managerial style they most commonly use. The last four phases of the Grid OD program concentrate on encouraging managers to adopt the 9,9 Management style and showing them how to use this style within their specific job situation. Emphasis throughout the program is on developing teamwork within the organization. Some evidence suggests that Grid OD is a useful technique because it is effective in enhancing profit, positively changing managerial behavior, and positively influencing managerial attitudes and values. Grid OD probably will have to undergo more rigorous testing for an extended period of time, however, before more conclusive statements can be made.

If the entire OD area is taken into consideration, changes that emphasize both people and the organization as a whole seem to have inherent strength. There are, however, several commonly voiced weaknesses of OD efforts. Some suggest, for example, that the effectiveness of an OD program is difficult to evaluate, that OD programs are generally too time consuming, that OD objectives are commonly too vague, that total costs of an OD program are difficult to pinpoint at the time the program starts, and that OD programs are generally too expensive. Common guidelines that managers can use to improve the quality of OD efforts are: (1) systematically tailoring OD programs to meet the specific needs of the organization, (2) continually demonstrating how people should change their behavior, and (3) conscientiously changing organizational reward systems so that organization members who change their behavior as suggested by an OD program are rewarded.

Managers have been using OD techniques for several decades. The broad and useful applications of these techniques continue to be documented in the more recent management literature. OD techniques are being applied to business organizations as well as many other types of organizations like religious organizations. In addition, OD applications are being documented throughout the world with increasing use being reported in countries like Hungary, Poland, and the United Kingdom.

Learning Objective 4 — *An appreciation for why individuals affected by a change should be considered when the change is being made*

A fourth major factor to be considered by managers when changing an organization is the people affected by the change. A good assessment of what to change and how to make the change probably will be wasted if organization members do not support the change. To increase the chances of employee support of a change, managers should be aware of the usual employee resistance to change, how this resistance can be reduced, and the three phases usually present when behavioral change occurs.

Resistance to change within an organization is as common as the need for change. Managers typically meet with employee resistance aimed at preventing the change from occurring. This resistance generally exists because organization members fear some personal loss, such as a reduction in personal prestige, a disturbance of established social and working relationships, and personal failure due to an inability to carry out new job responsibilities, as a result of the proposed change.

To ensure the success of needed organizational modifications, managers should try to reduce the effects of this resistance by following some general guidelines. First, managers should avoid surprises. People typically need time to evaluate proposed change before management implements it. Whenever possible, individuals who will be affected by a change should be kept informed of the type of change being considered and the probability that the change will be adopted.

Second, managers also should attempt to promote real understanding of a proposed change. This understanding may even generate support for a proposed change by focusing attention on possible individual gains that could materialize as a result of the change. Individuals should receive information that will help them to answer such change-related questions as: Will I lose my job? Will I have to work longer hours? Will it force me to betray or desert my good friends?

Third, perhaps the most powerful tool for reducing resistance to change is management's positive attitude toward change. This attitude should be displayed openly by top and middle management as well as by lower management. To emphasize this attitude toward change, some portion of organizational rewards should be earmarked for those organization members most instrumental in implementing constructive change.

Fourth, making changes on a tentative basis can help to reduce resistance to change. Permitting organization members to spend some time working under a proposed change before voicing support or nonsupport of the change is a good way of reducing feared personal loss. When this approach is used, those involved are able to test their reactions to the new situation before committing themselves irrevocably, are able to acquire more facts on which to base their attitudes and behavior toward the change, are in a better position to regard the change with greater objectivity, and are less likely to regard the change as a threat. In addition, management is better able to evaluate the method of change and make any necessary modifications before carrying it out more fully.

Almost any change will require that organization members modify the way in which they are accustomed to behaving or working. Therefore, managers must not only be able to decide upon the best people-structure-technology relationships for the organization but also to make corresponding changes in such a way that related human behavior is changed most effectively. Positive results of any change will materialize only if organization members change their behavior as necessitated by the change.

According to Lewin, behavioral change is caused by three distinct but related conditions experienced by an individual: (1) unfreezing, (2) changing, and (3) refreezing. **Unfreezing** occurs when individuals become ready to acquire or learn new behavior-they experience the ineffectiveness of their present mode of behavior and are ready to attempt to learn new behavior that will make them more effective. It may be especially difficult for individuals to "thaw out" because of positive attitudes they traditionally associated with their past behavior.

Changing occurs when individuals begin experimenting with new behavior. They try new behaviors they hope will increase their effectiveness. This changing is best effected if it involves both identification and internalization. Identification is a process in which individuals performing new behaviors pattern themselves after someone who already has expertise in those behaviors; that is, individuals model themselves after an expert. Internalization is a process in which individuals performing new behaviors attempt to use those behaviors as part of their normal behavioral pattern. In other words, individuals consistently try to make the new behaviors useful over an extended period of time.

Refreezing is a situation in which individuals see that the new behavior they have experimented with during "changing" is now part of themselves. They have developed attitudes consistent with performing the new behavior and now see that behavior as part of their normal mode of operations. Rewards individuals receive as a result of performing the new behavior are very instrumental in refreezing.

For managers to increase their success as change agents, they must be able to make their changes in such a way that individuals who will be required to modify their behavior as a result of the change live through Lewin's three conditions. In the example in your text, Ed Clark is faced with a change-related problem. Terry Lacey, a lower-level manager, believes that he can save time and effort by simply writing out his intracompany memos longhand rather than having them typed, proofread, corrected if necessary, and then sent out. However, some of Lacey's memos are written so poorly that words and sentences are misinterpreted. Clearly, some change seems necessary. While Clark simply could mandate change by telling Lacey to write more clearly or to have his memos typed, this strategy may not have enough impact to cause a lasting behavioral change and could conceivably create personal friction between Clark and Lacey. Clark, instead, had decided to approach the problem so that Lacey experiences unfreezing, changing, and unfreezing. To encourage unfreezing, Clark could direct all questions about Lacey's memos back to Lacey himself and make sure that Lacey is aware of all memo misinterpretations and the resulting mistakes. Once Lacey recognizes a need for changing the way in which he writes his memos, Clark could then give Lacey examples of effective intracompany memos (identification). Over time, Clark could also help Lacey to develop the method of transmitting memos that best suits his talents (internalization). After Lacey has developed an effective method of writing memos, Clark could take steps to ensure that positive feedback about his improved memo writing reaches Lacey. This feedback, of course, will be instrumental in refreezing Lacey's new method.

Learning Objective 5   *Some facility in evaluating change*

As with all other action managers take, they should spend some time evaluating the changes they make. The purpose of this evaluation is not only to gain insights on how the change itself might be modified to further increase organizational effectiveness, but also to determine if the steps taken to make the change can be modified to increase organizational effectiveness the next time they are used.

Evaluation of change often involves watching for symptoms that indicate that further change is necessary. For example, if organization members continue to be oriented more to the past then to the future, if they recognize the obligations of rituals more than the challenges of current problems, or if they owe allegiance more to departmental goals than to overall company objectives, the probability is relatively high that further change is necessary.

While symptoms such as those just listed generally indicate that further change is warranted, the decision to make additional changes should consider more objective information resulting from repeated and well-executed internal and external organizational diagnoses. Additional change generally is justified if it further improves the means for satisfying someone's economic wants, increases profitability, promotes human work for human beings, or contributes to individual satisfaction and social well-being.

Learning Objective 6   *An understanding of how organizational change and stress are related*

When implementing changes in organizations, managers should be very concerned about accompanying amounts of stress which they may be simultaneously creating. Such stress not only could be significant enough to completely eliminate any improved impact on the organization which was planned as a result of the change, it could also result in the organization being less effective than it was before any changes were attempted.

Stress is defined as bodily strain which an individual experiences as a result of coping with some environmental factor. Selye says that stress is simply the rate of wear and tear on the body. In organizations this wear and tear is primarily caused by an unconscious mobilization of an individual's energy when confronted with organizational or work demands.

There are several sound reasons for studying stress. First, stress can have damaging psychological and physiological effects on employees that will affect their health and contribution to the effectiveness of the organization. A second important reason to study stress is that it is a major cause of employee turnover and absenteeism. The third reason to study stress is that stress experienced by the employee can affect the safety of other workers or even the public itself. The final reason for studying stress is that it represents a very significant cost to organizations. Some estimates put the cost of stress-related problems in the U.S. economy at $150 billion a year. Since stress is felt by virtually all employees in all organizations, insights regarding how to manage stress which workers might feel are valuable to virtually all managers. Managers must understand how stress influences worker performance. Although having individuals experience some stress is generally considered advantageous and will tend to increase production, having individuals feel too much or too little stress is generally considered disadvantageous and will tend to decrease their production.

Managers should also be able to identify unhealthy stress in organizations. Most stress-related organizational problems reported are the result of employees experiencing too much stress. However, even with this fact in mind, identifying people in organizations who are experiencing detrimentally high levels of stress is a difficult task. People respond to stress in many different ways; the physiological reactions to stress are difficult, if not impossible, for managers to observe and monitor. Such reactions include high blood pressure, pounding heart, and gastrointestinal disorders.

However, there are several more easily **observable signs of unhealthy stress** which the manager can look for. These include: constant fatigue, low energy, moodiness, increased aggression, excessive use of alcohol, temper outbursts, compulsive eating, high levels of anxiety, and chronic worrying. If these signs are observed in employees, the manager should investigate further to determine if employees are experiencing too much stress and if so, assist them in reducing or managing this stress. **Stressors** are organizational situations in which individuals are confronted by circumstances where their usual behaviors are inappropriate or insufficient and where negative consequences are associated with not properly dealing with the situation. Organizational policies, structure, physical conditions and processes can act as stressors. In general, stress is not reduced significantly until the stressor(s) causing the stress has been coped with satisfactorily or withdrawn from the environment. There are several **strategies** which management can adopt to help prevent the development of unwanted stressors in organizations. Management can create an organizational climate which is supportive of individuals, make jobs interesting, and design and operate career counseling programs.

Knowing You Know

True/False   *Directions: On the lines provided, place a "T" for true or an "F" for false for each of the statements that follow.*

_____ 1. Not all managers will be faced with the tasks of changing an organization.

_____ 2. Perhaps the most overlooked skill necessary to be a successful change agent is deciding how much change organization members can withstand.

_____ 3. Stress is felt primarily by employees in upper management positions.

_____ 4. One disadvantage of making structural changes such as those reflected by the matrix organization is that project costs are usually higher.

_____ 5. The central theme of the managerial grid is that managers should have higher concern for people than they have for production.

_____ 6. There is conclusive evidence that Grid OD is a useful technique because it is effective in enhancing profit, positively changing managerial behavior, and positively influencing managerial attitudes and values.

_____ 7. Resistance to change within an organization is as common as the need for change.

_____ 8. Providing time to evaluate how proposed change may affect individual situations usually results in automatic opposition to change.

_____ 9. When evaluating change, the decision to make additional changes should be made solely on the basis of observed symptoms.

_____ 10. One major reason that Ed Clark did not mandate that Terry Lacey write more clearly or have his letters typed was that Clark believed that such a change would be relatively short-lived.

_____ 11. Emphasis throughout the Grid OD program is on developing teamwork within the organization.

_____ 12. Organizational structure is an overt component considered during OD efforts.

_____ 13. The difficulty in evaluating organizational change is due in part to the difficulty of obtaining reliable outcome data from individual change programs.

_____ 14. Stress is a major cause of employee turnover and absenteeism.

_____ 15. A major advantage of matrix organization is that it increases the consistency with which company policy is applied.

Fill-in-the-Blank   *Directions: Fill in the blanks with the appropriate word or phrase*

16. Hellriegel and Slocum present a change model that stresses that an organization has the greatest probability of survival and growth when both _____ and _____ are high within the organization.

17. Perhaps the most important factor to be considered by managers when changing an organization is determining who will be the _____.

18. It has been generally accepted for many years that organizational effectiveness is primarily the result of organizational activities centering around three main classes of factors. These classes are: _____, _____, and _____.

19. A _____ is an organizational situation in which individuals are confronted by circumstances where their usual behaviors are inappropriate or insufficient.

20. _____ entails implementing advantageous changes by clarifying and defining jobs; modifying organizational structure to fit the communication needs of the organization; and decentralizing the organization to reduce the cost of coordination, increase the controllability of subunits, increase motivation, and gain greater flexibility.

21. A _____ is a more traditional organization that is modified primarily for the purpose of completing some type of special project.

22. The process of people change can be referred to as _____.

23. _____ is a commonly used OD technique for changing people in organizations and involves a basic model describing various managerial styles.

24. According to Lewin, behavioral change is caused by three distinct but related conditions experienced by an individual: _____, _____, and _____.

25. Behavioral change occurs when individuals try new behaviors they hope will increase their effectiveness. This change is best effected if it involves both _____ and _____.

Applying What You Know

Experience 12-1   Unexpected Relief*

Introduction

When changes are made in an organization, employees react in various ways. In the incident that follows, three clerks in the accounting division of Regional Hospital were selected to receive technical training in a newly established special project unit. What follows is a description of what transpired when these changes were announced. Read the incident, and then complete the exercises as directed.

Incident

A new rate schedule from Medicare that required an unusual service-charge breakdown caused an overload in the insurance claims office of Regional Hospital. Even by scheduling all the overtime allowed by the budget, the section head was unable to keep the work from piling up. John Barker, accounting division director, requested a procedure change as soon as possible to reduce the burdensome workload. In response to his request, Ron Marks, an assistant hospital administrator

*Source of Experience 12-1: John M. Champion and John H. James, *Critical Incidents in Management* (Homewood, IL: Richard D. Irwin, 1975), pp. 200-202. © 1975 by Richard D. Irwin, Inc.

whose specialty was conversion to computer operations, was assigned to analyze the problem. On the recommendation of Marks, a special project unit was set up near the insurance office to convert the problem procedure to data processing. Marks took charge of the special project, assisted by staff personnel and one claims supervisor. Completion of the special conversion project within six months was necessary to meet audit requirements and to qualify for a federal hospital grant.

On Wednesday, the day after the special unit was set up, Marks asked Barker to send three reliable clerks from his division. General supervision of the clerks would be retained in the division from which they had been borrowed, but the clerks would receive technical supervision in the special project unit.

One of the clerks selected for the special project unit was Lin Buxby, who had graduated from high school one year earlier with a good achievement record. She had near-point vision corrected by contact lenses, a fact that was reflected on her personnel record. The supervisor to whom she was first assigned called personnel about the matter, but he was assured that Buxby's eyesight problem would not handicap her for general clerical work. At her first formal appraisal six months after being hired, Buxby's overall performance was rated "good" by the supervisor. Partly for this reason, she was selected as one of the three clerks to go to the special project unit.

On Thursday, the three clerks were told about their temporary reassignment by Barker shortly before they were to undertake their new duties. The type of work was not mentioned in his brief announcement. The reassignment was unexpected by them. Two of them readily accepted the reassignment with comments such as, "Our pay will be the same," and "We can still have lunch with our friends here because we're just going across the hall."

Lin Buxby, however, was noticeably upset by the turn of events. She asked Barker, "Why can't I stay here? When can I return?" Her questions went unanswered.

When the three clerks arrived at the special project unit on Friday, one of the staff members explained the work to be done, desks were chosen, and work was assigned. During the first coffee break, Buxby rushed back across the hall. Bursting into tears, she implored Barker to let her return and continue training in her original assignment. She said, "The confusion and pressure are too much. And we don't know what to expect next." Barker explained that the situation would soon settle down, that the experience would help her when she returned to her original training position, and that she might be able to make some overtime wages. Buxby seemed convinced and went back to work in the special project unit.

Two working days later, Marks called Barker and demanded that Buxby be replaced immediately. Marks said that Buxby was too slow, that she couldn't do anything right, and that Barker had sent an incompetent clerk for a top-priority project. This attracted Barker's attention because he did not want to make that kind of an impression on the assistant hospital administrator. He was upset and surprised and convinced that Buxby's poor performance was intentional. A replacement for Buxby was selected.

The next morning, Barker took Buxby's replacement to the special project unit, brought Buxby back, and talked to her. It appeared that Buxby didn't know why she had been replaced. When he referred to her being so slow and making so many mistakes, Buxby said, "No one said anything to me about making mistakes. But I know I was slow. The lines on the data sheet ran together due to the columns on the coding sheets being only a quarter inch wide. Everything seemed to swim in front of my eyes. Trying to make sure I didn't make mistakes slowed me up. I told the supervisor about my trouble and she said, 'I'll see what I can do.' The next thing I knew was that you came over and brought me back."

Barker could not avoid the conclusion that everyone connected with the Lin Buxby incident was partially responsible.

Exercise 1

Meet with three or four of your classmates and discuss the incident. Then prepare answers to questions that follow. One group in the class may be called upon to present its answers, so be prepared to support your suggestions.

a.   Why do you think Lin Buxby was so hesitant to leave her old position? Explain.

b. How could John Barker have helped Buxby to reduce the negative feelings she was having about the new position? Explain.

c. Who do you feel is to blame for the problems Buxby was encountering in the new position? Explain.

d. What effect do you feel this experience will have on Lin Buxby in the long run? Will she be more willing or less willing to venture into new areas and accept new challenges and responsibilities? Explain.

e.   If you were in John Barker's position at the beginning of the incident and you wanted Lin Buxby to fill the new position, how would you have approached the situation? Apply what you know about reducing resistance to change.

Exercise 2

Explain what you have gained from this experience.

Experience 12-2   Behavioral Change at Telectrics, Incorporated

Introduction

Behavioral change is caused by three distinct but related conditions experienced by an individual: (1) unfreezing, (2) changing, and (3) refreezing. Unfreezing occurs when individuals become ready to acquire or learn new behaviors. Changing occurs when individuals begin to experiment with new behaviors in the hope that they will increase their effectiveness. Refreezing is a situation in which individuals see that the new behavior they have experimented with during the changing phase is now part of themselves.

In this experience, assume that you and four or five of your classmates have been hired by Telectrics, Incorporated as consultants (external change agents). The job of your group is to assist Telectrics in solving suspected human relations problems that appear to be keeping the organization from perfecting a process to economically mass-produce a product. Read the incident that follows, and then complete the exercises as directed.

Incident

After two years of a four-year contract period, Telectrics, Incorporated had not yet perfected the production process to economically mass-produce the television telephone system for which it had contracted. While the plant manager believed that the corporation had the needed expertise to perfect the product, she felt that there were numerous human problems hindering the success of the effort. Therefore, six months ago she had contacted headquarters about hiring an outside OD consultant, and five months ago, Telectrics, Incorporated had contracted with LEAD Consulting (your consulting organization) for professional assistance in solving the suspected human relations problems.

A preliminary interview program conducted by your team substantiated some of the plant manager's suspicions; lack of leadership and human relations problems were identified as major sources of friction. In an attempt to more closely pinpoint the problem, your team and the plant manager decided to conduct interviews to more fully assess the leadership styles of the three top managers of the firm. Each manager was then to be given confidential feedback. The following report was the feedback given to the manager of microcircuitry design:

MEMORANDUM

To: Manager, Microcircuitry Design
From: LEAD Consulting
Re: Feedback (pro and con) from four of your subordinates and peers regarding your style of leadership as manager of microcircuitry design.

As I am sure you are aware, LEAD Consulting has been employed to help Telectrics identify and overcome problems that seem to be hindering progress on the television telephone system. The summary that follows is provided so that you may have a better perspective on your managerial style and the impact you have on others when carrying out your managerial responsibilities. You are the only person who will receive this confidential report. It is hoped that, through the insight gained from this information, you will be able to build on your strengths and work on your weaknesses to improve your effectiveness as a manager. Feel free to talk with us about these results.

Individual A
Pro:
   1. He has great technical competency.
   2. He is effective in handling administrative details and paperwork.
Con:
   1. He is not receptive to ideas that do not fit his conceptualization of how to do the job.
   2. He is rather arbitrary on technical points.
   3. He is weak in delegating job activities.

Individual B
Pro:
   1. He is knowledgeable in areas that require technical judgment.
   2. Attention to detail, when properly applied is an asset.
Con:
   1. Sometimes, a concern for detail antagonizes those who feel that too much detail is simply inefficient use of energy.
   2. He does not appear to have trust and confidence in the ability of subordinates.
   3. He has difficulty "letting go" of projects.

Individual C
Pro:
   1. He appears to be well organized.
   2. He knows the technical aspects of the business.
Con:
   1. He finds fault too easily, and his head-on approach to taking corrective action really antagonizes the professionals working on the project.
   2. If a job is not completed according to his "personal timetable," it frequently is given to someone else or, in many instances, he may work on it himself.

Individual D
Pro:
   1. His major strength is that he has a fine mind and is a very competent engineer.
   2. Usually, his decisions are well thought out—sometimes too well thought out.

Con:

1. His real problem is in human relations. His curt approach is not appreciated or needed.
2. People are reluctant to go to him with any kind of problem; it's not so much what he says but how he says it.
3. He just cannot continue to assign job activities to a professional and then look over the professional's shoulder continuously to see that the job is being done correctly.

Exercise 1

Now that you have familiarized yourself with the Telectrics incident, form a group with four or five of your classmates and answer the questions that follow.

a. What are the major problems your consulting team should attempt to help the manager of microcircuitry design deal with to improve his managerial effectiveness? Explain.

b. Assume that the major problem of the manager of microcircuitry design is his inability to effectively delegate authority and assign job activities. What are some of the arguments that the manager might be using to resist changing his present mode of operation? List as many reasonable explanations as you can.

c. What are some of the arguments you could present to the manager of microcircuitry design to encourage him to change his mode of operation?

d. Using the change terminology in your text, explain how you feel the LEAD Consulting report will affect the manager of microcircuitry design. Do you think that he will seek the counsel of the consulting team? Explain.

e. How might you, as external change agents, help the manager of microcircuitry design to become a more effective delegator?

f. Assuming that the interventions you suggested in question *e* above bring about the desired behavioral change. How might you help the manager "refreeze" his newly developed skills and attitude about delegation? Explain.

Exercise 2

Explain what you have gained from this experience.

Experience 12-3   Coping with Stress[**]

Introduction

The text suggests that stress can have negative effects on employee health which, in turn, can significantly impact employee contributions to the effectiveness of the organization. This experience will provide you with the opportunity to evaluate whether you are a person prone to stress tendencies, judge the amount of stress with which you presently cope, identify the situations you encounter that are particularly stressful, and determine techniques for coping with these stressful situations. Complete the experience as directed.

Exercise 1

Your instructor will provide you with additional information related to stress. Use the space provided below to record your reactions to this added stress-related information.

[**]Exercise presented by Lee A Graf and Masoud Hemmasi at the 1989 conference of the Associatoin for Business Simulation and Experiential Learning, Orlando, Florida, March 1-3, 1989.

Exercise 2

The first step in effectively managing stress is to take an inward look at yourself and make an evaluation of whether you are a person prone to stress tendencies. Please complete the "Type A-Type B Self-Test" and the "Self-Assessment Student Questionnaire" below following the directions provided. Your instructor will explain how to interpret the results of your efforts.

TYPE A-TYPE B SELF-TEST***

To determine your Type A or Type B profile, circle the number on the continuums (the verbal descriptions represent endpoints) that best represents your behavior for each dimension. Next, total the circled numbers and multiple this total by 3 to obtain your score. Finally, use the point total (number of points) to determine your personality type.

Am casual about appointments	1 2 3 4 5 6 7 8	Am never late
Am not competitive	1 2 3 4 5 6 7 8	Am very competitive
Never feel rushed, even under pressure	1 2 3 4 5 6 7 8	Always feel rushed
Take things one at a time	1 2 3 4 5 6 7 8	Try to do many things at once; think about what I am going to do next
Do things slowly	1 2 3 4 5 6 7 8	Do things fast (eating, walking, etc.)
Express feelings	1 2 3 4 5 6 7 8	"Sit" on feelings
Having many interests	1 2 3 4 5 6 7 8	Have few interests outside work

Total your score:_____. Multiply it by 3:_____The interpretation of your score is as follows:

Number of points	Type of personality
Less than 90	B
90 to 99	B+
100 to 105	A-
106 to 119	A
120 or more	A+

*** Source: Adapted from R. W. Bortner, "A Short Rating Scale as a Potential Measure of Pattern A Behavior," *Journal of Chronic Diseases*, vol. 22, 1966, pp. 87-91.

SELF-ASSESSMENT STUDENT QUESTIONNAIRE[****]

Below are listed events which occur in the life of a college student. Place a check in the left-hand column for each of those events that have happened to you during the last 12 months.

	Life Event	Point Values
_____	Death of a close family member	100
_____	Jail term	80
_____	Final year or first year in college	63
_____	Pregnancy (to you or caused by you)	60
_____	Severe personal illness or injury	53
_____	Marriage	50
_____	Any interpersonal problems	45
_____	Financial difficulties	40
_____	Death of a close friend	40
_____	Arguments with your roommate (more than every other day)	40
_____	Major disagreements with your family	40
_____	Major change in personal habits	30
_____	Change in living environment	30
_____	Beginning or ending a job	30
_____	Problems with your boss or professor	25
_____	Outstanding personal achievement	25
_____	Failure in some course	25
_____	Final exams	20
_____	Increased or decreased dating	20
_____	Change in working conditions	20
_____	Change in your major	20
_____	Change in your sleeping habits	18
_____	Several-day vacation	15
_____	Change in eating habits	15
_____	Family reunion	15
_____	Change in recreational activities	15
_____	Minor illness or injury	15
_____	Minor violations of the law	11

Score: _____

After checking the items above, add up the point values for all of the items checked. Your instructor will explain how to interpret your score.

[****]Source: T. H. Holmes and R. H. Rahe, "Social Readjustment Rating Scale," *Journal of Psychosomatic Research*, vol. 11, 1967, pp. 213-218.

Exercise 3

Record pertinent information from the "Extended Stress Lecturette" in the space provided below.

Exercise 4

a. Utilizing information provided in the stress lecturette, jot down the degree of stress with which you are faced (refer back to Exercise 2).

b. List below the situations that you're presently encountering that are particularly stressful. Number these situations using 1 to denote the most stressful situation, 2 the second most stressful, and so forth.

Exercise 5

From information provided in your textbook and that provided by your instructor in the "Extended Stress Lecturette", what technique(s) or approach(es) will you utilize to try to cope with each stressful situation identified in Exercise 4? Explain in the space provided below.

Exercise 6

Return to the stress quiz that you took earlier in the class period. Correct any mistakes that you made before having the insight gained from the "Extended Stress Lecturette." Your instructor will then provide you with the correct answers and reasoning behind those answers.

Exercise 7

Meet with 4 or 5 other classmates and discuss the two situations that you currently face that are most stressful for you and how you plan to cope with these stressful situations. Make notes in the space provided below on other suggestions made by group members that would appear helpful in dealing with the stressful situations you face. Be prepared to share the two most unique situations discussed in your group with the remainder of the class.

Exercise 8

Explain what you personally have gained from this experience and how you will apply what you have learned as a prospective manager. Use the space provided below for your answer.

13 FUNDAMENTALS OF INFLUENCING AND COMMUNICATION

Chapter Summary

The information in this chapter is divided into two main parts: (1) fundamentals of influencing and (2) communication.

Learning Objective 1   *An understanding of influencing*

Influencing is the process of guiding the activities of organization members in appropriate directions. Appropriate directions, of course, are those that lead to the attainment of management system objectives. Influencing involves focusing on organization members as people and dealing with such issues as morale, arbitration of conflicts, and the development of good working relationships among individuals. Influencing is a critical part of a manager's job. The ability of a manager to influence others is a primary determinant of how successful a manager will be.

As with the planning and organizing functions, the influencing function can be viewed as a subsystem of the overall management system process. The primary purpose of the influencing subsystem is to enhance the attainment of management system objectives by guiding the activities of organization members in appropriate directions. Input of this subsystem is comprised of a portion of the total resources of the overall management system, and output is appropriate organization member behavior. The process of the influencing subsystem involves the performance of four primary management activities: (1) leading, (2) motivating, (3) considering groups, and (4) communicating. Managers transform a portion of organizational resources into appropriate organization member behavior mainly by performing these four activities.

Leading, motivating, and considering groups are related influencing activities, each of which is accomplished, to some extent, by managers communicating with organization members. For example, managers decide what kind of leader they should be only after they analyze the characteristics of various groups with which they will interact and how these groups can best be motivated. Then, regardless of the strategy they adopt, their leading, motivating, and working with groups will be accomplished, at least to some extent, by communicating with other organization members. In fact, all management activities are at least partially accomplished through communication or communication-related endeavors. Because communication is used repeatedly by managers, communication skill often is referred to as the fundamental management skill.

Learning Objective 2   *An understanding of interpersonal communication*

Communication is the process of sharing information with other individuals. Information, as used here, represents any thought or idea that managers desire to share with other individuals. In general, communication involves one individual projecting a message to one or more others that results in all people arriving at a common meaning of a message. Since communication is a commonly used management skill and often is cited as the one ability most responsible for a manager's success, prospective managers must learn how to communicate. Communication activities of managers generally involve interpersonal communication-sharing information with other organization members.

To be a successful interpersonal communicator, a manager must understand how interpersonal communication works, the relationship between feedback and interpersonal communication, and the importance of verbal versus nonverbal interpersonal communication. The interpersonal communication process has three basic elements. The first element is the **source/encoder**. The source/encoder is that person in the interpersonal communication situation who originates and encodes information that he or she desires to share with another person. Encoding is the process of putting information in some form that can be received and understood by another individual. Until information is encoded, it cannot be shared with others.

The second element is the signal. Encoded information that the source intends to share constitutes a **message**. A message that has been transmitted from one person to another is called a **signal**.

The third element is the decoder/destination. The **decoder/destination** is that person with whom the source is attempting to share information. This individual receives the signal and decodes or interprets the message to determine its meaning. Decoding is the process of converting messages back into information. The source determines what information he or she intends to share, encodes this information in the form of a message, and then transmits the message as a signal to the destination. The destination decodes the transmitted message to determine its meaning and then responds accordingly.

Successful communication is an interpersonal communication situation in which the information the source intends to share with the destination and the meaning the destination derives from the transmitted message are the same. Conversely, **unsuccessful communication** is an interpersonal communication situation in which the information the source intends to share and the meaning the destination derives from the transmitted message are different. To increase the probability that communication will be successful, a message must be encoded to ensure that the source's experience concerning the way in which a signal should be decoded is equivalent to the destination's experience of the way it should be decoded. If this situation exists, the probability is high that the destination will interpret the signal as intended by the source.

Factors that decrease the probability that communication will be successful commonly are called communication barriers. A clear understanding of these barriers is helpful to managers in their attempt to maximize communication success. **Communication macrobarriers** are those that hinder successful communication in a general communication situation. These factors relate primarily to the communication environment and the larger world in which communication takes place.

One communication macrobarrier is *the increasing need for information*. To minimize the effects of this barrier, managers should take steps to ensure that organization members are provided with information critical to the performance of their jobs and that they are not overloaded with too much information. A second macrobarrier is the *need for increasingly more complex information*. If managers take steps to emphasize simplicity in communication, the effects of this barrier can be lessened. Also, furnishing organization members with adequate training to deal with more technical areas might be another strategy for overcoming this barrier. A third macrobarrier is that individuals in the United States are increasingly coming in contact with individuals *using other languages besides English*. As business becomes international in scope and as organization members travel more, this trend will accelerate. When dealing with foreigners, it becomes important to be familiar not only with their language but also their cultures. Knowledge of a foreign language may be of little value if individuals don't know which words, phrases, and actions are culturally acceptable for use. A fourth macrobarrier is that the *need for learning decreases time available for communication*. Many managers feel pressured to learn new and important concepts that they have not had to know in the past. Issues like learning about the intricacies of international business as well as computer usage continue to use significant amounts of managerial time. Many managers believe that because of the increased demands that training places on their time, there is simply less time available for communicating with other organization members.

Communication microbarriers are those that hinder successful communication in a specific communication situation. These factors relate directly to such variables as the communication message, the source, and the destination. One microbarrier is the *source's view of the destination*. The source in any communication situation has a tendency to view a destination in a specific way and to influence his or her messages by this view. For example, individuals tend to speak differently to people they think are informed about a subject than to those they think are uninformed. Another microbarrier is *message interference*. Message interference, or noise, is defined as stimuli that compete with the communication message for the attention of the destination. An example of message interference is a manager talking to an office worker while the worker is trying to input data into a word processor. Correcting the mistake is message interference because it competes with the manager's communication message for the secretary's attention. A third microbarrier is the *destination's view of the source*. The destination can have certain attitudes toward the source that also can hinder successful communication. When communicating, managers should attempt to consider the worth of messages transmitted to them independent of their personal attitudes toward the source.

Perception, another microbarrier to effective communication, is an individual's interpretation of a message. Different individuals can perceive the same message in very different ways. The two primary factors that influence the way in which a stimulus is perceived are the level of the destination's education and the destination's amount of experience. To minimize the negative effects of this perceptual factor on interpersonal communication, managers should try to send messages with precise meanings. Ambiguous words generally tend to magnify the detrimental outcome of the perceptual process on interpersonal communication.

A final microbarrier to effective communication results from *multi-meaning words*. Because many words in the English language have several different meanings, a destination may have difficulty deciding which meaning should be attached to the words of a message. On the average, each of the five hundred most common words in our language has over eighteen usages. When encoding information, managers should be careful to define the terms they use whenever possible and never use obscure meanings for words when designing messages. They also should also try to use words in the same way they see their destination use them.

Learning Objective 3   *A knowledge of how to use feedback*

Feedback is the destination's reaction to a message. In general, feedback can be used by the source to ensure successful communication. For example, if the destination's message reaction is inappropriate, the source can conclude that communication was not successful. On the other hand, if the destination's message reaction is appropriate, the source can conclude that communication was successful.

Feedback can be either verbal or nonverbal. For example, to gather verbal feedback, the source could simply ask the destination pertinent message-related questions. To gather nonverbal feedback, the source merely may have to observe the destination's nonverbal response to a message. An example would be a manager who has transmitted a message to a subordinate indicating new steps that must be taken in the normal performance of the subordinate's job. Assuming that no other problems exist, if the steps are not followed accurately, the manager has nonverbal feedback that indicates that he should clarify further the initial message.

Robert S. Goyer has suggested other uses for feedback besides determining if a message is perceived as intended. For example, over time the source can use feedback to evaluate his or her personal communication effectiveness. A formula called the **communication effectiveness index** is used to determine the proportion of the communication effectiveness of the source. If over an extended period of time managers discover that their communication effectiveness index is relatively low, they should assess their situation to determine how to improve their communication skills. One problem they may discover is that they are repeatedly using a vocabulary confusing to the destination. For example, in one study it was found that managers tended to repeatedly use certain words, like *facilitate* and *designate*, that generally were misunderstood by employees (steelworkers). To eliminate this confusion, the researchers suggested phrases or words that managers should use instead.

Besides analyzing their vocabulary, managers should attempt to increase their communication effectiveness by following the "ten commandments of good communication" as closely as possible. These commandments are:

1. *Seek to clarify your ideas before communicating.* The more systematically you analyze the problem or idea to be communicated, the clearer it becomes.

2. *Examine the true purpose of each communication.* Before you communicate, ask yourself what you really want to accomplish with your message--obtain information, initiate action, change another person's attitude?

3. *Consider the total physical and human setting whenever you communicate.* Meaning and intent are conveyed by more than words alone.

4. *Consult with others, when appropriate, in planning communications.* Such consultation often lends additional insight and objectivity to your message.

5. *Be mindful, while you communicate, of the overtones as well as the basic content of your message.* Your tone of voice, your expression, your apparent receptiveness to the responses of others--all have tremendous impact on those you wish to reach.

6. *Take the opportunity, when it arises, to convey something of help or value to the receiver.* Consideration of the other person's interests and needs--trying to look at things from the other person's point of view--frequently points up opportunities to convey something of immediate benefit or long-range value to the other person.

7. *Follow up your communication.* You can do this by asking questions, by encouraging the receiver to express his or her reactions, by follow-up contacts, and by subsequent review of performance.

8. *Communicate for tomorrow as well as today.* Communications must be planned with the past in mind if they are to maintain consistency in the receiver's view; however, they must be consistent with long-range interests and goals. While it is not easy to communicate frankly on such matters as poor performance, postponing disagreeable communications makes these matters more difficult in the long run and is actually unfair to your subordinates and your company.

9. *Be sure your actions support your communications.* In the final analysis the most persuasive kind of communication is not what you say, but what you do.

10. Last, but by no means least: *Seek not only to be understood but to understand--be a good listener.* Listening is one of the most important, most difficult, and most neglected communication skills. Thus, you must learn to listen with the inner ear if you are to know the inner person.

Learning Objective 4   *An appreciation for the importance of nonverbal communication*

Interpersonal communication generally is divided into two types: verbal and nonverbal. Up to this point, the main emphasis of the chapter has been on **verbal communication**--communication that uses either spoken or written words to share information with others. **Nonverbal communication** is sharing information without using words to encode thoughts. Factors commonly used to encode thoughts in nonverbal communication include gestures, vocal tones, and facial expressions.

In most interpersonal communication, both verbal and nonverbal communication modes are used. Generally, the destination's interpretation of a message is based not only on the words in the message but also on such factors as the source's gestures and facial expressions. In an interpersonal communication situation in which both verbal and nonverbal factors are present, nonverbal factors may have more influence on the total impact of a message than verbal factors. Mehrabian suggests that the total message impact equals .07 words plus .38 vocal tones plus .55 facial expressions. Of course, both vocal tones and facial expressions are nonverbal factors. Besides vocal tones and facial expressions, gestures, gender and dress can influence the impact of a verbal message.

Given the great potential influence of nonverbal factors on the impact of a message, managers should use nonverbal message ingredients to complement verbal message ingredients whenever possible. To this end, a head might be nodded or a voice might be toned to show either agreement or disagreement. Regardless of how managers decide to combine verbal and nonverbal factors, they must be sure that the two do not unknowingly present contradictory messages. This situation creates message ambiguity and leaves the destination frustrated.

Learning Objective 5   *Insights on formal organizational communication*

To be effective communicators, managers must not merely understand the more general interpersonal communication concepts discussed previously but also the characteristics of interpersonal communication within organizations. This organizational communication directly relates to the goals, functions, and structure of human organizations and, to a major extent, organizational success is determined by the effectiveness of organizational communication.

In general, communication that follows the lines of the organization chart is called formal **organizational communication.** The organization chart depicts relationships between people and jobs and shows the formal channels of communication between them. Communication that flows from any point on an organization chart downward to another point on the organization chart is called **downward organizational communication.** This type of formal organizational communication primarily relates to the direction and control of employees, and typically includes a statement of organizational philosophy, management system objectives, position descriptions, and other written information relating to the importance, rationale, and interrelationships of various departments.

Communication that flows from any point on an organization chart upward to another point on the organization chart is called **upward organizational communication.** This type of organizational communication primarily contains information managers need to evaluate the organizational area for which they are responsible. Techniques that managers commonly use to encourage upward organizational communication include informal discussions with employees, attitude surveys, the development and use of grievance procedures, suggestion systems, and an "open door" policy that is an invitation for employees to come in whenever they would like to talk to management. Organizational modifications based upon this feedback can be made to enable the organization to be more successful in the future.

Communication that flows from any point on an organization chart horizontally to another point on the organization chart is called **lateral organizational communication.** Communication that flows across the organization usually focuses on coordinating the activities of various departments and developing new plans for future operating periods.

By nature, organizational communication creates patterns of communication among organization members. These patterns essentially evolve from the repeated occurrence of various serial transmission of information. A serial transmission involves passing information from one individual to another; the originator and the ultimate recipient of the message are separated by middle people. One of the obvious weaknesses of a serial transmission is that messages tend to become distorted as the length of the serial transmission increases. Research has shown that, in a serial transmission, message details may be omitted, altered, or added.

The potential inaccuracy of messages transmitted is not the only weakness of a serial transmission. A serial transmission also can influence morale, the emergence of a leader, and the degree to which individuals involved in the transmission are organized and efficient.

Learning Objective 6   *An appreciation for the importance of the grapevine*

Organizational communication that does not follow the lines of the organization chart is called **informal organizational communication.** This type of communication typically follows the pattern of personal relationships among organization members. Informal organizational communication networks generally exist because organization members have a desire to know information that formal organizational communication does not furnish them. The informal organizational communication network, or **grapevine,** has several distinctive characteristics: (1) the grapevine springs up and is used irregularly within the organization; (2) it is not controlled by top executives, who may not even be able to influence it; and (3) it is used largely to serve the self-interests of the people within it. Understanding the grapevine is a prerequisite for a complete understanding of organizational communication. Some estimates indicate that 70% of all communication in organizations follows organizational grapevines. Not only do grapevines carry great amounts of communication, but they carry it at very rapid speeds. The company grapevine is commonly cited by employees as being the most reliable and credible source of information about company events. As with formal organizational communication, informal organizational communication involves serial transmissions. Organization members involved in these transmissions, however, are more difficult for managers to identify than those in the formal communication network.

Four different patterns of grapevines generally tend to exist in organizations. The first of these grapevine patterns is the *single-strand grapevine*: A tells B, who tells C, who tells D, and so on. This type of grapevine generally tends to distort messages more than any other. Another pattern is the *gossip grapevine:* A informs everyone else on the grapevine. A third pattern is the *probability grapevine*: A communicates randomly, for example, to F and D. F and D then continue to inform other grapevine members in the same way. In the *cluster grapevine*, A selects and tells C, D, and F. F selects and tells I and B, and B selects and tells J. Information in this grapevine travels only to selected individuals.

A grapevine can and often does generate rumors that can be detrimental to organizational success. On the other hand, when employees have what they view as sufficient organizational information it seems to build their sense of belonging to the organization and their level of productivity. Grapevines could be used to help managers to maximize information flow to employees. Other writers argue that managers should encourage the development of grapevines and strive to become grapevine members to gain information feedback that could be very valuable in improving the organization. Exactly how individual managers should deal with the grapevine, of course, depends on the specific organizational situation in which managers find themselves.

Learning Objective 7   *Some hints on how to encourage organizational communication*

Organizational communication often is called the "nervous system" of the organization. Since formal organizational communication is generally the most important type of communication that takes place in the organization, managers must encourage its free flow if the organization is to be successful. To encourage the flow of formal organizational communication, managers can listen attentively to messages that come through formal channels, support the flow of clear and concise statements through formal communication channels, ensure that all organization members have free access to the use of formal communication channels within the organization, and assign staff personnel specific communication responsibilities.

Knowing You Know

True/False   *Directions: On the lines provided, place a "T" for true or an "F" for false for each of the statements that follow.*

_____ 1. Informal communication typically follows the pattern of personal relationships among organization members.

_____ 2. The gossip grapevine tends to distort messages more than any other type.

_____ 3. Informal communication is often called the "nervous system" of the organization.

_____ 4. The process of the influencing subsystem involves the performance of four primary management activities: (1) communicating, (2) motivating, (3) cooperating, and (4) leading.

_____ 5. A message that has been transmitted from one person to another is called a signal.

_____ 6. Perception is a communication microbarrier.

_____ 7. There are over five hundred meanings for many of the common words in our language.

_____ 8. Gathering nonverbal feedback requires that the source delve much deeper than mere observance of the destination's nonverbal response to a message.

_____ 9. A formula called total message impact (TMI) is used to determine the proportion of the destinations' reactions that were intended by the source.

_____ 10. Nonverbal communication is sharing information without using words to encode thoughts.

Matching　　　　　*Directions: Match items 11-25 with items a-o. There is only one correct answer for each item.*

_____11.　Influencing
_____12.　Communication
_____13.　Source
_____14.　Decoding
_____15.　Communication macrobarrier
_____16.　Communication microbarrier
_____17.　Feedback
_____18.　Nonverbal communication
_____19.　Downward organizational communication
_____20.　Lateral organizational communication
_____21.　Perception
_____22.　Serial transmission
_____23.　Information
_____24.　Grapevine
_____25.　Message interference

a.　All management activities are at least partially accomplished through
b.　The process of converting a message back into information
c.　Facial expressions and gestures are examples of
d.　The need for increasingly more complex information
e.　The process of guiding the activities of organization members in appropriate directions
f.　Focuses on coordinating the activities of various departments and developing new plans for future operating periods
g.　Primarily relates to the direction and control of employees
h.　Message interference
i.　The destination's reaction to a message
j.　Encodes information that he or she desires to share with another person
k.　The network of informal organizational communication
l.　The passage of information from one individual, to the next individual, to the next, and so on
m.　Stimuli that compete with the message for the attention of the destination
n.　Any thought or idea to be shared with another individual
o.　The interpretation of a message by a particular individual

Applying What You Know

Experience 13-1　Communication: One-Way Versus Two-Way

Introduction

Information that flows from a source (encoder) through a signal to a destination (decoder) is called one-way communication. Communication becomes two-way when a fourth element, called feedback, is added to the three elements (source, signal, destination) of the one-way process. When a mechanism exists for information to flow from the destination back to the source, feedback is possible. In this experience, you learn more about one-way and two-way communication.

Exercise 1

Your instructor will pair you with another member of the class for this experience. Determine which team member will be the source (encoder) and which will be the destination (decoder). Then position two chairs so that the source sits facing the back of the destination. Since this experience will simulate a telephone conversation in which instructions are given, the source should not be able to see the destination or what the destination is writing. The destination should have two sheets of paper, one labeled "Form A: One-Way Communication" and the other "Form B: Two-Way Communication." The destination will use this paper to record the message communicated by the source. Your instructor will provide the source with the message to be communicated. For one-way communication, the source should pretend that the mouthpiece on the destination's phone is out of order. In other words, the source must provide all of the information, and the destination cannot ask any questions or provide any feedback. (The destination must make a conscious effort not to provide nonverbal feedback--no nodding of the head, etc.) Since the first communication experience is one-way, the destination should record the source's message on the sheet labeled "Form A: One-Way Communication." After one-way communication has been completed, the destination and the source should turn all materials facedown and should not refer back to this material until instructed to do so. At this point, no further interaction between source and destination is permitted.

Exercise 2

After completion of the one-way communication exercise, your instructor will provide the source with a new message to be communicated to the destination in two-way communication fashion. In this second situation, the hypothetical phone system functions properly, the source provides information, and the destination provides feedback to the source. However, because the information still is being passed by telephone, the source is not permitted to see what the destination is writing down, and the destination must make a conscious effort to provide only verbal feedback. The destination should record the message on the sheet labeled "Form B: Two-Way Communication." After two-way communication has been completed, all materials should again be turned facedown. Do not discuss your experiences or refer back to the materials used in the one-way or two-way communication exercises until instructed to do so.

Exercise 3

Answer the questions that pertain to the role (source or destination) you played in the experience. Please do not discuss these feelings with your partner at this time.

a.   If you acted as the source, how did you feel about giving information in the one-way communication setting? In the two-way communication setting? Use descriptive words like confident, powerful, etc.

b.   If you acted as the destination, how did you feel about receiving information in the one-way communication setting? In the two-way communication setting? Use descriptive words like confused, confident, uncertain, etc.

Exercise 4

You and your partner should now compare Form A to the original diagram for A and Form B to the original diagram for B to determine whether one-way or two-way communication was more effective. Which diagram came closest to matching the original? How can this be explained?

Exercise 5

Each team should discuss and answer the questions that follow.

a. Based on what you have just experienced, how can you explain the fact that supervisors still frequently use one-way communication? You may find it helpful to discuss what you jotted down in exercises 3 and 4 at this time.

b. Your instructor has recorded on the chalkboard the average team time for one-way and two-way communication. Does that information provide you with any further insight into question *a*?

c.   In some instances (for example, when speaking to a large group or in times of emergency), the situation may require that one-way communication be used. If this is the case, what can you suggest to make one-way communication as effective as possible?

d.   If two-way communication can be used, how can you make sure that you are communicating effectively? Explain.

Exercise 6

After you have discussed this experience in class, explain what you have gained from your involvement.

Experience 13-2   Giving and Getting Information*

Introduction

While managers have numerous oral communication activities, such as making assignments, leading conferences, negotiating with people, making corrections, giving commendations, and just participating in friendly office conversation, they generally agree that the giving and getting of information is the oral communication activity they spend the most time performing. Passing on information is one of the great verbal activities in any office.

This experience is designed to illustrate how you can become more skilled at giving and getting information. Some members of the class will be asked to involve themselves in a "giving and getting information" experiment; the remainder of the class will act as observers. Both participants and observers will then meet in small groups to discuss the experiment.

Exercise 1

Your instructor will select five people from the class to be participants in this experiment (these individuals will be numbered one through five). The remaining class members will serve as observers. Participants two through five will be asked to step out of the room while further instructions are being given to observers and participant one. Participants two through five will then be called in one at a time.

Exercise 2

Undoubtedly, some parts of the message in the experiment were lost or distorted as the information was passed from participant one through participants two, three, four, and five. Whenever information is passed from one person to another, there tends to be a falloff in the number of details that get through. Items *a---e* list five ways for information loss or distortion to occur. Meet with three or four other classmates, refer to the street scene used in exercise 1, and identify as many specific errors as you can that you observed under each classification.

a.   **Omissions**   These are the items that were *never* mentioned at all--details that either escaped participant one or that participant one considered unimportant. For example, the fence around the grassy area or the bell sign on the window of the telephone company may *never* have been mentioned.

b.   **Losses**   These are items that were mentioned at first but later dropped. For example, the time on the bank clock may have been mentioned by an earlier sender but dropped by a later one.

*Source of Experience 13-2: From *Handling Barriers in Communication* by Irving J. Lee and Laura L. Lee. Copyright © 1956, 1957 by Laura L. Lee. Reprinted by permission of Harper & Row, Publishers, Inc.

c.   **Changes**   These are items that were modified to have a different meaning or position in the picture. For example, building locations are often shifted to different corners in the street scene: the clothing store might have been repositioned on the telephone company corner or vice versa.

d.   **Additions**   These are items that were added by one participant or another. For example, oftentimes an armed bandit or an armored car is added to the scene.

e.   **Qualified statements that become definite statements**   These are statements where one of the participants said, "I think it was . . .," and the next participant stated it as fact. For example, the statement, "Some people *may have been waiting for a bus*," may have become, "Some people *were waiting* for a bus."

Exercise 3

As a group, explain why falloff occurs. How can this falloff phenomenon be explained?

Exercise 4

Your group should discuss ways of preventing loss of information. Think back to the experiment--the five people talking about the street scene. What could they have done to reduce the number of errors? What advice would you give another five people about to go through the same experiment? What would you do yourself if you were called upon to participate in the experiment?

Exercise 5

What implications does this exercise have for prospective supervisors or managers? Explain.

Experience 13-3   Effective Listening: A Key to Managerial Success

Introduction

Today, modern managers know that listening is as important, if not more important, than the effective transmission of information. How well do you think you listen? In this experience, you assess your listening skills and then develop strategies to overcome your listening deficiencies.

Exercise 1

In a few minutes, your instructor will give you instructions to take some specific actions. Make sure that you use your best listening skills.

Exercise 2

Use what you observed from your experience as well as what happened with others in exercise 1 to answer the questions that follow.

a.   Some individuals were not successful in following instructions in exercise 1. Why?

b.   What could the source (in this experience, your instructor) have done differently to increase the probability that the message would be decoded and interpreted more effectively? Explain.

Exercise 3

List as many obstructions to skillful and perceptive listening as you can.

Exercise 4

Evaluate your listening skills by completing the self-evaluation form in figure 13.1

Figure 13.1 Self-evaluation form for listening.[**]

How Do You Listen?

Listening Habit	Frequency					Score
	Almost Always	Usually	Sometimes	Seldom	Almost Never	
Shunning new experience	_____	_____	_____	_____	_____	_____
Faking attention to the speaker	_____	_____	_____	_____	_____	_____
Avoiding difficult material	_____	_____	_____	_____	_____	_____
Welcoming or creating distractions	_____	_____	_____	_____	_____	_____
Finding fault with the speaker	_____	_____	_____	_____	_____	_____
Listening only for details	_____	_____	_____	_____	_____	_____
Getting overstimulated by some point in the task	_____	_____	_____	_____	_____	_____
Letting bias or prejudice interfere	_____	_____	_____	_____	_____	_____
Note-taking faults (writing while someone is talking)	_____	_____	_____	_____	_____	_____
Failing to relate the speaker's ideas to your own situation	_____	_____	_____	_____	_____	_____

Score 2 points for almost Always, 4 for Usually, 6 for Sometimes, 8 for Seldom, and 10 for almost Never.
A total score of 90 or above indicates an extraordinarily good listener; 70-90, a good listener; below 70 indicates a need for listening training.

[**]"Are You Sure You're a Good Listener?" *Supervisory Management* (February 1969), pp. 33-36.

Exercise 5

What must a person do to become a more skillful listener?

Experience 13-4   Interpreting Nonverbal Communication: Can You "Read" These Classic Smiles?***

Introduction

Most people are bad liars because their feelings tend to "ooze out" of their faces, if only in minute changes of expression. Those most effective in interpreting communication analyze not only what has been said verbally but also what has been said nonverbally through those changing facial expressions. A smile is one of the most expressive gestures you can make. Sociologists have cataloged hundreds of different smiles signifying hundreds of different emotions. In this experience, you test your skill at "reading" smiles and also at interpreting other facial expressions and gestures.

Exercise 1

Closely examine the six smiles in figure 13.2. Below these pictures are six phrases that describe the "emotions" displayed in the pictures. Write the letter of the phrase that most closely matches the emotion in each picture in the box in the lower left corner of each picture. Each phrase is used only once.

***Source of Experience 13-4: Adapted from "Can You 'Read' These Classic Smiles?" *Xchange: Xerox Learning Systems* 4 (1976): 6.

Figure 13.2   Six smiles.

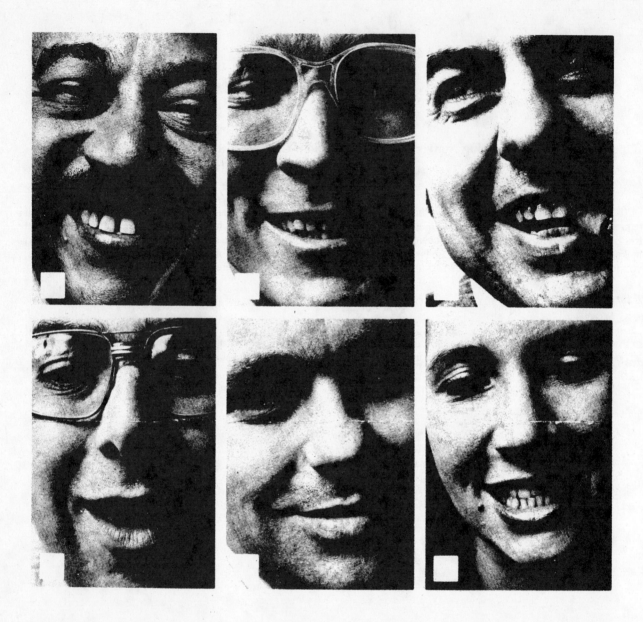

a. "Good talking to you, General."   d. "What a good time!"
b. "I'll fix your wagon."   e. "Hello, how are you?"
c. "This puzzle is intriguing."   f. "   "

Exercise 2

Pair off with a classmate and interpret the meaning of the facial expressions and gestures that follow.****
a. Hand wringing

b. Clenched fist

c. Opening one' s hands to another

d. Joining fingertips to form a "church steeple"

e. Tapping one's fingertips

f. Hand to mouth gesture

g. Covering one's mouth with hand

h. Resting a hand on one's face

i. Placing hands on hips

j. Crossed legs combined with crossed arms

k. Leg draped over the arm of a chair

l. Feet up on the desk

m. When talking, leaning toward the other person

n. Hair-smoothing on the part of a woman, or a hands-on-hips stance and squared shoulders on the part of a man

o. Furrowed forehead

p. Raised eyebrows together with a wide-eyed look

****Many of the examples in Exercise 2 were drawn from Anthony G. Athos and John J. Gabarro, *Interpersonal Behavior: Communication and Understanding in Relationships*, © 1978, pp. 27-32. Adapted by permission of Prentice-Hall, Englewood Cliffs, New Jersey.

q.   Wrinkled nose

r.   Flared nostrils

s.   Lips clamped, tightly drawn, or pursed

Exercise 3

Your instructor will randomly select different members of the class to stand up and act out the meaning they attach to one or more of the facial expressions or gestures in exercise 2. Other class members will be called upon to "read" and verbally interpret for the class the meaning of that acted out facial expression or gesture. Since some expressions may have more than one meaning, you must observe closely to get the precise meaning. During the acting out of these expressions, jot down in exercise 2 any meanings you did not originally identify for an expression.

Exercise 4

Explain what you have gained from this experience.

14 LEADERSHIP

Chapter Summary

This chapter discusses (1) how to define leadership, (2) the difference between a leader and a manager, (3) the trait approach to leadership, and (4) the situational approach to leadership, and (5) the recent emphasis now being placed on leadership.

Learning Objective 1   *A working definition of leadership*

Leadership is the process of directing the behavior of others toward the accomplishments of some objective. Directing, in this sense, means causing individuals to act in a certain way or to follow a particular course. Ideally, this course of action is perfectly consistent with such factors as established organizational policies, procedures, and job descriptions. The central theme of leadership is getting things accomplished through people. It is extremely important that managers have a thorough understanding of what leadership entails. Leadership has always been considered a prerequisite for organizational success. Given issues like the increased capability afforded by enhanced communication technology and the rise of international business, leadership is perhaps more important now than ever before.

Learning Objective 2   *An understanding of the relationship between leading and managing*

Leading is not the same as managing. Many executives do not understand the difference between leading and managing, and are therefore apprehensive about how to carry out their organizational duties. Management consists of the rational assessment of a situation and the systematic selection of goals and purposes (what is to be done); the systematic development of strategies to achieve these goals; the marshalling of the required resources; the rational design, organization, direction, and control of the activities required to attain the selected purposes; and, finally, the motivating and rewarding of people who do the work. Managing is much broader in scope than leading and focuses on behavioral as well as nonbehavioral issues. Leading mainly emphasizes behavioral issues. The most effective managers, over the long run, are also leaders. Merely possessing management skills is no longer sufficient for an executive to be successful in today's business world. Modern executives need a fundamental understanding of the difference between management and leading and how both activities must be combined to achieve organizational success. A manager makes sure that a job gets done and a leader cares about and focuses on the people who do the job. To combine management and leadership, modern executives should demonstrate a calculated and logical focus on organizational processes (management) along with a genuine concern for workers as people (leadership).

Learning Objective 3   *An appreciation for the trait and situational approaches to leadership*

The **trait approach to leadership** is based on early leadership research that seemed to assume that a good leader is born and not made. Researchers thought that, if a complete profile of the traits of a successful leader could be summarized, it would be fairly easy to pinpoint those individuals who should and should not be placed in leadership positions. One study concluded that successful leaders tend to be intelligent (with both judgment and verbal ability); to have past achievements in scholarship and athletics; to be emotionally mature and stable; to be dependable and persistent, with a drive for continuing achievement; to have the skill to participate socially and to adapt to various groups; and to have a desire for status and socioeconomic position. An evaluation of a number of these trait studies, however, concludes that the findings generally tend to be inconsistent. In essence, research indicates that no trait or combination of traits guarantees that a leader will be successful. Contemporary management writers and practitioners generally agree with the notion that leadership ability cannot be explained by an individual's traits or inherited characteristics. More popular current thought supports the notion that individuals can be trained to be good leaders.

The emphasis of leadership study has shifted from the trait approach to primarily the situational approach. The more modern **situational approach to leadership** is based on the assumption that all instances of successful leadership are somewhat different and require a unique combination of leaders, followers, and leadership situations. This interaction commonly is expressed in formula form: $SL = f(L,F,S)$. A translation of this formula is that successful leadership (SL) is a function (f) of the leader (L), the follower (F), and the situation (S).

Learning Objective 4   *Insights about using leadership theories that emphasize decision making situations*

Tannenbaum and Schmidt wrote one of the first and perhaps most well-quoted discussions on the situational approach to leadership. This discussion emphasizes situations in which a leader makes decisions. Since one of the most important tasks of a leader is making sound decisions, practical and legitimate leadership thought should contain some emphasis on decision making.

Tannenbaum and Schmidt's model of leadership behavior is actually a continuum, or range, of leadership behavior available to managers in making decisions. Each type of decision-making behavior on this model has both a corresponding degree of authority used by the manager and a related amount of freedom available to subordinates. Management behaviors at the extreme left of the model characterize the leader who makes decisions by maintaining high control and allowing little subordinate freedom, while those at the extreme right characterize the leader who makes decisions by exercising little control and allowing much subordinate freedom and self-direction. Behavior between the extreme left and right of the model reflects a gradual change from autocratic to democratic leadership, or vice versa. Managers displaying leadership behavior toward the left of the model are more autocratic and called boss-centered leaders, while managers displaying leadership behavior toward the right of the model are more democratic and called subordinate-centered leaders. The seven types of behavior in this model, beginning with the most autocratic and moving to the most democratic, are:

1. *The manager makes the decision and announces it.* This behavior is characterized by the manager identifying a problem, analyzing various alternatives available to solve the problem, choosing the alternative that will be used to solve the problem, and requiring followers to implement the chosen alternative. The manager may or may not use coercion, but the followers have no opportunity to participate directly in the decision-making process.

2. *The manager "sells" the decision.* As before, the manager identifies the problem and independently arrives at a decision. Rather than announce the decision to subordinates for implementation, however, the manager tries to persuade subordinates to accept the decision.

3. *The manager presents his or her ideas and invites questions.* The manager makes the decision and attempts to gain acceptance through persuasion. One additional step is taken, however, since subordinates are invited to ask questions about the decision.

4. *The manager presents a tentative decision subject to change.* The manager actually allows subordinates to have some part in the decision-making process. The manager, however, retains the responsibility for identifying and diagnosing the problem and arrives at a tentative decision that is subject to change based upon subordinate input. The final decision is made by the manager.

5. *The manager presents the problem, gets suggestions, and then makes the decision.* This is the first leadership activity described thus far that allows subordinates the opportunity to offer problem solutions before the manager offers a problem solution. The manager still, however, identifies the problem in the first place.

6. *The manager defines the limits and requests the group to make a decision.* This behavior is characterized by the manager first defining the problem and setting the boundaries within which a decision must be made. But the manager indicates that he or she and the group are partners in making an appropriate decision.

7. *The manager permits the group to make decisions within prescribed limits.* The manager actually becomes an equal member of a problem-solving group. The entire group identifies and assesses the problem, develops alternative problem solutions, and chooses an alternative to be implemented. Everyone within the group understands that the group's decision will be implemented.

The true value of the model developed by Tannenbaum and Schmidt can be realized only if a leader can use it to make practical and desirable decisions. According to these authors, the three primary forces that influence a manager's determination of which leadership behavior to use to make decisions are: (1) forces in the manager, (2) forces in subordinates, and (3) forces in the leadership situation.

Managers should be aware of four forces within themselves that influence their determination of how to make decisions as a leader. The first of these forces is a **manager's values,** such as the relative importance to the manager of organizational efficiency, personal growth, growth of subordinates, and company profits. For example, if subordinate growth is valued very highly, a manager may want to give group members the valuable experience of making a decision, even though the manager could have made the same decision much more quickly and efficiently alone. The second force within the manager is the **manager's level of confidence in subordinates.** In general, the more confidence a manger has in subordinates, the more likely the manager's style of decision making will be democratic or subordinate-centered. The reverse is also true. The third force within the manager that influences a manager's determination of how to make decisions as a leader is the **manager's personal leadership strengths.** Some managers are more effective in issuing orders than leading a group discussion and vice versa. A manager must be able to recognize his or her personal leadership strengths and to capitalize on them. The fourth influencing force within a **manager is tolerance for ambiguity.** As a manager moves from a boss-centered style to a subordinate-centered style, he or she loses some certainty about how problems should be resolved. If this reduction of certainty is disturbing to a manager, it may be extremely difficult for him or her to be successful as a subordinate-centered leader.

A second primary force that influences a manager's determination of how to make decisions as a leader is forces in subordinates. To understand subordinates adequately, a manager should keep in mind that all subordinates are both somewhat different and somewhat alike. Any cookbook approach for deciding how to lead all subordinates is, therefore, impossible. Generally speaking, however, a manager probably could increase his or her success as a leader by allowing subordinates more freedom in making decisions if (1) the subordinates have relatively high needs for independence, (2) the subordinates have a readiness to assume responsibility for decision making, (3) they have a relatively high tolerance for ambiguity, (4) they are interested in the problem and feel that it is important, (5) they understand and identify with goals of the organization, (6) they have the necessary knowledge and experience to deal with the problem, and (7) they have learned to expect to share in decision making. If these characteristics of subordinates do not exist in a particular situation, a manger probably should move toward a more autocratic or boss-centered approach to making decisions.

The third group of forces that influence a manager's determination of how to make decisions as a leader are forces in the leadership situation. The first such situational force involves the types of organization in which the leader works. Such organizational factors as the size of working groups and their geographical distribution become especially important in deciding how to make decisions as a leader. Extremely large work groups or a wide geographic separation of work groups, for example, could make a subordinate-centered leadership style impractical. Another such force in the leadership situation is the effectiveness of group members working together. To this end, a manger should evaluate such issues as the experience of the group in working together and the degree of confidence group members have in their ability to solve problems as a group. A manager should only assign decision-making responsibilities to effective work groups. A third situational force that influences a manager's determination of how to make decisions as a leader is the problem to be solved. Before acting as a more subordinate-centered leader, a manager should be sure that a group possesses the expertise necessary to make a decision about the existing problem. As a group loses the necessary expertise to solve a problem, a manager generally should move toward more boss-centered leadership. A fourth situational force involves the time available to make a decision. As a general guideline, the less time available to make a decision, the more impractical it becomes to have that decision made by a group.

An update to Tannenbaum and Schmidt's original work stresses that in modern organizations the relationship among forces within the manager, subordinates, and situation is becoming more complex and more interrelated than ever. As this relationship becomes increasingly complicated, it obviously becomes more difficult for the leader to determine how to lead. This update also stresses that both societal and organizational values, such as the development of minority groups and pollution control, should have some influence on leader decision making.

Another major decision-focused theory of leadership that has gained widespread attention was first developed in 1973 and refined and expanded in 1988. This theory, the **Vroom-Yetton-Jago Model (VYJ)**, focuses on how much participation to allow subordinates in the decision-making process. The VYJ model is built on two important premises: (1) organizational decisions should be of high quality (have a beneficial impact on organizational performance), and (2) subordinates should accept and be committed to organizational decisions that are made. Overall, the VYJ model suggests that there are five different decision styles or ways that leaders can make decisions. These decision styles range from the leader being autocratic (the leader makes the decision) to consultative (the leader makes the decision after interacting with the followers) to group-focused (the manager meets with the group and the group makes the decision). Of the five decision styles, two are autocratic in nature, two consultative, and the last group oriented.

The VYJ model is actually a method for determining when a leader should use which decision style. In order for a leader to determine which decision style to use in a particular situation, the leader starts at the left of the decision tree by stating an organizational problem being addressed. After the problem has been stated, the leader asks a series of questions about the problem as determined by the structure of the decision tree until a decision style appropriate for the situation is determined at the far right side of the model. For example, after stating an organizational problem, the leader determines that a decision related to that problem has low quality requirement, that it is important that subordinates are committed to the decision, and it is very uncertain that if the leader made the decision by himself or herself that subordinates would be committed to the decision. As a result of these factors, the model (or decision tree) suggests that the leader use the GII (group) decision style--the leader meets with the group to discuss the situation and the group makes the decision

The VYJ model seems promising. Research dealing with an earlier version of this model has yielded some evidence that decisions managers make that are consistent with the model tend to be more successful than decisions managers make that are inconsistent with the model. The model tends to be somewhat complex, however, and therefore somewhat difficult for practicing managers to apply.

Another stream of leadership thought focuses on leadership situations in more general terms. This stream of thought usually is discussed as beginning with two series of leadership studies. In one series researchers were affiliated with Ohio State University (OSU). The **OSU studies** are a series of leadership investigations that concluded that leaders exhibit two main types of behavior. The first type of behavior, called **structure behavior**, is any leadership activity that delineates the relationship between the leader and the leader's followers or establishes well-defined procedures that followers should adhere to in performing their jobs. Overall, structure behavior limits the self-guidance of followers int he performance of their tasks. Although it would be correct to conclude that structure behavior can be, and sometimes is, relatively firm, it would be incorrect to assume that it is rude and malicious. The second main type of leadership behavior described by the OSU studies, **consideration behavior**, is leadership behavior that reflects friendship, mutual trust, respect, and warmth in the relationship between the leader and the followers. Consideration behavior generally is aimed at developing and maintaining a more human relationship between the leader and the followers.

The OSU studies resulted in a model that depicts four fundamental leadership styles. A **leadership style** is the behavior a leader exhibits while guiding organization members in appropriate directions. Each of the four leadership styles in this model is a different combination of structure behavior and consideration behavior (see text figure 14.6). For example, the high structure/low consideration leadership style represents a leader who emphasizes structure behavior and de-emphasizes consideration behavior. The OSU studies have made a significant contribution to the understanding of leadership. The central thoughts and ideas generated by these studies still serve as the basis for modern leadership thought and research.

At about the same time that the OSU Leadership Studies were being conducted, researchers at the University of Michigan were also performing a series of historically significant leadership studies. Analyzing information based upon interviews of both leaders and followers or managers and subordinates, the **Michigan Studies** pinpointed two basic types of leader behavior; job-centered and employee-centered. **Job-centered behavior** focuses primary attention on the work a subordinate is doing. Such behavior indicated that the leader is very interested in the work the subordinate is performing and how well the subordinate is doing the work. **Employee-centered behavior** focuses primary attention on subordinates as people. Such behavior indicated that the leader is very attentive to the personal needs of subordinates and is interested in building cooperative work teams that are satisfying to subordinates and advantageous for the organization.

The results of the OSU Studies and the Michigan Studies are very similar. Both research efforts indicated two primary dimensions of leader behavior: a work dimension (structure behavior/job-centered behavior) and a people dimension (consideration behavior/employee-centered behavior).

An early investigation of high school superintendents concluded that more desirable leadership behavior seems to be associated with high leader emphasis on both structure and consideration, while more undesirable leadership behavior tends to be associated with low leader emphasis on both dimensions. Results of a more recent study indicate that high consideration is always preferred by subordinates. One should be extremely careful, however, in concluding that any one leadership style is more effective than any other. The overall leadership situation is so complex that pinpointing one leadership style as the most effective seems to be an oversimplification. In fact, a successful leadership style for managers in one situation may be ineffective for them in another situation.

The **Hersey and Blanchard life cycle theory of leadership** is a rationale for linking leadership style with various situations so as to ensure effective leadership. This theory uses essentially the same two types of leadership behavior as the OSU leadership studies, but calls these dimensions "task" rather than structure, and "relationships" rather than consideration. Life cycle theory is based primarily on the relationship between follower maturity, leader task behavior, and leader relationships behavior. In general terms, according to this theory, leadership style primarily should reflect the maturity level of the followers. **Maturity** is defined as the ability of the followers to perform their jobs independently, to assume additional responsibility, and to achieve success. The more of each of these characteristics that followers possess, the more mature they are said to be. Maturity, as used in life cycle theory, is not necessarily linked to chronological age.

The curved line in the life cycle theory of leadership model (see text figure 14.7) indicates the maturity level of the followers. As the maturity curve runs from right to left, the followers' maturity level increases. In more specific terms, life cycle theory suggests that effective leadership behavior should shift from high task/low relationships behavior to high task/high relationships behavior to high relationships/low task behavior to low task/low relationships behavior, as one's followers progress from immaturity to maturity. Life cycle theory suggests, therefore, that a style of leadership will be effective only if it is appropriate for the maturity level of the follower or followers.

Some exceptions to the general philosophy of life cycle theory do exist. For example, if there is a short-run deadline to meet, a leader may find it necessary to accelerate production through a high task/low relationships style rather than a low task/low relationships style, even though the leader's followers may be extremely mature. A high task/low relationships leadership style carried out over the long run with such followers, however, typically results in a poor working relationship between leader and followers. (Refer back to your text for an in-depth example of how life cycle theory would apply in an actual leadership situation--a man just hired as a salesperson in a men's clothing store.)

Learning Objective 6   *An understanding of alternatives to leader flexibility*

Situational theories of leadership such as life cycle theory are based on the concept of **leader flexibility**--that successful leaders must change their leadership style as they encounter different situations. Can leaders be so flexible as to span all major leadership styles? The only answer to this question is that some leaders can be flexible and some cannot.

Unfortunately, there are numerous obstacles to leader flexibility. One strategy, proposed by Fred Fiedler, for overcoming these obstacles is changing the organizational situation to fit the leader's style, rather than changing the leader's style to fit the organizational situation. Relating this thought to the life cycle theory of leadership, it may be easier to shift various leaders to situations appropriate for their leadership styles than to expect leaders to change styles as situations change. It probably would take three to five years to train managers to use effectively a concept such as life cycle theory. Changing the situation a particular leader faces, however, can be done in the short run simply by exercising organizational authority.

According to **Fiedler** and his **contingency theory of leadership**, leader-member relations, task structure, and the position power of the leader are the three primary factors that should be used for moving leaders into situations more appropriate for their leadership styles. Leader-member relations is the degree to which the leader feels accepted by his or her followers. Task structure is the degree to which goals--the work to be done--and other situational factors are outlined clearly. Position power is determined by the extent to which the leader has control over rewards and punishments the followers receive. These three factors can be arranged in eight different combinations. Each of these eight combinations is called an octant.

Fiedler suggests that management should attempt to match permissive, passive, and considerate leaders with situations reflecting the middle of the continuum containing the octants. He also suggests that management should try to match a controlling, active, and structuring leader with the extremes of this continuum. (See text figure 14.8.) Possible actions that Fiedler suggests to modify the leadership situation are: (1) change the individual's task assignment, (2) change the leader's position power, or (3) change the leader-member relations in the group.

Overall, Fiedler's work helps to destroy the old myths that there is one best leadership style and that leaders are born, not made. Further, Fiedler's work supports the theory that almost every manager in an organization can be a successful leader if placed in a situation appropriate for his or her leadership style. This, of course, assumes that someone within the organization has the ability to assess the characteristics of the organization's leaders and of other important organizational variables and then match the two accordingly. Fiedler's model, like any other theoretical model, has its limitations and criticisms. Although it may not provide any concrete answers, it does emphasize the contention that situational variables are very important in determining leadership effectiveness. It may actually be easier to change the leadership situation or move the leader to a more favorable situation than it is to try to change a leader's style.

Learning Objective 7   *An appreciation of both transformational and substitute leadership theory*

The **path-goal theory of leadership** suggests that the primary activity of a leader should be to make desirable and achievable rewards available to organization members as a result of attaining organizational goals and to clarify the kinds of behavior that must be performed to earn those rewards. In essence, the leader outlines the goals that followers should aim for and clarifies how (the path followers take) to earn those goals. Overall, the path-goal theory indicates that managers can facilitate job performance by showing employees how their performance directly affects their receiving desired rewards.

According to the path-goal theory of leadership, leaders perform four primary types of behavior. These are directive, supportive, participative or achievement behaviors. **Directive behavior** is leader behavior aimed at telling followers what to do and how to do it. The leader indicates what performance goals exist and precisely what must be done to achieve them. **Supportive behavior** is leader behavior aimed at being friendly with followers and showing interest in them as human beings. Through supportive behavior the leader shows sensitivity to the personal needs of followers. **Participative behavior** is leader behavior through which follower suggestions are sought regarding business operations and followers are involved in making important organizational decisions. Consistent with this type of leader behavior, followers often help to determine the rewards that will be available to them in organizations and what must be done to earn those rewards. Finally, **achievement behavior** is leader behavior aimed at setting challenging goals for followers to reach and expressing and demonstrating confidence that followers will meet the challenge. This leader behavior focuses on making goals difficult enough so that employees find achieving them challenging, but not so difficult that followers view them as impossible and, therefore, give up trying to achieve them.

As with other situational theories of leadership, the path-goal theory suggests that leaders can be successful if they are able to match appropriately the four types of behavior mentioned above to situations that they face. Overall, the primary focus of the path-goal theory of leadership is on how leaders can increase employee effort and productivity by clarifying performance goals and the path to be taken to achieve those goals. Over time, the path-goal theory of leadership has gained increased acceptance. Research suggests that the path-goal theory holds promising potential for helping managers to enhance employee commitment to achieving organizational goals and thereby gives managers a key for increasing the probability that organizations will be successful.

Two topics that have recently been getting more attention in the leadership literature are transformational leadership and trust. **Transformational leadership** is leadership that inspires organizational success by profoundly impacting follower beliefs like what an organization should be, as well as follower values like justice and integrity. In essence, transformational leadership creates a sense of duty within an organization, encourages new ways of handling problems, and promotes learning for all organizational members. Transformational leadership is closely related to terms like charismatic leadership of inspirational leadership.

Transformational leaders perform several important tasks. Transformational leaders raise the awareness of followers concerning organizational issues and their consequences. Organization member must understand the high priority issues that exist for an organization and what will happen if the issues are not faced successfully. Transformational leaders also create a vision of what the organization should be, build commitment to that vision throughout the organization, and facilitate changes throughout the organization that support the vision. In essence, transformational leadership is consistent with strategy developed through an organization's strategic management process.

Perhaps the most fundamental ingredient of successful leadership is a **trust** that followers have for the leader. Trust is the followers' belief in and reliance upon the ability and integrity of the leader. Without such trust in a leader, successful leadership seems difficult if not impossible. Today there is significant concern that managers are not developing the trust with subordinates that is necessary to ensure successful leadership. In general, trust that subordinates feel for organizational leaders seems to be critically low. Additionally, employee opinion polls seem to illustrate a trend indicating that this trust might decline even further in the future.

In an effort to maximize leadership success, managers should focus on reversing this trend by building trust between themselves and their followers. There are many strategies that managers can use to build trust relationships with their subordinates. One of the most popular strategies entails showing and expressing confidence in subordinates and being completely open about why important decisions are made. Such actions demonstrate that a manager values his or her subordinates and will not take actions that might penalize them in any unfair way. In addition, such actions allow managers to demonstrate their competence by helping subordinates to understand how and why decisions are made. Building trust is a gradual process that requires constant management attention.

There are times when leaders do not have to lead (or, for one reason or another, cannot lead). Situational substitutes can actually have as much influence on employees as any leader. Many of you have heard or observed situations in which the leader had little or no impact on the situation. This could be due to a number of reasons. In some instances, this could be due to factors outside the control of the leader. Because of various conditions such as strong subordinates, knowledge of the task and organizational constraints, subordinates do not need or even want leadership. This is causing some people to argue that leadership is actually irrelevant to many organization outcomes. **Substitute leadership theory** attempts to identify situations in which the input of leader behavior is cancelled out or made less significant by the subordinate. For example, a subordinate may have a very high level of ability, experience, education and internal motivation so that little or no leadership is required or desired. Task characteristics may be so routine that the subordinate does not require much, if any, leadership. Group cohesion and a high degree of formalization are several organizational characteristics which reduce the need for leadership. When policies and practices are very formal and inflexible, leadership may not be required. Substitute theory tends to down play the importance of leadership characteristics, situations and leader behavior. In some situations or with some people in some organizations, things just seem to get done regardless of the quality of leadership.

In 1970 only 15 percent of all managers were women. By 1989 this figure had risen to more than 40 percent. By 1995, women will make up some 63% of the total workforce. Just how many of these **women will become leaders** in their companies or industries remains to be seen. Only three of every 100 top jobs in the largest US companies are held by women, about the same number a decade ago. A Labor Department study showed that subtle negative attitudes and prejudices (*the glass ceiling*) keep many women from moving up in management and leadership positions. When people speak of the glass ceiling they mean that workers can see their way to the top and that these don't seem to be barriers to promotion. But, in reality, a subtle barrier stops them from being promoted to top management and leadership jobs. Women who have broken through the glass ceiling have found that leaders don't come from one mold. In the past, women leaders have molded their style after successful male managers. women often describe their leadership styles as transformational--getting subordinates to transform or subordinate their individual self interests into group consensus directed toward a broader goal. This leadership style attributes power to personal characteristics like charisma, personal contacts and intrapersonal skills rather than to the organizational structure. Men, on the other hand, are more likely to characterize their leadership as transactional. They see their job as involving a series of transactions between themselves and their subordinates. This leadership style involves exchanging rewards for services or dispensing punishment for inadequate performance.

Knowing You Know

Fill-in-the-Blank *Directions: Fill in the blanks with the appropriate word or phrase.*

1. _____ is the process of directing the behavior of others toward the accomplishment of some objective.

2. The OSU studies concluded that leaders exhibit two main types of behavior _____ behavior and _____ behavior.

3. From a situational perspective, successful leadership is a function of the _____, the _____, and the _____.

4. The life cycle theory of leadership is based primarily on the relationship between _____, _____, and _____.

5. Changing leadership styles as new situations are encountered is called _____.

6. Fred Fiedler suggested changing the _____ to fit the _____.

7. According to Fiedler and his contingency theory of leadership, _____, _____, and _____ are the three primary factors that should be considered for moving leaders into situations more appropriate for their leadership styles.

8. The Michigan Studies pinpointed two basic types of leader behavior; _____ and _____.

9. Tannenbaum and Schmidt identify four forces in the situation that influence a manager's determination of how to make decisions as a leader. These four forces are the _____, the _____, the _____, and the _____.

10. _____ is leadership that inspires organizational success by profoundly impacting follower beliefs like what an organization should be, as well as follower values like justice and integrity.

True/False *Directions: On the lines provided, place a "T" for true or an "F" for false for each of the statements that follows.*

____11. Maturity, as used in life cycle theory, is not necessarily linked to chronological age.

____12. Life cycle theory suggests that effective leadership behavior should shift from high task/high relationships behavior to high task/low relationships behavior to low task/low relationships behavior to low task/high relationships behavior, as one's followers progress from immaturity to maturity.

____13. The overall leadership situation is so complex that pinpointing one leadership style as the most effective seems to be an oversimplification.

____14. Tannenbaum and Schmidt's model of leadership behavior is actually a continuum, or range, of leadership behavior available to managers in making decisions.

____15. According to life cycle theory, a leader may find it necessary to accelerate production through a high task/low relationships style rather than a low task/low relationships style even though the leader's followers may be extremely mature.

____16. According to the path-goal theory of leadership, leaders perform four primary types of behavior; directive, supportive, participative, or achievement behaviors.

____17. Early leadership research seemed to be based on the assumption that you can teach an individual to be a good leader and that most good leaders are made, not born.

____18. Substitute leadership theory attempts to identify situations in which the input of leader behavior is supported by increased subordinate cooperation.

_____19. According to the life cycle theory of leadership model, if the follower's task-relevant maturity decreases from a high level of maturity to a high/moderate level of maturity, the leader should both increase task and relationships behaviors.

_____20. Leading is basically the same as managing.

_____21. There are five decision styles within the VYJ model; two are autocratic in nature, two consultative, and the last group oriented.

_____22. The trait approach to leadership assumes that among the traits of a good leader is the desire for status.

_____23. Tannenbaum and Schmidt's boss-centered leadership style is characterized by an autocratic leader who maintains control and allows little subordinate freedom.

_____24. The OSU studies made it possible to pinpoint the most effective leadership style for a given situation.

_____25. A characteristic of a leader's consideration behavior is that well-delineated relationships between leader and followers exist.

Applying What You Know

Experience 14-1   Looking at Ourselves as Leaders*

Introduction

In this experience, you learn more about yourself as a leader by completing an individual leader style questionnaire, plotting your style on a leadership grid form, and then reacting to what you have learned about yourself as a leader.

Exercise 1

The thirty-five items that follow describe aspects of leadership behavior. Respond to each item according to the way you would be most likely to act if you were the leader of a work group. Circle whether you would be likely to behave in the described way always (A), frequently (F), occasionally (O), seldom (S), or never (N). When you have completed the questionnaire, your instructor will tell you how to compute your score.

Individual Leader Style Questionnaire
If I were the leader of a work group. . .

A F O S N   1.   I would most likely act as the spokesperson for the group.
A F O S N   2.   I would encourage overtime work.
A F O S N   3.   I would allow members complete freedom in their work.
A F O S N   4.   I would encourage the use of uniform procedures.
A F O S N   5.   I would permit group members to use their own judgments in solving problems.
A F O S N   6.   I would stress being ahead of competing groups.
A F O S N   7.   I would speak as a representative of the group.
A F O S N   8.   I would needle members for greater effort.
A F O S N   9.   I would try out my ideas on the group.
A F O S N   10.   I would let the members do their work the way they think best.
A F O S N   11.   I would be working hard for a promotion.
A F O S N   12.   I would be able to tolerate postponement and uncertainty.
A F O S N   13.   I would speak for the group when visitors were present.
A F O S N   14.   I would keep the work moving at a rapid pace.
A F O S N   15.   I would turn the members loose on a job and let them go to it.
A F O S N   16.   I would settle group conflicts when they occur.
A F O S N   17.   I would get swamped by details.
A F O S N   18.   I would represent the group at outside meetings.
A F O S N   19.   I would be reluctant to allow group members any freedom of action.

*Source of Experience 14-1: Adapted from Gerald H. Goldhaber, Instructor's guide, Organizational Communication, Wm. C. Brown Company Publishers, 1974, by Certo-Dougherty in *Organizational Leadership: Skills Through Theory and Experience,* Kendall/Hunt Publishing Company, Dubuque, Iowa, 1975.

A F O S N	20.	I would decide what should be done and how it should be done.
A F O S N	21.	I would push for increased production.
A F O S N	22.	I would let some members have authority that I should keep.
A F O S N	23.	Things would usually turn out as I predict.
A F O S N	24.	I would allow the group a high degree of initiative.
A F O S N	25.	I would assign group members to particular tasks.
A F O S N	26.	I would be willing to make changes.
A F O S N	27.	I would ask the members to work harder.
A F O S N	28.	I would trust the group members to exercise good judgment.
A F O S N	29.	I would schedule the work to be done.
A F O S N	30.	I would refuse to explain my actions.
A F O S N	31.	I would persuade others that my ideas are to their advantage.
A F O S N	32.	I would permit the group to set its own pace.
A F O S N	33.	I would urge the group to beat its previous record.
A F O S N	34.	I would act without consulting the group.
A F O S N	35.	I would ask that group members follow standard rules and regulations.

T (score) _____   R (score) _____

Exercise 2

To locate yourself on the leadership grid in figure 14.1, find your T-score (from exercise 1) on the horizontal axis of the graph. Next, move up the column corresponding to your T-score to the cell that corresponds to your R-score from exercise 1. Place an X in the cell that represents your two scores. You have now categorized yourself as possessing one of the four basic leadership styles.

Figure 14.1 Leadership grid.

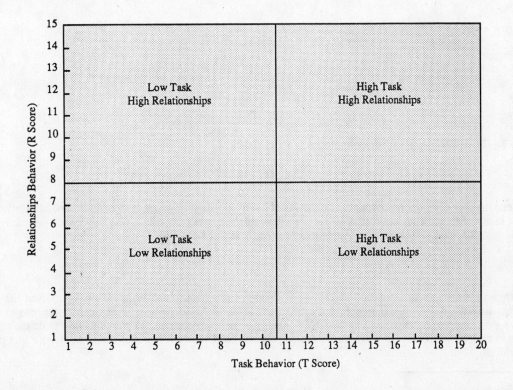

Exercise 3

Now that you have identified your leadership style, answer the questions that follow.

a.   Is this a valid measurement and categorization of your leadership style? Explain.

b.   Assuming that you could exhibit any of the four types of leadership styles that you wish, which would you choose?
     Why?

c.   Does this leadership style measurement and categorization give any indication of your ability to be flexible in your
     behavior? Are there situations where the ability to be flexible is important? Why?

Experience 14-2   Effective Leader Behaviors**

Introduction

   An infinite number of leader behaviors can be displayed in any situation in which leadership is needed. Unfortunately,
the display of many of these behaviors results in less than desirable follower responses. This experience provides you with
greater insight into the appropriateness or effectiveness of specific leader behaviors.

Exercise 1

Your instructor will hand your group a card describing a situation calling for a display of leadership. Given the situation
assigned (either situation A,B,C, or D), which of the following leader behaviors would most likely contribute to success?
Select the five most important choices and in the table column (see below) pertaining to your situation write the number of
those choices in rank order. Do not divulge the nature of your assigned situation to anyone outside of your group.

**Source of Experience 14-2: Adapted from an exercise developed by Peter D. Couch, Professor of Management, Illinois State University. Used with the
permission of the author.

Sit. A	Sit. B	Sit. C	Sit. D

1. Demonstrates decisiveness

2. Imposes rules and policies

3. Keeps quiet and calm

4. Behaves in an authoritarian way

5. Is verbally aggressive

6. Demonstrates courage

7. Is relaxed and fun-loving

8. Communicates clearly

9. Is analytical

10. Sets goals

11. Asks for group opinions

12. Is direct, frank, and candid

13, Shows sensitivity to feelings

14. States exactly what is wanted

15. Tells jokes

16. Schedules frequent meetings with group

17. Delegates authority

18. Shows employee how to do the job

19. Specifies work methods

20. Gives people a "pat on the back"

21. Talks with people individually

22. Holds a prayer meeting

23. Takes a vote

24. Emphasizes deadlines

25. Goes golfing

Exercise 2

What generalizations can you make about leadership from the data generated in exercise 1?

Exercise 3

a. If you had applied the life cycle theory of leadership to the situation you were assigned, which style of leadership would you have displayed? Explain.

b. Based upon your response to question *a*, does your group want to change any of the leader behaviors or rankings for the situation you were assigned? Give your reasoning for any changes you make.

c. Would you recommend that any other groups reconsider their list of behaviors and rankings? Be specific in your suggestions.

Exercise 4

Explain what you have gained from this experience.

Experience 14-3   Leadership Effectiveness: Fiedler's Contingency Theory***

Introduction

Fiedler's work supports the idea that almost all managers can be successful leaders if they are placed in situations appropriate for their leadership styles. A closer examination of Fiedler's model in text figure 14.8 indicates that a controlling, active, structuring leader is generally most effective if the situation is similar to that found in octants 1, 2, 3, or 8. A permissive, passive, considerate leader is most effective in the situations depicted in octants 4, 5, and 6. The situation in octant 7 does not strongly support either leadership style as being more effective.

***Source of Experience 14-3: Adapted from Fred E. Fiedler, "Engineer the Job to fit the Manager," *Harvard Business Review* Vol. 43, No. 5 (September/October 1965): pp. 115-22.

In this experience, you use Fiedler's model to asses leader effectiveness. You also are asked to suggest situational modifications to improve leader effectiveness. Carefully read the incident that follows. Then complete the exercises as directed.

Incident

Both Bill Johnson and Fred Ortega are supervisors at Eclipse Electric Company, a leading small electrical appliance manufacturer. Bill Johnson has been night supervisor of assembly line B for the past seven years. Line B consists of fifteen people who work from 3:30 P.M. to 12 midnight assembling electric knife sharpeners. Johnson always has been able to get along with his subordinates, and he feels they respect him. He attributes part of this respect to his knowledge and experience in the small appliance assembly plant. He also feels that his subordinates identify with him since he "came up through the ranks." The jobs of the employees on line B of small appliance assembly generally are closely defined. Each employee has a set work station and a specified number of tasks to perform as the knife sharpeners pass along the assembly line.

Fred Ortega was hired one year ago by the operations manager, Luis Sanchez. Ortega was recruited by Sanchez at Jason College to fill Alvin Jordan's position upon Jordan's retirement. Jordan's final assignment was to prepare Ortega for the responsibilities of the position he would shortly be filling. (Jordan retired about four months after Ortega was hired.) From the beginning, it was apparent that Ortega's three six-man teams assembling COMPTREX units did not like him. The comment that follows, found painted on the washroom wall about six months after Jordan's retirement, seems to sum up employee feelings toward Ortega:

Hey, Fred, you'll get ahead if you'll just shut your trap.
Your college jargon is no real bargain,
it's just a bunch of crap.

Ortega felt badly about the comments but knew there was little he could do about them. He could take no stronger action than an oral reprimand without first consulting with his immediate superior.

Exercise 1

After thoroughly familiarizing yourself with the situations of Bill Johnson and Fred Ortega, use Fiedler's contingency theory of leadership to answer the questions that follow.

a. Based on the given background information, which style of leadership would be most effective in each of the following situations. If you cannot determine the precise nature of a situation from information provided in the case (e.g., it is not abundantly clear whether the task is structured or unstructured), state where more information is needed and identify the appropriate leadership styles for all possible situations.

1) Bill Johnson's situation? Explain.

2) Fred Ortega's situation? Explain.

b.   If Bill Johnson felt more comfortable using a permissive, passive, considerate leadership style, what action could be taken to more closely match situation and style? Explain.

c.   If Fred Ortega felt more comfortable using a controlling, active, structuring leadership style, what action could be taken to more closely match situation and style? (Assume that the tasks in Ortega's department are highly structured.)

Exercise 2

Explain what you have gained from this experience.

Experience   14-4   Leadership and Decision Styles in "Operation Desert Storm:" The Vroom-Yetton-Jago Model****

Background

For a number of years, the styles or typical behaviors of leaders have been characterized as autocratic, democratic, or something in between the two. Autocratic leaders make decision by themselves while democratic leaders involve subordinates in the decision making process.

****A version of this exercise, coauthored by Lee A. Graf, Masoud Hemmasi, and Michael W. Winchell was submitted to the 1992 Conference of the Association for Business Simulation and Experiential Learning, Las Vegas, Nevada, March 25-27, 1992.

Historically, leadership behavior in military settings has been generally autocratic, especially under battle conditions. Recently, however, through the months of intense media coverage of the Desert Storm Operation, we have had the rare opportunity to observe a relatively large number of military leaders displaying a wide range of leadership styles in a variety of unique settings. From these observations, it would appear that the modern military has moved toward adopting more of **a situational approach** to providing effective leadership. Military leaders now seem to be more flexible, allowing their style/behavior to be molded by the unique situation with which they are faced.

Hypothetical "Desert Storm" scenarios can provide an effective vehicle to illustrate the utility of the Vroom-Yetton-Jago (VYJ) Model[*****] in analyzing and selecting appropriate leader behavior. The VYJ Model is a situational leadership approach with increasingly popular appeal. The model has practical value in helping one decide how much subordinate participation in problem solving and decision making is appropriate in a given situation. The VYJ approach emphasizes the following:

1. Five possible style choices for leaders ranging from highly autocratic to highly democratic (see Figure 14.2 below).

Figure 14.2 Five decision styles available to a leader[******]

Decision Style	Definition
AI	Manager makes the decision alone.
AII	Manager asks for information from subordinates but makes the decision alone. Subordinates may or may not be informed about what the situation is.
CI	Manager shares the situation with individual subordinates and asks for information and evaluation. Subordinates do not meet as a group, and the manager alone makes the decision.
CII	Manager and subordinates meet as a group to discuss the situation, but the manager makes the decision.
GII	Manager and subordinates meet as a group to discuss the situation, and the group makes the decision.
	A = autocratic; C = consultative; G = group

2. Eight questions that can be used to define any situation calling for leadership. Generally, the questions can be divided into those which affect the **quality** of the decision (Quality Requirement--QR, Leader's Information--LI, Problem Structure--ST, and Subordinate Information--SI) and those that affect the **acceptability of and commitment to** the decision (Commitment Requirement--CR, Commitment Probability--CP, Goal Congruence--GC, and Subordinate Conflict--CO). Figure 14.3 summarizes these eight important situational characteristics.

3. A "decision tree" which identifies the step-by-step sequence of questions to follow to ultimately select the most appropriate leadership style/behavior for that situation (again see Figure 14.3 below).

[*****] Victor H. Vroom and Arthur G. Jago, *The New Leadership: Managing Participation in Organizations*, Englewood Cliffs, NJ: Prentice-Hall, 1988.

[******] Adapted and reprinted from *Leadership and Decision-Making*, by Victor H. Vroom and Philip W. Yetton, by permission of the University of Pittsburgh Press. © 1973 by University of Pittsburgh Press.

Figure 14.3 The Vroom-Yetton-Jago Model[*******]

QR	Quality Requirement	How important is the technical quality of this decision? Are some alternatives going to be of higher quality than some other possible courses of action?	CP	Commitment Probability:	If you were to make the decision by yourself, is it reasonably certain that your subordinates would be committed to the decision? (Will subordinates commit themselves to the decision even without actively participating in making the decision?)
CR	Commitment Requirement:	How important is subordinate commitment to the decision? (Must subordinates commit themselves to the decision in order to have effective implementation of the decision?)	GC	Goal Congruence:	Do subordinates share the organizational goals to be attained in solving this problem? (Is it likely that if subordinates made the decision by themselves that their decision would be compatible with organizational goals?)
LI	Leader's Information:	Do you have sufficient information to make a high-quality decision? (Can the information needed to make a rational decision be obtained without involving subordinates?)	CO	Subordinate Conflict:	Is conflict among subordinates over preferred solutions likely? (Will subordinates be noncooperative if they do not get their way?)
ST	Problem Structure:	Is the problem well structured? (Does the leader know exactly what information is missing and how to get it?)	SI	Subordinate Information:	Do subordinates have sufficient information to make a high-quality decision? (Can subordinates make a rational decision without management input?)

Overall, the VYJ Model takes a situational approach--the leadership style which works best depends upon the characteristics of the situation. The VYJ approach is an attempt to develop a practical method for assessing the situation and selecting the most effective leadership style.

Exercise 1

Now that you have extended your background regarding the Vroom-Yetton-Jago Model, use the VYJ framework provided in Figure 14.3 to select the leadership style/behavior that would be most appropriate for each of the following two situations.******** Use the space provided to explain the logic used to move through the decision tree to the ideal leadership style for that particular situation.

Situation A   You are in charge of a large crew laying land mines through a remote northern region of Saudi Arabia. While having many different hats to wear as the project unfolds, the one presently carrying the greatest urgency involves estimating the rate of progress the team will make so that timely delivery of material (mines, food, etc.) can be made to the next field site. You have flown over the tract of land in question and know the nature of the terrain. You also have the standards book that covers burying mines in a variety of terrains that will permit you to calculate the mean and variance in the rate of speed (progress) you should be able to make. Given this information, it is a relatively simple matter to calculate the earliest and latest times at which materials will be needed at the next field site. It is important the estimate made be accurate because over-estimating the time results in materials simply sitting there waiting to go into production (very vulnerable to sabotage--the mines, and spoilage--the food) and underestimating results, in idle personnel (both officers and enlisted who are susceptible to attack and/or sniper fire). Progress on the project up to this time has been very good and both officers and enlisted men stand to receive a substantial leave (R&R in southern Greece) if the project is completed ahead of schedule.

******** Situations adapted from those presented in Victor H. Vroom, "A New Look at Managerial Decision-Making," *Organizational Dynamics*, Vol. 1, No. 4, Spring 1973, pp. 66-80.

Situation B   You are in charge of a large supply depot and maintenance facility in a permanent structure (not a tent) in central Saudi Arabia. Among other items, you store a number of flammable liquids and dangerous chemicals. While well outside the range of SCUD missile attack, there have been several minor fires and explosions, some of which have resulted in both minor injury to personnel and minor damage to the facility. You are technically responsible for overall operational safety. To date none of the explosions or fires have been serious, but you are concerned that unless the basic cause(s) are identified and managed that a real disaster could occur. Informal conversations with your subordinate officers suggest that there is probably no simple solution to the problem. While all junior officers in charge of separate departments under your command share your concern regarding safety, each has his own perspective on the problem and what should be done about it. Each junior officer believes he has a workable solution, but it is your opinion that each is looking at the problem from the perspective of the most beneficial impact to his own unit. Consequently, you have yet to implement any specific suggestions. Furthermore, it is your strong belief that whatever is done must meet with the full support from everyone.

Yesterday there was another minor explosion. Three enlisted men were sent to the base hospital for treatment of minor burns. If it had not been for the quick action of one NCO, far more serious injuries and significant damage to the facility could have resulted. You are now determined to initiate immediate actions to correct the situation and, have the authority to expend whatever resources are necessary to solve the problem.

Exercise 2

Now that you have had the opportunity to use the Vroom-Yetton-Jago Model to select a specific leadership style in two unique situations:

a. What specific advantages do you believe this model holds over others that you have been exposed to in the chapter on leadership? Concentrate specifically on the Fiedler Contingency Theory and the Hersey-Blanchard Life Cycle Theory of Leadership.

b. What shortcomings/difficulties do you see with utilizing the VYJ approach to change/adjust your leadership style to fit various real-world situations? Explain in the space provided below.

Exercise 3

In the space provided below, identify what you have learned from involving yourself in Experience 14-4.

15 MOTIVATION

Chapter Summary

The ability to motivate a work force is a skill that is extremely valuable to virtually all managers. The material in this chapter explains the motivation process and the steps that can be taken to motivate organization members.

Learning Objective 1   *A basic understanding of human motivation*

Motivation is an individual's inner state that causes him or her to behave in a way that ensures the accomplishment of some goal. In other words, motivation explains why people behave the way they do. The more managers understand organization members' behavior, the better able they should be to influence that behavior and to make it more consistent with the accomplishment of organizational objectives. Since productivity in all organizations is a result of the behavior of organization members, influencing this behavior is a manager's key to increasing productivity. Over the years, several different theories about motivation have been proposed. In general, these theories have been categorized into two basic types: process theories and content theories. **Process theories of motivation** are explanations of motivation that emphasize how individuals are motivated. In essence, the process theories focus on the steps that occur when an individual is motivated. Content theories of motivation are explanations of motivation that emphasize internal characteristics of people. The main focus of the content theories is understanding the needs that people possess and how they can be satisfied.

Four important theories that describe how motivation occurs have been developed. The **needs-goal theory** of motivation is the most fundamental of the motivation theories discussed. As its name implies, needs and goals are the two primary components of this theory. According to the theory, motivation begins with an individual feeling a need. This need is then transformed into behavior directed at supporting, or allowing, the performance of goal behavior to reduce the felt need. Theoretically, goal-supportive behavior and goal behavior continue until a felt need has been reduced significantly. For example, when an individual feels a hunger need, this need typically is transformed into behavior directed at supporting the performance of the goal behavior of eating. Examples of this supportive behavior could include such activities as buying, cooking, and serving the food to be eaten. Goal-supportive behaviors such as these and the goal behavior itself of eating typically continue until the individual's felt hunger need substantially subsides. If managers are to have any success in motivating employees, they must understand the personal needs that employees possess. When managers offer rewards to employees that are not relevant to the personal needs of employees, the employees will not be motivated. Managers must be familiar with needs that employees possess and offer rewards to employees that can satisfy these needs.

In reality, the motivation process is a more complex situation than depicted by the needs-goal motivation theory. A second theory, the **Vroom expectancy theory**, also is based on the premise that felt needs cause human behavior. In addition, however, the Vroom theory addresses the issue of motivation strength. **Motivation strength** is an individual's degree of desire to perform a behavior. As this desire increases or decreases, motivation strength is said to fluctuate correspondingly. In equation form, Vroom's expectancy theory is depicted as follows: motivation strength is determined by (equals) the perceived value of the result of performing a behavior multiplied by (times) the perceived probability that the behavior performed will cause the result to materialize. As both of these factors increase, the motivation strength, or the individual's desire to perform the behavior, increases. An illustration of how Vroom's theory applies to human behavior could be a college student who has been offered the summer job of painting three houses at the rate of two-hundred dollars a house. According to the model, the student's motivation strength or desire to paint the houses is determined by the student' perceived value of six-hundred dollars and the perceived probability that the student actually could paint the houses satisfactorily and, thus, receive the six-hundred dollars. As the perceived value of the six-hundred dollars reward and the probability that the houses could be painted satisfactorily increase, the student's motivation strength to paint the houses increases.

Equity theory, the third process theory, looks at an individuals's perceived fairness in an employment situation. Research on equity theory has found that perceived inequities can lead to changes in behavior. When individuals believe that they have been treated unfairly compared with co-workers, they will react in one of the following ways to attempt to bring the inequity into balance: (1) try to change their work inputs to better match the rewards they are receiving, (2) try to change the compensation they receive for their work by asking for a raise or through legal action, (3) try to change the perception of an inequality if attempts to change the actual inequality are unsuccessful, or (4) leave the situation rather than try to change it.

Perceptions of inequities can arise in any number of management situations such as work assignments, promotions, ratings reports, and office assignments but they occur most often in terms of money. Because these are emotionally charged issues that deal with human beings, even a minor inequity, in the mind of a manager, can be important in the minds of those affected. Effective managers attempt to keep equity issues in balance because the steps that a worker will take to try to "balance the scales" is not always the best for the organization.

Porter and Lawler developed a motivation theory that presents a more complete description of the motivation process than either the needs-goal theory or the Vroom expectancy theory. The **Porter-Lawler theory** of motivation, the fourth process theory that we have examined, is consistent with the prior theories in that it accepts the premises that felt needs cause human behavior and that effort expended to accomplish a task is determined by the perceived value of rewards that will result from the task and the probability that the rewards actually will materialize. However, the Porter-Lawler motivation theory stresses three other characteristics of the motivation process. According to the theory, the perceived value of a reward is determined by both intrinsic and extrinsic rewards that result in need satisfaction when a task is accomplished. **Intrinsic rewards** come directly from performing a task, while **extrinsic rewards** are extraneous to the task itself. For example, when a manager counsels a subordinate about a personal problem, the manager may get some intrinsic reward in the form of personal satisfaction simply from helping another individual. In addition to this intrinsic reward, however, the manager also would receive some extrinsic reward in the form of the overall salary the manager is paid. A second characteristic of the motion process that the Porter-Lawler theory stresses is that the extent to which an individual effectively accomplishes a task is determined primarily by the individual's perception of what is required to perform the task and the individual's actual ability to perform the task. Naturally, an individual's effectiveness at accomplishing a task increases as perception of what is required to perform the task becomes more accurate and as ability to perform the task increases. The third characteristic of Porter and Lawler's motivation theory is that the perceived fairness of rewards influences the amount of satisfaction produced by those rewards. The more equitable an individual perceives rewards to be, the greater the satisfaction the individual will experience as a result of receiving those rewards.

Learning Objective 2   *Insights on various human needs*

The motivation theories discussed thus far imply that a thorough understanding of motivation is based on a thorough understanding of human needs. There is some evidence that people in the general population typically possess strong needs for self-respect, respect from others, promotion, and psychological growth. While the task of precisely pinpointing all human needs is impossible, several theories have been developed to help managers better understand these needs.

Perhaps the most widely accepted description of human needs is the **hierarchy of needs** concept developed by **Abraham Maslow**. Maslow states that human beings possess five basic needs and that these five basic needs can be arranged in a hierarchy of importance or order in which individuals generally strive to satisfy them. The most basic needs are physiological needs. *Physiological needs* relate to the normal functioning of the body and include needs for water, food, rest, sex, and air. Until these needs are met, a significant portion of an individual's behavior is aimed at satisfying them. If these needs are satisfied, behavior becomes aimed at satisfying the security needs on the next level of Maslow's hierarchy. *Security or safety needs* are the needs individuals feel to keep themselves free from harm, including both bodily and economic disaster. As security needs are satisfied, behavior tends to be aimed at satisfying social needs. *Social needs* include an individual's desire for love, companionship, and friendship. Overall, these needs reflect a person's desire to be accepted by others. As these needs are satisfied, behavior shifts to satisfying esteem needs. *Esteem needs* are an individual's desire for respect and generally are directed into two categories: self-respect and respect for others. Once esteem needs are satisfied, an individual emphasizes satisfying self-actualization needs. The need to *self-actualize* is the desire to maximize whatever potential an individual possesses. For example, a high school principal who seeks to satisfy self-actualization needs would strive to become the best principal possible. Self-actualization needs are the highest level of Maslow's hierarchy.

Although many management theorists would admit readily that Maslow's hierarchy can be useful in understanding human needs, many concerns about the hierarchy also have been expressed. Maslow himself had some concerns about the legitimacy of making generalizations about labor in factories from his clinical study of neurotic people. Traditionally there have been concerns related to Maslow's hierarchy that are based on its lack of a research base, a questioning of whether Maslow has accurately pinpointed five basic human needs, and some doubt as to whether human needs actually are arranged in a hierarchy. Despite such concerns, Maslow's hierarchy is probably the most popular conceptualization of human needs to date and it continues to be positively discussed in the management literature. The concerns mentioned, however, indicate that Maslow's hierarchy should be considered a more subjective statement than an objective description of human needs.

Alderfer's ERG theory is similar to Maslow's theory except for three major respects. He identified three orders of human needs compared to Maslow's five orders of needs: (1) existence needs--the need for physical well-being, (2) relatedness needs--the need for satisfying interpersonal relationships, and (3) growth needs--the need for continuing personal growth and development. In contrast with Maslow, Alderfer found that workers may sometimes activate their higher level needs before they have completely satisfied all of the lower level needs. Alderfer also found that movement in his hierarchy in satisfying human needs is not always upward. He found, reflected in his frustration-regression principle, that people, frustrated by failing to satisfy an upper level need, might regress and try to fulfill an already satisfied lower-level need. Alderfer's work, in conjunction with Maslow's work, has implications for management. Job enrichment strategies can help an individual to meet the higher order needs. If an employee is frustrated by work which fails to provide the opportunity for growth or development on the job, that person might spend more energy trying to make more money, thus regressing to a lower level.

Argyris's maturity-immaturity continuum also furnishes insights on human needs. This continuum concept focuses on the personal and natural development of people to explain how needs exist. According to Argyris, as people naturally progress from immaturity to maturity, they have increasing needs for more activity, a state of relative independence, behaving in many different ways, deeper interests, considering a relatively long time perspective, occupying an equal position with other mature individuals, and more awareness of themselves and control over their own destiny. Unlike Maslow's hierarchy, Argyris's needs are not arranged in a hierarchy. Similar to Maslow's hierarchy, however, Argyris's continuum primarily represents a subjective position on the existence of human needs.

Another theory about human needs, called **McClelland's acquired-needs theory**, focuses on the needs that people develop through their life experiences--acquired needs. This theory focuses on three of the many needs humans develop in their lifetimes: (1) the need for achievement (*nAch*)--the desire to do something better or more efficiently than it ever has been done before, (2) the need for power (*nPower*)--the desire to control, influence them, or be responsible for others, and (3) the need for affiliation (*nAff*)--the desire to maintain close, friendly personal relationships. A person's early life experiences determine which of these needs will be highly developed and therefore dominate the personality. McClelland claims that in some business people the need to achieve is so strong that it is more motivating than a quest for profits. To maximize their satisfaction, individuals with high achievement needs tend to set goals for themselves that are challenging yet achievable. Although these individuals do not avoid risk completely, they assess it very carefully. Individuals motivated by the need to achieve do not want to fail and will avoid tasks that involve too much risk. Individuals with a low need for achievement generally avoid challenges, responsibilities, and risk. People with a high need for power are highly motivated to try to influence other people and to be responsible for subordinate behavior. They are likely to seek advancement and to assume increasingly responsible work activities. Power-oriented managers are comfortable in competitive situations and with their decision-making roles. Managers with a high need for affiliation, on the other hand, tend to have a cooperative, team-centered style of management where a task is completed through team efforts. However, a high need for affiliation could also sacrifice a manager's effectiveness when the need for social approval and friendship interfere with the manager's ability to make managerial decisions.

Learning Objective 3   *An appreciation for the importance of motivating organization members*

From a managerial viewpoint, motivation is the process of furnishing organization members with the opportunity to satisfy their needs by performing productive behavior within the organization. Unsatisfied needs of organization members can lead to either appropriate or inappropriate organization member behavior. Managers who are successful at motivating organization members minimize inappropriate organization member behavior and maximize appropriate organization member behavior. Correspondingly, these managers raise the probability that organization member productivity will increase and lower the probability that organization member productivity will decrease.

Learning Objective 4   *An understanding of various motivation strategies*

Managers have various strategies for motivating organization members. Each strategy is aimed at satisfying organization members' needs through appropriate organization member behavior. Perhaps the most basic motivation strategy for managers is simply to communicate with organization members. This **manager-subordinate communication** can satisfy such basic human needs as recognition, a sense of belonging, and security. For example, such a simple action as a manager attempting to become more acquainted with subordinates could contribute substantially to the satisfaction of each of these three needs. As another example, a communication message from a manager to a subordinate that praises the subordinate for a job well done can help to satisfy recognition and security needs of the subordinate. As a general rule, managers should strive to communicate often with other organization members, not only because communication is the primary means of conducting organizational activities, but also because it is a basic tool for satisfying the human needs of organization members.

Another motivation strategy involves a manager's assumptions about the nature of people. **Douglas McGregor** identified two sets of these assumptions: **Theory X** involves assumptions such as (1) people dislike work, (2) people must be threatened to get them to put forth any effort, and (3) people avoid responsibility but seek security. **Theory Y** involves assumptions such as (1) work is as natural as play or rest, (2) people will exercise self-direction and self-control if committed to the objective, and (3) people do not avoid responsibility--they seek it. McGregor feels that managers often use Theory X assumptions as the basis for dealing with people, while Theory Y represents the assumptions that McGregor feels management should strive to use. McGregor implies that managers who use Theory X assumptions are "bad" and that those who use Theory Y assumptions are "good."

Reddin, however, argues that production might be increased by using either Theory X or Theory Y assumptions, depending on the situation the manager faces. Reddin feels that McGregor has considered only the ineffective application of Theory X and the effective application of Theory Y. Using this argument, Reddin proposed a **Theory Z**--an effectiveness dimension that implies that managers who use either Theory X or Theory Y assumptions when dealing with people can be successful, depending upon their situation. Reddin's basic rationale for using Theory Y rather than Theory X in most situations is that managerial activity that reflects Theory Y assumptions generally is more successful in satisfying the human needs of most organization members than management activities that reflect Theory X assumptions. Therefore, management activities based on Theory Y assumptions generally are more successful in motivating organization members than management activities based on Theory X assumptions.

A third strategy managers can use to motivate organization members relates to the **design of jobs** that organization members perform. A movement has existed in the more recent history of American business to make jobs simpler and more specialized to increase worker productivity and efficiency. However, as work becomes simpler and more specialized, it typically becomes more boring and less satisfying to individuals performing the jobs. As a result, productivity suffers.

Perhaps the earliest major attempt to overcome this job boredom was job rotation. **Job rotation** entails moving individuals from job to job, or not requiring individuals to perform only one simple and specialized job over the long run. Although job rotation programs have been known to increase organizational profitability, they typically are ineffective because, over time, individuals become bored with all the jobs to which they are rotated. Job rotation programs, however, have been found to be useful training mechanisms to provide individuals with an overview of how various units of an organization function.

Job enlargement is another strategy developed to overcome the boredom of more simple and specialized jobs. Job enlargement advocates claim that jobs become more satisfying as the number of operations an individual performs increases. Some research supports the theory that job enlargement makes jobs more satisfying, while some does not. Job enlargement programs, however, generally have been more successful in increasing job satisfaction than job rotation programs.

A number of other job design strategies have evolved since the development of job rotation and job enlargement programs. **Frederick Herzberg** concludes from his research that the degrees of satisfaction and dissatisfaction that organization members feel as a result of performing a job are two different variables determined by two different sets of items. The set of items that influence the degree of job satisfaction are called **motivating factors**, or motivators, and includes such factors as responsibility, personal growth, advancement, and opportunity for recognition. The set of items that influence the degree of job dissatisfaction are called **hygiene, or maintenance, factors** and include such factors as salary, working conditions, and company policy and administration. Hygiene factors relate to the work environment, while motivating factors relate to the work itself. Herzberg indicates that, if hygiene factors are undesirable in a particular job situation, organization members will become dissatisfied. Making these factors more desirable by, for example, increasing salary generally will not motivate organization members to do a better job, but it will keep them from becoming dissatisfied. On the other hand, if motivating factors are high in a particular job situation, organization members generally are motivated to do a better job. In general, organization members tend to be more motivated and productive as more motivators are built into their job situation.

The process of incorporating motivators into a job situation is called **job enrichment**. Earlier reports indicated that such companies as Texas Instruments Incorporated and the Volvo Company have had notable success in motivating organization members through job enrichment programs. Although more current reports continue to support the value of job enrichment, experience indicates that, for a job enrichment program to be successful, it must be designed and administered carefully.

Herzberg's overall findings indicate that the most productive organization members are involved in work situations characterized by desirable hygiene factors and motivating factors. When Herzberg's theory and Maslow's hierarchy of needs are compared, it appears that hygiene factors satisfy lower-level needs, while motivating factors generally satisfy higher-level needs. Esteem needs, the fourth level of Maslow's needs hierarchy, can be satisfied by both types of factors. An example of esteem needs satisfied by a hygiene factor could be a private parking space--a status symbol and working condition evidencing the importance of the organization member. An example of esteem needs satisfied by a motivating factor could be an award received for outstanding performance--a display of importance through recognition for a job well done.

Another more recent job design strategy for motivating organization members is based on a concept called **flextime**. The main thrust of flextime, or flexible working hours programs, is that it allows workers to complete their jobs within a forty-hour workweek they arrange themselves. The choices of starting and finishing times can be as flexible as the organizational situation allows. Various kinds of organizational studies have indicated that flextime programs seem to have some positive organizational effects, such as greater job satisfaction, which typically results in greater production and higher motivation levels of workers. Lastly, because organization members generally find flextime programs to be desirable, such programs can help management to better compete with other organizations in recruiting qualified new employees. Although many well-known companies, such as Scott Paper, Sun Oil, and Samsonite, have adopted flextime programs, more research must be conducted to assess conclusively its true worth.

A fourth strategy that managers can use in motivating organization members is based primarily on a concept known as behavior modification. As stated by **B. F. Skinner, behavior modification** focuses on encouraging appropriate behavior as a result of the consequences of that behavior. According to the law of effect, behavior that is rewarded tends to be repeated, while behavior that is punished tends to be eliminated. Although behavior modification programs typically involve the administration of both rewards and punishments, the rewards generally are emphasized since they typically have more effective influence on behavior than punishments. Behavior modification theory asserts that if managers want to modify subordinates' behavior, they must ensure that appropriate consequences occur as a result of that behavior. For example, if a particular activity such as a worker arriving on time for work is positively reinforced, or rewarded, the probability increases that the worker will begin arriving on time with greater frequency. In addition, if the worker experiences some undesirable outcome related to arriving late for work, such as a verbal reprimand, the worker is negatively reinforced when this outcome is eliminated due to the worker arriving on time. According to behavior modification, positive reinforcement and negative reinforcement are both rewards that increase the likelihood that behavior will continue. **Positive reinforcement** is the presentation of a desirable consequence of a behavior, while **negative reinforcement** is the elimination of an undesirable consequence for a behavior. Conversely, **punishment** is the presentation of an undesirable behavioral consequence and/or the elimination of a desirable behavioral consequence that decrease the likelihood of a behavior continuing. Although punishment stops behavior quickly, it may be accompanied by undesirable side effects, such as employee turnover and absenteeism, if emphasized by managers over the long run.

The establishment and use of an effective feedback system is extremely important to a successful behavior modification program. This feedback should be aimed at keeping employees informed of the relationship between various behaviors and the consequences associated with them. Other ingredients that successful behavior modification programs include are: (1) giving different levels of rewards to different workers depending on the quality of their performance, (2) telling workers what they are doing wrong, (3) punishing workers privately so as not to embarrass them in front of others, and (4) always giving rewards and punishments when earned to emphasize that management is serious about behavior modification efforts.

Another strategy that managers can use for motivating organization members is based on the work of **Rensis Likert.** As a result of studying several types and sizes of organizations, Likert concludes that management styles in organizations can be categorized into **four systems** and placed on a continuum. *System 1* (treating people poorly) involves having no confidence or trust in subordinates. Subordinates do not feel free to discuss their jobs with superiors and are motivated by fear, threats, punishments, and occasional rewards. Information flow primarily is directed downward, with upward communication viewed with great suspicion. The bulk of all decision making is at the top of the organization. *System 2* (treating people less poorly) involves having condescending confidence and trust (such as master to servant) in subordinates. Subordinates do not feel very free to discuss their jobs with superiors and are motivated by rewards and some actual or potential punishment. Information flows mostly downward, while upward communication may or may not be viewed with suspicion. *System 3* (treating people fairly well) involves having substantial, but not complete, confidence in subordinates. Subordinates feel rather free to discuss their jobs with superiors and are motivated by rewards, occasional punishment, and some involvement. Information flows both up and down. Upward communication is often accepted but at times may be viewed with suspicion. While broad policies and general decisions are made at the top of the organization, more specific decisions are made at lower levels. *System 4* (treating people extremely well) involves having complete trust and confidence in subordinates. Subordinates feel completely free to discuss their jobs with supervisors and are motivated by such factors as economic rewards based on a compensation system developed through participation and involvement in goal setting. Information flows upward, downward, and horizontally. Decision making is spread widely throughout the organization and is well coordinated.

Likert suggests that, as management style within an organization moves from system 1 to system 4, the human needs of individuals within that organization tend to be more effectively satisfied over the long run. Thus, as management style within an organization moves toward system 4, the organization tends to become more productive over the long run. Managers may increase production in the short run by using a system 1 management style, since motivation by fear, threat, and punishment is generally effective in the short run. Over the long run, however, this style usually causes production to decrease, primarily because of the long-run nonsatisfaction of organization members' needs and poor working relationships that develop between managers and subordinates. Conversely, managers who attempt to initiate a system 4 management style probably face some decline in production initially, but an increase in production over the long run. This trend exists over the short run because managers must implement a new system to which organization members must adapt. The production increase over the long run materializes as a result of organization members becoming adjusted to the new management system, greater satisfaction of the human needs of organization members, and good working relationships that tend to develop between managers and subordinates. This long term production increase can also be related to decision making under the two management systems. Since decisions reached in system 4 are more likely to be thoroughly understood by organization members than decisions reached in system 1, decisions implementation is more likely to be efficient and effective in system 4 than in system 1.

Likert offers his **principle of supportive relationships** as the basis for management activity aimed at developing a system 4 management style. This principle states that the leadership and other processes of the organization must be such as to ensure a maximum probability that, in all interactions and in all relationship within the organization, each member in light of his or her background, values, desires, and expectations will view the experience as supportive and one that builds and maintains his or her sense of personal worth and importance.

Both **monetary** and some **non-monetary incentives** can also motivate employees to improve their organizational performance. A number of firms make a wide range of compensation programs (monetary incentives) available to their employees as a form of motivation. For instance, employee stock ownership plans (ESOPs) motivate the employee to boost production by offering shares of company stock as a benefit. Other incentive plans include lump sum bonuses--one-time cash payments and gain-sharing--a plan where members of a team receive a bonus when that team exceeds an expectation. All of these plans link the amount of pay closely to performance. A firm also has the opportunity to keep employees committed and motivated by non-monetary means. For instance, some companies have a policy of promoting from within. They go through an elaborate process of advertising jobs within before going to the outside to fill vacancies.

Knowing You Know

True/False   *Directions: On the lines provided, place a "T" for true and an "F" for false for each of the statements that follows.*

_____ 1. Although behavior modification programs typically involve the administration of both rewards and punishments, the administration of punishments generally is emphasized since rewards typically are considered to have less effective influence on behavior than punishments.

_____ 2. Process theories of motivation are explanations of motivation that emphasize how individuals are motivated.

_____ 3. The manager who attempts to initiate a system 1 management style probably will face some decline in production initially, but an increase in production over the long run.

_____ 4. There is some evidence that people in the general population typically possess strong needs for self-respect, respect from others, promotion, and psychological growth.

_____ 5. Equity theory looks at an individual's perceived fairness in an employment situation and has found that perceived inequities can lead to changes in behavior.

_____ 6. Alderfer identified three basic categories of needs: existence needs, relatedness needs, and growth needs.

_____ 7. McClelland's acquired-needs theory focuses on three of the many needs humans develop in their lifetimes: the need for achievement, the need for power, and the need for affiliation.

_____ 8. From a managerial viewpoint, motivation is the process of furnishing organization members with the opportunity to satisfy their needs by performing production behavior within the organization.

_____ 9. Both monetary and some non-monetary incentives can also motivate employees to improve their organization performance.

_____10. While flextime programs seem to have some positive organizational effects, research indicates that higher motivation levels of workers is not one of them.

Multiple Choice   *Directions: Circle the letter of the word or phrase that best completes each statement.*

11. Which of the following is an *incorrect* statement about motivation?
    a. Motivation is an individual's inner state that causes him or her to behave in a way that ensures the accomplishment of some goal.
    b. Motivation deals primarily with directing the behavior of others.
    c. Numerous models that describe how motivation occurs have been developed.
    d. The more that managers understand organization members' behavior, the better able they should be to influence that behavior and to make it more consistent with the accomplishment of organizational objectives.
    e. All of these are correct statements.

12. Which of the following is an example of supportive behavior for the individual who feels a hunger need?
    a. eating food
    b. buying food
    c. buying and eating food
    d. buying, cooking, and eating food
    e. none of these is an example of supportive behavior

13. According to Vroom, motivation strength is
    a. increased once a felt need has been significantly reduced
    b. determined by the perceived value of the result of performing a behavior and the perceived probability that the behavior performed will cause the result to materialize
    c. an individual's degree of desire to perform a behavior
    d. *b* and *c*
    e. all of these are correct

14. While the Porter-Lawler theory of motivation is consistent with the needs-goal theory and the Vroom expectancy theory, it stresses three other characteristics of the motivation process. Which of the following is *not* one of those characteristics?
    a. The perceived fairness of rewards influences the amount of satisfaction produced by those rewards.
    b. The extent to which an individual effectively accomplishes a task is determined primarily by the individual's perception of what is required to perform the task and the individual's actual ability to perform the task.
    c. The perceived value of a reward is determined by both intrinsic and extrinsic rewards that result in need satisfaction when a task is accomplished.
    d. The sum of gratification of various needs or satisfaction with various job facets constitutes the amount of total job satisfaction.
    e. All of these are characteristics of the motivation process.

15. Job enlargement entails
    a. moving an individual from job to job and not requiring the individual to perform only one simple and specialized job over the long run
    b. incorporating motivators into a job situation
    c. allowing workers to complete their jobs within a workweek they arrange themselves
    d. increasing the number of operations an individual performs
    e. none of these accurately describes job enlargement

16. According to Herzberg's motivating/hygiene theory, which of the following is *not* a motivator?
    a. working conditions
    b. responsibility
    c. opportunity for recognition
    d. personal growth
    e. work itself

17. According to Maslow, which of the following is the correct hierarchical ordering of human needs?
    a. physiological, security, social, esteem, self-actualization
    b. security, physiological, social, esteem, self-actualization
    c. security, physiological, esteem, social, self-actualization
    d. physiological, security, esteem, social, self-actualization
    e. none of the above

18. Select the incorrect statement. According to Argyris
    a. people naturally progress from immaturity to maturity
    b. people move from a state of activity as an infant to a state of passivity as an adult
    c. people move from a state of dependence on others as an infant to a state of relative independence as an adult
    d. people move from having a short time perspective as an infant to having a much longer time perspective as an adult
    e. all of these are correct statements

19. Perhaps the most basic strategy for managers in motivating other organization members is
    a. job rotation
    b. behavior modification
    c. communication
    d. making Theory Y assumptions
    e. none of these is a basic strategy

20. According to Reddin
    a. managers who use Theory X assumptions are "bad"
    b. motivation might be increased by using either Theory X or Theory Z
    c. Theory Z is actually an effectiveness dimension that implies that managers who use either Theory X or Theory Y assumptions when dealing with people can be successful, depending on their situation
    d. Theory Y represents the assumptions that management should strive to use
    e. all of these statements are correct

21. Which of the following statements correctly describes flextime?
    a. The major purpose of flextime is to reduce the total number of hours that an employee works.
    b. The use of flextime has resulted in greater job dissatisfaction among employees.
    c. Flextime is arranged by supervisors, not employees
    d. The main purpose of flextime is to allow employees to arrange their work schedule to meet their special needs while still working forty hours per week.
    e. All of the above statements correctly describe flextime.

22. Any successful behavior modification program would include all of the following components *except*
    a. giving rewards and punishments when earned
    b. punishing inappropriate behavior publicly
    c. varying the rewards to match the quality of performance
    d. providing feedback to keep employees informed about the relationship between various behaviors and associated consequences
    e. telling employees what they are doing wrong

23. Likert's system 4 is best described by which of the following?
    a. downward communication, with upward communication viewed with suspicion; condescending confidence in subordinates; workers motivated by rewards and actual or potential punishment
    b. downward communication only; no confidence in subordinates; workers motivated by rewards and some involvement
    c. upward and downward communication; complete confidence in subordinates; workers motivated by a compensation system based on participation in goal setting and decision making
    d. upward and downward communication; substantial confidence in subordinates; workers motivated by rewards and some involvement
    e. none of these accurately describes system 4

24. According to the text, which of the following is *not* a strategy for motivating organization members?
    a. job design strategy
    b. behavior modification
    c. Likert's management systems theory
    d. managerial communication
    e. social needs

25. Which of the following is *not* an example of McGregor's Theory Y assumptions?
    a. The average person will exercise self-direction in the service of objectives to which he or she is committed.
    b. Work is as natural as play for the average person.
    c. The average person will seek responsibility.
    d. The average person wants security above all else.
    e. The commitment to objectives is a function of the rewards associated with achievement.

Applying What You Know

Experience 15-1   What Do Employees Want from Their Jobs?

Introduction

"The devil with the recognition, give me the money!" What do employees **really** want from their jobs? While this question cannot always be answered in the same way for all situations, this experience is designed to help clarify the factors that generally motivate employee performance. It also is designed to provide you with an opportunity to explore why perceptions of these factors vary from situation to situation.

Exercise 1

Put yourself in the employee's shoes and figure out what he or she wants from the job. Then rank the ten items in figure 15.1 in order of importance to employees. Use the column headed "My Ranking." Place a 1 after the item you think employees want most, and so on. *Remember, it is not what you want, but rather, what you think employees will say they want.*

Figure 15.1 Ranking what employees want.

Items	What Employees Say they Want!			
	My Ranking	Class Ranking	Supervisor's Actual Ranking	Employee's Actual Ranking
1. Good working conditions				
2. Feeling "in" on things				
3. Tactful discipline				
4. Full appreciation for work done				
5. Management loyalty to workers				
6. Good wages				
7. Promotion and growth within company				
8. Sympathetic understanding of personal problems				
9. Job Security				
10. Interesting work				

Exercise 2

Now that you have individually ranked the ten items in exercise 1, your instructor will help you to determine the class ranking and will show you survey results of what supervisors think employees will say and actual employee rankings. Get together with four or five classmates and try to develop some reasonable explanations for these data.

Exercise 3

Once you have discussed as a class the rationale behind the rankings, discuss in your small group the possible implications of the data for managers. What should managers do to create situations in which employees feel motivated?

Exercise 4

Explain what you have gained from this experience.

Experience 15-2   Job Enlargement or Job Enrichment?

Introduction

One strategy managers can use to motivate organization members relates to the design of jobs that organization members perform. Two design changes that have been made to reduce job boredom and, thus, make jobs more meaningful are job enlargement and job enrichment. Supporters of job enlargement argue that, when a person performs a greater number of tasks, the job becomes less monotonous and, therefore, more satisfying. An example of job enlargement would be changing the job of an assembler so that the individual would assemble many different units rather than performing a single operation. Job enrichment, on the other hand, is designed to stimulate motivation by improving the nature of the work itself. For job enrichment to be effective, individuals must perceive their work as being meaningful. Meaningful work, from Herzberg's perspective, is able to satisfy needs for achievement, recognition, responsibility, growth, and learning.

In this experience, you test your understanding of job enlargement and job enrichment. Read the incident that follows and then complete the exercises as directed.

Incident

Sally Kentwood holds the title "Dietary Specialist-Vegetables" at Bakemont Retirement Village. An undergraduate degree in dietetics is required to be considered for a dietary specialist's position at Bakemont. For a fairly "stiff" fee, residents of the retirement village are provided with a special diet tailored to meet individualized needs.

The process of providing this specialized diet begins when the village physician recommends to the chief dietician that a particular menu be prepared for a certain retiree or retiree group. The chief dietician then decides on the food items to be prepared, the quantity of each item to be prepared, the method of preparation, and the type of seasoning called for to meet individualized needs. After these decisions have been made, a food prep form is handed to each dietary specialist. The job of the dietary specialist is then to prepare the item or items that fall within his or her specialty.

After the food item or items are prepared, they are sent by conveyor to the cafeteria serving area. Resident satisfaction or dissatisfaction with the dietary program is usually channelled back to the chief dietician, who uses this information to make any changes that could better satisfy individual demands and yet meet dietary requirements.

Exercise 1

List in the appropriate columns several suggestions for enriching and enlarging Sally Kentwood's job.

Suggestions for enrichment

a.

b.

Suggestions for enlargement

a.

b.

Suggestions for enrichment	Suggestions for enlargement
c.	c.
d.	d.
e.	e.
f.	f.

Exercise 2

a. If you were in Sally Kentwood's position, would you prefer an enlarged job or an enriched job? Explain.

b. What are the main differences between enriching factors and enlarging factors?

c. Which would be more difficult to enrich: a field sales job or an auto assembly job? Explain.

d.   Can you enrich the job of a janitor? Explain how.

e.   Discuss the statements that follow with a small group of your classmates. Then write a group response.

1) "Job rotation is a special case of job enlargement."
2) "Some jobs simply cannot be enriched."
3) "Flextime is a special case of job enrichment."

Exercise 3

Explain what you have gained from this experience.

Experience 15-3   Easy-Does-It Can Opener Company--A Case in (De)Motivation

Introduction

Performance is frequently stimulated through the distribution or withholding of rewards. By looking at the impact of a reward on members of the work group in Assembly Shop K at the Easy-Does-It Can Opener Company, you should be able to extend your understanding of motivation. Read the incident that follows and then complete the exercises as directed.

Incident

There are seven workers in Assembly Shop K of the Easy-Does-It Can Opener Company (see below). Each worker performs certain tasks as the can openers pass through different stages of assembly. All of the workers are paid an hourly wage. Claudine Raeff is the fifth person on the line. From management's perspective, Claudine is clearly the fastest and most efficient worker on the assembly line. Management has been able to make this judgment from observing the line.

Claudine sometimes must remain idle because the first four operatives do not feed her work fast enough. In other instances management has noticed that bottlenecks arise at the sixth position on the line because Raeff does her tasks so quickly (efficiently).

Last month, the shop supervisor, Andy Knapp, recommended Raeff for a raise in pay because of her performance. This raise was approved by higher management two weeks ago. During the last two weeks, the productivity of the other workers in the shop has declined noticeably; they seem to be upset that Raeff received a raise and they did not.

Assembly Shop K

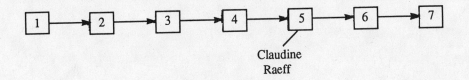

Claudine
Raeff

Exercise 1

a. Why do you feel productivity in Assembly Shop K has declined? Explain.

b. Looking at the case from a motivational perspective, do you feel that the compensation policy followed in this shop is sound? If not, what changes would you recommend and why?

c. What steps would you take to provide for a more efficient work flow and higher overall productivity in this shop? Explain.

Exercise 2

Your instructor will provide you with additional information on motivation. After you have performed as directed, answer the questions that follow.

a.   What basic principle(s) could be developed as a result of Miller and Hamblin's research?

b.   Can these principles be used to explain why productivity declined in Assembly Shop K? Explain.

Exercise 3

Explain what you have gained from this experience.

16 GROUPS AND CORPORATE CULTURE

Chapter Summary

This chapter focuses on managing groups. Managing work groups requires guiding the behavior of organization members so as to increase the probability of reaching organizational objectives. The chapter: (1) defines groups, (2) discusses the kinds of groups that exist in organizations, and (3) explains what steps managers should take to manage groups appropriately.

Learning Objective 1   *A definition of the term group as used within the context of management*

As used in management-related discussions, a **group** is not simply a gathering of people, but any number of people who interact with one another, are psychologically aware of one another, and perceive themselves to be a group. The study of groups is important to managers since the common ingredient of all organizations is people and since the most common technique for accomplishing work through these people is dividing them into work groups. Four additional reasons for the importance of studying groups are: (1) groups exist in all kinds of organizations; (2) groups inevitably form in all facets of organizational existence; (3) groups can cause either desirable or undesirable consequences within the organization; and (4) understanding groups can assist managers in increasing the probability that groups with which they work will cause desirable consequences within the organization.

Learning Objective 2   *A thorough understanding of the difference between formal and informal groups*

Groups that exist in organizations typically are divided into two basic types: formal and informal. A **formal group** is one that exists within an organization by virtue of management decree to perform tasks that enhance the attainment of organizational objectives. Placement or organization members in such areas as marketing departments, personnel departments, or production departments involves establishing formal groups. The coordination of and communication among these formal groups is the responsibility of managers or supervisors, commonly called "linking pins." Linking pins belong to two formal groups: they are the supervisor in one formal group and a subordinate in the other.

Informal groups are the second major kind of group that can exist within an organization. **Informal groups** are those that develop naturally as people interact. Organization members can belong to more than one information group at the same time. In contrast to formal groups, informal groups typically are not highly structured in terms of procedure and are not formally recognized by management.

Informal groups generally are divided into interest groups and friendship groups. **Interest groups** are informal groups that gain and maintain membership primarily because of a special concern each member possesses about a specific issue. An example might be a group of workers pressing management for better pay or working conditions. In general, once the interest or concern that causes this informal group to form has been eliminated, the group tends to disband. **Friendship groups**, on the other hand, are informal groups that form in organizations because of the personal affiliation members have with one another. As with interest groups, the membership of friendship groups tends to change over time. Here, however, group membership changes as friendships dissolve or new friendships are made.

In general, informal groups tend to develop in organizations because of various benefits that group members obtain. These benefits include the perpetuation of social and cultural values that group members consider important, status and social satisfaction that might not be enjoyed without group membership, increased ease of communication between group members, and increased desirability of the overall work environment. These benefits may be one reason why employees who are on fixed shifts or who continually work with the same group are sometimes more satisfied with their work than employees whose shifts are continually changing.

One tool managers may be able to use to assist in the development of informal groups is called a quality circle. **Quality circles** are simply small groups of factory workers who meet regularly with management to discuss quality-related problems. Naturally, during these meetings, management has opportunities to nurture relationships with various informal groups. In fact, quality circles may actually result in some managers and workers becoming members of the same informal groups.

Formal groups commonly are divided into command groups and task groups. **Command groups** are formal groups that are outlined on the chain of command on an organization chart. In general, command groups typically handle the more routine organizational activities. **Task groups**, on the other hand, are formal groups of organization members who interact with one another to accomplish mostly nonroutine organizational tasks. Although task groups commonly are considered to be made up of members on the same organizational level, they can consist of people from different levels of the organizational hierarchy.

Committees and work teams are examples of formal groups that can be established in organizations. Committees are a more traditional formal group, while work teams only recently have begun to gain popular acceptance and support. A **committee** is a group of individuals that has been charged with performing some type of activity. A committee, therefore, usually is classified as a task group. From a managerial viewpoint, the major reasons for establishing committees are: (1) to allow organization members to exchange ideas, (2) to generate suggestions and recommendations that can be offered to other organizational units, (3) to develop new ideas for solving existing organizational problems, and (4) to assist in the development of organizational policies. Committees typically exist within all organizations and at all organizational levels. The larger the organization, the greater the probability that committees are used within that organization on a regular basis.

Managers generally agree that committees have several uses in organizations. One is that committees can improve the quality of decision making. Generally speaking, as more people become involved in making a decision, the strengths and weaknesses of that decision are discussed in more detail, and the quality of the decision tends to increase. Another reason for committees is that they encourage honest opinions because committee members feel protected. Committees also tend to increase organization member participation in decision making and thereby enhance support of committee decisions. Also, as a result of this increased participation, committee work creates the opportunity for committee members to satisfy their social or esteem needs. Finally, committees ensure the representation of important groups in the decision-making process.

A recent study by McLeod and Jones indicates that some executives strongly favor using committees in organizations. Study results indicate that while executives get more information from other sources than committees, the value of information from committees is greater than that from other sources. However, some top executives show only qualified acceptance of committees as work groups, while still other executives express negative feelings. In general, however, executives who are negative about using committees are fewer in number than those who have positive feelings or display qualified acceptance of them.

Although committees have become a commonly accepted management tool, management action taken to establish and run committees is a major variable in determining a committee's degree of success. *Steps that can be taken to increase the probability that a committee will be successful are*: (1) the committee's goals should be clearly defined, preferably in writing; (2) the committee's authority should be specified; (3) the optimum size of the committee should be determined; (4) a chairperson should be selected on the basis of ability to run an efficient meeting; (5) a permanent secretary to handle communications should be appointed; (6) the agenda and all supporting material for the meeting should be distributed before the meeting; and (7) meetings should be started and ended on time. In addition, there are a number of more people-oriented guidelines managers can follow to increase the probability of a committee's success. In this regard, a manager can increase the quality of discussion in committees by rephrasing ideas already expressed, by bringing a member into active participation, and by stimulating further thought by a member. Managers should also help the committee to avoid a phenomenon called "groupthink." **Groupthink** is the mode of thinking that persons engage in when seeking agreement becomes so dominant in a group that it tends to override the realistic appraisal of alternative problem solutions. Groups operate under groupthink when group members are so concerned with being too harsh in their judgments of other group members that objective problem solving is lost.

Work teams are another example of task groups used in organizations. Work teams, in the U.S., have evolved from the problem-solving teams--based on Japanese-style quality circles--that were widely adopted in the 1970s. Problem-solving teams consist of five to twelve volunteer members from different areas of the department who meet weekly to discuss ways to improve quality and efficiency. Special-purpose teams, a hybrid type of problem-solving team, typically involve both workers and union representatives who meet together to collaborate on operational decisions at all levels, creating an atmosphere for quality and productivity improvements. These self-managing teams consist of five to fifteen employees who work together to produce an entire product. Members learn all the tasks and rotate from job to job on the project. The teams even take over such managerial duties as work and vacation scheduling and ordering materials. The concept of the work team is a fundamental change in how work is organized, giving the employees control over their jobs. As product quality becomes more and more important, managers will need to rely more on the team approach in order to stay competitive.

Another facet to managing formal groups is understanding the **stages of formal group development**. In a classic book, Bernard Bass has suggested that group development is a four-stage process influenced primarily by groups learning how to use their resources. The first stage, according to Bass, is the acceptance stage. In this stage, the initial mistrust within a group is transformed into mutual trust and the general acceptance of group members by one another. Next, in the communication and decision-making stage, group members learn to communicate frankly with one another. This frank communication provides the basis for establishing and using effectively some type of group decision-making mechanism.

The group solidarity stage is characterized by members becoming more involved in group activities and cooperating, rather than competing, with one another. Finally, the group control stage involves group members attempting to maximize group success by matching individual abilities with group activities and by assisting each other. In general terms, as a group passes through each of these four stages, it tends to become more mature, more effective, and, therefore, more productive. The group that reaches maximum maturity and effectiveness is characterized by the members functioning as a unit participating effectively in group effort; being oriented toward a single goal; having the equipment, tools, and skills necessary to attain the group's goals; and asking and receiving suggestions, opinions, and information from each other.

Learning Objective 4   *An understanding of how managers can determine which groups exist in an organization*

Informal groups, the second major kind of group that can exist within an organization, are groups that develop naturally as people interact. An **informal group** is defined as a collection of individuals whose common work experiences result in the development of a system of interpersonal relations that extend beyond those expected of them by management. Informal groups generally are divided into two types: interest groups and friendship groups. **Interest groups** are informal groups that gain and maintain membership primarily because of a special concern each member possesses about a specific issue. Once the interest or concern that causes an informal group to form has been eliminated, the group tends to disband. **Friendship groups**, on the other hand, are informal groups that form in organizations because of the personal affiliation members have with one another. Personal factors like personal interests, race, gender, and religion serve as foundations for friendship groups. As with interest groups, the membership of friendship groups tends to change over time. Here, however, group membership changes as friendships dissolve or new friendships are made.

Informal groups tend to develop in organizations because of various benefits that group members obtain. These benefits include: (1) perpetuation of social and cultural values that group members consider important, (2) status and social satisfaction that might not be enjoyed without group membership, (3) increased ease of communication among group members, and (4) increased desirability of the overall work environment. These benefits may be one reason that employees who are on fixed shifts or who continually work with the same groups are sometimes more satisfied with their work than employees whose shifts are continually changing.

To manage work groups effectively, managers must consider simultaneously the impact of both formal and informal group factors on organizational productivity. This consideration requires three steps. The first and perhaps the most important step that managers should take in managing work groups is determining what groups exist within the organization and who constitutes the membership of those groups. **Sociometry** is an analytical tool that managers can use to help determine such information. Sociometry also can provide information on the internal workings of an informal group, such as who leads the group, the relative status level of various members within the informal group, and the informal group's communication networks. This information on informal groups, along with an understanding of the established formal groups as shown on an organization chart, gives managers a complete picture of the group structure with which they must deal.

The procedure involved in performing a sociometric analysis in an organization is quite basic. Various organization members simply are asked, either through an interview or questionnaire, to state several other organization members with whom they would like to spend some of their free time. A **sociogram** then is constructed to summarize the informal relationships among group members that were uncovered. Sociograms are diagrams that visually link individuals within the group according to the number of times they were chosen and whether or not the choice was reciprocal.

Obviously, knowing what groups exist within an organization and what characterizes the membership of those groups is an extremely important prerequisite for managing groups effectively. A second prerequisite is understanding how informal groups evolve since this gives managers some insights on how to encourage informal groups to develop appropriately within an organization.

Perhaps the most widely accepted framework for explaining the evolution of informal groups was developed by George Homans. According to Homans, the sentiments, activities, and interactions that emerge as part of an informal group actually result from the sentiments, activities, and interactions that exist within a formal group. In addition, Homans says that the informal group exists to obtain the consequences of satisfaction and growth for informal group members. Feedback on whether or not these consequences are achieved can result in forces that attempt to modify the formal group so as to increase the probability that the informal group achieves these consequences. For example, as workers interact and perform their jobs on a formal basis, informal groups based on such factors as common interests and friendship tend to evolve to maximize the satisfaction and growth of informal group members. Once established, these informal groups tend to resist changes or established segments of formal groups that threaten the satisfaction and growth of informal group members.

Once managers determine which groups exist within an organization and understand how informal groups evolve, they should strive to maximize work group effectiveness. As work group size (the number of members of a work group) increases, forces usually are created within that group that can either increase or decrease its effectiveness. The ideal number of members for a work group depends primarily on the group's purpose. For example, the ideal size for a fact-finding work group usually is set at about fourteen members, while the maximum size for a problem-solving work group is approximately seven members. Work group size is a significant determinant of group effectiveness because it has considerable impact on three major components of a group: leadership, group members, and group process. When attempting to maximize group effectiveness by modifying formal group size, managers also should consider informal group factors. If, for example, a manager reduces the size of a formal group and in the process transfers the informal group leader, the effectiveness of the work group could diminish considerably due to the loss of its informal leader.

Another factor that can influence work group effectiveness is the degree of cohesiveness within the group. **Group cohesiveness** is the attraction group members feel for one another in terms of desires to remain a member of the group and resist leaving it. The greater these desires, the greater the cohesiveness within the group. In general, the cohesiveness of a work group is determined by the cohesiveness of the informal groups that exist within that work group. Group cohesiveness is extremely important to managers since the greater the cohesiveness within a group, the greater the probability the group will accomplish its objectives. In addition, some evidence indicates that groups whose members have positive feelings toward one another tend to be more productive than groups whose members have negative feelings toward one another. *Indicators of high group cohesiveness include:* (1) the members have a broad, general agreement on the goals and objectives of the informal group; (2) a significant amount of communication and interaction is evident among participating members; (3) there is a satisfactory level of homogeneity in social status and social background among the members; (4) members are allowed to participate fully and directly in the determination of group standards; (5) the size of the group is sufficient for interaction but is not too large to stymie personal attention; (6) the members have a high regard for their fellow members; (7) the members feel a strong need for the mutual benefits and protection the group appears to offer; and (8) the group is experiencing success in the achievement of its goals and in the protection of important values.

Since group cohesiveness of informal groups is such an influential determinant of cohesiveness within work groups and, as a result, of work group effectiveness, management should assist in the development of informal group cohesiveness whenever possible. If, however, managers determine that an informal group is attempting to attain objectives that are counterproductive within the organization, an appropriate strategy would be to attempt to reduce informal group cohesiveness. Overall, managers must keep in mind that, the greater the cohesiveness within informal groups with nonproductive objectives, the greater the probability that those nonproductive objectives will be attained.

Group norms are a third major determinant of work group effectiveness. **Group norms**, as used in this chapter, apply only to informal groups and can be defined as appropriate or standard behavior that is required of informal group members. These norms, therefore, significantly influence informal group members' behavior as members of their formal group. According to Hackman, group norms (1) are structured characteristics of groups that simplify the group influence processes, (2) apply only to behavior and not to private thoughts and feelings of groups members, (3) generally develop only in relation to those matters that most group members consider important, (4) usually develop slowly over time, and (5) sometimes apply only to certain group members. Systematic study of group norms has revealed that there is generally a close relationship between group norms and the profitability of the organization of which that group is a part. Although it would be impossible to state all possible norms that might develop in a group, most group norms relate to organizational pride, performance, profitability, teamwork, planning, supervision, training, innovation, customer relations, and honesty or security.

Norms usually are divided into two general types: negative norms and positive norms. **Negative norms** are required informal group behavior that limits organizational productivity, while **positive norms** are required informal group behavior that contributes to organizational productivity. Some managers consider group norms to be of such great importance to the organization that they develop profiles of group norms to assess the norms' organizational impact. A normative profile may be characterized by a number of norm differences. For example, a high level of organizational pride and good customer relations could contrast with a lower concern for profitability. To change existing norms within an informal group, characteristics of the formal work group of which that informal group is a part must be changed. An illustration of changing informal group norms could involve an informal group that has the negative norm: "Don't rush the work--they'll just give you more to do." For a manager to change this norm, the factor in the formal work group from which this norm probably arose should be eliminated. For example, the manager might find that this norm is a direct result of the fact that workers are formally recognized within the organization through pay and awards, regardless of the amount of work performed. Changing this formal policy so that the amount of work accomplished is considered in formal organizational recognition should help to dissolve this negative norm.

Status is the position of a group member in relation to other group members. Overall, an individual's status within a group is determined not only by the person's work or role within the group but by the nonwork qualities the individuals bring into the group. Work-related determinants of status include titles, work schedules, and, perhaps most commonly, amounts of pay group members receive. Nonwork-related determinants of status include education level, race, age, and sex. These status symbols generally are used within formal work groups to reward individual productivity and to clearly show different levels of organizational importance. To maximize the effectiveness of a work group, however, managers also should consider the status of members of the informal group or groups that exist within that formal group. Management usually finds that, to increase productivity within a formal work group, the support of both the formal and informal leaders must be gained. In fact, some evidence suggests that production is more associated with support from informal group leaders than from formal group leaders.

Learning Objective 6   *Insights about managing corporate culture to enhance organizational success*

Corporate culture is defined as a set of shared values and beliefs that organization members have regarding the functioning and existence of their organization. The evidence for the type or corporate culture present in any organization can be found by studying its own special combination of status symbols, traditions, history, and physical environment. By understanding the significance of this evidence of corporate culture, management can help to develop a culture which is beneficial to the firm. For example, by looking at the **status symbols**, the visible, external signs of one's social position, that are associated with the various positions in the firm, one can get a feeling for the social hierarchy in the organization. Status symbols such as size and location of one's office, use of executive clubs, and reserved parking are all indicators of status level of a job. Traditions and history developed over time in a firm can determine the special way that workers in that particular firm act on a daily basis. Typically, the traditions can help workers know exactly what is expected of them. By developing traditions, managers can help to steer everyday behaviors. The firm's physical environment also makes a statement about the firm's type of corporate culture. For instance, offices that are closed with few common areas for organization members to meet creates an image of a closed form of culture. A building with open offices and considerable common areas for the employees to interact indicates a more open culture. Whether the doors are consistently closed or open is another clue as to the type of formality that exists in an organization.

The significance of corporate culture for management is that it influences the behavior of everyone within an organization and, if carefully crafted, can have a positive and significant impact on organizational success. If not properly managed, however, corporate culture can help doom an organization to failure. Typically, top managements as well as other present or past leaders in an organization are the key agents for influencing corporate culture. Advice concerning how managers should handle corporate culture issues commonly appears in the current management literature. One example of such advice that seems especially practical and helpful suggests that managers can use five primary mechanisms to help develop and reinforce corporate culture. These mechanisms are: (1) what leaders pay attention to, measure, and control, (2) leaders' reactions to critical incidents and organizational crises, (3) deliberate role modeling, teaching, and coaching, (4) criteria for allocation of rewards and status, and (5) criteria for recruitment, selection, promotion, and retirement of employees.

The above information suggests that managers can influence the type of culture that exists within organizations. In general, a manager must first determine the characteristics of a culture that would be appropriate for an organization, and then take calculated and overt steps to encourage the establishment, growth, and maintenance of that culture. Simply allowing corporate culture to develop without planned management influence can result in the appearance of an inappropriate corporate culture that ultimately limits the degree of success that an organization can attain.

Knowing You Know

Fill-in-the-Blank   *Directions: Fill in each blank with the appropriate word or phrase.*

1. The study of groups is important to managers since the common ingredient of all organizations is _____ and since the most common technique for accomplishing work through these people is _____.

2. A _____ is a group that exists within an organization by virtue of management decree to perform tasks that enhance the attainment of organizational objectives.

3. A _____ is a group of individuals that has been charged with performing some type of activity.

4. _____ is the mode of thinking that persons engage in when seeking agreement becomes so dominant in a group that it tends to override the realistic appraisal of alternative problem solutions.

5. _____ are informal groups that gain and maintain membership primarily because of a special concern each member possesses about a specific issue.

6. Some managers are called _____ because they belong to two formal groups; they are the supervisor in one formal group and a subordinate in the other.

7. _____ is an analytical tool that managers can use to help determine information about informal groups and the internal workings of those informal groups.

8. _____ are formal groups that are outlined on the chain of command on an organization chart

9. _____ are groups that develop naturally as people interact.

10. _____ is defined as a set of shared values and beliefs that organization members have regarding the functioning and existence of their organization.

True/False   *Directions: On the lines provided, place a "T" for true and an "F" for false for each of the statements that follows.*

_____11. According to Homans, the sentiments, activities, and interactions that emerge as part of a formal group actually result from the sentiments, activities, and interactions that exist within an informal group.

_____12. The ideal size for a fact-finding work group usually is set at a maximum of seven members.

_____13. In general, the cohesiveness of a work group is determined by the cohesiveness of the informal groups that exist within that work group.

_____14. The greater the cohesiveness within informal groups with nonproductive objectives, the greater the probability that those nonproductive objectives will be attained.

_____15. According to your text, group norms apply to both formal and informal groups and can be defined as appropriate or standard behavior that is required of group members.

_____16. Negative norms are required informal group behavior that limits organizational productivity, while positive norms are required formal group behavior that contributes to organizational productivity.

_____17. To change existing norms within an informal group, characteristics of the formal work group of which that informal group is a part must be changed.

_____18. Overall, an individual's status within a group is determined by the nonwork qualities the individual brings into the group and not by the person's work or role within the group.

_____19. A committee's goals should be clearly defined, preferably in writing.

_____20. Bass suggests that group development is a four-stage process; he called the first stage "the acceptance stage."

_____21. To deal with groups appropriately, managers must have a thorough understanding of the nature of organizational groups.

_____22. Cohesion within informal groups is a determinant of work group effectiveness.

_____23. Work-related determinants of status include titles, work schedules, and education level.

_____24. The ideal number of members for a work group depends primarily upon the group leader's skills.

_____25. Most executives agree that, while committees may be useful, they frequently waste a great deal of time.

Applying What You Know

Experience 16-1   What to Look for in Groups*

Introduction

The two major ingredients in all group interactions are content and process. Content deals with subject matter or the task upon which the group is working. In most interactions, the focus of attention is on the content. Process, on the other hand, is concerned with what is happening between and to group members while the group is working toward task accomplishment. Group process or dynamics deals with such items as morale, feelings, tone, atmosphere, influence, participation, styles of leadership, leadership struggles, conflict, competition, cooperation, and so forth. *In most interactions,*

---

*Reprinted from J. W. Pfeiffer and J.E. Jones, (Eds.), *The 1972 Annual Handbook for Group Facilitators*, San Diego, CA: Pfeiffer & Company, 1972. Used with permission.

accomplishment. Group process or dynamics deals with such items as morale, feelings, tone, atmosphere, influence, participation, styles of leadership, leadership struggles, conflict, competition, cooperation, and so forth. *In most interactions, very little attention is paid to process, even when it is the major cause of ineffective group action.*

In this experience, you learn more about how to analyze group process behavior. Familiarize yourself with the thirty-four observation guidelines, grouped into nine major categories, that follow, and then complete the exercises as directed.

Process Guidelines

Participation--One indication of involvement is verbal participation. Look for differences among members in the amount of participation.
1. Who are the high participators?
2. Who are the low participators?
3. Do you see any shift in participation; for example, high participators become quiet; low participators suddenly become talkative. Do you see any possible reason for this in the group's interaction?
4. How are the silent people treated? How is their silence interpreted? Consent? Disagreement? Disinterest? Fear?
5. Who talks to whom? Do you see any reason for this in the group's interactions?
6. Who keeps the ball rolling? Do you see any reason for this in the group's interactions?

Influence--Influence and participation are not the same. Some people may speak very little, yet they capture the attention of the whole group. Others may talk a lot but generally are not listened to by other members.
7. Which members are high in influence? That is, when they talk, others seem to listen.
8. Which members are low in influence? Others do not listen to them or follow them. Is there any shifting in influence? Who shifts?
9. Do you see any rivalry in the group? Is there a struggle for leadership? What effect does it have on other group members?

Decision-Making Procedures--Many kinds of decisions are made in groups without considering the effects of these decisions on other members. Some members try to impose their decisions on the group, while others want everyone to participate or share in the decisions that are made.
10. Does anyone make a decision and carry it out without checking with other group members (self-authorized)? For example, does anyone decide on the topic to be discussed and start right in talking about it? What effect does this have on other group members?
11. Does the group drift from topic to topic? Whose topic jumps? Do you see any reason for this in the group's interactions?
12. Who supports other members' suggestions or decisions? Does this support result in the two members deciding the topic or activity for the group (handclasp)? How does this affect other group members?
13. Is there any evidence of a majority pushing a decision through over other members' objections? Do they call for a vote (majority decision)?
14. Is there any attempt to get all members participating in a decision (consensus)? What effect does this seem to have on the group?
15. Does anyone make any contributions that do not receive any kind of response or recognition (plop)? What effect does this have on the contributor?

Task Functions--These feelings illustrate behaviors concerned with getting the job done or accomplishing the task that the group has before them.
16. Does anyone ask for or make suggestions as to the best way to proceed or to battle a problem?
17. Does anyone attempt to summarize what has been covered or what has been going on in the group?
18. Is there any giving or asking for facts, ideas, opinions, feelings, feedback, or alternatives?
19. Who keeps the group on target, preventing topic jumping or going off on tangents?

Maintenance Functions--These functions are important to the morale of the group since they maintain good and harmonious working relationships among group members and create a group atmosphere that enables each member to contribute naturally. They promote smooth and effective teamwork within the group.

20. Who helps others get into the discussion (gate openers)?
21. Who cuts off others or interrupts them (gate closers)?
22. How well are members getting their ideas across? Are some members preoccupied and not listening? Are there any attempts by group members to help others clarify their ideas?
23. How are ideas rejected? How do members react when their ideas are rejected?

Group Atmosphere--Something about the way a group works creates an atmosphere which in turn is revealed in a general impression. In addition, people may differ in the kind of atmosphere they like in a group. Insight can be gained into the atmosphere characteristic of a group by finding words that describe the general impression held by group members.

24. Who seems to prefer a friendly, congenial atmosphere? Is there any attempt to suppress conflict or unpleasant feelings?
25. Who seems to prefer an atmosphere of conflict and disagreement? Do any members provoke or annoy others?
26. Do people seem involved and interested? Is the atmosphere one of work, play, satisfaction, taking flight, sluggishness?

Membership--A major concern for group members is the degree of acceptance or inclusion in the group. Different patterns of interaction may develop in the group that give clues to the degree and kind of membership.

27. Is there any subgrouping? Sometimes, two or three members may consistently agree and support each other or consistently disagree and oppose one another.
28. Do some people seem to be "outside" the group? Do some members seem to be most "in?" How are those "outside" treated?
29. Do some members move in and out of the group? Under what conditions do they come in or move out?

Feelings--During any group discussion, feelings frequently are generated by the interaction between members. These feelings, however, are seldom discussed. Observers may have to make guesses based on tone of voice, facial expressions, gestures, and many other forms of nonverbal clues.

30. What signs of feelings do you observe in group members? Anger? Irritation? Frustration? Warmth? Affection? Excitement? Boredom? Defensiveness? Competitiveness?
31. Do you see any attempts by group members to block the expression of feelings, particularly negative feelings? How is this done? Does anyone do this consistently?

Norms--Standards or group rules may develop in a group that controls the behavior of its members. Norms usually express the beliefs or desires of the majority of the group members as to what behaviors should or should not take place in the group. These norms may be clear to all members (explicit), known or sensed by only a few (implicit), or operating completely below the level of awareness of any group members. Some norms help group progress, and some hinder it.

32. Are certain areas of discussion avoided by the group (for example, sex, religion, talk about present feelings in group, discussing leader's behavior)? Who seems to reinforce this avoidance? How do they do it?
33. Are group members overly nice or polite to each other? Are only positive feelings expressed? Do members agree with each other too readily? What happens when members disagree?
34. Do you observe norms about participation or the kinds of questions allowed--for example, "If I talk, you must talk," "If I tell my problems, you have to tell your problems"? Do members feel free to probe each other about their feelings? Do questions tend to be restricted to intellectual topics or events outside the group?

Exercise 1

For this exercise, your instructor will segment the class into two groups: discussants and observers. Discussants will move their chairs into a circle in the center of the room and discuss a topic assigned by the instructor. (This arrangement is called a discussion "fishbowl.") Observers will sit on the outside of the circle and process-analyze what takes place in the "fishbowl." Each observer will concentrate on one of the nine major behavior categories from the preceding process guidelines. When the "fishbowl" discussion is completed, observers will provide specific feedback (answer the questions in their category) to discussants. Observers should jot down pertinent observations during the "fishbowl" discussion so that they can provide discussants with accurate feedback.

Exercise 2

Repeat exercise 1, reversing the roles of discussants and observers. A new discussion topic will be assigned.

Exercise 3

Explain what you have gained from this experience.

Experience 16-2   Using Sociometry

Introduction

Sociometry techniques are not new. In fact, they date back three decades. Yet, they still are perceived to be an effective means of depicting group interaction. Basically, the method involves asking group members who they like or dislike (who they do or do not like to work with). From this interview data, it is possible to develop interaction patterns that can be depicted in a graphic format called a sociogram. In this experience, you become more familiar with the technique of sociometry.

Exercise 1

Closely examine the simple sociogram in figure 16.1. Then list the "stars," the isolates, the most powerful individuals, the leader, and the most cohesive groups.

Figure 16.1   Sociogram

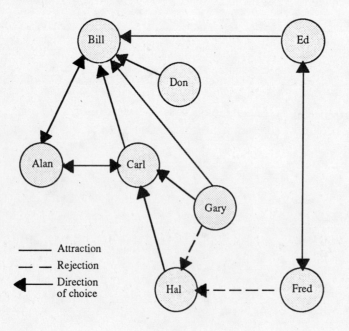

Exercise 2

Pair up with a class member who is also a member of a student group (fraternity group, sorority group, class project group, etc.). A group with six to twelve members is ideal. Interview members of the group (including your partner). Simply ask group members who they really like or dislike. Then construct a sociogram to represent what you discovered from the interview, and write a short interpretation of your sociogram.

Exercise 3

Ask you partner from exercise 2 to react to your sociogram and sociogram interpretation. Discuss those relationships in the group that you and your partner (a group member) perceived differently. Be prepared to share your experience with the class.

Exercise 4

Explain what you have gained from this experience.

Experience 16-3 The Work Group at Laird's Steak House[**]

Introduction

Informal groups develop naturally as people interact. In general, informal groups tend to develop in organizations because of various benefits individuals obtain as a result of being a member of such a group. In this experience, you test your understanding of the functioning of an informal group at Laird's Steak House. Read the incident that follows, and then complete the exercises as directed.

Incident

My name is Jenny Barker and I want to tell you about an experience I had working as a waitress my senior year in high school.

I was sixteen at the time and decided in early September to get a job because I had nothing to do and all my friends were working. When I saw an ad in the paper, placed by a restaurant that was within walking distance of my home, I decided to apply there.

The place was called Laird's Steak House, and it was a small, quality restaurant. It was owned and operated by Mrs. Martinelli (Mrs. M), aided by her son, Bob, his wife, Alice, Mrs. M's daughter, Marie, and occasionally, Marie's husband, Victor. Victor usually managed a larger family restaurant in the next town and only dropped in occasionally. Bob acted as host and fill-in cook, while Alice, Marie, and Mrs. M took turns hosting.

When I applied for the job, I had to talk to Bob and Alice as well as Mrs. M. Mrs. M struck me as grumpy but artificially sweet to the customers. She made a big point about being nice to the customers and also kept emphasizing cleanliness. When I finally got the job, she didn't give me any other instructions. She just gave me the menu and told me to memorize it completely.

Bob and Alice actually did most of the interviewing. At first I didn't think I had much of a chance at the job. They kept saying that I was too young to serve beer and that they were reluctant to hire me because of that fact. Eventually, I got the job because, as they said, they really needed someone. They said they would call me each week whenever they needed me.

I must say, I didn't feel very welcome at Laird's right from that interview on. Mrs. M made me feel like an intruder in her family and obviously favored the other waitresses who had worked there for several years.

The staff consisted of a night and day dishwasher, two cooks who rotated day and night shifts, and nine waitresses. The waitresses were: (1) Sally, a young wife; (2) Becky, a girl three years my senior whom I had known vaguely most of my life as a popular upperclassman (she was voted prettiest in her graduating class); (3) Shelly, Becky's friend, an attractive blonde; (4) Susan, a twenty-three-year-old who was the most experienced and best waitress of the bunch; (5) Nancy, Susan's sister; and (6) Dot, a middle-aged mother who seldom worked nights. There were two other daytime waitresses whom I never met.

All of these girls were attractive and seemed to me to put on airs, flirting with the customers and trying to act very sophisticated. I felt rather artless by comparison; Susan even nicknamed me "kid." Having worked at Laird's for several years, they all knew the routine by habit and had developed a close relationship among themselves. In addition, they sometimes worked for Victor in the larger restaurant and had a close social relationship with Bob, Marie, Alice, and Victor, going to the same weddings, and so forth. Susan was the most respected and the informal leader of the group, while Marie was glamorous, outgoing, and often talked with customers while they waited for meals.

The group did a lot of fooling around with one another and even kidded openly with Bob, Alice, and Marie. They were encouraging and friendly with Nancy, Susan's sister (who was also a high school senior in training as a waitress), but seemed snobby and insincere toward me. I didn't make friendships with any of them while I was there. I would sometimes stand near them when several were talking, but they never drew me into the conversation. Once in a while, I'd try to start a conversation myself, but I never got very far. Their outside interests seemed different than mine. Also, with some, I couldn't even say, "Did you have a nice weekend?" I felt that they would think, "What is this punk up to?"

I felt like an outsider from the beginning, and that never really changed. It's funny, because I'm a person who likes to please others, and I'm always able to fit in with groups. In school, I'm seen as talkative, aggressive, and something of a leader. The only other time something like this ever happened to me was when I joined the cheerleader squad. That was a group with a lot of status in my school, and when I joined them, I sort of held back and was quiet at first.

[**]Source of Experience 16-3: Allen Cohen, Stephen Fink, Herman Gadon, and Robin Willits, *Effective Behavior in Organizations: Learning from the Interplay of Cases, Concepts, and Student Experiences* (Homewood, IL: Richard D. Irwin, 1976), pp. 475-79. © 1976 by Richard D. Irwin, Inc.

One of the things that the waitresses did was to stand back of the counter together smoking cigarettes whenever there was a free minute. I didn't smoke, so I worked during my free minutes for lack of anything better to do. Besides, I didn't feel free to take breaks since I was new and couldn't feel as sure of my job as they did. My attempts at joking with Bob or Marie seemed feeble and formal. I always felt they compared me with Becky, Shelly, or even Nancy, who was older looking than I was and much like Susan in appearance and personality.

Mrs. M watched me closely. She seemed cold and critical, which made me feel even younger and more inexperienced compared to the others. Otherwise, she ignored me as a person. Her only comments were complaints which she'd pass on through Bob. She did comment favorably on Becky's smile, Susan's efficiency, and Shelly's popularity with the customers, but she never complimented me. I know I did a good job because Marie revealed several times that the clientele were pleased with me, too. Mrs. M's slight criticisms ("wipe that up") and attitude made me feel further degraded. Though I did my work well, the only encouragement I got were remarks like, "Busy night, good job," from Marie as she sped by. Being the youngest and newest and not part of the clique, I felt at the bottom of the totem pole.

As time passed, I decided that the group was closely knit and found it easier to make no effort to exert myself to become a part of it. My relations were formal. I would go to work at 4:30 P.M., set up, wait for the people to pour in, and busy myself doing the best job possible. The customers seemed satisfied and pleased with me, and I enjoyed the interaction with the public. I felt relaxed and outgoing with the customers, many of whom were regulars. Though my salary was $1.30/hour, I averaged $10 to $15 per night in tips working for five hours.

There were two shifts to the job--11 A.M. to 3:30 P.M. (which I never did) and 4:30 P.M. to 9:30 P.M. From 3:30 to 4:30, the restaurant closed to prepare for the dinner crowd. At 4:30, I was required to go to the back room, put the salad-dressing buckets on ice, and get rolls, salads, silverware, and coffee ready. I always worked the back section, which had booths and was the last to be filled with customers (see the floor plan in figure 16.2). The coffee machine was located in the back and was an added responsibility for me. Since Susan handled the section with tables next to my section, I helped her with salads and soda when she was busy. She, in turn, served beer to my customers for me. Otherwise, there was little interaction between waitresses. The waitress in front operated from her section alone. Each waitress was required to give her order to the cook, and while the order was prepared, serve salad, rolls, and beverages. The cook prepared the order over an open charcoal grill, then called our names out.

Figure 16.2 Laird's Steak House floor plan.

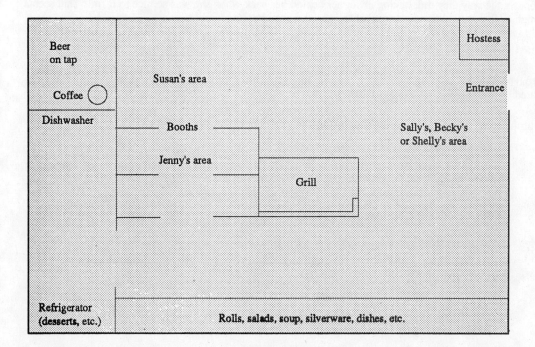

One thing I noticed was that Susan was more friendly than the others. She was nice to me when we were alone. When we were with the others, she would ignore me and make no effort to include me in the conversation. She seemed to be more interested in the topics the others wanted to talk about.

One cook was a middle-aged family man and the other a young Puerto Rican named Reggie. The former was friendly and fatherly, but Reggie was temperamental and derogatory. He often reprimanded me harshly in front of everyone, saying that he could not read my writing. One night, he played a practical joke in the back room by sticking spaghetti up his nose, which I felt was in *very* poor taste, not in keeping with Laird's standards. I found Reggie to be immature, yet his remarks often upset me ("Christ, you're dumb and ugly"). Nevertheless, he never showed his worst side to Mrs. M and frequently talked about "the old lady" behind her back.

The night dishwasher, a young black named Bill, with a wife and two children, was relatively new on the job. He and I became good friends, and in my spare time I talked with him. One day, Mrs. M came in the dishroom and reprimanded me harshly, saying I looked cheap talking to Bill. This particularly bothered me because no customers were in the restaurant and they could not have seen me if they were. To me, the girls looked more "cheap" smoking together at the back counter within sight of customers, but I said nothing. This seemed to confirm Mrs. M's attitude toward me. Her dislike of me and the superiority of the experienced older girls was a threat to my sense of adequacy. Their smoking really bothered me!

While the other girls seemed to be having fun and seemed satisfied, I felt excluded and unhappy. I often was pressured to work weekends because the other girls did not want to; this made me feel "stuck" doubly, because whenever they wanted a night off, I was expected to fill in. Their lack of appreciation made me feel even more inferior, even though I usually didn't mind working weekends. The weekends generally were busy, went quickly, and tips were especially good. nevertheless, I still felt extremely tense under Mrs. M's watchful eye and was never quite sure what Bob, Alice, or Marie actually thought of me. Our relationships were formal and limited to, "Hello, how are you?" I often felt flustered when Reggie needled me, but I always got my job done.

On two consecutive weekends in February I had to go away. I was quite worried since I had never asked for time off, even though the other girls often did so. After several days of pondering, Mrs. M and Bob consented. I wondered how they felt about this, whether they thought I was taking advantage of them or what. They must have been irritated because after the second weekend, they never called me to come in to work again. I suppose I could have called and asked, but I didn't know who was supposed to, so I didn't. . . .

Well, that's the story. I respected that gang because they were attractive, popular girls, but I sure didn't like the way they worked. They certainly were less than conscientious about keeping things clean, despite Mrs. M's making such a big thing about it. But at least I fulfilled my responsibilities; I get a better feeling when I act in a responsible manner. I didn't treat Mrs. M discourteously the way they did, talking about her behind her back when she was so nice to them! That seems unfair! But it was rough to feel so unwelcome and to always be the outsider.

Exercise 1

Now that you are thoroughly familiar with the incident, meet with three or four of your classmates and answer the questions that follow. Be prepared to present your answers to the class.

a.   What factors contributed to the situation experienced by Jenny? Explain.

b.   How does Jenny see herself? Explain.

c. How do the others at Laird's see Jenny?

d. Is Jenny of lower status? Higher status? Explain.

e. What group norms were operating at Laird's Steak House?

f. How would you explain Susan's behavior when alone with Jenny?

g.   If you were in Jenny's shoes, what would you have done to make the situation more satisfying to yourself? (Assume you have not yet asked for the two weekends off in February and that you are still working at Laird's Steak House.) Explain.

Exercise 2

In question *g* (exercise 1), you were asked to indicate the actions that you (as Jenny) would take to make your situation more satisfying. Now your group should prepare a role play to demonstrate the actions you would take to improve the situation. Be prepared to demonstrate the role play for the class if called upon to do so by your instructor. Instructions for role playing are in Appendix H.

Exercise 3

Explain what you have gained from this experience.

17 PRINCIPLES OF CONTROLLING

Chapter Summary

This chapter emphasizes four main topics: (1) fundamentals of controlling, (2) the controller and control, (3) power and control, and (4) performing the control function.

Learning Objective 1   *A definition of control*

Stated simply, **control** is making something happen the way it was planned to happen. As implied in this definition, planning and control are virtually inseparable, and, in fact, have been called the Siamese twins of management. For control activities to exist within an organization, some activity or a process must be taking place within that organization. Managers should continually control or check to make sure that organizational activities and processes are going as planned.

Controlling is the process managers go through to control. According to Mockler, controlling is a systematic effort by business management to compare performance to predetermined standards, plans, or objectives to determine whether performance is in line with these standards and, presumably, to take any remedial action required to see that human and other corporate resources are being used in the most effective and efficient way possible in achieving corporate objectives.

Learning Objective 2   *A thorough understanding of the controlling subsystem*

As with the planning, organizing, and influencing subsystems described previously, controlling can be viewed as a subsystem that is part of the overall management system. The purpose of the controlling subsystem is to help managers to enhance the success of the overall management system through effective controlling.

The **three main steps of the controlling process are:** (1) measuring performance, (2) comparing measured performance to standards, and (3) taking corrective action. Before managers can determine what must be done to make an organization more effective and efficient, they must *measure current organizational performance*. Before such a measurement can be taken, some unit of measure that gauges the performance must be established, and the quantity of this unit generated by the item whose performance is being measured must be observed. For example, if a manager wants to measure the performance of five janitors, the manager first has to establish units of measure that represent janitorial performance, such as the number of floors swept, the number of windows washed, and/or the number of light bulbs changed. After designating these units of measures for janitorial performance, the manager then has to determine the number of each of these units associated with each janitor. This process of determining the units of measure and the number of units per janitor furnishes the manager with a measure of janitorial performance. Managers also must keep in mind that a wide range of organizational activities can be measured as part of the control process. For example, the amounts and types of inventory kept on hand commonly are measured to control inventory, and the quality of goods and services being produced commonly is measured to control product quality. Performance measurements also can relate to various effects of production, such as the degree to which a particular manufacturing process pollutes the atmosphere. The relative degree of difficulty in measuring various types of organizational performance primarily is determined by the activity being measured.

Once managers have taken a measure of organizational performance, they should take the next step in controlling and *compare this measure against some standard*. A **standard** is the level of activity established to serve as a model for evaluating organizational performance. In essence, standards are the "yardsticks" that determine if organizational performance is adequate or inadequate. For example, American Airlines set the following standards for appropriate performance of airport ticket offices: (1) at least 95 percent of the flight arrival times posted should be accurate in that actual arrival times do not deviate fifteen minutes from posted times, and (2) at least 85 percent of the customers coming to the airport ticket counter do not wait more than five minutes to be serviced. As a general guideline, successful managers pinpoint all important areas of organizational performance and establish corresponding standards in each area.

Once managers have measured actual performance and compared this performance with established performance standards, they should *take corrective action if necessary*. **Corrective action** is managerial activity aimed at bringing organizational performance up to the level of performance standards. In other words, corrective action focuses on correcting the mistakes in the organization that are hindering organizational performance. Before taking any corrective action, however, managers should make sure that standards being used were properly established and that measurements of organizational performance are valid and reliable.

It seems fairly simple to state that managers should take corrective action to eliminate **problems**, factors within organizations that are barriers to organizational goal attainment. In practice, however, it may be extremely difficult to pinpoint the problem causing some undesirable organizational effect. For example, a performance measurement may indicate that a certain worker is not adequately relaying critical information to fellow workers. Once the manager is satisfied that the related communication standards are appropriate and that the performance measurement information is valid and reliable, he or she then must take some corrective action to eliminate the problem causing this substandard performance. However, what exactly is the problem causing substandard communication performance? Is the problem that the individual is not communicating because he or she doesn't want to communicate? Or is this individual not communicating adequately because the job being performed makes communication difficult? Does this individual have the training needed to enable him or her to communicate in an appropriate manner? The manager must determine whether this individual's lack of communication is a problem in itself or a **symptom**, a sign that some problem exists. For example, the individual's lack of communication could be a symptom of such possible problems as inappropriate job design or a cumbersome organizational structure.

Once an organizational problem has been identified, necessary corrective action can focus on one or more of the three primary management functions of planning, organizing, and influencing. Correspondingly, corrective action can include such activities as modifying past plans to make them more suitable for future organizational endeavors, making an existing organizational structure more suitable for existing plans and objectives, or restructuring an incentive program to make sure that high producers are rewarded more than low producers. In addition, since planning, organizing, and influencing are so closely related, there is a good chance that corrective action taken in one area will necessitate some corresponding change in one or both of the other two areas.

Learning Objective 3 — *An appreciation for various kinds of control and how each kind can be used advantageously by managers*

There are **three types of management control:** (1) precontrol, (2) concurrent control, and (3) feedback control. Each type primarily is determined by the time period in which the control is emphasized in relation to the work being performed. Control that takes place before work is performed is called *precontrol or feed-forward control*. In this regard, management creates policies, procedures, and rules aimed at eliminating behavior that will cause future undesirable work results. Precontrol focuses on eliminating predicted problems. Control that takes place as work is being performed is called *concurrent control*. Concurrent control relates not only to human performance but also to such areas as equipment performance or department appearance. Control that concentrates on past organizational performance is called *feedback control*. When exercising this type of control, managers are attempting to take corrective action within the organization by looking at organizational history over a specified time period. This history can concentrate on only one factor, such as inventory levels, or on the relationships among many factors, such as net income before taxes, sales volume, and marketing costs.

It is clear that managers have the responsibility to compare planned and actual performance and to take corrective action when necessary. In smaller organizations, managers may be completely responsible for gathering information about various aspects of the organization and developing necessary reports based on this information. In medium- or large-sized companies, however, an individual called the **controller** usually exists. The controller's basic responsibility is assisting line managers with the controlling function by gathering appropriate information and generating necessary reports that reflect this information. The information with which the controller usually works generally reflects the following various financial dimensions of the organization: (1) profits, (2) revenues, (3) costs, (4) investments, and (5) discretionary expenses. The controller is responsible for generating appropriate information on which a manager can base the exercising of control. Since the controller generally is not directly responsible for taking corrective action within the organization and typically advises a manager of what corrective action should be taken, the controller position is primarily a **staff position.**

As with all organizational endeavors, control activities should be pursued if expected benefits of performing such activities are greater than the costs of performing them. The process of comparing the cost of any organizational activity with the expected benefit of performing the activity is called **cost-benefit analysis.** In general, managers and controllers should collaborate to determine exactly how much controlling activity is justified within a given situation. Generally, controlling costs increase steadily as more and more controlling activities are performed. In addition, since the controlling function begins with the incurrence of related "start-up" costs, controlling costs usually are greater than increased income generated from increased controlling. As controlling starts to correct major organizational errors, however, increased income from increased controlling eventually equals controlling costs and ultimately surpasses controlling costs by a large margin. However, as more and more controlling activity is added, controlling costs and increased income from increased controlling eventually are equal again. As more controlling activity is added beyond that point, controlling costs again surpass increased income from increased controlling. The main reason why this last development takes place is that major organizational problems probably have been detected much earlier, and corrective measures taken now primarily are aimed at smaller and more insignificant problems.

Learning Objective 4   *Insights on the relationship between power and control*

To control successfully, managers must understand not only the control process itself but also how organization members relate to the control process. Up to this point, nonhuman variables of controlling have been emphasized. The focus now, however, is on power, perhaps the most important human-related variable in the control process.

Perhaps the two most often confused terms in management are power and authority. **Authority** is the *right* to command or give orders. The extent to which an individual is able to influence others so that they respond to orders is called **power**. The greater this *ability* to influence others, the more power an individual is said to have. Obviously, power and control are closely related. To illustrate, after a manager compares actual performance with planned performance and determines that corrective action is necessary, orders usually are given to implement this action. Although these orders are issued on the manager's allotted organizational authority, they may or may not be followed precisely, depending on how much power the manager has over those individuals to whom the orders are issued.

The **total power** a manager possesses is made up of two different kinds of power: position power and personal power. *Position power* is power derived from the organizational position a manager holds. In general, moves from lower-level management to upper-level management accrue more position power for a manager. *Personal power* is power derived from a manager's human relationships with others. Managers can increase their total power by increasing their position power and/or their personal power. Position power generally can be increased by achieving a higher organizational position, but managers usually have little personal control over moving upward in an organization. On the other hand, managers generally have substantial control over the amount of personal power they hold over other organization members. Personal power is critical to managerial success because managers are always dependent on some people over whom they have no formal authority, and because virtually no one in modern organizations will passively accept and completely obey a constant stream of orders from someone just because he or she is the "boss." To increase personal power, a manager can attempt to develop (1) a sense of obligation in other organization members that is directed toward the managers, (2) a belief in other organization members that the manager possesses a high level of expertise within the organization, (3) a sense of identification that other organization members have with the manager, and (4) the perception in other organization members that they are dependent upon the manager.

Learning Objective 5   *Knowledge of the various potential barriers that must be overcome for successful control*

Controlling can be an extremely detailed and intricate process, especially as the size of the organization increases. Managers should take steps to avoid the following **potential barriers to successful controlling**:

1. Control activities can create an undesirable overemphasis on short-run production as opposed to long-run production. As an example, in striving to meet planned weekly production quotas, a manager might "push" machines in a particular area and not allow these machines to stop running to be serviced properly.
2. Control activities can increase employee frustration with their jobs and thereby reduce morale.
3. Control activities can encourage the falsification of reports. Employees may perceive management as basing corrective action solely on department records with no regard to extenuating circumstances related to the records. If this is the case, employees may feel pressured to falsify reports so that corrective action regarding their organizational unit will not be too drastic.
4. Control activities can cause the perspective of organization members to be too narrow for the good of the organization. Although controls can be designed to focus on relatively narrow aspects of an organization, managers must keep in mind that any corrective action should be considered not only in relation to the specific activity being controlled but also in relation to all other organizational units.
5. Control activities can be perceived as the goals of the control process rather than the means by which corrective action is taken. Control activities only can be justified within the organization if they yield some organizational benefit that extends beyond the cost of performing them.

Learning Objective 6   *An understanding of steps that can be taken to increase the quality of a controlling subsystem*

In addition to avoiding the potential barriers to successful controlling, managers can perform certain activities to make their control process more effective. In this regard, managers should make sure that various facets of the control process are appropriate for the specific organizational activity being focused on, that control activities are used to achieve many different kinds of goals, that information used as the basis for taking corrective action is timely, and that the mechanics of the control process are understandable to all individuals who are in any way involved with implementing the process.

Knowing You Know

Matching *Directions: Match items 1-10 with items a-j. There is only one correct answer for each item.*

_____ 1. An ingredient of measurement in controlling
_____ 2. Comparing measured performance to standards
_____ 3. A means of increasing position power
_____ 4. An example of precontrol
_____ 5. Overemphasis on short-run production
_____ 6. An example of concurrent control
_____ 7. Taking corrective action
_____ 8. A means of increasing personal power
_____ 9. An individual's power
_____ 10. An example of feedback control

a. Managerial activity aimed at bringing organizational performance up to the level of performance standards
b. A manager moving from lower-level management to upper-level management
c. Potential barrier to successful controlling
d. Observation of the quantity of this unit generated by the item whose performance is being measured
e. Management creating policies, procedures, and rules aimed at eliminating behavior that will cause future undesirable work results
f. Stock manager making periodic visual checks to evaluate the status of sales shelves
g. Looking at inventory from a historical perspective
h. The second of the three steps of the control process
i. The ability to influence others
j. Creating the perception in organization members that they are dependent upon you

True/False *Directions: On the lines provided, place a "T" for true or an "F" for false for each of the statements that follow.*

_____11. Controlling and influencing are so inseparable that they have been called the Siamese twins of management.
_____12. According to your text, there are three steps in the control process: precontrol, concurrent control, and feedback control.
_____13. One ingredient needed to take a control measurement is the establishment of some unit of measure that gauges the performance.
_____14. Successful managers pinpoint all important areas of organizational performance and establish corresponding standards in each area.
_____15. It is fairly simple to discriminate between symptoms and problems.
_____16. Small- to medium-sized companies usually employ an individual with the title "controller."
_____17. As more and more controlling activity is added, controlling costs eventually will surpass the increased income from increased controlling.
_____18. While total authority comes from the organization, total power comes from the individual.
_____19. Control activities can encourage the falsification of reports.
_____20. Personal power is critical to managerial success because managers are always dependent on some people over whom they have no formal authority.
_____21. As the size of the organization increases, the controlling process generally becomes less detailed and intricate because of the increased number of managers available to provide control.
_____22. A plan is only as good as one's ability to control it.
_____23. Controllers and managers frequently collaborate to determine how much control is necessary in a given situation.
_____24. There is a good probability that corrective action taken in the area of organizing will necessitate some corresponding change in the area of planning but less change in the area of influencing.
_____25. To control successfully, a manager must understand the control process as well as how organization members relate to the control process.

Applying What You Know

Experience 17-1 Fare Discrepancies on Bus 41[*]

Introduction

Control is making something happen the way it was planned to happen. Controlling, the process managers go through to control, is simply the systematic effort by business management to measure performance; to compare performance to predetermined standards, plans, or objectives; and to take any corrective or remedial action required to see that human and other corporate resources are being used in the most effective and efficient way possible to achieve corporate objectives. In this experience, you apply your knowledge of the control process. Read the incident that follows, and then complete the exercises as directed.

Incident

Chief Inspector Halley boarded bus 41 and dropped a token into the fare box. It gave the usual satisfying "ting" as it passed through the mechanism. He sat in the first seat to the right of the driver and watched.

Halley was responsible for checking fare thefts for City-Suburban Transit. He liked the job, which involved his traveling extensively to the subsidiary companies, making sure that drivers were not taking cash fares instead of reporting them. None of the drivers knew who he was, and at times his job was much like a detective's.

The company had fare boxes that registered the fare with a small meter and a "ting." The meter was deliberately designed so that inspectors, such as Halley, could unobtrusively observe it from the front seat. At the moment, this meter showed twenty-seven fares collected.

The bus stopped, and six people boarded. One gave a transfer; the others dropped tokens and coins into the box. There were five "tings" as they did so, but the man with a transfer blocked Halley's view of the fare box. When he moved away, the register showed thirty fares.

Halley was on the scent now. He carefully noted the next stops, mentally keeping track of the fares collected by counting the "tings." At the end of the run, he had counted 226 fares, but the meter showed only 122. He recalled that Jackson, the supervisor, had been complaining about the low earning power of this run, considering its traffic potential.

Halley got up to leave the bus as five people boarded. Deliberately, he situated himself so that he could watch the driver. There was a slight bulge in the driver's jacket pocket. The driver took four fares in his hand and held his hand over the box. Four "tings" registered, but the meter moved only once. Halley's trained ear caught several "tings" coming from the driver's pocket. It was the old familiar game in the transit business--the bell machine in the pocket. This one was quite small and pretty good. Halley smiled as he got off to phone in his preliminary report to the main office and to prepare the written report that would be the basis of action against the driver.

[*]Source of Experience 17-1: From *Incidents in Applying Management Theory* by Richard N. Farmer, Barry M. Richman, and William G. Ryan. © 1966 by Wadsworth Publishing Company, Belmont, CA. Reprinted by permission of the authors.

Exercise 1

Now that you have thoroughly familiarized yourself with the incident, group with three or four other class members and analyze the situation at City-Suburban Transit. (Assume that you are the top management group that will have to decide what to do about the situation on bus 41.) Be prepared to explain in management terminology what has transpired at City-Suburban Transit and what actions, if any, you would take to rectify the situation. Your instructor may select one group to present its analysis of the situation to the class.

Exercise 2

Maintaining discipline is one of the perennial problems of management. In general, there are two approaches that can be used in resolving disciplinary problems: a *judicial approach*--determining the rightness or wrongness of an act as defined by a specific rule and applying the penalty prescribed--and a *human relations approach*--an emphasis on problem solving with an ultimate goal of improving the employee's behavior.

a. Which approach do you feel that you (or your group) used in dealing with the bus driver?

b.   Why did you use this approach?

Exercise 3

Explain what you have gained from this experience.

Experience 17-2 Correcting without Punishment[**]

Introduction

The act of making corrections may very well be the most distasteful task that supervisors and managers must perform because, no matter how tactfully it is handled, it is generally perceived by subordinates to be punishment. And managers know that there is a reaction to the action of punishment, often with dysfunctional consequences for the organization and, more specifically, the manager. Yet, all effective managers are faced with having to take corrective action when they discover that actual subordinate performance does not coincide with planned performance. Fortunately, there are ways to correct subordinates that do not generate these negative reactions. This experience begins with an actual corrective interview with an employee.

Interview with Miss Winkler

This conversation takes place in the office of Mr. Zurch, Director of Personnel for an organization employing about 3,500 persons. Miss Winkler has been reported by her supervisors as doing unsatisfactory work; they ask that she be transferred on the basis of a list of charges outlined in a memorandum. Mr. Zurch has sent for Miss Winkler, who enters his office while he is talking to an assistant about another matter. Also present in the office at the time of the interview, but presumably not able to hear the conversation and doing other work, are Mr. Zurch's secretary, his assistant, and the recorder of the interview. Inasmuch as Miss Winkler speaks in a low tone, all her comments are not audible to the recorder, especially as she becomes more emotional and finally tearful, but the conversation is substantially as follows:

W: Did you send for me, Mr. Zurch?

Z: Yes, I did; I'll be with you in just a minute. (Mr. Zurch continues to talk to his assistant for seven minutes. During this time, there is considerable confusion in the office, with the telephone ringing often, and with Mr. Zurch becoming more and more concerned over some matter about which he talks loudly, interspersing his rather definite comments with considerable swearing. This, it may be noted, is his usual manner under stress. Mr. Zurch continues.) Now, look, Miss Winkler (takes several minutes to look over her file and to talk to his assistant about another matter), you remember we talked together in March, and at that time B Division was not satisfied, and since you have been with Mr. Newton, and he was not altogether satisfied.

W: He didn't tell me anything like that. (Speaks in a low, courteous voice.) He told me after I left that he wanted me back. . . .

Z: Now you have been in C Division, and there is a report on your work there. Now, Miss Winkler, we take each employee and try to fit her in where she can do the best job. We realize that people sometimes can't get along because of the supervisor, or fellow employees, and we try to make adjustments. (This comment is given in Mr. Zurch's usual direct and rather belligerent manner.) Now you have been in a number of positions. How many have you occupied?

W: (After thinking a moment) Four or five.

Z: Do you agree with the comments made in this report? (Quotes from report before him on the desk:) "Shows little interest in work and says she doesn't care for filing."

W: (Miss Winkler's voice is growing husky now and her response is almost inaudible, but she explains that she doesn't like filing and that she wasn't hired to do that kind of work. She was to be a stenographer.)

Z: We don't have the work always to everyone's satisfaction.

W: But I wasn't told that was what the job would be.

Z: But we can't give someone a job he wants. . . . (Interview has turned into something of an argument at this point; Mr. Zurch presents next charge:) "Deliberately slows down on the job."

W: No, I do not. (Miss Winkler seems quite incensed at this charge.)

Z: "Uses business hours to write letters."

W: I did that *once*.

Z: "Doesn't keep up-to-date with her work."

W: They put in a new system up there, and the supervisor asked me to help with it, and I said I would. But I couldn't keep up-to-date on my own work and do that too. The supervisor asked me to do this at the same time that I had more than enough work of my own to do. (Though deeply disturbed at these charges, Miss Winkler's responses are direct; by this time, however, she is on the verge of tears.)

[**]Source of Experience 17-2: Adaption from pages 93-116 from *Handling Barriers in Communication* by Irving J. Lee and Laura L. Lee. Copyright © 1956, 1957 by Laura L. Lee. Reprinted by permission of Harper & Row, Publishers, Inc.

Z: "Leaves fifteen minutes before noon and returns twenty to twenty five minutes late."

W: If I went before noon, I returned earlier.

Z: "Uses restroom facilities on second floor instead of third as required by the rules."

W: They were dirty on the third floor.

Z: We can't be in these rooms every minute of the day. When I went in there (apparently at an earlier complaint), it wasn't dirty--only a few papers thrown around. It wasn't like any bathroom at home, but it wasn't dirty.

W: I have seen it at times when you couldn't use it.

Z: Why didn't you report it?

W: I did--but that's a petty thing (i.e., the complaint).

Z: Yes, but it means five to ten minutes more away from your desk. Listen, Miss Winkler, I think the supervisor doesn't have an axe to grind; maybe all of these things aren't true, but a certain amount is.

W: I did the work I was told to do, but some had to be left over. They expected me to get the mail out, and certain work had to be left.

Z: That's right, but there are those times when you were away from your work. (Mr. Zurch explains the limitations on the number of persons the organization may hire, that each girl must do her work, or the organization will get behind.)

W: I still think the charges aren't fair.

Z: Well, tell me, are there any differences between you and Jones (her immediate supervisor)?

W: I'd rather not say.

Z: Don't you get along?

W: Oh, sometimes.

Z: Please tell me the story. . . . (When apparent there will be no response:) Did you go over this with Miss Counce (the counselor)?

W: (Miss Winkler replies that she did, but by this time she is crying softly, and the exact words are not heard.)

Z: We have a reputation of being fair. We try to analyze every factor in a report of this kind. . . . You have been here two years, long enough to know the whole story. . . . Do you think you aren't in the right job?

W: I want to leave the job.

Z: (In a milder tone:) Now, that's not the right attitude. We won't get anywhere that way. Has Mr. Achen (a higher supervisor) ever talked to you?

W: Not once.

Z: Has the principal clerk of the department talked to you about it?

W: Yes, once. (Two sentences are not heard.)

Z: Do you think your work too heavy?

W: I can keep it cleaned up at times, but not all the time. There are days when with dictation, etc., I can't.

Z: Well, why don't we have the job analyzed on a week's basis and see if there is too much for one person.

W: A week wouldn't be right; once I was behind for three weeks.

Z: Honestly, haven't you taken extra time off?

W: No, absolutely not. I've noticed other girls going out when they weren't support to, though.

Z: Are you getting along with other employees?

W: Yes.

Z: Well, I'll tell you, go back upstairs after you get set (i.e., after she has made repairs on her face because of the crying). Do you have any other comment to make?

W: I feel he (supervisor) has been very unfair about my slowing down on my work.

Z: All right, O.K., now you stay down until, let's see, it's 3:30 now, until 3:45. I'll call them to expect you at 3:45.

Mr. Zurch's comment after the interview: "This girl comes from a good family and environment and apparently feels that she has a better head than the other workers. Our problem is to get her adjusted. I disagree with this report that she purposely slowed down on the job. The fact that she didn't like filing is nothing against her; we have that trouble all the time. But there is no question that she takes time off. I think 50 to 60 percent of the charges are correct, and the rest is put on for a good story. We'll find that the supervisor hasn't talked to her correctly. She would be a better employee under a girl who could handle her or a smart-looking man. You noted that she was especially indignant at charges of slowing down, but not so indignant on spending extra time out."

Mr. Zurch calls the immediate supervisor and the next higher supervisor into his office to discuss the situation.

Z: What is it all about, this Winkler case?

MR. ACHEN: Her attitude is wrong. She wants to be a stenographer, and she was hired as a clerk-typist, and there isn't a 100 percent steno job up there. We give her some dictation but can't give her full time. She doesn't want to do filing.

JONES: She gets behind. (Telephone call interrupts.)

MR. ACHEN: She said to someone, "I'll let this filing pile up and just see what happens." I think for the good of the department she should be transferred. (Another telephone call interrupts.)

Z: But we can't transfer her all the time.

MR. ACHEN: We spoke to her about the restrooms, but she disregards the rules. We have given her a fair chance.

Z: O.K., thanks a lot. (Apparently, the decision is to transfer Miss Winkler to another department. Mr. Zurch goes off to a meeting.)

Exercise 1

What impressed you (or may be depressed you) about this corrective interview? Explain.

Exercise 2

What should be accomplished in a good corrective interview? Explain.

Exercise 3

What guidelines can you develop from exercise 2 that can be used to structure a good corrective interview?

Exercise 4

Do you think you can apply the corrective guidelines you developed in exercise 3? In this exercise, you will be given the opportunity to test your ability by role playing a corrective interview. One member of your triad will take the role of the boss (person making the correction), one the role of the employee (person being corrected), and the third person an observer who will give feedback to the "corrector" on the guidelines that were overlooked and *how* the interview could have been improved. Solutions to three different situations will be played out, so each person will be given the opportunity to play each role (corrector, correctee, and observer). Use the space provided to write observer comments when that is your role.

Exercise 5

Explain what you have gained form this experience.

18 PRODUCTION MANAGEMENT AND CONTROL

Chapter Summary

This chapter emphasizes the fundamentals of production control, which is ensuring that an organization produces goods and services as planned. The three primary discussion areas in this chapter are: (1) production, (2) operations management, (3) operations control, and (4) selected operations control tools.

Learning Objective 1 *Definitions of production, productivity, and quality*

Production is simply defined as the transformation of organizational resources into products. Within this definition, organizational resources are all assets available to a manager to generate products, transformation is the set of steps necessary to change organizational resources into products, and products are various goods or services aimed at meeting human needs.

Productivity, on the other hand, is the relationship between the total amount of goods or services being produced (output) and the organizational resources needed (input) to produce the goods and services. This relationship is expressed by the equation:

Productivity = Outputs/Inputs.

The higher the value of the ratio of outputs to inputs, the higher the productivity of the operation. Some of the more *traditional strategies for increasing productivity* include improving the effectiveness of the work force through training, improving the production process through automation, improving product design to make products easier to assemble, improving the production facility by purchasing more modern equipment, and improving the quality of workers being hired to fill open positions. **Quality** can be defined as how well a product does what it is intended to do--how closely and reliably it satisfies the specifications to which it is built. In a broad sense, quality is a degree of excellence on which products or services can be ranked on the basis of selected features or characteristics.

During the last several years, managerial thinking about the relationship between quality and productivity has changed drastically. Managers once saw little relationship between improving quality and increasing productivity. Improving quality was viewed largely as a controlling activity that took place somewhere near the end of the production process. Since this emphasis on improving quality typically resulted in simply rejecting a number of finished products that could otherwise be offered to customers, efforts to improve product quality were generally believed to lower productivity. Many earlier managers chose to achieve higher levels of productivity simply by producing a greater number of products given some fixed level of available resources.

Management theorists have more recently found that improving product quality during all phases of a production process actually improves the productivity of the system that manufactures the product. As early as 1948, Japanese companies observed that such improvements in product quality normally resulted in improved productivity. How does this happen? According to Dr. W. Edwards Deming, a world-renowned quality expert, a serious and consistent quality focus normally reduces nonproductive variables like the reworking of products, production mistakes, delays and production snags, and poor use of time and materials.

According to Deming, for continual improvement to become a way of life, management needs to understand the company and its operations. Most managers feel they know their company and its operations, but when they begin drawing flowcharts, they discover that their understanding of strategy, systems, and processes is not complete. Deming recommends that managers question every aspect of an operation and involve workers in discussion before improving operations. Deming believes that a manager who seriously focuses on improving product quality throughout all phases of a production process initiates a set of chain reactions that benefits not only the organization but the society in which the organization exists.

Deming's flow diagram introduces the customer to the operations process and introduces the idea of continually refining knowledge, design, and inputs to the process so as to constantly increase customer satisfaction. The diagram shows the whole process as an integrated operation. From the first input to actual use of the finished product, it is one process; a problem at the beginning will impact on the whole and the end product. There are no barriers between the company and the customer, between the customer and its suppliers, between the company and its people. The process is unified: the greater the harmony along all components, the better the results.

Quality assurance involves a broad group of activities that are aimed at achieving the organization's quality objectives. An organization's interpretation of quality is expressed in its strategies. Quality, cost, availability, flexibility, and dependability are competitive weapons.

Quality assurance is a much broader concept than statistical quality control. **Statistical quality control** is the process used to determine how many products from a larger number should be inspected to calculate a probability that the total number of products meets organizational quality standards. Quality is a characteristic that makes something what it is. Product quality determines an organization's reputation. It is the customer who determines what quality is. Customers define quality in terms of appearance, performance, availability, flexibility, and reliability.

Quality assurance is a continuum of activities that start when quality standards are set and end when quality goods and services are delivered to the customer. An effective quality assurance strategy reduces the need for quality control and subsequent corrective actions. Quality assurance is best when a "no rejects" philosophy is adopted by management. Unfortunately, for most mass-produced products, this is not economically feasible. Employees should approach production with a "do not make the same mistake once" mind-set. Mistakes are costly. Detecting defective products in the final quality control inspection is too late and too expensive. Emphasizing quality in the early stages--during product and process design-- will reduce rejects.

Recently, managers have involved all of a company's employees in quality control. In general, management solicits the ideas of employees in judging and maintaining product quality. This trend toward more involvement of employees in quality control developed from a control system originating in Japan called quality circles. Although many corporations are now moving beyond the concept of the quality circle to the concept of the work team, as discussed in chapter 16, many of the ideas generated from quality circles continue to be valid. **Quality circles** are simply small groups of workers who meet to discuss a particular project in terms of quality assurance. Solutions to the problems are communicated directly to management at a formal presentation session.

Most quality circles are similar in the way they operate. Each circle is usually under eight members in size, and leaders of the circles are not necessarily the members' supervisors. Members may be outsiders or task members. The focus is on operational problems rather than interpersonal ones. Although the problems to be discussed are sometimes assigned by management, they can also be uncovered by the group itself.

Automation--including **robots**, mechanical devices built to perform repetitive tasks efficiently, and **robotics**, an area of study dealing with the development and use of robots--shows promising signs of increasing organizational productivity in a revolutionary way. Over the past twenty years, a host of advanced manufacturing systems have been developed and implemented to support operations. Most of these advanced systems are automated systems that combine hardware-industrial robots and computers--and software. **Automation** means that electro-mechanical devices replace human effort. Human effort in operations includes welding, materials handling, design, drafting, and decision making. The goals of new automation include reduced inventories, higher productivity, and faster billing and product distribution cycles. The Asian countries appear to be doing the best job of making optimal use of company resources through automation.

Learning Objective 2   *An understanding of the importance of operations and production strategies, systems, and processes*

According to Kemper and Yehudai, an effective and efficient operations manager is skilled not only in management, production, and productivity but also in strategies, systems, and processes. A **strategy** is a plan of action. A **system** is a particular linking of organizational components that facilitates carrying out a process. A **process** is a flow of interrelated events toward a goal, purpose, or end. Strategies create interlocking systems and processes when they are comprehensive, functional, and dynamic--when they designate responsibility and provide criteria by which to measure output.

Learning Objective 3   *Insights on the role of operations management concepts in the work place*

Operations management deals with managing production in organizations. According to Chase and Aquilano, operations management is the performance of the managerial activities entailed in selecting, designing, operating, controlling, and updating production systems. These activities can be categorized as either periodic (performed from time to time) or continual (performed without interruption).

Operations management is the systematic direction and control of operations processes that transform resources into finished goods and services. The concept conveys three key notions: First, operations management involves managers, people who get things done by working with or through other people. Second, operations management takes place within the context of objectives and policies that drive the organization's strategic plans. Third, the criteria relevant for judging the actions taken as a result of operations management are standards for effectiveness and efficiency. **Effectiveness** is the degree to which managers attain organizational objectives--"doing the right things." **Efficiency** is the degree to which organizational resources contribute to productivity--"doing things right." A review of performance based on these standards (feedback) is essential.

Operations strategies--*capacity, location, product, process, layout,* and *human resources*--are designed to assure that resources are obtained and used effectively and efficiently. An **operational strategy** is implemented by people who get things done with and through people. It is achieved in the context of objectives and policies derived from the organization's strategic plan.

Capacity strategy is a plan of action aimed at providing the organization with the right facilities to produce the needed output at the right time. The output capacity of the organization determines its ability to meet future demands for goods and services. *Insufficient capacity* results in loss of sales that in turn affects profits. *Excess capacity* results in higher production costs. The *optimal capacity strategy*, where quantity and timing are in balance, provides an excellent basis for minimizing operating costs and maximizing profits.

Capacity flexibility enables the company to deliver its goods and services to its customers in a shorter time than its competitors. Capacity flexibility is part of capacity strategy and includes having flexible plants and processes, broadly trained employees, and easy and economical access to external capacity such as suppliers.

Managers use capacity strategy to balance the costs of overcapacity and undercapacity. The inability to accurately forecast long-term demand makes the balancing task difficult and risky. Modifying long-range capacity decisions while in production is difficult and costly. In a highly competitive environment, construction of a new high-tech facility might take longer than the life cycle of the product. In the case of overcapacity, closing a plant saddles management with a high economic cost and an even higher social cost. Closing a plant is a tremendous burden on employees and the community in which the plant operates. These high social costs will have an adverse effect on the firm.

Traditionally, the concept of economies of scale has led to large plants that tried to do everything. More recently, the concept of the focused facility has suggested that better performance can be achieved if the plant is more specialized, concentrates on fewer tasks, and is therefore smaller.

A five-step process can aid management in making sound strategic capacity decisions: (1) measure the capacity of currently available facilities; (2) estimate future capacity needs based on demand forecasts; (3) compare future capacity needs and available capacity to determine whether capacity must be increased or decreased; (4) identify ways to accommodate long-range capacity changes (expansion or reduction); and (5) select the best alternative based on a quantitative and qualitative evaluation.

Location strategy is a plan of action that provides the organization with a competitive location for its headquarters, manufacturing, service, and distribution activities. A competitive location results in lower transportation and communication costs among the various facilities, costs that may run as high as 20 to 30 percent of a product's selling price. These costs greatly affect the volume of sales and amount of profit generated by a particular product. Additionally, many other quantitative and qualitative factors are important when formulating location strategy.

A successful location strategy requires a company to consider the following major location factors in its location study: the nearness to market and distribution centers; the nearness to vendors and resources; the requirements of federal, state, and local governments; the character of direct competition; the degree of interaction with the rest of the corporation; the quality and quantity of labor pools; the environmental attractiveness of the area; the requirements of taxes and financing; the kinds of existing and potential transportation; and the quality of utilities and services. The dynamic nature of these factors could make what is a competitive location today an undesirable location in five years. **Product strategy** is a way of deciding which goods and services an organization will produce and market. Product strategy is a main component of the operations strategy and the link between the operations strategy and the other functional strategies, especially marketing and research and development. Product, marketing, and research and development strategies fit together to build an effective overall operations strategy. Together, they form the product aspect of the business strategy. The product strategy and the operations strategy of the business should take into account the strengths and weaknesses of operations, which are primarily internal, as well as those of other functional areas which deal more with external opportunities and threats.

Cooperation and coordination among marketing, operations, and research and development from the inception of a new product is beneficial to the company. As the very least, it ensures a smooth transition from research and development to production. Operations people are able to contribute to the quality of the total product, not just attempt to improve the quality of the components. Even the most sophisticated product can be designed so that it is relatively simple to produce, reducing the number of units that must be scrapped or reworked during production and reducing the need for highly trained and highly paid employees. The product's price competitiveness or profits can thus increase.

Process strategy determines the means and the methods that the organization uses to transform resources into goods and services. Materials, labor, information, equipment, and managerial skills are resources that must be transformed. A competitive process strategy will ensure the most efficient and effective use of the organization's resources.

Manufacturing processes may be grouped into three different types. The first type is the *continuous process*, a product-oriented high volume, low-variety process, used for example, in producing chemicals, beer, and petroleum products. The second type is the *repetitive process*, a product-oriented production process that uses modules, used for producing items in large lots. This mass-production or assembly-line process is used in the auto and appliance industries. The third manufacturing process is used to produce small lots of custom-designed products such as furniture and is commonly known as the *job-shop process*, a high variety, low volume system. The production of one-of-a-kind items is included in this type of process, as is unit production. Spaceship and weapons system production are considered job-shop activities. It is common for an organization to use more than one type of manufacturing process at the same time and in the same facility.

Process strategy is directly linked to product strategy. The decision to select a particular process strategy may be the result of external market opportunities or threats. When this is true, the product takes center stage and the process becomes a function of the product. The corporation decides what it wants to produce then it selects a process strategy to produce it. The function of process strategy is to determine what equipment will be used, what maintenance will be necessary, and what level of automation will be most effective and efficient. The type of employees and the level of employee skills needed are a direct result of the process strategy.

Layout strategy is concerned with the location and flow of all organizational resources around, into, and within production and service facilities. A cost-effective and cost-efficient layout strategy is one that minimizes the cost of processing, transporting, and storing materials throughout the production and service cycle. A layout strategy is closely linked, directly and indirectly, to the rest of the components of operations strategy--capacity, location, product, process, and human resource. The layout strategy is usually one of the last to be formulated. It must target capacity and process requirements It must satisfy the organization's product design, quality, and quantity requirements. Finally, it must target facility and location requirements. An effective layout strategy will be compatible with the organization's available quality of work life. A **layout** is the overall arrangement of equipment, work areas, service areas, and storage areas within a facility that produces goods or provides services. The three basic types of layouts for manufacturing facilities are product, process, and fixed position.

1. **A product layout** is appropriate for organizations that produce and service a limited number of different products. It is not appropriate for an organization that is involved with constant or frequent changes of products. A product layout is most appropriate when the production volumes are high, equipment is highly specialized, and the employees' skills are narrow.
2. **A process (functional) layout** is appropriate for organizations involved in a large number of different tasks. It best serves an organization whose production volumes are low, equipment is multipurpose, and employees' skills are broad.
3. The **fixed position layout** is most appropriate for an organization whose product is stationary while resources flow.

A *group technology layout* is a cell of a product layout within a larger process layout. It benefits organizations that require both types of layout. Most manufacturing facilities are a combination of two or more different types of layouts. Various techniques assist in designing an efficient and effective layout that meets the required specifications.

Human resources are individuals engaged in any of the organization's activities. There are two human resource imperatives: (1) the need to optimize individual, group, and organizational effectiveness; and (2) the need to enhance the quality of organizational life. A **human resource strategy** is a plan to use the organization's human resources effectively and efficiently while maintaining or improving the quality of work life.

The human resource management function is about employees. Employees are the means of enhancing organizational effectiveness. Human resource management (personnel management) attempts to increase organizational effectiveness through the establishment of personnel policies, education and training, procedures, and management methods.

Operations management attempts to increase organizational effectiveness by the methods used in the manufacturing and service processes. The skill level of the operations employees must be compatible with operations tasks. **Manpower planning** is the primary focus of the operations human resource strategy. Hiring the right employees for a job and training them to be productive is a lengthy and costly process. Fair treatment and trust are the basis of a human resource strategy. The employee, not operations, takes center stage.

Job design, on the other hand, is concerned with who will do a specific job and with how and where the job will be done. The goal of job design is to facilitate productivity. Successful job design takes into account efficiency and behavior. Job design must also guarantee that working conditions are safe and that the health of the employees will not be jeopardized in the short or long run. **Work methods analysis** is used to improve productivity and can be performed for new or existing jobs. **Motion study techniques** are also used to improve productivity. **Work measurement methods** are used to establish labor standards, These standards can be used for planning, control, productivity improvements, costing and pricing, bidding, compensation, motivation, and financial incentives.

Learning Objective 4　　*An understanding of how operations control procedures can be used to control production*

Once a decision is made to design an operational plan of action, resource allocations are considered. After the functional operations strategy has been determined using marketing and financial plans of action, specific tasks to accomplish the functional objectives are considered. This is known as operations control.

Operations control specifies the activities to be carried out. Operations control includes *just-in-time inventory control, maintenance control, cost control; materials control, advanced manufacturing support, aggregate planning and master scheduling, inventory control, and resource requirements planning.*

Just-in-time (JIT) inventory control is a control technique that reduces inventories to a minimum by arranging for them to be delivered to the production facility "just in time" to be used. The concept, developed primarily by the Toyota Motor Company of Japan, is also called "zero inventory" and "kanban"--the latter, a Japanese term referring to purchasing raw materials by using a special card ordering form.

JIT is based on the management philosophy that products should be manufactured when customers need them and in the quantities customers need in order to minimize levels of raw materials and finished goods inventories kept on hand. Overall, JIT emphasizes maintaining operations within a company by using only the resources that are absolutely necessary to meet customer demand. JIT works best in companies that manufacture relatively standardized products and that have consistent product demand. Such companies can comfortably order materials from suppliers and assemble products in several small, continuous batches. The result is a smooth, consistent flow of purchased materials and assembled products and little inventory buildup. Companies that manufacture nonstandardized products that have sporadic or seasonal demand generally must face more irregular purchases of raw materials from suppliers, more uneven production cycles, and greater accumulations of inventory.

If implemented successfully, JIT can enhance organizational performance in several important ways. First, it can reduce unnecessary labor expenses generated by products manufactured but not sold. Second, it can minimize the tying up of monetary resources needed to purchase production related materials that do not result in sales on a timely basis. Third, it can help management minimize expenses normally associated with maintaining an inventory--for example, storage and handling costs. Better inventory management and improved control of labor costs are two of the most commonly cited benefits of JIT. Experience indicates that successful JIT programs tend to have certain common characteristics:

1. *Closeness of suppliers.*
2. *High quality of materials purchased from suppliers.*
3. *Well-organized receiving and handling of materials purchased from suppliers.*
4. *Strong management commitment to JIT.*

The goal of **maintenance control** is to keep the organization's facility and equipment at predetermined work levels. In the planning stage, managers must select a strategy that will direct personnel to fix equipment before it malfunctions or after it malfunctions. Fixing equipment before it malfunctions is referred to as a **pure-preventive maintenance policy**. At the other end of the maintenance continuum is the **pure-breakdown policy**--fixing equipment after it malfunctions.

Most organizations implement a maintenance strategy somewhere in the middle of the maintenance continuum. An attempt is made to select a level and a frequency of maintenance that minimizes the cost of preventive maintenance and of breakdowns (repair). Since no level of preventive maintenance can eliminate breakdowns completely, repair is always an important activity. Whether management decides on a pure-preventive or pure-breakdown policy, or something in between, the prerequisite for a successful maintenance program is the availability of maintenance parts and supplies or replacement (standby) equipment. Some organizations choose to keep standby machines to protect themselves against the consequences of breakdowns. Plants that use special-purpose equipment are more likely to invest in standby equipment than plants that have general-purpose equipment.

Cost control is an important responsibility of every manager. Operations functions are cost intensive--the most cost intensive of all management activities. When cost savings are realized, they are realized at the operations level. The importance of cost control cannot be overstated. Operations managers, in general, are responsible for the cost of goods sold. Producing goods and services at or below standard costs is the prime objective of operations managers. An operations manager is evaluated on the basis of cost. When costs are above expectations and standards, a change in leadership may be necessary. Cost control is a major component of an organization's business strategy. This emphasis on cost must filter into each functional activity of an organization--research and development, operations, marketing, and finance. Managers in each functional area must focus on cost control.

Any control process involves four stages: establishing standard values, measuring actual values, comparing actual values to standard values, and implementing needed changes. To control the cost of goods sold, cost standards must be established for labor, materials, and overhead. The collection and allocation of costs into different accounts are part of the measurement process. There are two basic methods of compiling costs: job costing and continuous processing. Each depends on the type of production process being used. Job costing requires data appropriate to a specific job or specific customer. Continuous processing costs are compiled for a specific operations activity or a specific department.

A **budget** is a single-use financial plan that covers a specified length of time. The budget of an organization is the financial plan outlining how funds in a given period will be obtained and spent. In addition to being a financial plan, however, *a budget is also a control tool.* As managers gather information on actual receipts and expenditures within an operating period, significant deviations from budgeted amounts may be uncovered. In such a case, managers can develop and implement a control strategy aimed at making actual performance more consistent with planned performance. This, of course, assumes that the plan contained in the budget is appropriate for the organization.

To maximize the benefits of using budgets, managers must be able to avoid several potential pitfalls. These **pitfalls** include:

1. *Placing too much emphasis on relatively insignificant organizational expenses.* In preparing and implementing a budget, managers should allocate more time for dealing with significant organizational expenses and less time for relatively insignificant organizational expenses.
2. *Increasing budgeted expenses year after year without adequate information.* It does not necessarily follow that items contained in last year's budget should be increased this year. Perhaps the best-known method developed to overcome this potential pitfall is zero-base budgeting. **Zero-base budgeting** is the planning and budgeting process that requires managers to justify their entire budget requests in detail rather than simply to refer to budget amounts established in previous years.
3. *Ignoring the fact that budgets must be changed periodically.* Managers should recognize that such factors as costs of materials, newly developed technology, and product demand constantly are changing and that budgets should be reviewed and modified periodically in response to these changes. A special type of budget called a **Variable budget** outlines various levels of resources to be allocated for each organizational activity, depending on the level of production within the organization. It follows, then, that a variable budget automatically indicates increases or decreases in the amount of resources allocated for various organizational activities, depending on whether production levels increase or decrease. Variable budgets also have been called **flexible budgets.**

Many managers believe that although budgets are valuable planning and control tools, they can result in major human relations problems in an organization. Depending on the severity of such problems, budgets may result in more harm to the organization than good. Several strategies have been suggested to minimize the human relations problems caused by budgets. The most often recommended strategy is to design and implement appropriate human relations training programs for finance personnel, accounting personnel, production supervisors, and all other key people involved in the formulation and use of budgets. These training programs should be designed to emphasize both the advantages and disadvantages of applying pressure on people through budgets and the possible results of using budgets to imply organization member success or failure.

Another tool to control costs is ratio analysis. A *ratio* is a relationship between two numbers that is calculated by dividing one number into the other. **Ratio analysis** is the process of generating information that summarizes the financial position of an organization through the calculation of ratios based on various financial measures that appear on the organization's balance sheet and income statements. The ratios available to managers for controlling organizations typically are divided into four categories: (1) liquidity ratios, (2) leverage ratios, (3) activity ratios, and (4) profitability ratios.

Managers can use ratio analysis in three ways to control an organization. *First managers should evaluate all ratios simultaneously.* This strategy ensures that managers will develop and implement a control strategy appropriate for the organization as a whole rather than one that suits only one phase or segment of the organization. *Second, managers should compare computed values for ratios in a specific organization with the values of industry averages for those ratios.* Managers can increase the probability of formulating and implementing appropriate control strategies by comparing their financial situation to that of competitors. *Third, managers' use of ratios to control an organization also should involve trend analysis.* Managers must remember that any set of ratio values is actually only a determination of relationships that exist in a specified time period, perhaps a year. To use ratio analysis to its maximum advantage, values for ratios should be accumulated for a number of successive time periods to uncover specific organizational trends. Once these trends are uncovered, managers can formulate and implement appropriate strategies for dealing with them.

Materials control supports the flow of materials from vendors through an operations system to customers. The ability to achieve the desired level of product cost, quality, availability, dependability, and flexibility depends heavily on the effective and efficient flow of materials. In its broadest form, materials management activities can be organized into six groups or functions: purchasing, receiving, inventorying, floor controlling, trafficking, and shipping and distributing. This structure is a result of a long process of organizational evolution. Over 50 percent of the expenditures of a typical manufacturing company are spent on procurement of materials, including raw materials, parts, sub-assemblies, and supplies, and the purchasing department is engaged in several activities. Purchasing of production materials is largely automated and linked to a resources requirement planning system. Purchasing of all other materials is based on a requisition from the user. Purchasing does not end with the placement of an order; order follow-up is equally crucial.

Receiving activities may include unloading, identifying, inspecting, reporting, and storing inbound shipments. Shipping and distribution activities are similar to receiving. They may include preparing documents, packaging, labeling, loading, and directing outbound shipments to customers and to distribution centers. Shipping and receiving activities are sometimes organized as one unit. A traffic manager's main activities include selection of the transportation mode, coordination of arrival and departure of shipments, and audit of freight bills.

Inventory control activities ensure the continuous availability of purchased materials. Work-in-process and finished-goods inventory are inventory control subsystems. Inventory control specifies what, when, and how much to buy. Held inventories buffer a variety of uncertainties that can disrupt supply. Since holding inventory is costly, an optimal inventory control policy must provide a predetermined level of certainty of supply at the lowest possible cost. Shop-floor control activities include input/output control, scheduling, sequencing, routing, dispatching, and expediting.

While many materials management activities can be programmed, it is the human factor that is the key to a competitive performance. Skilled and motivated employees are crucial.

Learning Objective 5

Insights concerning operations control tools and how they evolve into a continual improvement approach to production management and control

In addition to understanding production, operations management, and operations control, managers also should be aware of various operations control tools that can be used within an operations facility. A **control tool** is a specific procedure or technique that presents pertinent organizational information in a way that helps managers and workers develop and implement appropriate control strategy. That is, a control tool helps managers and workers pinpoint the organizational strengths and weaknesses on which a useful control strategy must focus. Continual improvement of operations is not theoretical. On a daily basis, organizations struggle with new ways of doing things. Organizations have different goals and strategies, but in many respects they are the same. The goal of continual improvement applies not just to money-making enterprises, but to those with other missions as well.

On the one hand, organizational leaders are continually changing systems and personal styles of management. And on the other, everyone within the organization is learning to live with change. **Continuous improvement** is nothing but the development and use of better methods.

Traditionally, managers believed that if you wanted good quality, you hired many inspectors. These inspectors made sure an operation was producing at the quality level expected. Inspectors simply examined and graded finished products or components, parts, or services at any stage of operation by measuring, tasting, touching, weighing, disassembling, destroying, and testing. The goal of inspection was to detect unacceptable quality levels before a bad product or service reached a customer. When inspectors found more defects they blamed the workers and increased the number of inspectors. Today, managers know that inspection will not catch problems built into the system. The traditional inspection process is not improvement and does not guarantee quality. **Inspection**, according to Deming, is a limited, grossly overused, and often misused tool. Further, Deming recommends that management stop relying on mass inspection to achieve quality. Deming advocates either 100 percent inspection in those cases where defect-free work is impossible or no inspection where the level of defects is acceptably small.

Management by exception is a control technique that allows only significant deviations between planned and actual performance to be brought to a manager's attention. Actually, management by exception is based on the exception principle, a management principle that appears in early management literature. The *exception principle* recommends that subordinates handle all routine organizational matters, leaving managers to handle only nonroutine, or exceptional, organizational issues.

Although exceptional issues might be uncovered when manages themselves detect significant deviation between standards and performance, some managers establish rules to ensure that exceptional issues surface as a matter of normal operating procedure. It is important to establish the rules carefully, so that a true deviation is always brought to the manager's attention. Such rules can be established in virtually any organizational area.

If appropriately administered, management by exception yields the added advantage of ensuring the best use of a manager's time. Because it brings only significant issues to the manager's attention, the possibility that the manager will spend valuable time working on relatively insignificant issues is automatically eliminated.

Management by objectives (MBO), as discussed in chapter 4, is a control tool in which the manager assigns a specialized set of objectives and action plans to the workers and then rewards the individuals on the goals that are reached. It is a control technique that has been implemented successfully in some corporations in order to use an employee-participative means to improve productivity.

Other well known quantitative tools commonly used to control the production of organizational goods and services include *decision-tree analysis, process control, value analysis, computer aided design (CAD)* and *computer aided manufacturing (CAM)*. **Decision-tree analysis**, as discussed in chapter 6, is a statistical and graphical multiphase decision-making technique containing a series of steps. Decision trees allow a decision maker to deal with uncertain events by determining the relative expected value of each alternative course of action. The probabilities of different possible events are known, as are the monetary payoffs that result from a particular alternative and a particular event. Decision trees are best used where capacity decisions involve several capacity expansion alternatives and where the selection of the alternative with the highest expected profit or the lowest expected cost is necessary.

Process control, also known as **statistical process control**, is a technique that assists in monitoring production processes. Production processes must be monitored continuously in order to assure that the quality of their output will be acceptable. An early detection of a faulty production process is preferred. It is less costly than the detection of parts that do not meet quality standards and must be scrapped or reworked. If a production process is out of control or shows unstable performance, corrective action must be taken. Process control can be implemented with the aid of graphical charts known as control charts.

Value analysis is a cost-control and cost-reduction technique that focuses primarily on material costs. The analysis is performed by examining all the parts and materials, and their functins. The analysis is aimed at reducing costs through cheaper components and materials in a way that will not affect product quality or appeal. Simplification of parts is also included in these efforts. Value analysis can result not only in cost savings, but sometimes in an improved product at the same time. Value analysis requires a team (company-wide) effort. The team should at least include personnel from operations, purchasing, engineering, and marketing.

Computer-aided design (CAD) systems include several automated design technologies. *Computer graphics* is used to design geometric specifications for parts. *Computer-aided engineering (CAE)* is used to evaluate and perform engineering analyses on a part. CAD also includes technologies that are used in process design. The design of parts for computer-controlled machine tools is an appropriate CAD function.

Computer-controlled machine tools and computer-aided inspection are examples of **computer-aided manufacturing (CAM) systems.** CAD and CAM processes can be linked through a computer, which can be very beneficial when production processes must be altered. The linkage enables design changes to be implemented in a very short period of time because CAD and CAM systems have the ability to share information easily.

Another control tool commonly used by managers is break-even analysis. **Break-even analysis** is the process of generating information that summarizes various levels of profit or loss associated with various levels of production. Break-even analysis typically includes seven basic ingredients: **Fixed costs** are expenses incurred by the organization regardless of the number of products produced. Examples of these costs would be real estate taxes, upkeep to the exterior of a business building, and interest expenses on money borrowed to finance the purchase of equipment. **Variable costs** are expenses that fluctuate with the number of products produced. Examples of variable costs include costs of packaging a product, costs of materials needed to make the product, and costs associated with packing products to prepare them for shipping. **Total costs** are simply the sum of fixed costs and variable costs associated with production. **Total revenue** is all sales dollars accumulated from selling manufactured products or services. Naturally, total revenue increases as more products are sold. **Profits** are defined as that amount of total revenue that exceeds the total costs of producing the products sold. **Loss** is that amount of the total costs of producing a product that exceeds the total revenue gained from selling the product. The **break-even point** is defined as that situation wherein the total revenue of an organization equals its total costs; the organization is generating only enough revenue to cover its costs. The company is neither gaining a profit nor incurring a loss.

There are two somewhat different procedures for determining the same break-even point for an organization: algebraic break-even analysis and graphic break-even analysis. Algebraic break-even analysis involves using a simple formula to determine that level of production at which an organization breaks even. In formula form, the break-even point is equal to fixed costs divided by the price minus variable costs. Graphic break-even analysis entails the construction of a graph that shows all critical elements within a break-even analysis.

The situation managers face usually determines which break-even method they should use. If managers simply desire a quick yet accurate determination of a break-even point, the algebraic method generally suffices. On the other hand, if managers desire a more complete picture of the cumulative relationships between a break-even point, fixed costs, and escalating variable costs, the graphic break-even method probably is more useful. Break-even analysis is a useful control tool because it helps managers to understand the relationships between fixed costs, variable costs, total costs, and profit and loss within an organization. Once these relationships are understood, managers can take steps to modify one or more of these variables to reduce significant deviation between planned profit levels and actual profit levels.

Knowing You Know

True/False   *Directions: On the lines provided, place a "T" for true or an "F" for false for each of the statements that follow.*

_____ 1. A budget is a multiple-use financial plan that covers a specific length of time.

_____ 2. From a human relations perspective, budgets may result in more harm to the organization than good.

_____ 3. The exception principle recommends that managers handle all routine matters, while subordinates are permitted to handle only nonroutine issues.

_____ 4. Algebraic break-even analysis is generally more useful than graphic break-even analysis because it gives managers a more complete picture.

_____ 5. A ratio is a relationship between two numbers that is calculated by dividing one number into the other.

_____ 6. Quality circles are often used to determine how many products from a larger number should be inspected to calculate a probability that the total number of products meets organizational quality standards.

_____ 7. The use of appropriate human relations training programs is recommended to overcome many of the human relations problems often associated with the use of budgets.

_____ 8. Robots are mechanical devices built to efficiently perform non-repetitive tasks.

_____ 9. Just-in-time (JIT) inventory control is also called "zero inventory" and "kanban."

_____ 10. Fixing equipment before it malfunctions is referred to as "pure-breakdown policy."

_____ 11. Process layout is a layout pattern that has workers, tools and materials rotating around a stationary product.

_____ 12. According to Chase and Aquilano, operations management is the performance of the managerial activities entailed in selecting, designing, operating, controlling, and updating production systems.

_____ 13. Statistical quality control and quality assurance are virtually synonymous themes.

_____ 14. One common characteristic of successful JIT programs is closeness of suppliers.

_____ 15. A "layout" is the overall arrangement of equipment, work areas, service areas, and storage areas within a facility that produces goods or provides services.

Multiple Choice   _Directions: Circle the letter of the word or phrase that best completes each statement._

16. Which of the following is both an important planning and control tool?
    a. management by exception
    b. break-even analysis
    c. ratio analysis
    d. budget
    e. human asset accounting

17. Productivity, the relationship between the total amount of goods or services being produced and the organizational resources needed to produce these goods and services is represented by the following formula:
    a. Productivity = Inputs/Outputs
    b. Productivity = Total Cost/Fixed Cost Plus Variable Cost
    c. Productivity = Outputs/Fixed Cost minus Variable Cost
    d. Productivity = Outputs/Inputs
    e. none of the above are correct

18. Which of the following is _not_ a traditional strategy for increasing productivity?
    a. improve the effectiveness of the organizational workforce through training.
    b. improve the productivity process through automation
    c. improve the quality of workers hired to fill open positions
    d. improve the production facility by purchasing more modern equipment
    e. all of the above are viable means of increasing productivity

19. One pitfall to effective budgeting is increasing budgeted expenses year after year without adequate information. One well-known method to overcome this potential pitfall is called
    a. zero-base budgeting
    b. flexible budgeting
    c. fixed budgeting
    d. variable budgeting
    e. none of the above are correct

20. When using ratios to control organizations, managers should
    a. evaluate all ratios simultaneously
    b. compare the computed values for ratios in a specific organization to the values of industry averages for those same ratios
    c. accumulate ratio information for a number of successive time periods to uncover specific trends
    d. all of these are correct statements
    e. none of the above are correct statements

21. The layout pattern based on grouping together similar types of equipment is known as
    a. product layout
    b. process layout
    c. fixed position layout
    d. generic layout
    e. none of the above are correct

22. Operations strategies include all of the following *except*:
    a. location strategy
    b. layout strategy
    c. product strategy
    d. service strategy
    e. capacity strategy

23. Included in human resources strategy would be all of the following *except:*
    a. manpower planning
    b. motion study techniques
    c. job-shop process
    d. job design
    e. work measurement methods

24. Which of the following statements is true of break-even analysis?
    a. Examples of variable costs might be packaging costs and real estate taxes.
    b. Total cost is simply the sum of all variable costs.
    c. Profits are all sales dollars accumulated from selling the products manufactured.
    d. The break-even point is defined as that situation wherein total variable costs are equal to the total revenue.
    e. None of these is correct.

25. Which formula for algebraic break-even analysis is correct?
    a. $BE = \dfrac{FC}{P - VC}$

    b. $BE = \dfrac{FC}{VC + P}$

    c. $BE = \dfrac{VC}{FC - P}$

    d. $BE = \dfrac{P - VC}{FC}$

    e. none of these is the correct formula

Applying What You Know

Experience 18-1   Quality Is Job 1: An Introduction to Statistical Process Control[*]

Introduction

In recent years, the quality of Japanese products has been impressive. One reason for Japan's success has been its widespread use of statistical process control (SPC), that is, the use of statistical methods to evaluate and improve production processes. This experience consists of four exercises designed to increase your understanding of SPC. Read the "Introduction to Statistical Process Control" that follows, and then complete the exercises as directed.

Introduction to Statistical Process Control

Concern about America's low productivity growth, in combination with the Japanese success in business and industry, has provoked much discussion about possible cures. One productivity improvement approach that has gained prominence recently is statistical process control (SPC). SPC is comprised of a set of systematic procedures for evaluating and improving quality, and hence--in the long run--productivity. SPC is most closely associated with W. Edwards Deming.

Deming, a statistician with a Ph.D. degree from Yale, developed SPC from earlier work done by Walter A. Shewhart, a Bell Laboratories physicist, in the 1920s and 1930s. When American managers didn't respond to SPC, Deming took his approach to Japan, where he became a national hero. (The Japanese government annually awards the prestigious Deming Prize to the company with the largest gain in productivity.) The Japanese have assiduously used Deming's approach to quality control in both the industrial and service sectors of their economy. Many attribute the success of the Japanese largely to their effective use of Deming's teachings.

Deming finally received widespread recognition in this country in June 1980 when he was featured in a popular NBC documentary titled "If Japan Can, Why Can't We?" Since then, several prominent American companies, including Ford and General Motors, have begun to use SPC to upgrade quality and productivity. These large companies have now required that their suppliers also implement SPC.

The following excerpt from a memo written by an executive of a major organization illustrates just how important SPC has become to many American companies:

> Due to automobile customer demand and foreign competition, the quality expectations of our vendors are changing. Our policy follows:
>
> 1. The Products Purchasing Department intends to purchase 100 percent good parts. No defects are expected. Our sources will be developed or eliminated until this goal is achieved.
> 2. Statistical process controls are to be implemented by vendors as soon as possible. . . .
> 3. It is mandatory that vendors' material meet all specifications. Vendors shipping nonconforming material are liable for contingent liability. This includes cost of downtime, sorting charges, premium transportation, and costs of product recalls.
> 4. Vendor failure to comply with this program or their deliberate falsification of records will be cause for elimination of the vendor as a future supplier.

There are two major aspects to Deming's approach. The first concerns Deming's overall philosophy of productivity improvement; the second concerns the specific statistical techniques used in SPC. To Deming, these two aspects are inseparable and mutually reinforcing; one cannot achieve sustained productivity improvement without applying both the philosophy of management and the special statistical techniques of SPC. Deming set forth his philosophy of management in his "fourteen points." These fourteen points contain the following three major themes:

1. *Constancy of purpose*--Deming emphasizes long-term planning as opposed to the more prevalent short-term orientation found in U.S. organizations. Constancy of purpose requires that managers have a long-term commitment to their company and that they become intimately familiar with and care deeply about the business and its products or services. Finally, constancy of purpose requires that top management make consistent and sustained efforts to keep the

---

[*]Source of Experience 18-1: This exercise was developed by Larry E. Mainstone, Valparaiso University, and Ariel S. Levi, Indiana University, South Bend. Used with the permission of the authors.

company current in new technology and procedures. This necessitates an emphasis on research and development and on training employees in new skills.

2. *Systems orientation*--A second major theme in Deming's approach is a strong systems orientation. According to Deming, 85 percent of the problems in products or services are due to faults within the system rather than to faults of the employee. Employees simply work in the system that management created. Thus, blaming workers is deemphasized, and responsibility for product or service quality is placed largely in the hands of management. Management's task is to provide or develop the organizational system (that is, the procedures, tools, raw materials) that enables workers to do their best.

3. *Objective measurement and standards*--The third theme running through Deming's fourteen points is an emphasis on objective measurement and standards. Ad hoc, "seat-of-the-pants" standard setting, judgement, diagnosis, and problem solving is distrusted. Precise operational definitions of product and service quality are to be developed, and objective, quantitative measurements of work outcomes are to provide the basis for evaluation and attempts at quality improvement. Various statistical techniques, taught to both workers and managers, are the "tools" by which work processes and outcomes are evaluated.

The second part of Deming's approach involves using statistical techniques to monitor in-process quality and research methods to isolate specific causes for the quality level. The most crucial elements of process control are described in the paragraphs that follow.

The most important assumption of SPC is that all processes exhibit variation. This variation, which is manifest both in tangible products (for example, the length of steel rods) and intangible performances (for example, the quality of a gymnast's routine), has two sources: normal and abnormal. *Normal variation* reflects numerous, natural, extraneous, and unsystematic factors that characterize the production or performance system. Such factors can be regarded as "chance" or "noise" in the system. When a process is in *statistical control* and the outcome being measured is continuous (for example, inches, ounces, degrees), it will exhibit a certain amount of variability around a modal (that is, most frequent) outcome. Generally, this variability, when graphed, will appear as a normal bell-shaped distribution.

Abnormal variation, in contrast, reflects the existence of a special or unusual factor affecting the system's process. The special factor (for example, a new employee operating the machine; a defective batch of components from a vendor) throws the systems "out of whack," producing outcomes that differ greatly from the modal outcome. A graph of the product variability will now be abnormal (that is, bimodal or skewed in one direction).

A primary objective of SPC is to determine whether variation in a product or service is due to normal or abnormal causes. If the variation is within normal bounds, the system should be left as is. Intervening in a system that is in statistical control is counter productive--it will merely result in greater variability and will not improve quality. However, if the variation is abnormal, intervention is called for to bring the process back into statistical control. This is done by identifying the special cause and eliminating it.

Determining whether variation is normal or abnormal is accomplished by statistical techniques and by control charts. These charts serve as signaling devises that tell the worker or manager when to intervene to diagnose and remove special causes. Without objective data and this charting method, it is easy to confuse normal and abnormal causes. This, in turn, has two unfortunate consequences. First, when normal variation is mistaken for abnormal variation, attempts to improve quality by greater effort or by tampering with the current work procedures are doomed to failure. The only result is increased variability, higher costs, and increased frustration as workers and managers try unsuccessfully to "remedy" the system. Second, when normal variation is attributed to the worker rather than to the system, the worker can be incorrectly rewarded or punished for the results that are beyond his or her control.

The histogram and the control chart are the main devices for distinguishing between normal and abnormal variation. You will learn how to construct and interpret a histogram in exercise 2, and how to construct and interpret a control chart in exercises 3 and 4.

Exercise 1

In small groups, answer each of the questions that follow.

a. Do you think American industry is in trouble? Why?

b. Many American managers believe that quality comes at the expense of productivity. Deming, however, believes that improving quality automatically improves productivity. Explain Deming's argument.

c. Why is it unfair and demoralizing to hold workers accountable for their performance when the process is in statistical control?

d. In your own words, explain the difference between normal variation and abnormal variation?

e. Compare and contrast Deming's management philosophy with another theory of management (for example, Theory X and Theory Y).

Exercise 2

The simplest way of determining whether a process is in statistical control is to measure the product and plot a histogram of the data. The process is said to be in statistical control if the histogram appears to approximate a normal distribution. However, if the histogram is bimodal or skewed, it signals the presence of an unusual cause that must be found and eliminated.

John Smith is the quality control engineer for the Patterson Rubber Company. A particular gasket is to be $.066 \pm .004$ inches. Some customers, however, are saying that they are receiving gaskets that are too thin. To investigate this claim, Smith has had a technician take a random sample of fifty gaskets and measure the thickness of each. The results are as follows (unit of measure = inches):

.063	.065	.059	.062	.061
.066	.063	.062	.063	.065
.062	.060	.062	.067	.063
.058	.062	.064	.061	.063
.061	.063	.064	.059	.062
.063	.067	.060	.062	.063
.064	.059	.066	.063	.061
.067	.065	.061	.062	.065
.058	.060	.061	.063	.062
.064	.061	.064	.065	.063

a. Construct a histogram of Smith's rubber gasket situation. First, make a frequency distribution of the random sample of gaskets by making tally marks in figure 18.1. Then convert the frequency distribution into a histogram in figure 18.2.

Figure 18.1 Frequency distribution table.

Class No.	Class Interval	Tally	Total
1	.058-.059		
2	.060-.061		
3	.062-.063		
4	.064-.065		
5	.066-.067		
6	.068-.069		
			N = 50

Figure 18.2   Histogram of rubber gaskets.

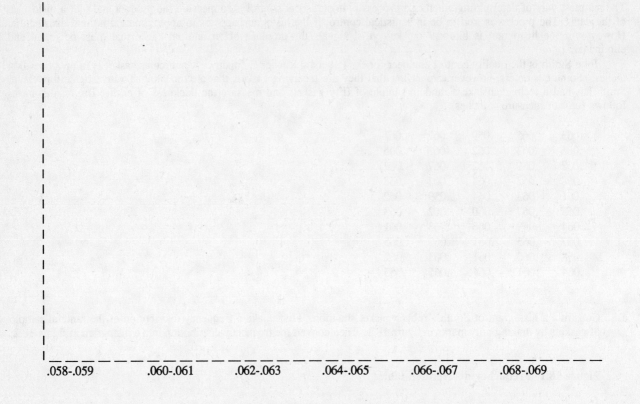

.058-.059	.060-.061	.062-.063	.064-.065	.066-.067	.068-.069

b. Now compare the histogram to the manufacturing specifications and determine whether or not corrective action is necessary. If corrective action is necessary, explain what should be done.

c. In small groups, answer each of the questions that follow.

1) Can a process be in statistical control and still produce defective parts?

2) What are some special causes that could affect this process?

3) Smith wants to introduce an incentive plan that would pay operators a five-cent bonus for every gasket produced within .063 and .065. What advise would you give Smith? Why?

Exercise 3

The goal of the SPC is to make products that consistently conform to specifications. The most economical way to achieve this goal is to implement a defect prevention strategy that emphasizes doing it right the first time. To do it right the first time, the process must be in statistical control and capable (a process is said to be **capable** when the spread of the distribution is less than the product specification tolerances). When these two conditions have been achieved, the chances of producing a nonconforming product are extremely rare. For example, when the process is just barely capable, only about three out of every one thousand products are nonconforming. Improving the capability of the process (that is, reducing the spread of distribution) further decreases the chances of producing a nonconforming product. This is illustrated in figure 18.3.

If a capable process should suddenly go out of statistical control, then the chances that the process will produce nonconforming products are increased. The sooner this condition can be detected, the fewer the number of defects produced. If the process goes out of control gradually, then it may be possible to make modifications to the process before any defects are produced. Therefore, it is desirable to have an early warning system that provides a statistical signal to identify when a special cause has entered the system. If detected early enough, the special cause can be found and removed before many (if any) nonconforming products are produced. This is known as process control.

Process control could be achieved by periodically constructing histograms. However, since histograms require relatively large samples, it would be expensive to keep close tabs on the process by taking frequent samples (for example, one every hour). Taking less frequent samples (for example, one a day) would reduce the costs, but it would also delay the detection, and thus correction, of the trouble in the process.

In the 1920s, Dr. Walter A. Shewhart of the Bell Telephone Laboratories solved the problem by developing a simple process control tool known as a control chart. The control chart is a special graph that allows production personnel to continuously monitor the process and detect when the process has gone out of statistical control. In this exercise, you learn how to construct and interpret one type of control chart--the $\bar{X}$ & R control chart.

The $\bar{X}$ & R control chart tracks the operating level (average or $\bar{X}$) and dispersion (range or R) of a process and displays them on graphs for easy visualizing and interpretation. If the process is in statistical control, the $\bar{X}$ and R values vary

Figure 18.3 Various degrees of process capability.

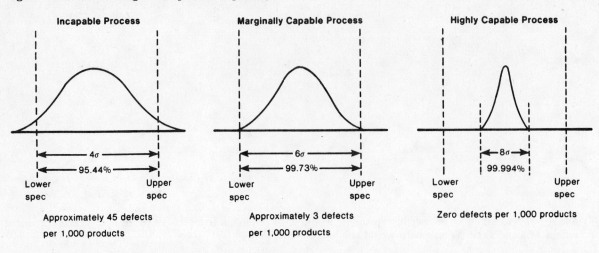

randomly around their modal value. If either the operating level or the dispersion vary more than could be expected by chance alone, the process is said to be out of statistical control.

The $\bar{X}$ & R control chart consists of two graphs--an average chart and a range chart. To construct the average chart, same-sized samples (for example, four) are drawn at regular intervals from the process or output. The product dimension (diameter, weight, length, etc.) of each piece in each sample is measured. The sample mean of each sample is calculated and plotted, in temporal order (from left to right) on graph paper. Next, the grand mean(of the sample means) is calculated. The grand mean becomes the center line on the chart.

To determine whether or not a process is in statistical control, one must determine whether the sample means are normally distributed around the grand mean or deviate significantly from the grand mean. Significant deviations are indicated by values that lie outside upper and lower *control limits* (CL). Typically, the upper control limit (UCL) is set at three standard deviations above the grand mean; the lower control limit (LCL) at three standard deviations below the grand mean (standard deviations are based on the sample means.) By chance alone, only about three out of one thousand outcomes would lie outside these control limits. Thus, any sample value lying outside these control limits indicates the presence of abnormal variation and the possibility that the process is out of statistical control. Figure 18.4 shows an average chart that has gone out of statistical control. Since the construction and interpretation of the range chart is almost identical to the average chart, we will not discuss it here.

Figure 18.4   Average chart with abnormal variation (process is out of statistical control).

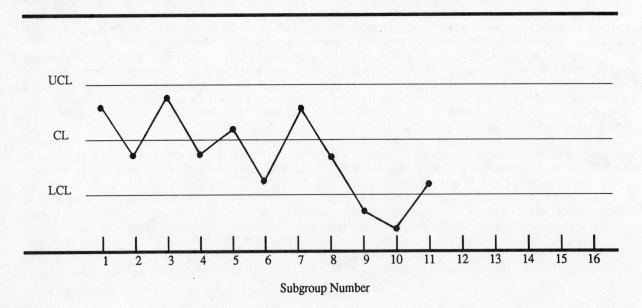

Subgroup Number

Assume that you are the quality control inspector for print samples. You will be looking at twenty-four subgroups with four print samples of the word QUALITY in each subgroup. Your job is to rate the quality of each of these print samples on a 100-point scale with 1 = inferior quality and 100 = excellent quality. Your ratings will serve as the data for construction of a control chart. Follow steps 1-10.

Step 1: Rate the quality of the print samples for the first ten subgroups in figure 18.5. Place your ratings in figure 18.6 beneath the headings X_1, X_2, X_3, X_4.

Figure 18.5   Print samples of the word QUALITY.

Figure 18.6   Data sheet

(1)	(2) Sample Ratings				(3)	(4)
Subgroup No.	X1	X2	X3	X4	$\bar{X}$	R
1						
2						
3						
4						
5						
6						
7						
8						
9						
10						
					(5) $\bar{\bar{X}} =$	(6) $\bar{R} =$

Step 2: Compute the mean value for each of the ten samples. Enter the results in column 3 of figure 18.6. Compute the range for each of the samples and enter the results in column 4 of figure 18.6.

Step 3: Compute the grand average (average of averages) and enter the results in space 5 in figure 18.6. Compute the average range and enter the results in space 6 in figure 18.6.

Step 4: Given your ratings, develop an appropriate scale and plot the $\bar{X}$ values from column 3 on the average chart portion of figure 18.7. Plot the R values from column 4 on the range chart portion of figure 18.7.

Figure 18.7 X̄ - R control chart

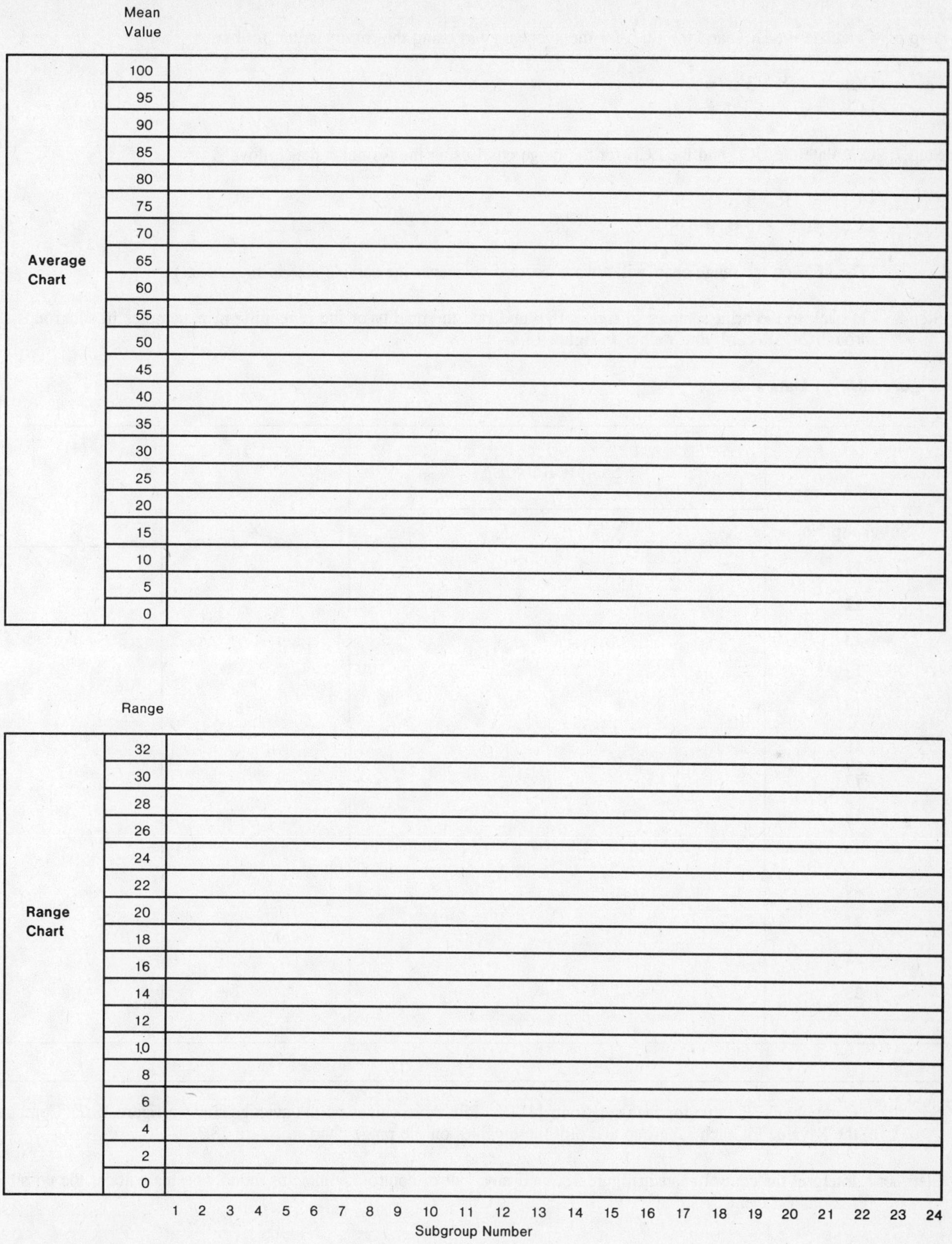

Mean
Value

	100	
	95	
	90	
	85	
	80	
	75	
	70	
Average	65	
Chart	60	
	55	
	50	
	45	
	40	
	35	
	30	
	25	
	20	
	15	
	10	
	5	
	0	

Range

	32	
	30	
	28	
	26	
	24	
	22	
Range	20	
Chart	18	
	16	
	14	
	12	
	10	
	8	
	6	
	4	
	2	
	0	

1 2 3 4 5 6 7 8 9 10 11 12 13 14 15 16 17 18 19 20 21 22 23 24
Subgroup Number

Step 5: Draw the center line on the average chart (X double bar value from space 5 in figure 18.6). Draw the center line on the range chart ($\bar{R}$ value from space 6 in figure 18.6).

Step 6: Calculate the UCL and the LCL for the average chart using the formulas that follow.

$$\text{UCL} = \bar{\bar{X}} + 3\,\sigma =$$
$$\text{LCL} = \bar{\bar{X}} - 3\,\sigma =$$

Step 7: Calculate the UCL and the LCL for the range chart using the formulas that follow.

$$\text{UCL} = \bar{R} + 3\,\sigma$$
$$\text{LCL} = \bar{R} - 3\,\sigma = 0.0$$

(The LCL on the range chart will always be zero whenever the sample size is six or less.)

Step 8: Go back to the print samples in figure 18.5 and rate the quality of the remaining print samples in subgroups 11 through 24. Record your ratings in figure 18.8.

Figure 18.8   Data sheet.

(1) Subgroup No.	(2) Sample Ratings				(3) $\bar{X}$	(4) R
	X_1	X_2	X_3	X_4		
11						
12						
13						
14						
15						
16						
17						
18						
19						
20						
21						
22						
23						
24						

Step 9: Compute the $\bar{X}$ value for each subgroup 11--24. Plot these values on the average chart in figure 18.7. Compute the R value for each subgroup and plot these values on the range chart in figure 18.7.

Step 10: Interpret the control chart in figure 18.7. If any "out of control" points are found, speculate about the possible reasons for them.

Exercise 4

For this exercise, assume that you are working in a manufacturing setting. In general, the process you are working on will follow the sequence shown in figure 18.9.

Figure 18.9   Flow diagram of process.

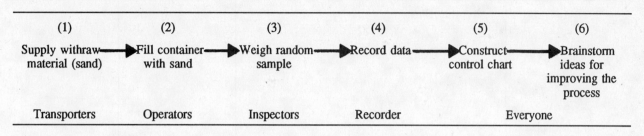

Your instructor will assign you to one of four positions. These are:

1. *Operator (10-30 people)*: Your task is to fill small containers with sand. When you have filled 10 containers halfway to the top, set them aside for the transporter to take to the inspectors. All operators will be filling 250 containers (25 lots consisting of 10 containers per lot).
2. *Transporter (2-3 people)*: Your task is to transport the half-filled containers produced by the operators in lot sizes of 10, to one of the inspectors. Once the inspector has taken the sample, return the sand and the containers to the operators for recycling.
3. *Inspectors (3-4 people)*: Your task is to take a random sample of 4 containers from each of the 25 lots. Weigh these 4 containers and give the weights to the recorder.
4. *Recorder (1 person)*: Your task is to take the inspection data and record in figure 18.10. These data will be used to construct a control chart.

Figure 18.10 Data sheet.

(1)	(2) Sample Ratings				(3)	(4)
Subgroup No.	X_1	X_2	X_3	X_4	$\bar{X}$	R
1						
2						
3						
4						
5						
6						
7						
8						
9						
10						
11						
12						
13						
14						
15						
					$\bar{\bar{X}} =$	$\bar{R} =$
16						
17						
18						
19						
20						
21						
22						
23						
24						
25						

After positions have been assigned, the operators should produce 150 containers (15 lots consisting of 10 half-filled containers in each lot). Once the production run has been completed, the recorder should use the data generated to construct a control chart in figure 18.11. Fill in the missing information from the details provided here and above. (Your instructor may generate the control chart using a microcomputer.)

At this point, a special cause will be introduced. The special cause in this case will be a change in the raw material from sand to pebbles. (Keep in mind that, normally, you would not be told that a special cause was being introduced into the process.) Except for this change, the production procedures should remain as before. The operators should produce 10 new lots, replacing the sand with pebbles. Each lot size should remain 10, and each random sample should continue to be 4. The recorder should then plot the new data on the control chart in figure 18.11.

Figure 18.11 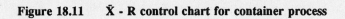 $\bar{X}$ - R control chart for container process

Average
Chart

Range
Chart

As a group, answer the questions that follow:

a. Did either the average chart or the range chart go out of statistical control? Why?

b. How can the control chart be used to prevent defects?

Exercise 5

Explain what you have learned from this exercise.

Experience 18-2   Using Materials Requirements Planning[**]

Introduction

Materials requirements planning (MRP) is basically a computer-operated system for planning and controlling manufacturing operations. MRP can, however, be done manually or with microcomputers in smaller firms. Datatram and Ethan Allen Furniture Company are two examples of smaller organizations that successfully have used manual MRP systems for several years. The basic components of an MRP system include: (1) a master production schedule, (2) a bill of materials or product structure tree, and (3) an inventory transaction or record file.

In this experience, you play the role of the production planner and scheduler at the "Arkansaw" Do-nothin' Company. The Do-nothin' Company produces a very simple product that is used throughout the world whenever someone has extra time

---

[**]Source of Experience 18-2: This exercise was developed by C. E. Kellogg, University of Arkansas, Little Rock. Used with permission of the author.

to waste. Read the information that follows, which was compiled from company records, and then complete the exercises as directed.

Master Production Schedule

The Do-nothin' Company uses a production schedule that matches orders. The completed Do-nothin's are delivered immediately to distributors who ordered the product. Do-nothin's are not placed in inventory at the plant. The firm, on occasion, accepts special orders. The production schedule (based on promised orders) for the next eight weeks is:

	Week							
	1	2	3	4	5	6	7	8
Production Schedule (Gross Requirements)	43	38	33	41	67	44	33	18

Bill of Materials

The Do-nothin' is a very simple product (as would be expected). It consists of only two separate parts (neither of which work). Part B is a six-inch diameter piece of 3/4-inch wood. Part C is an eight-inch length of one-inch diameter wood. A Do-nothin' consists of two each of Part B and Part C (See Figure 18.12 for the product structure tree for the Do-nothin'). The bill of materials consist of:

Level	Part	Description	Quantity Per
00	A	Completed Do-nothin'	1
01	B	Base and top (6" X 3/4")	2
01	C	Handle (1" X 8")	1
02	C	Handle (1" X 8")	1

Figure 18.12   Product structure tree for Do-nothin'

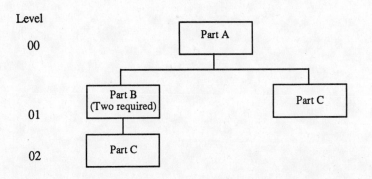

The manufacturing process for a Do-nothin' is quite simple. At level 02, Part C has a 3/4-inch groove cut in both ends. Level 01 consists of gluing Part B to each end of the grooved Part C. A second ungrooved Part C is then glued to the top of the assembled Parts B and C. The production process is then complete. It takes one week to completely assembly a Do-nothin'. A completed Do-nothing' is shown in figure 18.13.

Figure 18.13   A Completed Do-nothin'.

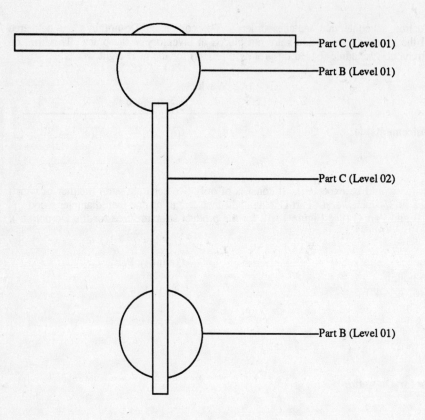

Inventory Transaction Files

Part A (Completed Do-nothin's):

On hand: 28
Quantity per production run: 60
Lead time: 1 week

Part B:

On hand: 140
Quantity per order: 125
Lead time: 1 week
Scheduled receipts: 105 during week 1

Part C:

On hand: 180
Quantity per order: Order the exact number needed
Lead time: 1 week
Scheduled receipts: 0

Exercise 1

Complete the MRP records provided in Figure 18.14 for the weeks indicated.

Figure 18.14 MRP records (1)

Part A		1	2	3	4	5	6	7	8
Gross Requirements									
Scheduled Receipts									
On Hand									
Planned Order Releases									

Part B		1	2	3	4	5	6	7	8
Gross Requirements									
Scheduled Receipts									
On Hand									
Planned Order Releases									

Part C		1	2	3	4	5	6	7	8
Gross Requirements									
Scheduled Receipts									
On Hand									
Planned Order Releases									

Exercise 2

a. An MRP system produces output reports that indicate the parts that need to be ordered, when they should be ordered, and how many should be ordered during the time frames examined. Develop an output report for each part. Do the reports indicate that any orders should be rushed or slowed down? Explain.

b. Assume that a new customer comes to you requesting a special order of seventy-five units to be delivered at the end of week 4. If you accept the order, how will the MRP records changes? Use the forms provided in figure 18.15 to show the changes.

Figure 18.15 MRP records (2).

Part A

	1	2	3	4	5	6	7	8
Gross Requirements								
Scheduled Receipts								
On Hand								
Planned Order Releases								

Part B

	1	2	3	4	5	6	7	8
Gross Requirements								
Scheduled Receipts								
On Hand								
Planned Order Releases								

Part C

	1	2	3	4	5	6	7	8
Gross Requirements								
Scheduled Receipts								
On Hand								
Planned Order Releases								

c.   Would the output reports change? If so, how? Would there be any exception reports? (Exception reports indicate materials or parts that will not be available in sufficient quantities, items that are overstocked, and customer orders that cannot be met at the scheduled date.) If so, what would they be?

d.   As the production planner and scheduler, what should be done about this special order? Why?

Exercise 3

Explain what you have learned about MRP as a production planning and control tool from this experience.

Experience 18-3   Solve the Dilemma of the Management Club with Break-Even Analysis

Introduction

A control tool is a specific procedure or technique that presents pertinent organizational information in such a way that managers are aided in developing and implementing appropriate organizational control strategy. One such control tool commonly used by management is break-even analysis. In this experience, you use break-even analysis to solve the dilemma of the management Club. Read the incident that follows, and then complete the exercises as directed.

Incident

Second semester was already underway, and the Management Club at Michael University was two days into a five-day spring recruiting drive that was to culminate with a new member/old member get-acquainted party at a local pizzeria the evening of the fifth day. While checking on funding for the pizza party, Bill Pack, the new club treasurer, discovered that most of the club's funds were already committed for scheduled activities during the semester and that there was only enough money left in the treasury to cover the $1.50 (per person) refreshment fee for *old club members*. Any other charges, including the $34.00 room rental fee (to reserve a private room for the activity) and the $1.50 refreshment fee for each new member in attendance, would have to come from new members dues (dues were $5.00).

At this point, only five new students had been recruited. All five indicated that they would attend the pizza party. A number of other individuals had indicated considerable interest in the club, but for one reason or another, had not yet paid their dues. The pizzeria required three days advance notification and payment in advance of the room rental fee to reserve the private room. The nonrefundable rental fee was due today. Pack wondered if new member dues would eventually cover the cost of the event. He also wondered if he should commit the club to the party by paying the $34.00 nonrefundable room rental fee. Pack saw this as an unsolvable dilemma. If he did not pay the rental fee, the party would have to be cancelled. On the other hand, if he did pay the nonrefundable rental fee and the break-even point was not reached, other scheduled activities might have to be cancelled.

Exercise 1

Use figure 18.16 to draw a break-even analysis of Bill Pack's situation.

Figure 18.16   Chart for break-even analysis.

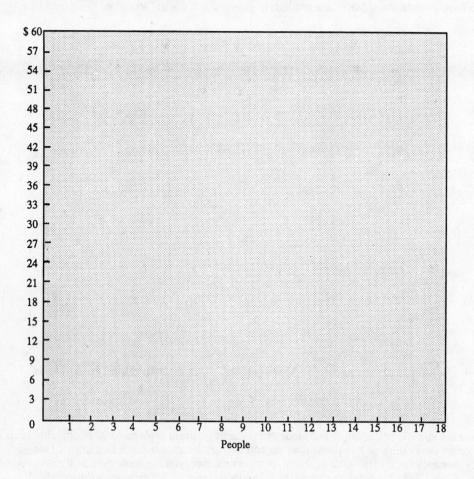

Exercise 2

Questions *a-g* can be answered from a properly drawn break-even chart.

a.   What is the break-even point in dollars? In people? How do you know this is the break-even point?

b.   How much additional money (that is already allocated to other activities) will the club have to use to cover the cost of the pizza party if no one else joins the club? Explain.

c.   Assume that seven additional new members (in addition to the five original new members) join the club and attend the pizza party. Describe the club's financial situation if this were to occur.

d. If the pizzeria offered the club a special $25.00 rate to reserve the private room, what impact would this have on the situation? (Show this change on the break-even chart with dashed lines.) Explain.

e. If the pizzeria management told Bill Pack that the charge per person would be $1.75 instead of the originally quoted figure of $1.50 (assume that the club could still absorb the per person charge for old members and that the nonrefundable room rental fee remained at $34.00):

1) What impact would this have on the break-even point? (Use dotted lines to represent this change on the break-even chart.) Explain.

2) How much of a loss would the organization incur with only five new members? Explain.

3) Describe the club's financial picture if a total of twelve new members join the club and attend the pizza party.

f. If you assume the original break-even situation and you use what you know about the means available for clubs and organizations to raise funds at your university or college, would you recommend cancellation or continuation of the pizza party? (Remember, there are only five dues-paying new members.) Explain.

g. Explain how the break-even chart can be used as a control tool.

Exercise 3

Explain what you have gained from this experience.

Experience 18-4   J. R. Manufacturing Company

Introduction

A ratio is a relationship between two numbers that is calculated by dividing one number into the other. Ratio analysis is the process of generating information that summarizes the financial position of an organizational by calculating ratios based on various financial measures that appear on the organization's balance sheet and income statement. If significant differences are found between calculated ratios of the firm and industry ratios, further examination and possibly corrective action may be necessary.

In this experience, you familiarize yourself with the specific ratios that are ordinarily included in each ratio category (liquidity, leverage, activity, profitability). Then using the financial statements of J. R. Manufacturing Company, compute selected ratios from these statements, compare computed ratios to industry ratios, and suggest areas where further examination or, possibly, corrective action would be necessary. The balance sheet and income statement of J. R. Manufacturing Company appear below in figures 18.17 and 18.18.

Introduction to Ratio Analysis

Liquidity Ratios. Ratios that indicate an organization's ability to meet upcoming financial obligations are called liquidity ratios. The better an organization is at meeting these obligations, the more liquid it is said to be. As a general rule, organizations should be liquid enough to meet their obligations, yet not so liquid that too many financial resources are sitting idle in anticipation of meeting upcoming debts. The two main types of liquidity ratios are the current ratio and the quick ratio.

The **current ratio** is calculated by dividing the dollar value of the organization's current assets by the dollar value of its current liabilities:

$$\text{Current ratio} = \frac{\text{Current assets}}{\text{Current liablities}}$$

Current assets typically include cash, accounts receivable, and inventory. Current liabilities generally include accounts payable, short-term notes payable, and any other accrued expenses. The current ratio indicates to managers the organization's ability to meet its financial obligations in the short term.

The **quick ratio,** sometimes called the acid-test ratio, is computed by subtracting inventory from current assets and then dividing the difference by current liabilities:

$$\text{Quick ratio} = \frac{\text{Current assets - Inventory}}{\text{Current liabilities}}$$

The quick ratio is the same as the current ratio except that it does not include inventory in current assets. Because inventory can be difficult to convert into money or securities, the quick ratio gives managers information on the organization's ability to meet its financial obligations with no reliance on inventory.

Leverage Ratios. Leverage ratios indicate the relationships between organizational funds supplied by the owners of an organization and organizational funds supplied by various creditors. The more organizational funds furnished by creditors, the more leverage an organization is said to be employing. As a general guideline, an organization should use leverage to the extent that borrowed funds can be used to generate additional profit without a significant amount of organizational ownership being established by creditors. Perhaps the two most commonly used leverage ratios are the debit ratio and the times interest earned ratio.

The **debt ratio** is calculated by dividing total organizational debt by total organizational assets:

$$\text{Debt ratio} = \frac{\text{Total debts}}{\text{Total assets}}$$

In essence, this ratio gives the percentage of all organizational assets provided by organizational creditors.

The kind of business an organization is in may help to determine whether a particular debt ratio is too high. As an example, the debt ratio at Unisys Corporation, a company that designs and manufactures computer-related equipment, recently reached 41.7 percent. Some think that this level of financing is somewhat high for Unisys because no one knows for sure what kind of computers will be popular in ten years, and the ability of Unisys to repay this level of debt therefore becomes questionable. In contrast, this level of debt would probably be considered more acceptable for a basic food processing company like Heinz. Because many products Heinz now offers, such as ketchup, will probably still be in demand in ten years, the company's ability to repay its debt is less suspect.

The **times interest earned ratio** is calculated by dividing gross income, or earnings before interest and taxes, by the total amount of organizational interest charges incurred from borrowing needed resources:

$$\text{Times interest earned ratio} = \frac{\text{Gross income}}{\text{Interest charges}}$$

This ratio indicates the organization's ability to pay interest expenses directly from gross income.

Activity Ratios. Activity ratios indicate how well an organization is selling its products in relation to its available resources. Obviously, management's goal is to maximize the amount of sales per dollar invested in organizational resources. Three main activity ratios are (1) inventory turnover, (2) fixed assets turnover, and (3) total assets turnover.

Inventory turnover is calculated by dividing organizational sales by inventory:

$$\text{Inventory turnover} = \frac{\text{Sales}}{\text{Inventory}}$$

This ratio indicates whether an organization is maintaining an appropriate level of inventory in relation to its sales volume. In general, as sales volume increases or decreases, an organization's inventory level should fluctuate correspondingly.

Fixed assets turnover is calculated by dividing fixed assets, or plant and equipment, into total sales:

$$\text{Fixed assets turnover} = \frac{\text{Sales}}{\text{Fixed assets}}$$

This ratio indicates the appropriateness of the amount of funds invested in plant and equipment relative to the level of sales.
Total assets turnover is calculated by dividing sales by total assets:

$$\text{Total assets turnover} = \frac{\text{Sales}}{\text{Total assets}}$$

The focus of this ratio is on the appropriateness of the level of funds the organization has tied up in all assets relative to its rate of sales.

Profitability Ratios. Profitability ratios focus on assessing overall organizational profitability and improving it wherever possible. Major profitability ratios include the profit to sales ratio and the profit to total assets ratio.
The **profit to sales ratio** is calculated by dividing the net profit of an organization by its total sales:

$$\text{Profit to sales ratio} = \frac{\text{Net profit}}{\text{Sales}}$$

This ratio indicates whether the organization is making an adequate net profit in relation to the total dollars coming into the organization.
The **profit to total assets ratio** is calculated by dividing the net profit of an organization by its total assets:

$$\text{Profit to total assets ratio} = \frac{\text{Net Profit}}{\text{Total assets}}$$

This ratio indicates whether the organization is realizing enough net profit in relation to the total dollars invested in assets.

Figure 18.17   J. R. Manufacturing Company balance sheet, December 31, 1993.

J. R. Manufacturing Company
Balance Sheet
December 31, 1993

Assets		*Claims on Assets*	
Cash	$5,000	Accounts payable	$ 6,000
Marketable securities	15,000	Notes payable, 8%	10,000
Receivables, net	20,000	Accrual	1,000
Inventories	30,000	Provisions for federal income taxes	13,000
Total current assets	$70,000	*Total current liabilities*	$30,000
Gross plant and equipment	$180,000	First mortgage bonds, 5%	$50,000
Less reserve for depreciation	50,000	Debentures, 6%	20,000
Net plant and equipment	$130,000	Preferred stock, 7% $10,000	
		Common stock 50,000	
		Retained earnings 40,000	
		Total net worth	$100,000
Total assets	$200,000	*Total claims on assets*	$200,000

Figure 18.18   J. R. Manufacturing Company income statement, December 31, 1993.

J. R. Manufacturing Company
Income Statement
December 31, 1993

Net sales			$300,000
Cost of goods sold			258,000
Gross profit			$ 42,000
Less operating expenses:			
Selling	$2,200		
General and administrative	4,000		
Rent on office	2,800		9,000
Gross operating profit			33,000
Depreciation			10,000
Net operating profit			23,000
Add Other income:			
Royalties			1,500
Gross income			$ 24,500
Less Other expenses:			
Interest on notes payable	$ 800		
Interest on first mortgage	2,500		
Interest on debentures	1,200		4,500
Net income before income tax			$ 20,000
(Tax at 40 percent)			8,000
Net income after income tax			$ 12,000

Exercise 1

Calculate the following ratios for J. R. Manufacturing Company:

a. Liquidity ratios:
    1) Current ratio

    2) Quick ratio

b. Leverage ratios:
    1) Debt ratio

    2) Times interest earned ratio

c. Activity ratios:
    1) Inventory turnover ratio

    2) Fixed assets turnover ratio

3) Total assets turnover ratio

d. Profitability ratios:
    1) Profit to sales ratios (sales margin)

    2) Profit to total assets ratio

Exercise 2

Compare the computed ratios for J. R. Manufacturing Company to the average industry ratios provided in figure 18.19. In what areas would you suggest further examination or possibly even corrective action?

Figure 18.19 Average industry ratios.

Name of Ratio	Industry Average	
1. Liquidity ratios:		
a) Current ratio	2.5	times
b) Quick ratio	1	times
2. Leverage ratios		
a) Debt ratio	50	percent
b) Times interest earned ratio	8	times
3. Activity ratios:		
a) Inventory turnover ratio	9	times
b) Fixed assets turnover ratio	5	times
c) Total assets turnover ratio	2	times
4. Profitability ratios:		
a) Profit to sales ratio (sales margin)	5	percent
b) Profit to total assets ratio	10	percent

Exercise 3

Describe another way (other than comparing company ratios to industry ratios) in which managers could use ratio analysis for control purposes.

Exercise 4

Explain what you have gained from this experience.

19 INFORMATION

Chapter Summary

Controlling is the process of making things happen as planned. Of course, managers cannot make things happen as planned if they lack information on the manner in which various events occur within both the organization and the organizational environment. This chapter discusses the fundamental principles of handling information within an organization. Major topics discussed are: (1) essential of information, (2) the management information system (MIS), and (3) the management decision support system (MDSS).

Learning Objective 1   *An understanding of the relationship between data and information*

The process of developing information begins with the gathering of some type of facts or statistics, called **data**. Once gathered, data typically are analyzed in some manner. Generally speaking, **information** can be defined as conclusions derived from data analysis. In management terms, information can be defined as conclusions derived from the analysis of data that relate to the operation of an organization. As examples to illustrate the relationship between data and information, managers gather data regarding: (a) pay rates that individuals are receiving within industries to develop information about competitive pay rates, (b) hazardous-materials accidents in order to gain information about how to improve worker safety, and (c) customer demographics in order to gain information about product demand in the future. The information managers receive heavily influences managerial decision making, which in turn determines what activities will be performed within the organization, which in turn dictates the eventual success or failure of the organization. Some management writers consider information to be of such fundamental importance to the management process that they define management as the process of converting information into action through decision making.

Learning Objective 2   *Insights on the main factors that influence the value of information*

Some information managers receive is more valuable than other information. The value of information is defined in terms of how much benefit can accrue to the organization through the use of information. The greater this benefit, the more valuable the information. **Four primary factors determine the value of information:** (1) information appropriateness, (2) information quality, (3) information timeliness, and (4) information quantity. In general, management should encourage the generation, distribution, and use of organizational information that is appropriate, of high quality, timely, and of sufficient quantity. Following this guideline will not necessarily guarantee sound decisions, but it will ensure that important resources necessary to make such decisions are available.

Information appropriateness is defined in terms of how relevant the information is to the decision-making situation that faces the manager. If information is quite relevant to the decision-making situation, then it is said to be appropriate. As a general rule, as the appropriateness of information increases, the value of that information increases. The three main decision-making situations that commonly face managers in organizations relate to making operational control decisions, management control decisions, and strategic planning decisions. Operational control decisions relate to assuring that specific organizational tasks are carried out effectively and efficiently. Management control decisions relate to obtaining and effectively and efficiently using the organizational resources necessary to reach organizational objectives. Strategic planning decisions relate to determining organizational objectives and designating the corresponding action necessary to reach those objectives.

The characteristics of appropriate information change as managers shift from making operational control decisions to management control decisions to strategic planning decisions. Strategic planning decision makers need information that focuses on the relationship of the organization to its external environment, emphasizes the future, is very wide in scope, and is aggregate or presents a broad view of all information. Also, appropriate information for this type of decision is usually quite old and not completely accurate. Information appropriate for making operational control decisions has dramatically different characteristics than information appropriate for making strategic planning decisions. Operational control decision makers need information that focuses for the most part on the internal organizational environment, emphasizes the performance history of the organization, is well defined, narrow in scope, and quite detailed. In addition, appropriate information for this type of decision is both highly current and highly accurate. Information appropriate for making management control decisions generally has characteristics that fall somewhere between the extreme characteristics of appropriate operational control information and appropriate strategic planning information.

The second primary factor that determines the value of information is **information quality**, which is the degree to which information represents reality. The more closely information represents reality, the higher the quality and the greater the value of the information. In general, the higher the quality of information available to managers, the better equipped managers are to make appropriate decisions and the greater the probability that the organization will be successful over the long run. Perhaps the most significant factor in producing poor quality information is data contamination. An issue like inaccurate data gathering can result in information that is of very low quality, a poor representation of reality.

Information timeliness is the third primary factor that determines the value of information. The timeliness of information refers to the extent to which the receipt of information allows decisions to be made and resulting action to be taken so that the organization can gain some benefit from possessing the information. Information received by managers at a point when it can be used to the advantage of the organization is said to be timely.

The fourth and final determinant of the value of information is called **information quantity**. Information quantity refers to the amount of decision-related information managers possess. Before making a decision, managers should assess the quantity of information they possess that relates to the decision being made. If this quantity is judged to be insufficient, more information should be gathered before the decision is made. If the amount of information is judged to be as complete as necessary, managers can feel justified in making the decision.

Learning Objective 3   *Knowledge of some potential steps for evaluating information*

Evaluation of information is the process of determining whether or not the acquisition of specified information is justified. As with all evaluations of this type, the primary concern of management is to weigh the dollar value of benefit gained from using some quantity of information against the cost of generating that information. The first major step in evaluating organizational information is determining the value of that information by pinpointing the data to be analyzed and then determining the expected value or return to be received from obtaining perfect information based on this data. Next, this expected value should be reduced by the amount of benefit that will not be realized because of deficiencies and inaccuracies expected to appear in the information. Then the expected value of organizational information should be compared with the expected cost of obtaining that information. If the expected cost does not exceed the expected value, managers must either increase the information's expected value or decrease its expected cost before the information gathering can be justified. If neither of these objectives is possible, management cannot justify gathering the information. One generally accepted strategy for increasing the expected value of information is to eliminate those characteristics of the information that tend to limit its usefulness. For example, if the language or format of information is not understandable, managers should translate, revise, or change the format to make it understandable.

Learning Objective 4   *An appreciation for the role of computers in handling information*

Managers have an overwhelming amount of data to gather, analyze, and transform into information before making numerous decisions. In fact, many managers in the U.S. as well as the United Kingdom and other foreign countries are currently complaining that they are *overloaded* with information. A **computer** is a tool managers can use to assist in the complicated and time-consuming task of generating this information. A computer can be defined as an electronic tool capable of accepting data, interpreting data, performing ordered operations on data, and reporting on the outcome of these operations.

A computer function is a computer activity that must be performed to generate organizational information. Computers perform five main functions: (1) the input function, (2) the storage function, (3) the control function, (4) the processing function, and (5) the output function. The **input function** consists of computer activities whereby the computer enters the data to be analyzed and the instructions to be followed to analyze that data appropriately. The purpose of the input function is to provide data and instructions to be used in the performance of the storage, processing, control, and output functions. The **storage function** consists of computer activities involved with retaining the material entered into the computer during the performance of the input function. The storage unit, or "memory," of a computer is similar to the human memory in that various facts can be stored until they are needed for processing. In addition, facts can be stored, used in processing, and then restored as many times as necessary. Storage, processing, and control activities are dependent on one another and ultimately yield computer output. The **processing function** consists of the computer activities involved with performing both logic and calculation steps necessary to analyze data appropriately. Calculation activities include virtually any numerical analysis. Logic activities include such analysis as comparing one number to another to determine which is larger. Data, as well as directions for processing the data, are furnished by input and storage activities. Computer activities that dictate the order in which other computer functions are performed comprise the **control function**. Control activities indicate when data should be retrieved after it has been stored, when and how this data should be analyzed, if and when the data should be restored after analysis, if and when additional data should be retrieved, and when output activities should begin and end. The **output function** is comprised of those activities that take the results of the input, storage, processing, and control functions and transmit them outside of the computer. These results can appear in such diversified forms as data on punched computer cards or words typed on paper tapes. Obviously, the form in which output should appear primarily is determined by how the output is to be used. Output that appears on punched computer cards, for example, can be used as input for another computer analysis but is of little value for analysis by human beings.

The computer is a sophisticated management tool with the potential of making a significant contribution to organizational success. For this potential to materialize, however, the following possible pitfalls should be avoided: thinking that a computer is capable of independently performing creative activities, spending too much money on computer assistance, and overestimating the value of computer output.

Learning Objective 5   *An understanding of the importance of a management information system (MIS) to an organization*

In simple terms, a **management information system (MIS)** is a network established within an organization to provide managers with information that will assist them in decision making. In more complete terms, Holmes states that an MIS is a system designed to provide selected decision-oriented information needed by management to plan, control, and evaluate the activities of the corporation. It is designed within a framework that emphasizes profit planning, performance planning, and control at all levels. It contemplates the ultimate integration of required business information subsystems, both financial and nonfinancial, within the company.

The title of the specific organization member responsible for developing and maintaining an MIS varies from organization to organization. In smaller organizations, a president or vice-president may possess this responsibility. In larger organizations, an individual with a title such as "Director of Information Systems" may be solely responsible for appropriately managing an entire MIS department. The term *MIS manager* is used in the text to indicate that person within the organization who has the primary responsibility for managing the MIS. The term *MIS personnel* is used to designate those nonmanagement individuals within the organization who possess the primary responsibility of actually operating the MIS. Examples of these nonmanagement individuals could be computer operators and computer programmers.

The MIS is perhaps best described by summarizing the steps necessary to properly operate an MIS and by discussing the different kinds of information various managers need to make job-related decisions. MIS personnel generally perform six sequential and distinct steps to properly operate an MIS. The first of these steps is to determine what information is needed within the organization, when it will be needed, and in what form it will be needed. Since the basic purpose of the MIS is to assist management in making decisions, one way to begin determining management information needs is to analyze (1) decision areas in which management makes decisions, (2) specific decisions within these decision areas that management actually must make, and (3) alternatives that must be evaluated to make these specific decisions. The second step is pinpointing and collecting data that will yield needed organizational information. This step is just as important as determining the information needs of the organization. If data collected do not relate properly to information needs, it will be impossible to generate needed information. After the information needs of the organization have been determined and appropriate data have been pinpointed and gathered, summarizing the data and analyzing the data are, respectively, the third and fourth steps MIS personnel generally should take to properly operate an MIS. It is in the performance of these steps that MIS personnel find computer assistance of great benefit. The fifth and sixth steps are transmitting the information generated by data analysis to appropriate managers and having managers actually use the information. The performance of these last two steps results in managerial decision making. Although each of these six steps is necessary if an MIS is to run properly, the time spent on performing each step naturally varies from organization to organization.

For maximum benefit, an MIS must collect relevant data, transform that data into appropriate information, and transmit that information to appropriate managers. Appropriate information for one manager within an organization, however, may not be appropriate for another. Murdick suggests that the degree of appropriateness of MIS information for a manager depends on the activities for which the manager will use the information, the organizational objectives assigned to the manager, and the level of management at which the manager functions. All of these factors, of course, are closely related.

Learning Objective 6   *A feasible strategy for establishing an MIS*

The process of establishing an MIS can be broken down into four stages: (1) planning for the MIS, (2) designing the MIS, (3) implementing the MIS, and (4) improving the MIS. Perhaps the most important stage of establishing an MIS is the planning stage. Commonly cited factors that make planning for the establishment of an MIS an absolute necessity are the typically long periods of time needed to acquire MIS-related data-processing equipment and to integrate it within the operation of the organization, the difficulty of hiring competent personnel to operate the equipment, and the major amounts of financial and managerial resources typically needed to operate an MIS. The specific form that plans take for an MIS varies from organization to organization.

Although data-processing equipment is normally an important ingredient of management information systems, the designing of an MIS should not begin with a comparative analysis of various types of such equipment available. Many MIS managers mistakenly think that data-processing equipment and an MIS are synonymous. Stoller and Van Horn indicate that, since the purpose of an MIS is to provide information that will assist managers in making better decisions, the designing of an MIS should begin with an analysis of the types of decisions managers actually make in a particular organization. These authors suggest that designing an MIS should consist of four steps: (1) defining various decisions that must be made to run an organization, (2) determining the types of existing management policies that may influence the ways in which these decisions should be made, (3) pinpointing the types of data needed to make these decisions, and (4) establishing a mechanism for gathering and appropriately processing this data to obtain needed information.

The third stage in the process of establishing an MIS within an organization is implementation: that is, putting the planned for and designed MIS into operation. In this stage, the equipment is acquired and integrated into the organization. Designated data are gathered, analyzed as planned, and distributed to appropriate managers within the organization. And line managers are making decisions based on the information they receive from the MIS. Management of the implementation process of the MIS can determine the ultimate success or failure of the system. To help ensure that this process will be successful, management can attempt to find an executive sponsor, a high-level manager who understands and supports the MIS implementation process. The support of such a sponsor will be a sign to all organization members that the MIS implementation is important to the organization and that all organization members should cooperate in making the implementation process successful. In addition, making sure that the MIS is as simple as possible and serves information needs of management is critical in making the implementation of an MIS successful. If the MIS is overly complicated or does not meet information needs of management, the implementation will meet with much resistence and likely have only limited success.

Once the MIS is operating, MIS managers continually should strive to maximize its value. To improve an MIS, MIS managers must first find symptoms or signs that the existing MIS is inadequate. Colbert divides these symptoms into three types: operational symptoms, psychological symptoms, and report content symptoms. Operational symptoms and psychological symptoms relate, respectively, to the operation of the organization and the functioning of organization members. Report content symptoms relate to the actual makeup of information generated by the MIS. Although the symptoms are clues that an MIS is inadequate, the symptoms themselves may not actually pinpoint MIS weaknesses. Therefore, after such symptoms are detected, MIS managers usually must gather additional information to determine what MIS weaknesses exist. Answering such questions as (1) Where and how do managers get information? and (2) Do managers tend to act before receiving information? probably would be of some help to MIS managers in determining those weaknesses.

MIS inadequacies vary from situation to situation, depending on such factors as the quality of an MIS plan, the appropriateness of an MIS design, and the type of individuals operating an MIS. However, several activities have the potential of improving the MIS of most organizations. One such activity involves building cooperation among MIS personnel and line managers. Cooperation of this sort encourages line managers to give MIS personnel honest opinions of the quality of information being received. A second activity involves constantly stressing that MIS personnel should strive to accomplish the purpose of the MIS: providing managers with decision-related information. In this regard, it probably would be a great benefit to hold line managers responsible for continually educating MIS personnel on the types of decisions organization managers make and the corresponding steps taken to make these decisions. The better that MIS personnel understand the decision situations that face operating managers, the higher the probability that MIS information will be appropriate for decisions these managers must make. A third activity involves holding, wherever possible, both line managers and MIS personnel accountable for MIS activities on a cost-benefit basis. In effect, this accountability emphasis helps to increase the cost conscientiousness of both line managers and MIS personnel. Finally, management should operate an MIS in a "people conscientious" manner. In addition to logic considerations, MIS activities also should include people considerations. After all, even if MIS activities are well thought out and completely logical, an MIS can be ineffective simply because people do not use it as intended. Traditionally, the concept of an MIS that uses electronic assistance in gathering data and providing related information to managers has been invaluable. This MIS assistance has been especially useful in areas where more programmed decisions are necessary and the computer continually generates the information which helps managers make them.

Learning Objective 7   *Information about what a management decision support system is and how it operates*

Closely related to the MIS is the Management Decision Support System (MDSS). A **management decision support system** is an interdependent set of decision aids that assist managers in making more non-programmed decisions. An MDSS is typically characterized by:

1. **One or More Corporate Data Bases.** A **data base** is a reservoir of corporate facts consistently organized to fit the information needs of a variety of organizational members. Corporate data bases tend to contain facts regarding all important facets of company operations and typically include financial as well as nonfinancial information. This data is used to explore issues which are important to the corporation.

2. **One or More User Data Bases.** In addition to the corporate data base, an MDSS tends to contain several additional user data bases. A **user data base** is a data base developed by individual managers or users. These user data bases may be derived from but not necessarily limited to the corporate data base and tend to address specific issues which are peculiar to the individual users.

3. **A Set of Quantitative Tools Stored in a Model Base.** A **model base** is a collection of quantitative programs which can assist MDSS users in analyzing data within data bases. A desirable feature of the model base is the ability of the user to perform a **"what if" analysis**--the simulation of a business situation over and over again using somewhat different data for selected decision areas. Popular software like LOTUS or the Interactive Financial Planning System (IFPS) allows managers to ask as many "what ifs" as desirable and save their answers without every changing their original data.

4. **A Dialogue Capability.** A **dialogue capability** is the ability of a MDSS user to interact with an MDSS. Such interaction typically involves extracting data from a data base, calling various models stored in the model base, and storing analysis results in a file.

The continued technological developments related to microcomputers have made the use of the MDSS concept feasible and its application available to virtually all managers. In addition, the continued development of extensive software to support information analysis related to more subjective decision making is contributing to the popularity of the MDSS.

Knowing You Know

Matching *Directions: Match items 1-10 with items a-j. There is only one correct answer for each item.*

____1. Control function
____2. Information
____3. Model base
____4. Transmitting the information generated by data analysis to appropriate managers
____5. Implementation
____6. Planning
____7. The designing of an MIS
____8. Collecting or gathering appropriate data
____9. Data
____10. Processing function

a. A collection of quantitative programs which can assist MDSS users in analyzing data within data bases
b. Computer activities involved with performing both logic and calculation steps necessary to analyze data appropriately
c. Fifth step for proper operation of an MIS
d. Conclusions derived from data analysis
e. Should not begin with a comparative analysis of the various types of equipment available
f. Probably the most important stage in establishing an MIS
g. During this stage of establishing an MIS, equipment is acquired and integrated into the organization
h. Computer activities that dictate the order in which other computer functions are performed
i. Second step for proper operation of an MIS
j. Facts or statistics

True/False *Directions: On the lines provided, place a "T" for true or an "F" for false for each of the statements that follow.*

____11. A reduction in cooperation among MIS personnel and line managers may very well be a means to improve the MIS in many organizations.

____12. Information appropriateness is defined in terms of how much benefit can accrue to the organization through the use of the information.

____13. A computer is a tool managers can use to assist in the complicated and time-consuming task of generating information.

____14. According to the text, the computer performs six main functions to generate organizational information.

____15. Information quality is the degree to which information represents reality.

____16. If managers discover that the expected cost of gathering information exceeds the information's expected value, they have little choice but to decide against gathering the information.

____17. MIS personnel use the acronym GIGO (garbage in--garbage out) to disguise their feelings when they discover that top management has purchased equipment that does not meet organizational needs.

____18. The management decision support system is an interdependent set of decision aids that assist managers in making more programmed decisions.

____19. Murdick suggests that the degree of appropriateness of MIS information for a manager depends on the activities for which the manager will use the information, the organizational objectives assigned to the manager, and the level of management at which the manager functions.

____20. Once the MIS is operating, MIS managers should minimize the number of changes or improvements made because such changes necessitate significant retraining of MIS personnel.

____21. Management control decisions are decisions that relate to assuring that specific organizational tasks are carried out effectively and efficiently.

____22. A computer's value to management is dependent upon management's ability to input quality data and appropriately instruct the computer.

____23. MIS improvements are appropriate as soon as operational, psychological, or report content symptoms arise.

____24. The storage, control, and processing functions of a computer are dependent on one another and ultimately yield computer output.

____25. To improve MIS effectiveness, managers may have to reduce such factors as threats to employees' power and status that might be discouraging MIS use.

Applying What You Know

Experience 19-1   DC-10 Disaster in Chicago: FAA Information*

Introduction

Various factors can influence the value of information or the degree of benefit that can accrue to an organization through the use of information. To maximize the degree of this benefit, management should encourage the generation, distribution, and use of organizational information that is appropriate, of high quality, timely, and of sufficient quantity.

In this experience, you evaluate Federal Aviation Administration (FAA) information about the DC-10 crash that occurred in Chicago on May 25, 1979 and determine the value of that information to the builder of the DC-10--McDonnell Douglas Corporation. Read the incident that follows, and then complete the exercises as directed.

Incident

The following information appeared in the Wall Street Journal on June 1, 1979, one week after the crash:

> Just how McDonnell Douglas's problems develop depends, to a large extent, on what investigators find in seeking the cause of the crash. To some extent, the investigators are in uncharted waters. This is the first time in the history of commercial jets that an engine has fallen off a plane and caused a crash. It is also the first time in the history of commercial jets that a U.S. plane has been grounded by the Federal Aviation Administration.
>
> The problems, which McDonnell Douglas declines to comment on, extend far beyond the American Airlines plane that went down in Chicago. The FAA said that, as a result of the latest round of inspections, some DC-10s remain on the ground. It said, further, that while other DC-10s could start flying again, they had to undergo additional, frequent checks . . .
>
> At first, the Chicago crash looked as though it had been caused by a simple problem that could easily be fixed. An official of the National Transportation Safety Board went on television holding a small bolt that, he suggested, had failed because of metal fatigue, causing the engine to fall off.
>
> But investigators have already found that there is much more to it than that. Within the pylon that attached the engine to the left wing, investigators have found a cracked forging, which is a heavy metal plate, and a cracked web, which is a lighter sheet-metal structure. These failures may have set off a complex sequence of events, including fracture (rather than metal fatigue) of the bolt, and this chain of events may have caused the loss of the engine . . .

What the cure might be isn't certain. "It might require just a tightening of certain bolts, or it might require a complete redesign of the pylon, but I suspect it will be somewhere in between," says one federal expert. "I think we'll all wind up beefing up our DC-10 pylons," says the senior vice-president of one big airline flying the plane.

More than the pylon may have to be fixed. Even with the loss of one engine, the DC-10 should have been able to keep flying with its other engines. And for a while, it did. After the loss of the engine, the DC-10 kept soaring upward for twenty-four seconds. "For those twenty-four seconds, the pilot handled it just beautifully," a safety official says.

But the engine that flew off had provided the pressure that drove hydraulic system number one, which powers the flaps and slats that control the DC-10's movements. Hydraulic system number two doesn't power slats. That left only hydraulic system number three as the backup. When the engine flew back and up over the wing, however, the pylon was wrapped back over the wing, apparently cutting system three's hydraulic pipes. These pipes run along the front of the wing.

Hydraulic fluid leaked from the left wing. Eventually, the slats, lacking power to remain in proper position, presumably failed to supply lift to the left wing. The plane was forced into a violent leftward roll and then dove into the ground. "The pilot did all he could, applying full right rudder and ailerons, but it just wasn't enough," the safety official says . . . .

This raises questions as to whether the DC-10's hydraulic system should be modified or at least be better protected. Failure of the pylon was bad enough, says Wolfgang Demisch, an aerospace analyst at the securities firm of Smith Barney, Harris Upham & Co. "The more salient concern is that control of the airplane was lost, suggesting massive hydraulic failure," Demisch says. "That might call for redesign of the hydraulic system."

Repair of the DC-10 may not be cheap. United Airlines, with a DC-10 grounded in Chicago due to pylon defects, has asked McDonnell Douglas for a brand new pylon. A complete pylon, United was told, would cost $500,000. The DC-10 has two engines mounted on pylons and a third in the tail structure.

Whatever the cost of repairs, the problems uncovered as a result of the Chicago crash are proving so complex that they have touched off a series of investigations of the DC-10. "We're going to look into basic design, the static testing, the dynamic testing, and any engineering changes involving the DC-10 pylon," one federal investigator says. The government also will review the service history of the plane in an attempt to pinpoint defects . . . .

Exercise 1

Assume that you and three of your classmates make up the top management group at McDonnell Douglas. As a group, evaluate the value of the information in the *Wall Street Journal* article to your company.

Exercise 2

If you were president of McDonnell Douglas Corporation, how would you use the present findings of the FAA? Explain.

Exercise 3

Explain what you have gained from this experience.

Experience 19-2   Information Loss?

Introduction

   The process of developing information begins with the gathering of some type of facts or statistics, called data. Once gathered, data typically are analyzed in some manner. Generally speaking, information can be defined as conclusions derived from data analysis. The information managers receive heavily influences managerial decision making, which in turn determines what activities will be performed within the organization.

   In this experience, Joan Doe, manager of Hypothetical Company, has gathered some data, analyzed it, and been influenced enough by the information to suggest to you that some action may be appropriate. Read the incident that follows, and then complete the exercises as directed.

Incident

   Fifteen minutes ago, your boss, Joan Doe, entered your office and plopped down in front of you the open page of an old edition of Industry Week magazine. On that page was a highlighted clipping from a section entitled "Memo to Managers: What's Your Communication Average?" She indicated to you that, if the data collected by the communication consultant in the clipping are accurate, a major program to improve communication effectiveness should be initiated by the company. Since you are in charge of corporate training and development, she has dropped this "bomb" in your lap. The clipping reads:

What's Your Communication Average?

How good is your internal communication system? How much of the important information is lost as messages pass down the line? In many cases, about 80 percent of the content is lost in transmission, reports the Dartnell Institute of Management. Robert A. Whitney, communications consultant, explains that, typically, a vice-president passes on only 66 percent of the message to a general supervisor or a sales director. By the time the message gets down to the supervisors or district sales managers, only 30 percent remains--and by the time it reaches production workers and salespeople, only 20 percent is left.

Exercise 1

Interpret the meaning of the clipping from an information perspective. Then write a memo to your boss giving your reaction to or explanation of the clipping.

Exercise 2

Explain what you have gained from this experience.

Experience 19-3   The Office of the Future: The Impact of Innovation in Information Technology**

Introduction

The term "Office of the Future" refers to office automation made possible by electronic information processing equipment. Office technology has advanced more rapidly in the past ten years than it has in all the rest of history. In the days of the abacus and quill pen, information processing was extremely slow and tedious. Since these hand-processing days, office technology has moved through mechanical (manual typewriter, adding machine) and electrical (electric typewriter) information processing phases to the most recent phase, electronic processing (computers in industry). Automated teller machines and computerized airline ticket booking are representative examples of electronic information processing. Even the routine chore of purchasing groceries involves application of electronic information processing. When one purchases groceries, the store clerk runs the universal product code (UPC) over an optical scanner at the service counter. The scanner reads the information on the code and relays it to the cash register, which displays the price and prints the item name and its price on a receipt. The same information is simultaneously relayed to a central computer, which keeps track of inventory and reorders the item when the supply of those items become low.

What will the office of the future be like? How will it differ from most offices of today? What role will information technology play in the office of the future? This experience is designed to expand your awareness of electronic office technology and the impact that it will have on the way the more successfully business organizations will operate. Complete the experience as directed.

Exercise 1

Listed below are fourteen terms associated with electronic office technology. Group together with 4 or 5 of your classmates, divide this list among members of your group, and find a definition/explanation for each term. Assign each term to at least two group members so that you obtain a check (control) on the accuracy of definitions/explanations. Exercise 1 will probably require you to spend some time in the library; many of these terms are not in your textbook. Use the spaces below to record your definitions.

Microcomputers:

Minicomputers:

Mainframe Computers:

Computer Software:

**Experience 19-3 developed from information provided in Kae H. Chung, *Management: Critical Success Factors*, Boston: Allyn and Bacon, Inc., 1987, pp. 540-552.

Word Processing:

Database Management:

Spreadsheet Analysis:

Graphic Analysis:

Databanks:

Electronic Mail:

Facsimile Communication:

Teleconferencing:

Local Area Network:

Centralized Network:

Exercise 2

Now that you have found definitions for the above terminology, identify the apparent changes that this electronic office technology will have on business organizations as they exist today. List and explain your major points in the space provided below. Through your library research you may also come across other information technology innovations. Also make note of the impact of these innovations below.

Exercise 3

Specifically, what impact do you see electronic office technology having on information processing workers? List your major points in the space provided below.

Exercise 4

Your instructor will initiate a general class discussion on the observations/reactions of all groups to the listed innovations in electronic office technology. Use the space below to record points made in the discussion that your group did not consider.

Exercise 5

Using the space provided below, indicate what you have learned from this experience.

20 INTERNATIONAL MANAGEMENT

Chapter Summary

The material in this chapter provides insights about the international management process. Topics covered include fundamentals of international management, the multinational corporation, management functions and multinational corporation, and comparative management.

Learning Objective 1   *An understanding of both international management and its importance to modern managers*

International management is simply defined as performing management activities across national borders. In essence, international management entails reaching organizational objectives by extending management activities to include an emphasis on organizations in foreign countries. Outstanding progress in areas like transportation, communication, and technology makes access to foreign countries more feasible and attractive as time passes. As a result, many modern managers face numerous international issues that can have a direct and significant impact on organizational success.

The notable trend that already exists in the United States and other countries toward developing business relationships in and with foreign countries is expected to accelerate even more in the future. The amount of U.S. investment in foreign countries as well as the amount of investment by foreign countries in the United States has been growing since 1970 and is expected to continue growing with only slight slowdowns or setbacks in recessionary periods. Many management educators as well as practicing managers voice the opinion that an understanding of international management is necessary to have a thorough and contemporary understanding of the fundamentals of management.

Learning Objective 2   *An understanding of what constitutes a multinational corporation*

The term multinational corporation, having first appeared in the dictionary about 1970, has been defined in several different ways in conversation and textbooks alike. For the purposes of this text, **a multinational corporation** is a company that has significant operations in more than one country. The multinational corporation carries out its activities on an international scale that disregards national boundaries and on the basis of a common strategy from a corporation center. A list of multinational corporations in this country includes four corporations whose business is energy (Exxon, Texaco, Chevron and Mobile). The largest foreign investments in the U.S. includes such well-known organizations as Seagram, Shell, BP, A&P, (Tenglemann), Hardee's (Imasco), Smith Corona and Ground Round (Hanson), Sony, Burger King and Pillsbury (Grand Metropolitan). Although a worldwide recession lasting into the early 1990s reduced multinational direct investment in the U.S., the North American Free Trade Agreement between the U.S., Canada, and Mexico will make the northern hemisphere the largest free trade zone in the world, surely a strong magnet attracting foreign investment from Europe and Asia.

Neil H. Jacoby implies that there are **six stages a company goes through to reach the highest degree of multinationalization.** According to Jacoby, multinationalization can range from a slightly multinationalized organization that simply exports products to a foreign country to a highly multinationalized organization that has some of its owners in other countries.

International management differs from domestic management because it involves operating within different national sovereignties, under widely disparate economic conditions, with peoples living within different value systems and institutions, in places experiencing the industrial revolution at different times, often over greater geographical distance, and in national markets varying greatly in population and area.

Learning Objective 3   *Insights concerning the risk involved in investing in international operations*

Developing a multinational corporation requires a substantial investment in foreign operations. Normally, managers who make foreign investments feel that such investments reduce or eliminate high transportation costs; allow participation in the rapid expansion of a market abroad; provide foreign technical, design, and marketing skills; and earn higher profits. Some risk, however, is associated with the decision to invest in foreign operations. For example, political complications between the **parent company**, the company investing in international operations, and various factions within the **host country, the** country in which the investment is made, could prohibit the previously mentioned outcomes from materializing. The likelihood of desirable outcomes related to foreign investments probably always will be somewhat uncertain and will vary from country to country. Nevertheless, managers faced with the decision of foreign investment must assess this likelihood as accurately as possible. A poor decision to invest in another country can cause serious financial problems for the organization.

Learning Objective 4   *Knowledge about planning and organizing in multinational corporations*

Planning is defined in text chapter 5 as determining how the management system will achieve its objectives. This definition is applicable to the management of either domestic or multinational organizations. The use of such management tools as policies, procedures, rules, budgets, forecasting, Gantt charts, and the program evaluation and review technique (PERT) are equally valuable in planning for either domestic or multinational organizations. Perhaps the primary difference between planning in multinational versus domestic organizations involves strategic planning. Organizational strategy for a purely multinational organization must include provisions that focus on the international arena, while such strategy for the domestic organization does not. Increased environmental uncertainties along with a growing sense of international competition are causing more and more managers to carefully evaluate internationalization as an organizational strategy. The most significant challenge facing modern managers may be how to plan strategically in order to survive in a multinational business world.

To develop appropriate international strategies, managers explore issues like: (1) establishing a new sales force in a foreign country, (2) developing new manufacturing plants in other countries through purchase or construction, (3) financing international expansion, and (4) determining which countries represent the most suitable candidates for international expansion. Although organizations' international strategies vary, most include some emphasis in one or more of the following areas: imports/exports, license agreements, direct investing, and joint venture.

Strategy in imports/exports emphasizes attempting to more successfully reach organizational objectives by **importing**-- buying goods or services from another country--or **exporting** selling goods or services to another country.

A **license agreement** is a right granted by one company to another to use its brand name, technology, product specifications, and so on in the manufacture or sale of goods and services. Naturally, the company to whom the license is extended pays some fee for the privilege. International strategy in this area involves more successfully reaching organizational objectives through either the purchase or sale of licenses at the international level.

Direct investing is using the assets of one company to purchase the operating assets (for example, factories) of another company. International strategy in this area emphasized the more successful reaching of organizational objectives through the purchase of operating assets in another country.

An international **joint venture** is a partnership formed by a company in one country with a company in another country for the purpose of pursuing some mutually desirable business undertaking. International strategy that includes joint ventures emphasizes the attainment of organizational objectives through partnerships with foreign companies.

Organizing is defined in text chapter 9 as the process of establishing orderly uses for all resources within the organization. Two important organizing topics regarding multinational corporations bear further discussion: organization structure and the selection of managers. **Organization structure** is defined in text chapter 9 as established relationships among resources within the management system, and the **organization chart** is the graphic illustration of organization structure. Chapter 9 also notes that departments as shown on organization charts are most commonly established according to function, product, territory, customers, or manufacturing process. Internationally oriented organizations also normally establish structure based upon these five areas (see text figure 20.3).

There is no one best way to organize all multinational corporations. Instead, managers of these organizations must analyze the multinational circumstances that confront them and develop an organization structure that best suits those circumstances. Naturally, for multinational organizations to thrive, they must select competent managers. Over the years, management theorists have identified **three basic managerial attitudes toward the operations of a multinational corporation:** ethnocentric, polycentric, and geocentric. The *ethnocentric attitude* reflects a feeling that multinational corporations should regard home country management practices as superior to foreign country management practices. Managers with an ethnocentric attitude seem prone to make the mistake of stereotyping home country management practices as sound and reasonable and foreign management practices as faulty and unreasonable. The *polycentric attitude* reflects a feeling that, since foreign managers are closer to foreign organizational units, they probably understand them better, and, therefore, foreign management practices should generally be viewed as more insightful than home country management practices. Managers with a *geocentric attitude* believe that the overall quality of management recommendations, rather than the location of managers, should determine the acceptability of management practices used to guide multinational corporations.

The ethnocentric attitude, although perhaps having the advantage of keeping the organization simple, generally causes organizational problems since feedback from foreign operations is eliminated. In some cases, the ethnocentric attitude even causes resentment toward the home country within the foreign society. The polycentric attitude can create the advantage of tailoring the foreign organizational segment to its culture, but can lead to the sizeable disadvantage of creating numerous individually run, relatively unique, and therefore more difficultly controlled foreign organizational segments.

The geocentric attitude is generally thought to be the most appropriate for managers in multinational corporations. This attitude promotes collaboration between foreign and home country management and encourages the development of managerial skill regardless of the organizational segment or country in which managers operate. An organization characterized by the geocentric attitude generally incurs high travel and training expenses, and many decisions are made by consensus. Although risks like wide distribution of power in such an organization are real, payoffs like better quality products, worldwide utilization of best human resources, increased managerial commitment to worldwide organizational objectives, and increased profit generally outweigh the potential harm of such risks. Overall, managers with a geocentric attitude tend to create organizations that contribute more to the long-run success of the multinational corporation.

Learning Objective 5   *Knowledge about influencing and controlling in multinational corporations*

Influencing is defined in text chapter 13 as guiding the activities of organization members in appropriate directions through such activities as communicating, leading, motivating, and managing groups. Influencing people within a multinational corporation, however, is more complex and challenging than within a domestic organization.

The one factor that probably most contributes to this increased complexity and challenge is culture. **Culture** is the total characteristics of a given group of people and their environment. Factors generally designated as important components of a culture include customs, beliefs, attitudes, habits, skills, state of technology, level of education, and religion. As a manager moves from a domestic corporation involving basically one culture to a multinational corporation involving several cultures, the task of influencing usually becomes progressively more difficult. To successfully influence people, managers in multinational corporations should acquire a working knowledge of the languages used in countries that house foreign operations, understand the attitudes of people in countries that house foreign operations, and understand the needs that motivate people in countries that house foreign operations. Multinational managers must understand their employees' need priorities and mold such organizational components as incentive systems, job design, and leadership style to correspond to these priorities.

Controlling is defined in text chapter 17 as making something happen the way it was planned to happen. As with domestic corporations, control in multinational corporations requires that standards be set, performance be measured and compared to standards, and corrective action be taken if necessary. Control in such areas as labor costs, product quality, and inventory is very important to organizational success, regardless of whether the organization is domestic or international.

Control of a multinational corporation, however, has additional complexities. First, there is the problem of different currencies. Another complication is that organizational units within multinational corporations are generally more geographically separated. This increased distance normally makes it more difficult for multinational managers to keep a close watch on operations in foreign countries. One action managers are taking to help overcome the difficulty of monitoring geographically separated foreign units is to carefully design the communication network or management information system (MIS) that links them. A significant part of this design is to require all company units to acquire and install similar MIS equipment in all offices, both foreign and domestic, in an effort to ensure the likelihood of network hookups when communication becomes necessary. In addition, such standardization of MIS equipment seems to provide the additional advantages of facilitating communication among all foreign locations as well as making MIS equipment repair and maintenance problems more understandable, more easily solved, and therefore more inexpensive.

Learning Objective 6   *Insights about what comparative management is and how it might help managers do their jobs better*

Perhaps the most popular international management topic today is comparative management. Comparative management is the study of the management process in different countries to examine the potential of management action under different environmental conditions. Comparative management emphasizes analysis of management practices in one country for their possible application in another country.

Learning Objective 7   *Ideas on how to be a better manager through the study of Japanese management techniques*

The one country being studied the most from a comparative management viewpoint is Japan. Before World War II, huge industrial conglomerates called *zaibatsus* controlled the Japanese economy. The *zaibatsus* were outlawed after the war, and a variation emerged known as *keiretsus,* collections of a number of major business organizations, whose managers effectively motivate organization members. The Japanese are so successful in this area that Americans are traveling to Japan to try to gain insights on Japanese motivation strategies.

Japanese managers seem to be able to motivate their subordinates by hiring an employee for life rather than some shorter period of time, elevating employees to a level of organizational status equal to that of management, and making them feel that they are highly valued by management and that the organization will provide for their material needs. Japanese managers obviously go to great lengths to build positive working relationships with their employees. In addition, there is some evidence that actions similar to those discussed in the previous paragraph have been applied successfully by Japanese managers in motivating American employees at the Nissan plant in Smyrna, Tennessee. Since the general Japanese culture has been shown to be a significant factor influencing the success of Japanese management, however, managers of other countries should imitate Japanese actions with extreme caution. What Japanese workers feel are desirable or need satisfying actions by management may not be the same as what workers from other countries feel are desirable or need satisfying.

Given the recent success of organizations like Nissan and Toshiba, many U.S. management writers have been carefully analyzing Japanese organizations and comparing them to American organizations. The purpose of this analysis and comparison is to make recommendations regarding how Japanese management practices can be used to improve the operation of American organizations.

One such recommendation, called **Theory Z**, was introduced by William Ouchi in 1981. Theory Z suggests integration of significant management practices in the United States and Japan into one, middle-ground, improved framework. Ouchi studied the following management practices in American and Japanese organizations: (1) the length of time workers were employed, (2) the way in which decisions were made, (3) where responsibility existed within the organization, (4) the rate at which employees were evaluated and promoted, (5) the type of control tools used, (6) the degree to which employees had specialized career paths, and (7) the type of concern organizations showed for employees. Text figure 20.4 summarizes Ouchi's findings regarding how these management practices differ in American and Japanese organizations.

Ouchi also made suggestions for how to integrate American and Japanese management practices to develop a new, more successful American organization, called a Type Z organization. The Type Z organization is characterized by the "individual responsibility" of American organizations, as well as the "collective decision making, slow evaluation and promotion, and holistic concern for employees" of Japanese organizations. The length of employment, control, and career path characteristics of the Type Z organization are essentially compromises between American and Japanese organizations.

Ouchi's Theory Z concept has gained much popularity not only among management theoreticians but also among practicing managers. As indicated by Organization Type J, employee participation in decision-making involved the evolution of teamwork or work teams, effectively introduced by such U.S. multinational organizations as Ford, Digital Equipment, General Electric, Champion International, and Boeing in the 1980s. Similarly, flexible work practices and cross-trained workers, the basis of teamwork as practiced in Japan, were introduced by Japanese operators of U.S. subsidiaries.

Japanese management has taught U.S. business to consider new approaches to compete with the Japanese high standard of industrialization. For example, leading American Management consultants are developing and proposing future changes for U.S. managers' consideration in the areas of strategies, organization, group cooperation, and competitive advantage.

Knowing You Know

True/False   *Directions: On the lines provided, place a "T" for true or an "F" for false for each of the statements that follow.*

_____ 1. International management is defined as performing management activities across national borders.

_____ 2. The smaller organization has a greater likelihood of participating in international operations of some sort.

_____ 3. International management differs from domestic management because it often involves working over greater geographical distances.

_____ 4. Planning is defined as determining how the management system will achieve its objectives.

_____ 5. Indirect investing is using the assets of one company to purchase the operating assets of another company.

_____ 6. The attainment of organizational objectives through a partnership with a foreign company is known as a joint venture.

_____ 7. There is usually only one best way to organize a multinational company.,

_____ 8. An ethnocentric attitude reflects a feeling that foreign management practices should generally be viewed as more insightful than home country management practices.

_____ 9. Multinational corporations should strive to select managers with geocentric attitudes rather than either polycentric or ethnocentric attitudes.

_____10. Influencing in a multinational corporation is not as complex or challenging as in a domestic corporation.

_____11. Control of labor costs, product quality, and inventory is much more important in a multinational corporation than a domestic one.

_____12. Comparative management is the study of the management process in different countries to examine the potential of management action under different environmental conditions.

_____13. One action managers are taking to help overcome the difficulty of monitoring geographically separated foreign units is to carefully design the communication network or management information system (MIS) that links them.

_____14. A main Japanese motivation strategy is to hire a person for a short period of time to maintain the job mobility of an individual.

_____15. Theory A suggests integration of significant management practices in the United States and Japan into one, middle-ground, improved framework.

Multiple Choice   *Directions: Circle the letter of the word or phrase that best completes each statement.*

16. William Ouchi, the developer of the Theory Z concept,
    a. wants to separate the Japanese and American styles of management
    b. feels that the integration of Japanese and American management practices would develop a better American organization
    c. believes that Japanese practices are better than American management practices
    d. *a* and *c*
    e. none of the above

17. Japanese motivation strategies include
    a. hiring employees for life rather than some shorter period of time
    b. elevating employees to a level of organizational status equal to that of management
    c. making employees feel that they are highly valued by management and that the organization will provide for their material needs
    d. none of the above
    e. all of the above

18. Managers attempting to influence people in multinational corporations should
    a. use specially trained translators instead of developing a working knowledge of the language used in a particular country
    b. ignore the attitudes of people in countries that house foreign operations
    c. understand the needs that motivate people in countries that house foreign operations
    d. all of the above
    e. none of the above

19. Three basic managerial attitudes toward the operations of a multinational corporation are
    a. ethnocentric, polycentric, and egocentric
    b. polycentric, geocentric, and egocentric
    c. geocentric, egocentric, and ethnocentric
    d. ethnocentric, polycentric, and geocentric
    e. none of the above

20. International management differs from domestic management because it involves operating
    a. within different national sovereignties
    b. under widely disparate economic conditions
    c. often over greater geographical distance
    d. in national markets varying greatly in population and area
    e. all of the above

21. Normally, managers who make foreign investments feel that such investments will
    a. increase transportation costs
    b. earn higher profits
    c. ignore foreign technical, design, and marketing skills
    d. allow participation in rapid market expansion at home
    e. all of the above

22. A license agreement is
    a. using the operating assets of one company to purchase another
    b. forming a partnership between companies in different countries
    c. a relationships among resources in a management system
    d. a right granted by one company to use its brand name, technology, product specifications, and so on in the manufacture and sale of goods and services
    e. *a* and *b*

23. Which of the management functions is the most important to a multinational corporation?
    a. planning
    b. organizing
    c. influencing
    d. controlling
    e. all of these are important

24. The feeling that the overall quality of management recommendations, rather than the location of managers, should determine the acceptability of management practices reflects a(n)
    a. ethnocentric attitude
    b. polycentric attitude
    c. geocentric attitude
    d. egocentric attitude
    e. none of the above

25. Which foreign country have managers from the United States been studying the most for the past few years?
    a. Germany
    b. Britain
    c. Taiwan
    d. Japan
    e. all of the above

Applying What You Know

Experience 20-1   Planning for International Operations

Introduction

The management process remains the same whether performed in Chicago, Illinois, or in Bangkok, Thailand. However, the issues that must be considered as each function of the process is carried out may change based upon differences in variables in the international system under consideration. In this experience, you develop a plan for conducting an international business operation or venture in a particular country or region of the world.

Exercise 1

Your instructor will break the class into small groups and assign each group one of the international business ventures that follow. Use the library and/or contact available resource persons from the country (area) in which your business operation is to be conducted to obtain information pertinent to your plan. Use the framework provided in figure 20.1* below to increase the chances that your group considers the more important variables as you develop your plan. Then jot down next to the appropriate variable in figure 20.2 the more important issues that your group identifies.

---

*Reprinted by permission of the author from Richard D. Robinson, *International Management* (Hinsdale, IL: Dryden Press, 1967).

International Business Venture	Location
1. Selling boxed cake mixes designed for use in electric rice cookers	Japan
2. Selling American made canned soups	Brazil
3. Selling American made refrigerators	Japan
4. Selling prepared baby food (in traditional glass jars)	Uganda

Figure 20.1 Management implications based on six variables in international systems and relationships among them.

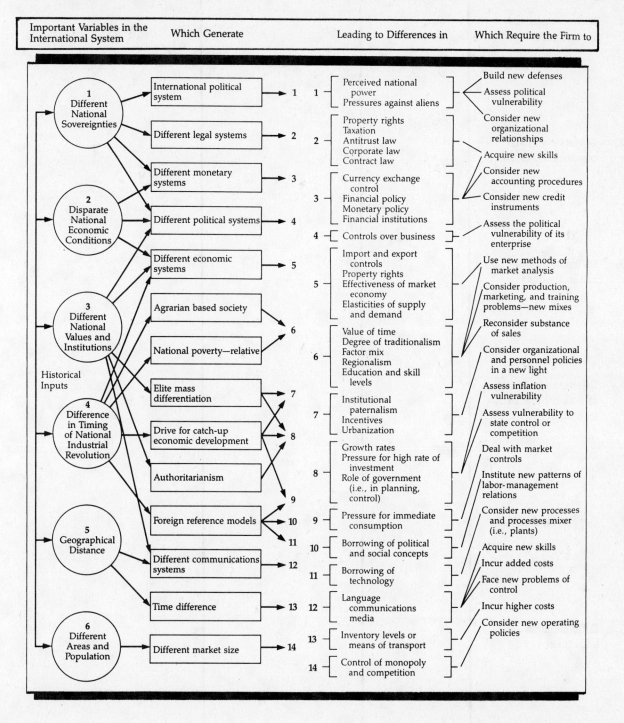

Figure 20.2 Management implications based on six variables in the international system.

Important Variables in the International System	Which Generate	Leading to Differences in	Which Require the Firm to
1. Different national sovereignties			
2. Disparate national economic conditions			
3. Different national values and institutions			
4. Difference in timing of national industrial revolution			
5. Geographical distance			
6. Different areas and population			

Exercise 2

Present your group's analysis of the assigned international business venture to the class. Then compare your analysis to that of other groups. Use the space below to note similarities and differences.

Exercise 3

Your instructor will present you with the scenario of an international business venture similar to the one your group investigated/analyzed. Write the factor(s) that your group omitted from its analysis.

Exercise 4

What have you gained from this experience?

Experience 20-2 Kuwait or Not?[**]

Introduction

As the world gets "smaller" because of progress in areas like transportation, communication, and technology, more and more business organizations are finding opportunities in international markets. This experience permits you to apply your knowledge of international management to a situation in which you might well find yourself in the future. Read the incident that follows, and then complete the exercises as directed.

Incident

He does not know it yet, but Leonard Ulrich soon will be facing a major career decision. As a design engineering manager for Builders International, a large multinational construction firm, Leonard has worked on numerous contract projects in the United States and Canada. He always has moved his family to the project locations, which caused few problems when his children were younger.

Last Friday, Harold Chamberlain, president of Builders International, decided to offer Leonard a promotion to project manager of a large housing construction project in Kuwait. Leonard would be allowed to take his wife and two daughters (ages fourteen and sixteen) with him. The Kuwait assignment would be for eighteen months, and then Leonard would return to corporate headquarters in the United States. Harold is unsure of what the reactions of Leonard and his family will be.

The move would be a unique cultural experience for Leonard and his family. In addition, the promotion would give Leonard sufficient international experience to replace a corporate vice-president who is scheduled for retirement in three years.

However, there are definite drawbacks. One major concern that Harold anticipates is the restrictions that commonly are placed on Western women in Arab countries. Also, even though good U.S.-operated private schools are available in Kuwait and the company would pay the tuition for Leonard's daughters, Harold knows that teenagers often resist leaving their friends. Furthermore, Leonard does not speak Arabic, although he is moderately proficient in French.

Harold knows that the choice of project manager is crucial because of the scope and the potential profitability of the project. At the same time, he wishes that he had thought of more factors when he approved the decision to bid on the project. Harold must discuss the "opportunity" with Leonard tomorrow, and he is trying to decide how to handle the conversation.

Exercise 1

a.   What political, economic, and cultural factors are present in the case?

[**]Reprinted by permission from p. 552 of *Management: Concepts and Effective Practice* by Michael Hitt, et al.; Copyright © 1992 by West Publishing. All rights reserved.

b. What specific factors should be considered in choosing someone for an overseas position?

c. What mistakes have Builders International and Harold Chamberlain already made?

d. If you were Leonard Ulrich, what would you do? Why?

Exercise 2

Explain what you have gained from this experience.

Experience 20-3 Preparing Managers for Overseas Assignments***

The amount of U.S. investment in foreign countries as well as the amount of investment by foreign countries in the United States has been growing since 1970 and is expected to continue growing. Furthermore, the notable trend that already exists in the United States toward developing business relationships in and with foreign countries is expected to accelerate even more in the future. Accompanying this increase in internationalization of operations is an increasing need for personnel capable of managing, or at least managing in, these overseas companies. While multinational corporations have learned many lessons over the years, there have been none more noteworthy than "preparation pays off." Companies have discovered that a well prepared employee is more productive, more satisfied, and more well adjusted.

Management at Hewlett-Packard (HP), one of the largest of the multinational corporations in terms of dollar value of goods and services sold, is one company that has learned this "preparation pays" lesson well. While it would be interesting to "sit in" on one of HP's briefing sessions for employees and their families scheduled for overseas assignment, physical distance from HP's International Office in Palo Alto, California and other limiting factors make this virtually impossible for most of us. However, the next best thing "to being there" may very well be to have the opportunity to be exposed to the framework utilized for such briefing sessions. Please find below Hewlett-Packard's "Foreign Service Employee (FSE) Briefing Checklist." After thoroughly familiarizing yourself with the "FSE Briefing Checklist," complete the experience as directed.

Foreign Service Employee (FSE) Briefing Checklist

1. Discussion of preview trip

2. Discussion of tax issues
   - tax equalization policy
   - personal income
   - 50% rule
   - working spouse
   - state taxes
   - rental of personal residence

3. U.S. payroll
   - changes/differences in paycheck
   - stay on U.S. payroll (corporate), paid in U.S. dollars
   - we become personnel and payroll department for duration of assignment

4. U.S. vs. foreign bank account
   - open account in U.S. outside of home state to avoid state tax
   - open account locally in transfer location
   - direct deposit of paycheck to U.S. bank account
   - usually no waiting period for U.S. checks to clear in transfer location

5. ORC cost-of-living tables

6. Compensation worksheet
   - explain about relocation allowance timing

7. Salary review/repatriation manager

Show first movie here
(followed by discussion of psychological aspects of environmental adjustment)

***Experience adapted from Arthur W. Sherman, Jr., George W. Bohlander, and Herbert J. Chruden, *Practical Study Experiences in Managing Human Resources*, Cincinnati: South-Western Publishing Company, 1988. pp. 319-321. Used with permission.

8. Household goods move

9. U.S. house vs. transfer location home
   - U.S. home is the responsibility of FSE
   - transfer location home includes furnishings, utilities

10. Language lessons
    - 150 hours per family members
    - start lessons in U.S. and take more in transfer location as needed

11. Physical exams
    - for physical, see doctor of your choice
    - dental, eye, ear, and EKG not covered unless recommended by doctor
    - give bill to home division to pay and they will bill to transfer location

12. Children's education
    - make arrangement at new location
    - HP will support K-12 to include tuition, books, uniforms, school bus
    - supports summer school for remedial help or to learn language

13. Temporary living expenses
    - 30 days from the time U.S. home is vacated until settled in FSE location
    - local management to extend beyond 30 days if necessary
    - full expense report status
    - covers hotel, meals, rental car
    - will cover groceries, dinner if staying in someone's home

14. Local holiday schedule

15. U.S. vacation schedule
    - report all vacation to Corporate International Relocations by HP Desk

16. Home leave
    - eligible after completing one year if staying six more months
    - HP pays round-trip economy air fare to point of origin
    - alternative location paid up to amount of air fare to return home
    - report usage to Relocations Administrator

17. Stock program
    - fill out form indicating address to send stock information
    - may sell stock by sending a desk message to Relocations Administrator

18. Medical/dental insurance
    - all FSEs must be insured by US Administrators
    - take supply of medical/dental/prescription forms with you
    - indicate exchange rate on date bill is paid/translate as necessary
    - send bills directly to U.S. administrators and keep copies

19. Mail disposition
    - post office forwards for one year within the U.S. only
    - have friend, relative, or HP person sort and forward first class through HP bulk mail
    - HP will support forwarding up to three magazine subscriptions till expirations

Show the rest of the movies here
(followed by discussion of country specifics)

Exercise 1

Now that you have studied the Foreign Service Employee (FSE) Briefing Checklist, meet with three or four of your classmates and prepare answers to the following questions.

a. Why is it desirable for a company that will be sending managers and their family on overseas assignments to have a checklist similar to the FSE briefing checklist?

b. You should have noticed that after #7 on the checklist a movie was shown and a discussion was initiated. Assume that you were asked to prepare materials to be covered on the psychological aspects of environmental adjustment. What topics should be addressed?

c. After #20 on the checklist, the remainder of a movie is to be shown, followed by discussion of country specifics. What topics should be included in a discussion of specifics for a particular country?

Exercise 2

The problem facing MNCs is to find managers who can succeed in a foreign environment. But what are the requirements that one should meet to be considered for a managerial position in a foreign country. Heller[****] provides a somewhat humorous profile of the ideal international manager:

[****]From Jean E. Heller, "Criteria for Selecting an International Manager," *Personnel*, Vol. 57, No. 3, (May-June, 1980), p. 48.

Ideally, it seems, he (she) should have the stamina of an Olympic swimmer, the mental agility of an Einstein, the conversational skill of a professor of languages, the detachment of a judge, the tact of a diplomat, and the perseverance of an Egyptian pyramid builder. . . . And if he (she) is going to measure up to the demands of living and working in a foreign country, he (she) should also have a feeling of culture; his (her) moral judgments should not be too rigid; he (she) should be able to merge with the local environment with chameleon-like ease; and he (she) should show no signs of prejudice.

a. Using the space below, identify what your group feels to be the ideal profile for the American international manager. Make sure you include sex, education, experience, feelings about local culture, concern for morality and ethics, pay, citizenship, languages spoken, and degree of independence in the profile that you develop.

b. As you can see, an overseas assignment asks a great deal of a manager. It also asks a lot of their families. In your group, develop a list of reasons for failure of American managers on foreign assignment.

c. What could a corporation do to increase the chances of U.S. managers succeeding in overseas assignments. Develop a list of the actions that a corporation could take.

Exercise 3

Explain what you gained from this experience in the space provided below.

Experience 20-4   Organizational Structures for International Operations[*****]

Introduction

In multinational business ventures, as in domestic operations, organizational structure is determined by corporate strategy--**structure follows strategy.** The organization, reflected by the organization chart, provides the vehicle for implementing strategic plans. The portion of the strategic plan related to international operations may range from simple export to worldwide operations. Resultingly, the organization structure used to carry out the strategy may range from a small export department to a chart reflecting a fully integrated multinational operation based on geography, product, or function.

The purpose of this experiential exercise is to give participants the opportunity to extend their understanding of the organizing function to international applications. More specifically, participants will be asked to develop (diagram) organization charts that will be effective in carrying out various business strategies for servicing international markets. For example, how would the organizational structure be charted if the strategy of the firm was to simply export some portion of its products to a foreign country?

Background

Before one is ready to begin charting organization structures for various international strategies, both a review of some of the more fundamental issues associated with selecting a pattern of organizational design (called departmentation) and background on the various methods of servicing foreign markets appear merited.

A. Patterns of Organizational Design

While there are a number of patterns from which managers may choose, the summary below will concentrate on the three most popular and frequently utilized types of departmentation. These patterns are titled functional, product, and geographical departmentation (Bedian, 1989, 201-207; 154-157; Pringle et al., 1988, 190-194; Szilagyi, 1988, 284-289).

The **functional pattern** is the organizational form in which business functions such as sales, finance, and production serve as the basic building blocks (see Figure 20.2). Consider using a functional structure if:

1. Product superiority is critical to the firm's strategy.
2. The environment is stable.
3. The work is best accomplished by one specialized task or sequence of tasks.

Figure 20.2 Functional Pattern of Organization

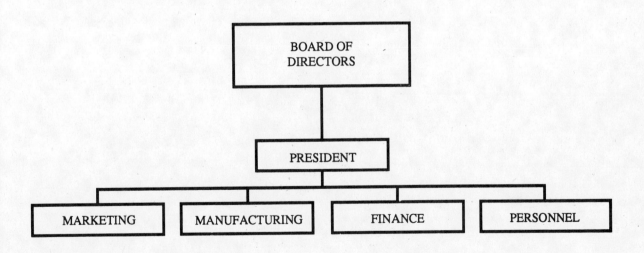

[*****]This exercise, coauthored by Lee A. Graf and Masoud Hemmasi, was presented at the 1990 Conference of the Association for Business Simulation and Experiential Learning, Honolulu, Hawaii, January 7-9, 1990.

Efficiency and economy are two of the more important advantages of functional organization. These benefits are derived primarily from improved communication flow between those with common interests and expertise. In addition, since all functional specialists are grouped together in a single department, the within-group synergy is magnified. A potential weakness in the functional pattern is its tendency to encourage a narrowness of viewpoint and, in turn, to deemphasize interdepartmental cooperation.

The **product pattern** involves grouping together all activities associated with a particular product or product line (see Figure 20.4). Consider using a product structure if:

1. Meeting schedules and controlling costs is very important.
2. Innovation is important (innovation requires the close cooperation and communication of various groups associated with the product; such product-centered cooperation can be achieved through a product structure).
3. Coping with an unstable environment is an important issue.
4. The organization is pursuing or plans to pursue a product diversification strategy (if corporations plan to diversify their product line--offer more products--such diversity can be more effectively managed through a product structure).
5. Technical expertise in various specialties is critical.

Figure 20.4 Product Pattern of Organization

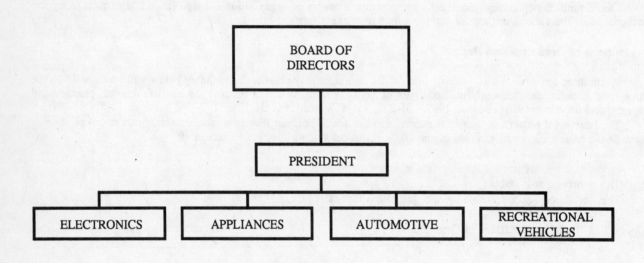

Among the advantages of product divisionalization is executive development (acquiring experience outside ones own field). Because the general manager of a product department is responsible for dealing with problems in various functional areas including marketing, R&D, finance, and production, this individual obtains a much broader purview of the entire operation. On the other hand, product structure has more insecure subordinates, for example, about such issues as possible unemployment and career retardation. In addition, employees in product structures are often more frustrated by ambiguity, conflict, and multiple levels of management and, therefore, less loyal to their organizations than are subordinates in functional structures. Furthermore, because the product structure does not emphasize or nurture interaction among similar professionals, it is likely to weaken functional expertise.

Some organizations use a **geographical pattern** rather than functional or product departmentation. Geographical departmentation groups tasks according to the place where the work is being done or the territorial location upon which the management system is being focused (see Figure 20.5). Consider using geographic structure if:

1. One is interested in fixing profit responsibility in a single business unit (just as in a product structure).
2. One wishes to take advantage of local or regional variations.

Figure 20.5 Geographical Pattern of Organization

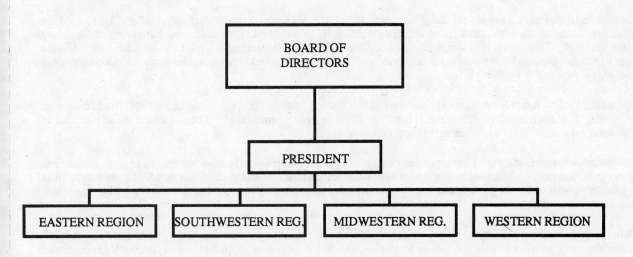

Geographical divisionalization has certain advantages in common with the product pattern, including breadth of manager experience. One additional advantage associated with adopting a geographical pattern relates to response time to customer needs. If the markets are widely dispersed in different regions, response time to customer needs will improve if the particular units in each region are grouped together.

B. Methods of Servicing Foreign Markets

Before an organization structure can be built to carry out an international corporate strategy, the organizational analyst also needs some background on the traditional methods utilized to service foreign markets (Murdick et al., 1984,274-280). These methods can be grouped under two major headings: "Export" and "Multinational Production."

Export of products to foreign countries involves primarily marketing-centered issues. The establishment of channels of distribution, effects of trade barriers, and an effective marketing mix abroad are some of the more significant sales related issues that must be taken into consideration in making export related decisions. However, the major concern appears to be designing the marketing mix to fit the target market. Export can be carried out by dealing through a(n):

1. **Export Management Company**--the simplest means to utilize because all foreign problems are handled by the export house. While a good way to begin exporting, consideration should be given to other channels as the market grows.

2. **Foreign Import House**--if one can identify a reliable importer who will effectively market ones' product, this is a good way to break into export. The U.S. Department of Commerce and the international departments of major banks can be very helpful in this regard.

3. **Manufacturer's Representative Abroad**--similar to the import house, but one may expect more individual effort to be put forth on the exporter's part.

4. **Marketing Subsidiary Abroad**--the domestic organization establishes an overseas marketing subsidiary. This subsidiary could be either wholly owned or a joint venture (see below for more indepth information on these types of subsidiary arrangements). This course of action is usually not considered unless the market potential has been firmly established through export or considerable multinational experience. This option provides maximum sales potential, but considerable volume is required to make it profitable.

5. **Domestic International Sales Corporation**--the DISC is a wholly owned domestic subsidiary which affords the parent company the opportunity to shelter export earnings from federal income taxes. The tax incentive is provided to encourage domestic firms to pursue export opportunities.

Multinational Production often evolves to service a market which has previously been serviced by export. In this case, the channels of distribution already exist and the extent of the market that can be captured can usually be estimated. It is at this time that consideration is given to moving the production function to foreign soil. There are several ways to get into multinational production:

1. **Licensing**--the company licenses use of its patents and know-how to foreign firms that will make and sell its products. Licensing may be used to generate profits from a market which cannot be tapped effectively through export or the creation of an overseas marketing subsidiary. It involves granting a license to a foreign firm to produce and market a product, for which the licensee pays royalties to the parent firm. Some of the major disadvantages of licensing include loss of control of quality, a diminished opportunity for the parent to effectively enter that foreign market at a later date, and the possibility of creating its own competitors in foreign markets.

2.. **Minority participation with a management contract**--this form may be used in those countries which require majority local ownership. The firm owns a minority interest but manages the venture under the terms of a contract with the majority owners. While not a popular mechanism to carry out production on foreign soil, this form may be the best available means of entering some markets.

3. **Joint venture**--in this form the parent organization owns a part interest (presumably majority) in a manufacturing subsidiary. The major advantage of this form is that the local partner may be able to provide special expertise or assistance. Expertise may relate to how to negotiate with local suppliers and how to penetrate local markets; special assistance might relate to special arrangements made possible through political contacts. The major disadvantage is that the foreign partner can be a source of conflict. For example, the interests of minority shareholders constitute a reduction in profitability; they can also interfere with the parent's investment and dividend decisions.

4. **Wholly owned subsidiary**--in this form, the parent company owns 100% of the overseas production facility. The most popular form for U.S. based multinationals, the major advantages are that the parent receives 100% of the profits and avoids major complications with foreign partners. Unfortunately, this form of organization is prohibited in some

countries. In addition, if politics play a major role in some country, the parent company may need local assistance to succeed.

Building Organizational Structures for International Operations

Once the most appropriate methods of servicing individual foreign markets have been found, a crucial policy area still remains. That is, how to organize diverse divisions into an integrated whole with the parent company. To maximize performance for the multinational firm, the organization structure must be appropriate for the firm's strategy and stage of international operation. Typically, the structure of the multinational firm evolves through a series of stages.

Exercise 1

In this exercise you will be asked to draw the organization charts for a hypothetical firm, Koca Cola, as it evolves through various stages from early international involvement to production and marketing through subsidiaries companies in host countries. Familiarize yourself with the setting provided for each stage, then draw the organization chart that would be most appropriate for each setting. Make reference to the "Background" section when choosing a basis for departmentation and for a refresher on the methods of servicing foreign markets.

Stage 1: Early Export--Koca Cola (KC) is an American soft drink manufacturer that has had considerable market success in the slowly expanding soft drink market. KC's strategic plan has always placed heavy emphasis on product superiority. "Koke," as it is sometimes called, has recently decided to expand its market by selling its soft drink in a large South American country. However, the company wants to get a better "handle" on the true demand for its product before establishing a marketing subsidiary abroad. Draw an organization chart that reflects the above outlined strategy.

Stage 2: Later Export--KC has now been exporting its product to Kantagua (our hypothetical South American country) for 14 months. Unfortunately, the import house being used also services a number of other clients from whom, we have surmised, it feels it can gain greater economic advantage. Resultingly, the import house has done an acceptable but not outstanding job of servicing our product line. Fortunately, however, by working through the import house arrangement, we have become far more aware of the untapped sales potential in Kantagua. The time seems 'ripe' to set up marketing subsidiaries in the three major cities in Kantagua (Kan, Tag, and Gua). In addition, you see growing opportunity for export to sister country, Tankagua, and decide to market your product line through a manufacturer's representative in that country. Draw the organization chart that reflects the revised strategy (all other strategic issues remain as they were in Stage 1).

Stage 3: Early International Production--Three years have now passed since setting up subsidiaries in Kantagua and establishing a relationship with an manufacturer's rep in Tankagua. During this time Koke's product line has expanded significantly. Koke's competition has also grown considerably. There is far less certainty today regarding business activity than has existed in the past. In addition, implementation of the firm's diversification strategy at home has resulted in the purchase of two other companies, "Folks" and "Jokes," each with a radically different product line utilizing different production facilities and marketing channels than that of Koke. Folks is a manufacturer of whole-hog sausage; Jokes, a company that produces and markets novelty items (gag and party gifts). While thought has been given to exporting the products of Folks and Jokes to foreign markets, no decision has yet been made. The only firm international decision made by corporate management is that it will establish a joint venture arrangement with Tagua Industries located in the city of Kan to produce Koke for sale and distribution in Kantagua's three major cities (Kan, Tag, and Gua) and in the expanding markets in more rural areas. Draw the organization chart that reflects this revised strategy (all other strategic issues remain as they were in Stage 2).

Stage 4: Later International Production--Three additional years have now passed since initiating production of Koke through a joint venture in Kantagua and exporting it from the U.S. to Tankagua. One of the lessons well learned over these years was that while in close proximity to each other, Kantagua, Tankagua, and all of its South American neighbors have major differences in markets, cultures, and laws. These national variations necessitate that business ventures in each country be handled very differently. During this period, company executives have learned a great deal about the wants and desires of the people of Kantagua; they also have had the opportunity to assess more accurately the market for Koke in Tankagua. Furthermore, business executives in Tankagua's northern neighbor, Guatanka, have expressed interest in setting up a bottling plant in that country. Government regulations in Guantanka, however, prohibit foreign (U.S. in this case) firms from owning or managing production facilities. Licensing arrangements for production and marketing are legal in Guatanka and such an agreement is reached with this group of executives. Because of significantly improved relations with government officials in Tankagua and very flexible laws associated with business practices there, Koke's corporate officials have decided to build a bottling facility and establish sales outlets in Nat, Tankagua's capitol. This will be a wholly owned subsidiary of Koca Cola. Company officials also have succeeded in negotiating an import arrangement for Folks' sausage with the import house that had previously handled the Koke account in Tankagua. Because of the significant growth in international activity (now generating more than 35% of the net profit of the corporation), the company has decided to divisionalize its international operations, separating it from its domestic businesses. Draw an organizational chart that reflects the above outlined strategy (all other strategic issues remain as they were in Stage 3).

Exercise 2

As you have just experienced through Exercise 1, the evolution of the organizational structure of an international enterprise can be viewed as a series of stages, with each stage a modification or adaptation of the structure in the previous stage. While Stage 4 above depicted a fully internationalized operation, with an international division of equal status to domestic divisions, continued growth of these divisions accompanied by enlarging interests of top management in international opportunities may lead some firms to abandon their international divisions in favor of a more global organization structure. At the global stage, responsibilities for both foreign and domestic business are moved to the top echelons and new subdivisions are specified on either a functional, geographic, or product basis. In the global stage, no single national market draws greater interest or attention than any other (Robock et al., 1977, 428-440). Your task in Exercise 2 is to construct organization charts from a functional, a geographic, and a product basis to reflect the more global philosophy just expressed. Assume that the corporation now has wholly owned subsidiaries for Koke, Folks, and Jokes in the United States, Kantagua, Tankagua, and Guatanka (use only the business functions of production and marketing in the construction of your charts). Use the space provided below for your organization charts.

Exercise 3

Explain what you have learned about designing organization structures for international operations from involving yourself in this experiential exercise.

SOURCES

Bedeian, Arthur G., *Management* (Chicago: The Dryden Press, 1989), 201-207.

Murdick, Robert G., R. Carl Moor, Richard H. Eckhouse, and Thomas W. Zimmerer, *Business Policy: A Framework for Analysis* (Columbus, Ohio: Grid Publishing, Inc., 1984), 274-280.

Pringle, Charles D., Daniel F. Jennings, Justin G. Longenecker, *Managing Organizations: Functions and Behaviors* (Columbus, Ohio: Merrill Publishing Company, 1988), 190-194.

Robock, Stefan H., Kenneth Simmonds, Jack Zwick, *International Business and Multinational Enterprises* (Homewood, Illinois: Richard D. Irwin, Inc., 1977), 428-440.

Szilagyi, Andrew D., Jr., *Management and Performance* (Glenview, Illinois: Scott, Foresman and Company, 1988), 284-289.

21 QUALITY: BUILDING COMPETITIVE ORGANIZATIONS

Chapter Summary

This chapter: (1) defines quality and total quality management (TQM), (2) explains the importance of quality, (3) discusses how to achieve quality, (4) describes how strategic planning can improve quality, and (5) outlines skills useful in achieving quality.

Learning Objective 1   *An understanding of the relationship between quality and total quality management*

Quality was defined in Chapter 18 as how well a product does what it is supposed to do--how closely and reliably it satisfies the specifications to which it is built. In general, quality was presented as the degree of excellence on which products or services can be ranked.

Total Quality Management (TQM) is the continuous process of involving all organization members in ensuring that every activity related to the production of goods or services has an appropriate role in establishing product quality. In essence, all organization members emphasize the appropriate performance of activities throughout the company in order to maintain the quality of products offered by the company. Under the TQM concept, all organization members work both individually and collectively to maintain the quality of products offered to the marketplace.

Although the TQM movement actually began in the United States, the establishment, growth, and development of the movement throughout the world is largely credited to the Japanese. The Japanese believe that a TQM program must include the cooperation of all people within a company. TQM is generally credited as a major factor in Japan's undeniable success in establishing itself as a major competitor in the world marketplace.

Overall, TQM is a means to the end of product quality. The excellence or quality of all management activities (planning, organizing, and controlling) inevitably influences the quality of final goods or services offered by organizations to the marketplace. In general, the more effective a TQM program within an organization, the higher the quality of goods and services that an organization can offer to the marketplace.

Learning Objective 2   *An appreciation of the importance of quality.*

Many managers and management theorists believe that organizations without high quality products will be unable to compete in the world marketplace of today. Producing high quality products is not an end in itself. Successfully offering high quality goods and services to the marketplace typically results in **three important benefits for the organization:** positive company image, lower costs and higher market share, and decreased product liability costs.

To a significant extent, an organization's reputation for high quality results in a positive image for the organization. Overall, organizations gain many advantages from having a positive company image. A *positive image*, for example, can be instrumental in recruiting valuable new employees, accelerating sales of a product newly offered to the marketplace, and obtaining needed loans from financial institutions. To summarize, high quality products generally result in a positive company image, which in turn results in numerous organizational benefits.

Overall, activities that support product quality benefit the organization by yielding *lower costs and greater market share*. Greater market share or gain in product sales is a direct result of customer perceptions of improved product quality. Activities within an organization that contribute to product quality result in such benefits as increased productivity, lower rework and scrap costs, and lower warranty costs, which in turn result in lower manufacturing costs and lower costs of servicing products after they are sold. The other important point is that both greater market share and lower costs due to high quality normally result in greater organizational profits.

Product manufacturers are increasingly facing *legal suits over damages caused by faulty products*. Organizations that design and produce faulty products can be and are being held liable for damages resulting from the use of such products.

Learning Objective 3   *Insight about how to achieve quality*

Recognizing these benefits of quality, companies in recent years have increased their emphases on manufacturing high-quality products. Several major awards have been established to recognize those organizations producing exceptionally high quality products and services. The most prestigious international award is the **Deming Award**, established in Japan in honor of W. Edwards Deming, who introduced Japanese firms to statistical quality control and quality improvement techniques after World War II. The most widely known award in the United States is the **Malcolm Baldridge National Quality Award**, awarded by the American Society of Quality and Control. This award was established in 1988. A few major awards recognize outstanding quality in particular industries. One example is the **Shingo Prize for Excellence in American Manufacturing**, sponsored by several industry groups, including the Association for Manufacturing Excellence and the National Association of Manufacturers, and administered by Utah State University. Another example, in the health care industry, is the **Healthcare Forum/Witt Award: Commitment to Quality.** The President of the United States and several states also have established a variety of quality awards. NASA gives an award for outstanding quality to its exceptional subcontractors. As these examples suggest, quality is an increasingly important element in an organization's ability to compete in today's global marketplace.

Ensuring that all company operations play a productive role in maintaining product quality seems like an overwhelming task. Although the task is indeed formidable, several useful and valuable guidelines have been formulated to make the task more achievable.

According to **Philip B. Crosby**, in order to achieve product quality, an organization must be "injected" with certain ingredients relating to integrity, systems, communications, operations, and policies. By adding these ingredients to an organization, the organization should be able to achieve significant progress in achieving product quality. Crosby calls these ingredients the "vaccination serum" that prevents the disease of low company-wide quality.

W. Edwards Deming advocates that the way to achieve product quality is to continually improve the design of a product and the process used to manufacture it. According to Deming, top management has the primary responsibility in achieving product quality. Deming advises that if management follows his 14 point approach, it will achieve a high level of success in improving and maintaining product quality.

Joseph M. Juran's philosophy emphasizes that management should pursue the mission of quality improvement and maintenance on two levels: (1) the mission of the firm as a whole to achieve and maintain high quality, and (2) the mission of individual departments within the firm to achieve and maintain high quality. According to Juran, quality improvement and maintenance is a clear process. Managers must be involved with studying symptoms of quality problems, pinpointing the quality problems inferred by the symptoms, and applying solutions to these problems. For maximum impact of a quality effort, strategic planning for quality should be similar to an organization's strategic planning for any other organizational issue like finance, marketing, or human resources. That is, strategic planning for quality should include setting short-term and long-term quality goals, comparing quality results with quality plans, and integrating quality plans with other corporate strategic areas.

Shigeo Shingo, of Toyota Production Systems, first learned quality production techniques from the Americans, who advocated statistical techniques. He later broke with this approach, however, in favor of what he called "mistake-proofing," or in Japanese, *poka yoke*. The essence of *poka yoke* is that production systems should be made mistake-proof, so that it is impossible for a system to produce anything except good product. Previously, quality was governed primarily by inspecting work after it was done, to catch and then fix defects, if possible. Even statistical quality control is dependent upon inspecting products to diagnose problems with production systems. Shingo recognized the wasted effort and cost of inspections, so he developed methods to assure that products are produced correctly the first time, every time.

Armand V. Feigenbaum is credited with originating the term "total quality control," today more often referred as "total quality management," or TQM. The basic idea of TQM is that every operation in an organization can benefit from the application of quality improvement principles. Defects are costly and unacceptable throughout any organizations, not just on the manufacturing floor.

Learning Objective 4   *An understanding of how strategic planning can be used to promote quality*

The *initial step* of the strategic management process is **environmental analysis.** Environmental analysis was defined in chapter 7 as the study of organizational environment to pinpoint factors that can significantly influence organizational operations. In establishing the role of environmental analysis to enhance product quality, special attention can be given to studying quality related environmental factors. Consumer expectations about product quality, the quality of products offered by competitors, and special technology being developed to enhance the quality of organizational activities are all examples of such factors.

Suppliers are often given special attention during environmental analysis by managers who stress quality. Suppliers are those companies that sell materials to be used in the final assembly of a product by another company. Basically, the satisfactory performance of a final product will only be as good as the quality of parts obtained from company suppliers.

Defective parts from suppliers can result in delayed delivery schedules, reduced sales, and reduced productivity. Special study of suppliers during environmental analysis can alert management to suppliers who can help to improve product quality through the quality of the parts that they furnish.

The *second step* of the strategic management process is **establishing organizational direction**. In this step the results of environmental analysis are used as the basis for determining the path that the organization will take in the future. This path is them documented and distributed throughout the organization in the form of a mission statement and related objectives. Assuming that environmental analysis results indicate that product quality is important for an organization, a manager can use an organizational mission statement and its related objectives to give general direction to organization members regarding the organization's focus on product quality.

In studying how different companies establish the direction of product quality focus, it becomes apparent that different companies define product quality in different ways. For example, at some companies product quality is defined as a stronger product that will last longer, or a heavier more durable product. At other companies, product quality can be the degree to which a product conforms to design specifications, or product excellence at an acceptable cost. In still other companies, quality is defined as the degree to which a product meets consumer requirements. Whatever management decides that its definition of product quality might be, this definition must be communicated to all organization members in order that they might work together in a focused and efficient way to achieve predetermined product quality.

After determining organizational direction, the *third step* of the strategic management process is **strategy formulation**-- deciding what steps should be taken to best deal with competitors. Incorporating the issue of product quality as part of the focus of a SWOT analysis (Strength, Weaknesses, Opportunities, Threats) can help managers develop quality-based strategies. As an example, it may be pointed out as a result of a SWOT analysis that organization members are not adequately trained to handle product quality issues with which they deal. Naturally, a strategy based upon this organizational weakness would suggest a need to improve quality oriented training.

Several **management strategies** have proven especially successful in improving and maintaining high quality operations and products. These include *value adding, leadership, empowerment, partnering, the right information right now,* and *continuous improvement and innovation.*

In **value adding,** all assets and effort should, as much as possible, directly add value to the product or service. All activities, processes, and costs that do not directly add value to the product should, as much as possible, be eliminated. Non-value-adding costs are wasteful and can be very costly. This particular strategy is largely responsible for the drastic reductions in staff positions in most large organizations in recent years.

The traditional vision of "The Boss," with whip in hand, *driving* lazy, reluctant workers to ever-higher production goals set from on high by management, is disappearing. In quality-focused organizations, "associates" (no longer called "workers" in many quality-focused organizations) are led. Through this **leadership**, management establishes vision and organizational values, and works with the associates to perfect the production process.

With **empowerment,** associates are organized into self-directed teams and empowered to do and improve their jobs, even to change work processes. They are trained, retrained, and cross trained in a variety of jobs. "Facilitators" (formerly called "supervisors") work with the associates to provide the resources necessary to meet customer needs.

In **partnering,** the organization establishes what are described as "partnerships" with suppliers and customers, (i.e., actively working with suppliers and customers) to find ways to improve the quality of products and services. Efforts are made to reduce the number of suppliers as much as possible to only those that are *reliable and cost-effective,* and *can prove the sustained quality of their products.*

The right information right now suggests that in a quality management environment, information systems are required that provide immediate access to critical nonfinancial and financial information, specifically tailored to the needs of the manager. Computerized information systems are answering this need. Everyone is trained in computers, from executive management through production staff. Computer terminals are now as commonplace on factory floors as they are in offices.

Finally, the clarion themes of the quality movement are **continuous improvement and constant innovation.** Last year's best performance is not good enough today, and today's best practices will not be good enough perhaps even next month. **Tom Peters** reported in *Thriving on Chaos: Handbook for a Management Revolution* that in 1982 Toyota, the company establishing the ideal for quality in automobile manufacturing, was implementing an average of five thousand employee suggestions (i.e., improvements) every day. That number does not include improvements initiated by management. Peters further advocated, "as a starting point," companies should target the percentage of revenues stemming from new products and services introduced in the previous twenty-four months at 50 percent. While these numbers might seem extreme--and perhaps they are for some companies--they clearly suggest the rapidly changing market place in which today's organizations compete.

The *fourth step* of the strategic management process is **strategy implementation**. Once the results of environmental analysis indicate that product quality is important for an organization, product quality direction has been established through its mission statement and related objectives, and strategy has been developed for achieving or maintaining product quality, management is ready to implement its product quality strategy. Implementation simply involves putting product quality strategy into action. Although implementing product quality strategy seems like a straightforward step, in reality it is quite complex. In order for managers to be successful at implementing product quality strategy, they must meet challenges like being sensitive to the fears and frustrations of employees in implementing new strategy, providing organizational resources needed to implement the strategy, monitoring implementation progress, and creating and using a network of individuals throughout the organization who can be helpful in overcoming implementation barriers.

Two tools managers commonly use to implement product quality strategy are policies and organizational structure. A policy was defined in chapter 8 as a standing plan that furnishes broad, general guidelines for channeling management thinking toward taking action consistent with reaching organizational objectives. A quality oriented policy is a special type of policy. A **quality oriented policy** is a standing plan that furnishes broad, general guidelines for channeling management thinking toward taking action consistent with reaching *quality* objectives. Quality-oriented policies can be made in virtually any organizational area. Such policies can focus on issues like the quality of new employees recruited, the quality of plans developed within the organization, the quality of decision-related information gathered and distributed within the organization, the quality of parts from suppliers to be used in the final assembly of products, and the quality of training used to prepare employees to work in foreign subsidiaries.

Juran says that "to create a revolutionary rate of quality improvement requires...a special organization structure." He suggests organizing a *"quality council,"* consisting largely of upper managers, to direct and coordinate the company's quality improvement efforts. The quality council's main job is to establish an appropriate infrastructure, which would include: (1) a process for nominating and selecting improvement projects, (2) a process for assigning project improvement teams, (3) a process for making improvements, (4) a variety of resources, such as time for diagnosis and remedy of problems, facilitators to assist in the improvement process, diagnostic support, and training, (5) a process for review of progress, (6) a process for dissemination of results and for recognition, (7) an appropriate employee merit rating system to reward quality improvement, and (8) extension of business planning to include goals for quality improvement. Juran points out that upper management's role in quality improvement includes active involvement in each element of the infrastructure, including serving on some improvement project teams. Notice that such a structure involves employees at all levels. All employees, including managers, serve on quality improvement teams. The quality council comprises mostly upper management, but also may include other employees as well.

Structure, on the other hand, was defined in chapter 9 as designated relationships among resources of the management system. Quality oriented structure is designated relationships among organizational resources that emphasize the achievement of quality objectives. One means of illustrating relationships among organizational resources as they are intended to help management accomplish product quality objectives is an organization chart, a graphic illustration of structure.

Strategic control, the *fifth step* of the strategic management process, emphasizes monitoring the strategic management process to make sure that it is operating properly. In terms of product quality, strategic control would focus on monitoring company activities to ensure that product quality strategies are operating as planned. In achieving strategic control in the area of product quality, management must measure how successful it has become in achieving product quality. Insights offered by Philip Crosby imply that in order to control efforts in achieving product quality, several organizational areas should be monitored. These areas include management's understanding and attitude toward quality, how quality appears within an organization, how organizational problems are handled, the cost of quality as a percentage of sales, quality improvement actions taken by management, and how management summarizes the organization's quality position.

According to Crosby, organizations go through five successive stages of quality maturity as they approach the maximum level of quality in all phases of organizational activity. Each of the stages represents variations of the above monitoring areas. Crosby's **Quality Management Maturity Grid** is a rating grid which contains five stages of quality and different variations of monitoring areas represented with each stage (see Figure 21.3). Overall, strategic control concerning quality would focus on ensuring that an organization evolves to Stage V of the Quality Management Maturity Grid.

Learning Objective 5   *Knowledge about the quality improvement process and reengineering*

Two approaches may be taken to improve quality. The first is the one advocated by most of the quality experts, such as Deming, Juran, Crosby, and Feigenbaum. This process can be described as *incremental improvement*. One thing is improved at a time. Of course, many of these incremental improvements may be undertaken simultaneously throughout an organization. Toyota's average of five thousand improvements per day in 1982 already has been mentioned. The second approach is advocated by Michael Hammer, who advocates the complete reengineering of a process. This requires starting with what sometimes is described as *a clean sheet of paper*. The question is asked, "If we were to start over today, how would we do this?"

A variety of researchers and consultants have advocated a variety of incremental approaches to achieving excellent quality in products and processes. Regardless of their differences, almost all **incremental improvement processes** bear some remarkable similarities. In *Step 1, an area of improvement is chosen, which often is called the improvement "theme."* This may be chosen by management, or an improvement team may choose the theme. The point is that an improvement objective must be chosen. In *Step 2, if a quality improvement team has not already been organized, one is organized.* Members of this team might include one or more associates directly responsible for the work being done, one or more customers receiving the benefit of the work, one or more suppliers providing input into the work, a member of management, or perhaps one or more experts in areas particularly relevant to solving the problem and making the improvement. In *Step 3, the team*

this team might include one or more associates directly responsible for the work being done, one or more customers receiving the benefit of the work, one or more suppliers providing input into the work, a member of management, or perhaps one or more experts in areas particularly relevant to solving the problem and making the improvement. In *Step 3, the team "benchmarks" the best performers; that is, the team identifies how much improvement is required in order to match the very best.* Suppose current performance of the company is an average of thirty-five minutes compared to the twenty-minute benchmark. There is a minimum possible improvement of fifteen minutes on the average. In *Step 4, the team performs an analysis to find out how current performance can be improved to meet, or beat, the benchmark.* Factors to be analyzed include potential problems related to equipment, materials, work methods, people, and environmental factors, such as legal constraints, physical conditions, and weather. In *Step 5, the team performs a pilot study to test the selected remedies to the problem.* Suppose the team conducted a pilot program for a month. The question then becomes, "is the improvement worth the cost?" If the company beats the benchmark, that performance level can become the standard. Finally, in *Step 6, management implements the improvements.*

Many such incremental improvements can greatly enhance a company's competitiveness. Of course, as more and more companies achieve better and better quality, the market becomes more and more demanding. The key, using the incremental approach, is to continually be improving both product and process.

Hammer argues that significant improvement requires "breaking away from...outdated rules and...assumptions...." It requires a complete rethinking of the process. He, too, recommends organizing a team representing the functional units involved in the process being **reengineered,** as well as other units depending upon the process. One important reason to reengineer is the need to integrate computerized production and information systems, which can be expensive and very difficult to accomplish piecemeal with an incremental approach. Hammer outlines **seven principles of reengineering:**

Principle 1. Organize around outcomes, not tasks. Traditionally, work has been organized around different tasks, such as sawing, typing, assembling, and supervising. This first principle of reengineering would have one person or team performing all the steps in a process. The person or team would be responsible for the outcome of the total process. *Principle 2.* Have those who use the output of the process perform the process. For example, a production department may do its own purchasing, and even its own cost accounting. This principle would require a broader range of expertise from individuals and teams, and a greater integration of activities.

Principle 3. Subsume information-processing work into the real work that produces the information. Modern computer technology now makes it possible for a work process to process information simultaneously. For example, scanners at checkout counters in grocery stores both process customer purchases and update accounting and inventory records at the same time.

Principle 4. Treat geographically dispersed resources as though they were centralized. Hammer uses Hewlett-Packard as an example of how this principle works. Each of the company's fifty manufacturing units had its own separate purchasing department, which prevented scale discounts. But rather than centralize purchasing, which would have reduced responsiveness, the company simply introduced a corporate unit to coordinate local purchases, so that scale discounts could be achieved. The local purchasing units retained their decentralized authority and thereby preserved the responsiveness to local manufacturing needs.

Principle 5. Link parallel activities instead of integrating their results. Several processes are often required to produce products and services. Too often, companies segregate these processes so that only at the final stage does the product come together. If problems occur in one or more processes, those problems may not become apparent until too late, at the final step. It is better, Hammer says, to link and coordinate the various processes so that such problems are avoided.

Principle 6. Put the decision point where the work is performed, and build control into the process. Traditional bureaucracies place decision authority separate from the work. This new principle suggests that the people doing the work should also make the decisions. The salesman should have the authority and responsibility to approve credit, for example. This principle saves time and helps the organization respond to customer needs. While some managers worry that such practices would reduce control over the process, control can be built into the process. In the example, criteria for credit approval can be built into a computer program, giving the salesman specific guidance on the decision.

Principle 7. Capture information once and at the source. Computerized on-line databases help make this principle achievable. Computers now make it easy to collect information when it originates, store it, and send it to those who need it.

Reengineering allows major improvements to be made all at once. While reengineering can be expensive, today's rapidly changing markets sometimes demand such drastic response.

Knowing You Know

True/False **Directions:** *On the lines provided, place a "T" for true or an "F" for false for each of the statements that follow.*

_____ 1. The Total Quality Management (TQM) movement began in Japan.

_____ 2. One important benefit of successfully offering high quality goods and services to the marketplace is positive company image.

_____ 3. According to Philip B. Crosby, organizations go through six successive stages of quality maturity as they approach the maximum level of quality in all phases of organizational activity.

_____ 4. W. Edwards Deming advocates that the way to achieve product quality is to continually improve the design of a product and the process used to manufacture it.

_____ 5. In essence, TQM is a means to the end of product quality.

_____ 6. The initial step of the strategic management process is establishing organizational direction.

_____ 7. The most prestigious international quality award is the Deming Award.

_____ 8. The definition of product quality must be communicated to all organization members in order that they might work together in a focused and efficient way to achieve predetermined product quality.

_____ 9. Although implementing a product quality strategy seems quite complex, in reality it is a relatively straightforward step.

_____ 10. Two tools managers commonly use to implement product quality strategy are policies and organizational structure.

_____ 11. A quality oriented policy is a standing plan that furnishes broad, general guidelines for channeling management action that is consistent with reaching quality objectives.

_____ 12. Armand V. Feigenbaum is credited with originating the term "total quality control."

_____ 13. "The Right Information Right Now" is the idea that tailor-made computerized information systems will be required to provide managers immediate access to critical nonfinancial and financial information.

_____ 14. One important reason to seriously consider reengineering over the incremental improvement process is the need to integrate computerized production and information systems which is difficult to accomplish piecemeal.

_____ 15. Tom Peters, in *Thriving on Chaos: Handbook For a Management Revolution*, suggests that companies target the percentage of revenues stemming from new products and services introduced in the previous twenty-four months at 80 percent.

Matching

Directions: Match items 16-25 with items a-j. There is only one correct answer for each item.

_____16. Total Quality Management (TQM)

_____17. Quality

_____18. Decreased product liability costs

_____19. W. Edwards Deming's perspective on how to achieve quality

_____20. Philip B. Crosby's perspective on how to achieve quality

_____21. Joseph M. Juran's perspective on how to achieve quality

_____22. Establishing organizational direction

_____23. Shigeo Shingo's perspective on how to achieve quality.

_____24. "Empowering" and "Partnering"

_____25. Step 1 in the Incremental Improvement Process

a. If management follows his 14 point approach it will achieve a high level of success in improving and maintaining product quality.

b. Management must mistake-proof so that it is impossible for a system to produce anything except good products.

c. An area of improvement, called the improvement "theme," is chosen.

d. How closely and reliably a product satisfies the specifications to which it is built.

e. To achieve quality, management should pursue the mission of quality improvement and maintenance on two levels: (1) the firm as a whole, and (2) individual departments within the firm.

f. Management strategies that have proven successful in improving and maintaining high quality operations and products.

g. The continuous process of involving all organizational members in ensuring that every activity related to the production of goods or services has an appropriate role in establishing product quality.

h. The second step of the strategic management process

i. An organization must be "injected" with certain ingredients relating to integrity, systems, communications, operations, and policies in order to achieve product quality.

j. An important benefit from successfully offering high quality goods and services to the marketplace.

Applying What You Know

Experience 21-1   Harley-Davidson Builds in Quality to Beat Back the Japanese

Introduction

Achieving overall quality requires an overall organizational commitment. To achieve overall quality or "total quality management" involves establishing quality related policies, standards, and procedures, setting up quality control training, soliciting quality assistance from suppliers, controlling quality in the production, purchasing, and warehousing processes, and usually transforming the inventory system to a JIT focus. In addition, employee participation and commitment to quality is necessary to make a total quality control or total quality management approach work. Finally, each worker must possess the authority to stop a production process or assembly line if a quality related deviation is discovered.

The condensed *Fortune* magazine article entitled "How Harley Beat Back the Japanese"* documents how management at Harley-Davidson, the last U.S. motorcycle maker, was able to pull off one of America's most celebrated turnarounds. As you will soon discover, at the core of this turnaround was heavy emphasis on employee involvement, JIT inventory control, and a dominant focus on quality. Read the article that follows, then complete the experience as directed.

*Article by Peter C. Reid, "How Harley Beat Back the Japanese," (condensed by Peter C. Reid from "Well-Made in America: How Harley Beat the Japanese at Their Own Game," *Fortune*, September 25, 1989), *Annual Editions: Management 91/92*, Fred Maidment, Editor, Guilford, Connecticut: The Dushkin Publishing Group, Inc., 1991, pp. 21-24.

HOW HARLEY BEAT BACK THE JAPANESE

Quality was awful, manufacturing a mess, and the Japanese were gobbling market share. The managers who bought the company pulled off one of America's most celebrated turnarounds.

Peter C. Reid

At the start of the 1980s few people gave Harley-Davidson much chance to survive. The last U.S. motorcycle maker was being bettered by the Japanese. Its share of the super-heavyweight motorcycle market had fallen from 75% in 1973 to less than 25%. Yet today the Milwaukee-based company, 86 years old and running full throttle, has nearly 50% of the market. Well-Made in America, a book commissioned by Harley and written by business journalist Peter C. Reid, is the authentic and candid tale of how a beleaguered company beat the Japanese, beat the bankers, and beat the odds (McGraw-Hill, $19.95, to be published in October). These passages are adapted from the first half. In specialized nuts-and-bolts detail, the second half tells how to make use of Harley's lessons.

AMERICA WAS WILD about motorcycles in the mid-1970s, which should have been great for Harley-Davidson. The Harley was unique, an American institution with raw power and a "voice"--a basso-profundo thump from its big V-twin engine that made other motorcycles sound like sewing machines. Harley riders were fanatically devoted to their mounts, and the American tradition they represented.

But Harley-Davidson, then owned by AMF, was in trouble. AMF had almost tripled production to 75,000 units annually over four years. Quality had deteriorated sharply--more than half the cycles came off the line missing parts, and dealers often had to fix them up to sell. The virile voice could not disguise an engine sorely in need of modern engineering. It leaked oil, vibrated, and couldn't match the performance of the flawlessly smooth Japanese bikes that were getting most of the growth. Hard-core enthusiasts were willing to fix their Harleys and modify them to perform better, but newcomers had no such devotion or skill. If Harley-Davidson was to expand its market, it had to improve the quality of its machines and update the engine design.

In late 1975, AMF put Vaughn Beals in charge of Harley. Beals found an ally in chief engineer Jeff Bleustein, who had felt like a lone voice trying to wake up top managers to the engineering realities they had to face. Beals set up a quality control and inspection program that began to eliminate the worst of the problems, but at a cost--on one new model, for example, the company had to spend about $1,000 extra per bike to get the first hundred into shape for dealers to sell at around $4,000.

Then he took a group of senior managers to Pinehurst, North Carolina, to devise a long-range product strategy--the first time the company had looked ten years ahead. At the top of the list were engines that would provide better performance as well as meet impending noise and emission rules. Harley would improve its existing power plants and start work on a new family to compete with the faster Japanese high-performance bikes. But upgrading would take years. What to do in the meantime?

The answer was a series of cosmetic innovations created by William G. Davidson, Harley's styling vice president. Known as Willie G., this grandson of one of the company's founders is not the only Harley executive who mingles with bikers, but with his beard, black leather, and jeans he's the most convincing. He understands his customers to a rare degree. Says Willie G.: "They really know what they want on their bikes: the kind of instrumentation, the style of bars, the cosmetics of the engine, the look of the exhaust pipes, and so on. Every little piece on a Harley is exposed, and it has to look just right. A tube curve or the shape of a timing case can generate enthusiasm or be a total turnoff. It's almost like being in the fashion business."

HE HAD ALREADY created a new model, called the Super Glide, that emulated the look of the choppers Harley fanatics put together in their own garages. This factory-built custom bike was a huge success, and the company 1 developed it at minimal cost by combining modified components of its two principal bikes, the heavy Electra Glide touring bike and the lighter Sportster. After Pinehurst, Beals asked Willie G. to spin out more such variations. Davidson came up with a succession of custom cruiser models--the Low Rider, with special paint and trim, low handlebars, and a lower seat; the Wide Glide, which took the chopper look even further than the Super Glide; and several other variations.

Other Harley executives credit Davidson's skill with saving Harley. "The guy is an artistic genius," says Bleustein, now senior vice president for parts and accessories. "In the five years before we could bring new engines on stream, he performed miracles with decals and paint. A line here and a line there and we'd have a new model. It's what enabled us to survive."

Though Harley's sales remained strong, its market share dwindled steadily as the Japanese continued to pour new bikes into the heavyweight market. By 1980, AMF was losing interest in the company. Early in 1981, Beals persuaded 12 other Harley executives to join him in taking over the company in an $81.5 million leveraged buyout. The group found a willing lead lender in Citicorp, and after several months of tough bargaining with AMF, the independent Harley-Davidson Motor Co. began business on June 16, 1981.

Manufacturing was still a major problem. Management had done everything it knew to boost quality and cut costs, but the Japanese were still producing better bikes at lower cost. How did they do it? Though Beals and other managers had visited Japanese plants in 1980, it wasn't until they got a chance to tour Honda's assembly plant in Marysville, Ohio, after the buyout that they began to understand. Says Beals: "We were being wiped out by the Japanese because they were better managers. It wasn't robotics, or culture, or morning calisthenics and company songs--it was professional managers who understood their business and paid attention to detail."

In October, 3.5 months after Beals and his group took charge, the manufacturing team began a pilot just-in-time inventory program in the Milwaukee engine plant. When that showed promise, Tom Gelb, senior vice president of operations, called a series of meetings with employees, telling them bluntly, "We have to play the game the way the Japanese play it or we're dead." But when he explained his plan to convert to just-in-time, many managers at the York, Pennsylvania, assembly plant reacted with disbelief. Some workers laughed out loud. After all, York already had a computer-based control system with overhead conveyors and high-rise parts storage--and the new system would replace all this with push carts. The new owners appeared to be taking the company back to 1930.

Just-in-time, however, eliminates the mountains of costly inventory that require elaborate handling systems and at the same time clears away many other manufacturing problems. For example, parts at York were made in large batches for long production runs, stored until needed, then loaded onto the 3.5-mile conveyor that rattled endlessly around the plant. "Sometimes we couldn't even find the parts we needed, " says Gelb. "Or if we found them they were rusted or damaged. Or there had been an engineering change since the parts were made and they didn't even fit."

IN DESIGNING the system, Harley started with the new wisdom that employees would have to be involved in planning it and working out the details. Management met for months with groups from all departments, from engineering to maintenance. Says Gelb: "No changes were implemented until the people involved understood and accepted them. It took two months before the consensus decision was made to go ahead. That was a Friday--and we started making the changes on Monday." About three weeks later Beals walked around the plant asking workers on the line how the conversion was going. To his surprise and delight, he says, the answer was generally, "Well, we have some problems, but it's a lot better than it was before, and we will get those problems fixed."

Says Beals: "That reaction demonstrated the true value of employee involvement. Normally, the engineers would figure out how to make the changes. They would have made them with the usual number of errors, and the reaction then would have been, 'Those dummies screwed up again.' And worse yet, the employees wouldn't have lifted a finger to help solve the problems."

It took more than just-in-time and employee involvement to make Harley a competitive manufacturer--the company learned that it also had to teach workers the statistical tools for monitoring and controlling the quality or their own work, train skeptical plant managers to become team leaders instead of bosses, and help its suppliers to adopt similar methods. Even today the company says the process won't be complete until employees are thinking perpetually about their own responsibility for doing the job better. But the dramatic quality improvements and cost reductions that resulted were the foundation of the company's comeback.

Finally on its way to leveling the playing field in manufacturing, Harley shifted its focus to marketing. The company abandoned a notion held by some senior managers of trying to compete broadly against the Japanese, and threw all of its resources into developing the big-bike niche. And it won protection against the Japanese heavyweights. Extra tariffs were slapped on the biggest ones, adding 45% to the existing 4.4%, and declining in stages before expiring in five years. But the Japanese manufacturers quickly found ways to evade the most onerous duties--for example, by assembling more heavyweight bikes in their U.S. plants. Harley was still losing market share.

One big hurdle was convincing potential buyers that Harley had truly solved its quality problems. To bring home the message, the company in 1984 committed $3 million to an unprecedented demonstration program it called SuperRide. A series of TV commercials invited bikers to come to any of the company's 600-plus dealers for a ride on a new Harley. Over three weekends, the company gave 90,000 rides to 40,000 people, half of whom owned other brands. The venture didn't sell enough bikes to cover its cost, but it made the point nonetheless. Many who rode the demonstrators came back to buy a year or two later when they were ready for new motorcycles. Today SuperRide is the only such consistent program in the industry, and so successful as a sales generator that Harley has a fleet of demo bikes that it takes to motorcycle rallies.

HARLEY also spent heavily to bolster its dealers and develop a close relationship with customers. In another industry first, the company in 1983 formed the Harley Owners Group (the acronym HOG, by no coincidence, is the affectionate name Harley riders give their mounts). Today HOG has some 100,000 members and a bimonthly newsletter. Run by Harley-Davidson employees, HOG sponsors some kind of motorcycle event almost every weekend from April to November all over the country. Harley managers participate, along with their spouses. "We try to run our business by the maxim 'The sale begins after the sale,'" says marketing chief Kathleen Lawler-Demitros. "HOG is one way we differentiate ourselves from our Japanese competitors." Apparently so. A similar group Honda tried to form soon faded away.

After losing $25 million in 1982, Harley edged into the black in 1983 and earned $2.9 million on sales of $294 million in 1984. It was catching up with Honda in the heavyweight market, improving its quality, reducing its breakeven, and marketing more aggressively. Then Citicorp decided it wanted out. The bank's analysts were concerned about the economy, and Citicorp officials began to worry about what would happen when the tariffs on big Japanese bikes ended in 1988. Harley's friendly loan officer was transferred to another division; his replacement took a dim view of the motorcycle maker's future. Citicorp reasoned that it had the best chance of selling off Harley's assets and recovering its money while the company was still on the upswing. In November of 1984, it told Harley that starting early the following year the bank would no longer provide overadvances--loans in excess of the conservative lending formula--and that Harley should start looking for another lender.

"Overadvance was our lifeline at that point," says Beals. "Telling us we'd get no more was the same as telling us to hire some lawyers and prepare to file for Chapter 11." Beals and the others persuaded Citicorp to extend the privileges for another six months--though they later concluded that the bank acquiesced mainly because it thought the extra months would be useful in preparing the company for liquidation. Over the summer of 1985, Beals and Richard Teerlink, who was then chief financial officer and later succeeded Beals as CEO, chased fruitlessly after new lenders. Knowing that Citicorp was trying to get rid of the account, other bankers held back.

In October, Beals and Teerlink met with their Citicorp loan officer to argue for more time, but they might as well have been talking to a wall. During a break they wandered into the men's room. "Look," Teerlink told Beals, "if they want out so badly, maybe they'll take a write-off on part of the loan. Then we have a better chance of inducing another lender to come in." Beals was dubious, but back in the conference room Teerlink proposed a $5 million write-off by Citicorp. The loan officer hardly batted an eyelash, and Beals quickly raised the amount to $10 million. Again, the officer was amenable. "We won't say no to anything if it gets us out of this deal," he said. Rather than making it easier to arrange new financing, the agreement turned off potential lenders even more. If Citicorp was willing to take a $10 million write-off, they figured, then Harley must be in a real mess.

As payments to creditors stretched out and lawyers worked on a bankruptcy plan, Dean Witter Reynolds put Beals and Teerlink together with Heller Financial Corp. Major events often turn on chance, and it happened that Heller's No. 2 executive, Bob Koe, was a Harley buff. Willing to listen, Koe probed hard for weak points but ended the meeting favorably impressed. After weeks of hard bargaining--Heller CEO Norm Blake turned the idea down at first--Harley and Heller struck a deal on December 23, 1985. The new lenders, including Heller and the three secondary banks that participated in the original buyout, would pay Citicorp $49 million--the bank took an $8 million write-off--and supply Harley with $49.5 million.

Citicorp had badly misjudged Harley's outlook. Management's long struggle--the manufacturing improvements, the multiple models, and the aggressive marketing--had transformed the company and secured its niche in the motorcycle business. After rebounding to almost 28% in 1985, Harley's share of the market for super-heavyweight bikes headed on a steady upward trajectory to today's level. By 1986 profits were up to $4.3 million on sales of $295 million. Harley went public, raising $20 million in its stock offering and refinancing its debt (since then, the shares have almost tripled). Cashing in Harley warrants it held, Citicorp recovered $6 million of its loan loss. Harley then acquired a motor-home maker, Holiday Rambler, and in 1987 asked to have the tariffs on Japanese bikes removed a year ahead of schedule.

Last year management celebrated Harley's 85th birthday with a party that reflected their unique way of getting close to customers.

Every motorcyclist was invited--even those who didn't ride Harleys. All they had to do was contribute $10 to Harley-Davidson's favorite philanthropic organization, the Muscular Dystrophy Association. More than 40,000 bikers accepted the invitation. Starting from as far away as San Francisco and Orlando, Florida, groups of cyclists headed for Milwaukee. Each was led by a Harley-Davidson executive, including Vaughn Beals, Rich Teerlink, Jeff Bleustein, Willie G. Davidson, and Jim Paterson, president of the motorcycle division. Along the way, the executives auctioned off Harley memorabilia for the benefit of muscular dystrophy. Beals rode into Milwaukee with his pants held up by a rope. The night before he had sold his pewter belt buckle for $100. (In all, the event raised more than $500,000 for charity.)

Thousands of Harleys, many flying American flags, rumbled into Milwaukee on June 18, shaking the air with the sound of their engines. Some riders had dogs perched on the back, others their children. Clothing ranged from minimal to a staggering variety of T-shirts and black leather vests covered with Harley buttons, emblems, and other mementos. Riders were all ages, from young gas pump jockeys to octogenarians. Every kind of Harley customer was represented, including a sprinkling of hard-core biker clubs such as the Sinners and the Saracens. The parking lots at the edge of Lake Michigan were agleam with chrome and flamboyant colors.

OFF THEIR BIKES, the celebrants spent the day participating in such activities as slow races--the winner was the last to cross the finish line after riding his bike as slowly as possible without falling over. Beals and Teerlink, among other executives, submitted themselves to the celebrity dunk tank, where they were unceremoniously dumped into the water by on-target baseball throwers.

Music resounded, starting with Booze Brothers Revue and ending with the Charlie Daniels Band. At the final ceremonies, 24,000 bikers watched videotapes of their ride to Milwaukee projected onto two giant screens. A continuous roar from the crowd was punctuated by shouts of recognition as riders saw their own groups. Thousands of Harley owners rose to their feet, clenched fists aloft, in a clamorous demonstration of product loyalty probably unrivaled anywhere in the world. They were celebrating the rebirth of a legend.

Investor's Snapshot Harley-Davidson

SALES (Latest four quarters) .... $810.1 million
    Change from year earlier .... up 13.2%
NET PROFIT .... $26.9 million
    Change .... up 16.4%
RETURN ON COMMON STOCKHOLDERS' EQUITY 19.4%
    Five-year average .... N.A.*
STOCK PRICE RANGE (Last 12 months) .... $21.50-$31.50
RECENT SHARE PRICE $30.125
PRICE/EARNINGS MULTIPLE 9
TOTAL RETURN TO INVESTORS (12 months to 8/18) 21.7%

* First public offering made in 1964

Exercise 1--Companywide Quality

a. Is there any evidence in the above article that Harley-Davidson's (H-D) turnaround was a result of a Total Quality Management (TQM) emphasis? Explain.

b. Would you argue that H-D's position on TQM is closer to the Tradition or the TQM position (see Table 21.1 in your text)? Explain.

c. In the text, Certo suggests that "offering high-quality" goods and services to the marketplace typically results in three important benefits for the organization. What are these benefits, and do you in fact see any evidence in the article that quality improvement has had such an impact? Explain.

Exercise 2--Quality from the Crosby and Deming Perspectives

a.   Which of Crosby's ingredients for injecting quality into an organization (Table 21.2) were evident at Harley-Davidson? Explain.

b.   Which of Deming's 14 points appear to have been followed in bringing about the Harley-Davidson turnaround? Explain.

Exercise 3--Strategic Quality Focus

Is there any evidence in the article that Harley-Davidson's strategic planning process included a product quality focus? Explain.

Exercise 4--Using the "Quality Management Maturity Grid"**

a. Check the appropriate boxes to position Harley-Davidson on the "Quality Management Maturity Grid"* below. In some instances you may need to intimate from statements made to be able to check a box; in a few instances there simply may be insufficient information to make a judgement.

QUALITY MANAGEMENT MATURITY GRID

Rater _____   Unit _____

Measurement Categories	Stage I: Uncertainty	Stage II: Awakening	Stage III: Enlightenment	Stage IV: Wisdom	Stage V: Certainty
Management understanding and attitude	No comprehension of quality as a management tool. Tend to blame quality department for "quality problems."	Recognizing that quality management may be of value but not willing to provide money or time to make it all happen.	While going through quality improvement program learn more about quality management; becoming supportive and helpful.	Participating. Understand absolutes of quality management. Recognize their personal role in continuing emphasis.	Consider quality management an essential part of company system.
Quality organization status	Quality is hidden in manufacturing or engineering departments. Inspection probably not part of organization. Emphasis on appraisal and sorting.	A stronger quality leader is appointed but main emphasis is still on appraisal and moving the product. Still part of manufacturing or other.	Quality department reports to top management, all appraisal is incorporated, and manager has role in management of company.	Quality manager is an officer of company; effective status reporting and preventive action. Involved with consumer affairs and special assignments.	Quality manager on board of directors. Prevention is main concern. Quality is a thought leader.
Problem handling	Problems are fought as they occur; no resolution; inadequate definition; lots of yelling and accusations.	Teams are set up to attack major problems. Long-range solutions are not solicited.	Corrective action communication established. Problems are faced openly and resolved in an orderly way.	Problems are identified early in their development. All functions are open to suggestion and improvement.	Except in the most unusual cases, problems are prevented.
Cost of quality as % of sales	Reported: unknown Actual: 20%	Reported: 3% Actual: 18%	Reported: 8% Actual: 12%	Reported: 6.5% Actual: 8%	Reported: 2.5% Actual: 2.5%
Quality improvement actions	No organized activities. No understanding of such activities.	Trying obvious "motivational" short-range efforts.	Implementation of the 14-step program with thorough understanding and establishment of each step.	Continuing the 14-step program and starting Make Certain.	Quality improvement is a normal and continued activity.
Summation of company quality posture	"We don't know why we have problems with quality."	"Is it absolutely necessary to always have problems with quality?"	"Through management commitment and quality improvement we are identifying and resolving our problems."	"Defect prevention is a routine part of our operation."	"We know why we do not have problems with quality."

**From Philip B. Crosby, *Quality is Free* (New York: McGraw-Hill), 1979, pp. 38-39. Used with permission.

b.   From the boxes you were able to check on the "Quality Management Maturity Grid," which "Stage" would appear to most closely reflect Harley-Davidson's level of maturity? Explain.

Exercise 5--Personal Insights Into Quality Issues

What specific personal lessons have you learned about the issue of quality from involving yourself in this experience? Explain.

Experience 21-2 The Real Estate Development Project: An Integrative Exercise with an Emphasis on Quality***

YOU ARE ONE OF THE MANAGERS OF THE FUTURE!! You have now been exposed to all of the fundamental concepts related to the management process through the material presented in the 21 chapters of the Certo text/activity manual package. While it may not be obvious to you, you have changed significantly over the past semester. But can you actually integrate your newly developed knowledge and skills and successfully apply them in the many and varied situations that you will encounter throughout your management career?

The experience that follows is designed to permit you to test your skills and to integrate your knowledge of the management process through a simulated real world situation called "The Real Estate Development Project." In this experience, you will work in teams and compete with other groups in constructing "buildings" out of index cards. (Used computer cards can be substituted if they are available.) Like in the "real world," the success of your group will be measured by the "profit" you make (determined by the appraised value of the building less the costs involved in production). Because a number of factors including quality enter into determining the appraised value, it is essential that your group analyze the task carefully, set some objectives, and plan the best organization possible. In other words, "practice" what you've learned about management.

Take this assignment seriously; you will be surprised how closely it mimics the real world. A conscientious effort will permit you (and other group members) to somewhat assess your personal strengths and weaknesses in carrying out the management process.

Exercise 1

Become familiar with the task directions that follow. Discuss them until everyone in the group understands them and then proceed to exercise 2.

Task Directions
Each group will construct a building or buildings out of index cards. When the construction period is over, the appraised value of the property will be determined by a real estate board following pre-established standards. The winning group will be the group with the greatest profit, regardless of the appraised value.

Materials
Each group will use index cards, one ruler, one scissors, one stapler, and a limited supply of tape. Extra staples are free.

Cost of Cards
Index cards cost $70 each. At the beginning of the exercise, each group will receive a package of one hundred cards and be charged $7,000 as an initial start-up investment. Additional cards may be purchased at the regular price. At the end of the exercise, you may redeem any unused (and undamaged) cards at $50 each. If you need to purchase or redeem cards, only one person from your group may go to the "supply depot" to carry out the transaction. (The location of the supply depot will be designated by your instructor.)

Construction and Delivery Time
After the planning period is completed, your instructor will announce the amount of time you will be allotted for construction. No group is allowed to build until your instructor announces, "Begin production." When the time is up, a "Stop production" order will be given; no construction will be allowed after this point. You will have thirty seconds in which to deliver your completed structure to the real estate board for appraisal. Except for the board members, no group members are allowed to remain with the building after it is delivered.

Real Estate Board
Each group should designate one member to serve on the real estate board. The board is responsible for appraising each structure and assuring that building codes are met. Board members will be allowed to work with their groups during the first part of the construction period, but they will be called together during the last ten minutes of the construction period. The board will convene to decide on criteria for the "drop-shock" test and aesthetic valuation. The board must appraise one building before going on to the next. Once a building is appraised, it cannot be reappraised later.

***Adapted from Douglas T. hall, Donald D. Bowen, Roy J. Lewicki, and Francine S. Hall, *Experiences in Management and Organizational Behavior*, 2nd. edition, Copyright © 1982 John Wiley & Sons, Inc. Reprinted by permission of John Wiley & Sons, Inc.

Building Code

All buildings must be fully enclosed (floors, roofs, and sidewalls). They also must have ceilings that are at least three inches from the floor and be capable of withstanding a "drop-shock" test. The "drop-shock" test may consist of dropping the building or dropping an object (e.g., heavy book) on the building. It will be the real estate board's responsibility to decide on the test. Buildings that do not meet code will be eliminated from competition.

Appraisal Values

Buildings are appraised on the basis of quality and aesthetics. The total of the quality and aesthetic values is then multiplied by the total square inches of floor space in the building to obtain the total appraised value.

Quality Valuation

Quality is determined by subjecting the building to the "drop-shock" test. Various qualities are assigned values as follows:

Minimal quality:	$12 per square inch of floor space
Good quality:	$14 per square inch of floor space
Better quality:	$16 per square inch of floor space
Top quality:	$18 per square inch of floor space

Aesthetic Valuation

The real estate board can set the aesthetic value anywhere from zero to $3 per square inch of floor space, depending on its appraisal of aesthetic value.

Other Instructions

Once construction begins (exercise 4), you will not be allowed to ask your instructor to clarify any game rules or to resolve any group difficulties. You will be on your own. Five minutes before construction is to stop, the group leader will notify you of the time remaining. While the real estate board is appraising buildings, each group will be expected to clean up leftover raw materials and return them to the supply depot. All unused cards should be redeemed.

Exercise 2

Your group should discuss the following:
    a. What are your objectives in the project?
    b. What plan will you use to achieve your objectives?
    c. How will group members be organized and coordinated?
    d. How will you utilize resources?
    e. Who will serve on the real estate board?

One member of the group should be designated to report on your objectives, plan, and organization structure during the discussion in exercise 6.

Exercise 3

Each group should assemble at one workplace (table, cluster of desks, or floor area). Your instructor will designate the following: (a) supply depot and supply person(s), (b) construction time, and (c) delivery station for real estate board appraisals. In addition, your instructor will distribute all materials and tools to the groups. Finally, the people designated to serve on the real estate board will be asked to convene briefly. No one is to use any materials or tools at this point.

Exercise 4

When you instructor announces, "Begin production," you may build. When your instructor announces, "Stop production," you must deliver your building to the real estate board.

Exercise 5

While the real estate board appraises the buildings, your group should clean up and return unused raw materials. Your instructor and supply person(s) will enter total cost figures and the real estate board will enter total appraisal values on a summary matrix. The profit for each group will then be computed by subtracting the total costs from the total appraisal value for each building. The most profitable group wins.

Exercise 6

As a class, discuss the results of exercise 5 in terms of the objectives, plan, and organization structure of each group to determine how these factors affected output and profits.

Exercise 7

Quality is a critical ingredient in all profitable ventures today. Certainly this will be even more the case for managers of the future than for managers of the past or present. To gain a fuller understanding of the dimensions of quality and how to structure an operation to assure quality, meet again in groups as outlined below and prepare to respond to the following questions related to quality:

1) Real estate board:

    a) Discuss how you (the real estate board) reached your decisions on the quality of the buildings that you were required to evaluate. What specific quality dimensions did you consider?

    b) What other dimensions of quality could/should you have included in your quality assessments?

2) All other (non-real estate board) class participants in their project teams:

    a) What additional dimensions of quality would you have liked to have seen the real estate board use in appraising your structure?

    b) What could your group or, for that matter, any organization do to assure the quality of the product of its efforts?

Exercise 8

After the class discussion is completed, individually answer the questions that follow.

a.   What major factors contributed to the success (or lack of success) of your group?

b.   Which of the management functions were most clearly illustrated in your group? Explain.

c.   In what ways was this experience similar to the real world (realistic)? In what ways did it lack realism?

d.   If there was a significant cash prize of, say, $10,000 for wining this game, and if the allotted game time was anywhere form one to eight hours, what would you do differently?

Exercise 9

What have you gained from involving yourself in the last experiential exercise in this manual?

22 MANAGEMENT AND DIVERSITY

Chapter Summary

This chapter can help a manager understand the challenges that a diverse workforce poses for American business. It discusses (1) the definition and social implications of diversity, (2) advantages of diversity in organizations, (3) challenges facing managers, (4) managerial strategies for promoting organizations, and (5) the role of the manager in promoting effective workforce diversity.

Learning Objective 1   *A definition of diversity and an understanding of its importance in the corporate structure*

Diversity refers to characteristics of individuals that shape their identities and the experiences they have in society. Workforce diversity is not a new issue. Historically, immigration of people from specific regions and cultures has been happening since the United States was a colony. The American population has always been a multifaceted mix of individuals and groups who varied by gender, race, ethnicity, religion, social class, physical ability, sexual orientation, and age. These basic human differences are among those comprising what we refer to as diversity. The purpose of exploring diversity issues is to learn how to include members of diverse groups equally, accepting the differences and utilizing the talents of all employees.

Diversity includes understanding the relationships between majority group members and minority group members. **Majority group** refers to the group of people holding the majority of the positions of decision-making power, control of resources and information, and access to system rewards. The majority group is not *always* the group representing a numerical majority. The term **minority group** refers to a group of people who lack critical power, resources, acceptance, and social status within the overall organization or system. Together, minority and majority group members form an entire social system. Minority group members are often, but not always, lesser in number than members of the majority group. For example, women are seen as a minority group in most organizations because they do not have the critical power to shape organizational decisions and to control resources. Moreover, women are still working to achieve full acceptance and social status within the workplace. In some instances white males are numerical minorities. For example, in most health care organizations, women outnumber men. Although men are numerical minorities, they are unlikely to be denied social status because men tend to hold the positions of power in the health care system hierarchy, such as physician and health care administrator.

Learning Objective 2   *An understanding of the advantages of a diverse workforce*

Managers are becoming increasingly dedicated to seeking a wide range of talents from every group represented within the nation's culture. In addition we learned in chapter 16 that group decisions improve the quality of decision making. Work groups or teams, drawing on the right contributions of a multicultural workforce, enhance the pool of information and approaches available to the group.

Ann Morrison, author of *The New Leaders: Guidelines on Leadership Diversity in America* carried out a comprehensive study of sixteen private and public organizations in the United States. The purpose of the study was to identify the most effective strategies for fostering diversity. One of the outcomes of the research was an outline of the **advantages of diversity.**

Because markets are becoming increasingly diverse, managers must understand their customers' preferences. Failing to do this could result in loss of business in the United States and internationally. Some argue that one of the best ways to ensure that the organization has the ability to **not only keep, but gain market share** is to include diversity among the organization's decision makers. Diversity among the managerial ranks might enhance company credibility. For example, a manager who is of the same gender or ethnic background as a customer may imply to the customer that his or her day-to-day experiences will be understood. One African-American female manager said that she used her influence to change the name of a product that her company intended to sell at Wal-Mart. "I knew that I had shopped for household goods at Wal-Mart, whereas the CEO of this company, a white, middle-upper-class male, had not. He listened to me and we changed the name of the product." Morrison's study cites a case in which one company lost an important opportunity for new business in a southwestern city's predominantly Hispanic community. The business ultimately went to a competitor, whose Hispanic manager in charge of the project solicited input from the Hispanic community.

There are high costs involved in recruiting, training, relocating, and replacing employees in and in providing competitive compensation packages. According to Morrison, the cost of Corning's high turnover among women and people of color was estimated at $2 to $4 million a year. Many managers in her study felt that **significant costs** associated with turnover (often using as much as two-thirds of an organization's budget) **could be saved** by instituting diversity practices that would give non-traditional managers more incentive to stay. When non-traditional managers remain with the organization, other non-traditional employees at lower levels feel more committed to he company. In addition to the personnel costs, executives are distressed by legal fees and staggering settlement amounts.

Many executives in Morrison's study expect **greater productivity and innovation** from employees in organizations that focus on diversity. These managers feel that employees who feel valued, competent, and relaxed in their work setting will enjoy coming to work and will perform at a high level. Morrison also cites a study by Donna Thompson and Nancy DiTomaso which states that a multicultural approach has a positive effect on employees' perception of equity. This in turn, affects their morale, goal setting, effort, and performance. The manager's in Morrison's Study see innovation as another strength of a diverse workforce.

Morrison's study also found that including non-traditional employees in fair competition for advancement can **improve the quality of management** by providing a wider pool of talent. According to the research cited in Morrison's study, exposure to diverse colleagues can help managers develop breadth and openness. The quality of management can also be improved by building more effective personnel policies and practices. Once developed, they will eventually benefit all employees in the organization. Morrison's study found that many of the programs initially developed for non-traditional managers resulted in improvements that were later applied throughout the organization. Ideas such as adding training for mentors, improving techniques for developing managers, and improving processes for evaluating employees for promotion (a concept originally developed for non-traditional managers), were later adopted for wider use. Other advantages of a diverse workforce are summarized in Table 22.1.

Learning Objective 3   *An awareness of the challenges facing managers within a diverse workforce*

Before a manager can begin to implement strategies to promote diversity, it is important to understand some of the **challenges facing managers within a diverse workforce.** An understanding of *changing demographics*, the statistical characteristics of a population, is an important tool used by managers to study workforce diversity. According to *Workforce 2000: Work and Workers for the Twenty-First Century,* a report developed for the United States Department of Labor by the Hudson Institute, the contemporary workforce and the jobs it will perform will parallel changes in the economy. This report, published in 1987, projected the following five demographic facts as "most important" in relation to workers and jobs by the year 2000: (1) the population and the workforce will grow more slowly than at any time since the 1930s; (2) the average age of the population and the workforce will rise, and the pool of young workers entering the labor market will shrink; (3) more women will enter the workforce; (4) minorities will make up a larger share of new entrants into the labor force; and (5) immigrants will represent the largest share of the increase in the population and the workforce. This study clearly emphasizes the growth of nonwhites, women, immigrants, and older workers within the workforce.

The changing demographics described by the *Workforce 2000* report set the stage for social dynamics, *(ethnocentrism, prejudices, stereotypes, and discrimination)*, which can interfere with a productive workforce. Our natural tendency for judging other groups less favorably than our own is one of the problems inherent in coping with diversity. This tendency is the source of **ethnocentrism,** the belief that one's own group, culture, country or customs are superior to others'. Two related dynamics are **prejudices** and **stereotypes.** A prejudice is a preconceived judgment, opinion or assumption about issues, behaviors, or groups of people. Stereotypes may be positive or negative assessments or perceived attributes toward members of a group. It is important for managers to recognize these ways of perceiving others so that they can monitor their own perceptions and help their employees to view others more accurately. When verbalized or acted upon, these dynamics can cause discomfort and stress for the judged individual. In some cases, these processes can result in outright **discrimination.** Discrimination refers to treating an issue, person, or behavior unjustly or inequitably. Discrimination often stems from stereotypes and prejudices. For example, consider a disabled person who is turned down for promotion because the boss feels that this employee would not be able to handle the regular travel accompanying this particular job. Prejudging this employee's capabilities based on his or her "difference" and implementing the preconception through differential treatment is considered discrimination.

Discrimination occurs when stereotypes are acted upon in ways that affect hiring, pay, or promotion (for example, steering older employees into less visible job assignments which are unlikely to provide opportunities for advancement). Other challenges facing minorities and women include the pressure to conform to the organizations' culture, high penalties for mistakes, and tokenism. **Tokenism** refers to being one of very few members of your group in the organization. "Token" employees experience either very high or very low visibility in the organization. In other cases, minorities are seen as representatives or "spokespeople" for all members of their group. Many are subject to high expectations and scrutiny from members of their own group.

Women's experiences differ from those of people of color. Women in organizations confront **gender-role stereotypes.** Gender-role stereotypes are perceptions about people based on what our society believes are appropriate behaviors for their gender. Both men and women's self-expression are constrained by gender role stereotyping. For example, women in organizations are often thought to be good listeners. This attribution is based on our societal view that women are nurturing. Although this is a positive assessment, it is not true of all women or of any woman all the time. Women managers also describe the subtle sanctioning they experience from both men and women when they do not respond to the expectation that they portray a nurturing component within their management style. In general, ethnocentrism, prejudices, and stereotypes-- when not applied consciously and constructively--inhibit our ability to accurately process information. A major pattern of discrimination affecting women in organizations is described as the "glass ceiling." The **glass ceiling** refers to an invisible "ceiling," or limit to advancement. This term, originally coined to describe barriers facing women, can also describe the experiences of other minorities. *Sexual harassment* is another form of discrimination disproportionately affecting female employees. Sexual harassment is any unwanted sexual language, behavior or imagery affecting an employee.

Minorities experience stereotypes about their group. They too encounter misunderstandings and expectations based on ethnic or cultural differences. Members of ethnic or racial minority groups are socialized within their particular culture. Many are socialized as members of two cultural groups--the dominant culture and their racial or ethnic culture. Ella Bell, professor of organizational behavior at MIT, refers to this dual membership as "biculturalism." In her study of African-American women, she identifies the stress of coping with membership in two cultures simultaneously, as **bicultural stress**. She indicates that **role conflict**--competing roles from two cultures--and **role overload**--too many expectations to comfortably fulfill--are common characteristics of bicultural stress. Although these issues can be applied to many minority groups, they are particularly intense for women of color. This is because this group experiences dynamics affecting *both* minorities and women. Socialization in one's culture of origin can lead to misunderstandings in the workplace. This is particularly true when the manager relies solely on the cultural norms of the majority group. According to these norms, within American culture it is acceptable--even positive--to publicly praise an individual for a job well done. However, in cultures that place primary value on group harmony and collective achievement, this method of rewarding an employee causes emotional discomfort. Employees feel that, if praised publicly they will "lose face" within their group.

In addition to women minorities, *older workers* represent a significant and valuable component of the labor force. Management is faced with significant questions concerning how to tap the rich knowledge and experience base of these workers, and how to help older workers avoid the occupational stagnation of later years. With respect to diversity, older workers bring some specific challenges for managers. Stereotypes and prejudices of older workers link age with senility, incompetence, and lack of worth in the labor market. Jeffrey Sonnenfeld found that co-workers and managers view older workers as "deadwood," and seek to "weed them out" through pension incentives, biased performance appraisals, or other methods. However, Sonnenfeld found that while older managers were more cautious, less likely to take risks, and less open to change, many are high performers. Studies which tracked individuals' careers over the long term indicate that there is a peak in performance occurring around age forty-five to fifty and a second peak around age fifty-five to sixty. It is the manager's responsibility to see that older workers are valued for their contribution to the organization and that they are treated fairly. This means that the manager needs some understanding of and sensitivity to the very real physiological and psychological changes that older workers are adjusting to. In order to support older workers, the manager must pay attention to performance appraisal processes, retirement incentives, training programs, blocked career paths, union insurance pensions, and affirmative action goals.

People with *disabilities* are also subject to the dynamics that affect minority groups, such as stereotyping, prejudices, and discrimination. One disabled professional indicated that she was always received warmly by phone, and was told that her background was exactly what companies were looking for. When she showed up for job interviews, however, she was not well received and was sometimes told that her credentials were lacking in some way.

Learning Objective 4   *An understanding of the strategies for promoting diversity in organizations*

This section looks at several approaches to diversity and strategies that organizations can consider in their plans for **promoting cultural diversity in their organizations**. The Hudson Institute, in its *Workforce 2000* report, offers *six strategies that corporations can undertake to implement diversity*. These issues include the need to: (1) stimulate balanced world growth--the U.S. must pay less attention to its share of the world trade and more attention to the growth of the economies of the other nations of the world, including those nations in Europe, Latin America, and Asia with whom the U.S. competes; (2) accelerate productivity increases in service industries--prosperity will depend much more upon how fast output per worker increases in health care, education, retailing, government, and other services, than on gains in manufacturing; (3) maintain the dynamism of an aging workforce--as the average age of American workers climbs toward forty, the nation must insure that its workforce does not lose its adaptability and willingness to learn; (4) recognize the conflicting needs of women, work, and families--despite the huge increases in the numbers of women in the workforce, many of the policies and institutions that cover pay, fringe benefits, time away from work, pensions, welfare, and other issues have not yet been adjusted to the new realities; (5) fully integrate into the economy black and Hispanic workers--the shrinking numbers of young people, the rapid pace of industrial change, and the rising skill requirements of the emerging economy make the task of fully utilizing minority workers particularly urgent between now and 2000; and (6) improve the education and skills of all workers--human capital (knowledge, skills, organizations, and leadership) is key to economic growth and competitiveness.

Many of the demographic shifts and the challenges which lie ahead are based upon complex societal issues. Organizations--and, ultimately, their leaders and managers--will find it necessary to clarify their own social values. These six challenges imply the need for organizations to become more inclusive, that is, include a broader mix of employees and to develop an organizational culture that maximizes the value and potential of each worker. As with any major initiative, tcommitment to developing an inclusive organization begins with those in positions of authority at the top of the organizational hierarchy. However, on a day-to-day operational basis, each manager's level of commitment is critical in determining how well or how poorly the organization's strategies and approaches are implemented.

Equal employment and affirmative action programs are intended to be positive steps forward in the area of managing diversity and have created many opportunities for both women and minority groups. However, some employees feel that these programs have been misused to create **reverse discrimination**. Reverse discrimination refers to inequalities affecting members of the majority group as an outcome of programs designed to help underrepresented groups and women. When an organization stops short of developing a multicultural organization, individuals' feelings and intergroup conflicts continue, even through the organization may have implemented the appropriate legal approaches.

Figure 22.3 shows the range of *organizational commitment to multiculturalism*. The figure depicts, at the base of the pyramid, organizations that have committed resources, planning, and time to the ongoing shaping and sustaining of a multicultural organization to, at the top of the pyramid, organizations which are directing very little attention toward managing diversity. Most organizations exist somewhere between the extremes. Some organizations make no efforts to promote diversity and do not comply with affirmative action and EEOC standards. The lack of attention to diversity needs within such organizations sends a strong message to their employees that the dynamics of difference are not important. The most effective diversity efforts are based on managerial implementation of affirmative action and EEOC policies that are developed in conjunction with an organization-wide assessment of the company's systems and structures. Such assessment is necessary to determine how the organization's systems support or hinder diversity goals. Generally, for such a comprehensive assessment to take place, top management must "buy in" to the idea that diversity is important to the company. This support from the top is critical to all successful diversity efforts and underlies tying organizational rewards to manager's commitment to diversity. Ongoing processes of organization assessment and continuing programs are also necessary to create an organizational climate which is inclusive and supportive of diverse groups.

Pluralism refers to an environment in which differences are acknowledged, accepted, and seen to be a significant contribution to the whole. A diverse workforce is most effective when managers are able to guide the organization toward achieving pluralism. Approaches, or strategies to achieve effective workforce diversity, can be classified in five major categories: (1) the "Golden Rule" approach, (2) assimilation, (3) righting the wrongs, (4) the culture-specific approach, and (5) the multicultural approach.

The **"Golden Rule"** approach to diversity relies on the biblical dictate "Do unto others as you would have them do unto you." The major strength of this approach is that it emphasizes individual morality. Its major flaw is that individuals apply the Golden Rule from their own particular frame of reference without knowledge of the cultural expectations, traditions, and preferences of the other person. The **assimilation approach** advocates shaping organization members to fit the existing culture of the organization. This approach pressures those who are not members of the dominant culture to conform. This must be done at the expense of their own cultures and worldviews. The result is the creation of a homogeneous culture that suppresses the creativity and diversity of views that could benefit the organization. **"Righting the wrongs"** is an approach that addresses past injustices experienced by a particular group. When a group's history places them at a disadvantage to achieving career success and mobility, policies are developed to create a more equitable set of conditions. This approach most closely parallels the affirmative action policies discussed in chapter 11. However, this approach also goes beyond affirmative action in that it emphasizes tapping the unique talents of each group in the service or organizational productivity. The **culture-specific approach** teaches employees the norms and practices of another culture to prepare them to interact effectively. This approach is often used to assist employees in making the transition for international assignments. Finally, the **multicultural approach** provides opportunities for employees to raise their awareness and develop an appreciation of differences of culture or personal characteristics. The focus is on how interpersonal skills and attitudinal changes relate to organizational performance. A strength of this approach is the assumption that individuals--as well as the organization itself-- will be required to make changes to accommodate the diversity of the organization's members. The multicultural approach may be the most effective approach managers can utilize because it advocates change on the part of management, employees, and organization systems and structures.

Learning Objective 5   *Insights into the role of the manager in promoting diversity in the organization*

Managers play an essential role in tapping the potential capacities of each person within their departments. To do this requires multiple competencies and commitments which are anchored within the four basic management functions of planning, organizing, influencing, and controlling. *Planning* is an ongoing process that includes troubleshooting and continually defining areas of improvement. Planning for diversity may involve selecting diversity training programs for the organization or setting diversity goals for employees within the department. Setting recruitment goals for members of underrepresented groups is a key example of planning. A manager's role might be to establish goals and objectives for the increased representation of Hispanic employees within five years. To achieve this five-year vision, the manager needs to establish benchmark goals for each year. *Organizing* is the process of establishing orderly uses for all resources within the management system. To achieve a diverse work environment, the manager will need to work with human resource professionals in the areas of recruitment, hiring, and retention, so that the best match is made between the company and the employees it hires. Responsibilities may lead to establishing task forces or committees to explore issues and provide ideas, carefully choosing work assignments to support the career development of all employees, and evaluating the extent to which goals are being achieved. Once managers begin to hire from a diverse pool of employees, they will need to turn their attention to retaining them. This means paying attention to the many concerns within a diverse workforce. In the case of working women and men with families, skillfully utilizing the organization's policies to support their needs, granting family leave time, allowing flexible work arrangements in keeping with company policy, and assigning and re-assigning work responsibilities equitably to accommodate family leave usage are all examples of managers applying the organizing function.

Influencing is the process of guiding the activities of organization members in appropriate directions. This management function is integrally tied to an effective leadership style, good communication skills, knowledge about how to motivate others, and an understanding of organizational culture and group dynamics. Influencing organization members with respect to valuing diversity generally requires encouraging and supporting employees in their efforts to participative constructively within a diverse work environment. This necessitates that the manager, too, engage in the career development and training processes that will provide the skills for facilitating smooth operation of a diversive work community. Managers are also accountable for informing their employees of breaches of organizational policy and etiquette. The manager's role includes holding employees accountable for learning about policies and complying with them. The manager might accomplish this through regular meetings, consultations with staff, or one-on-one meetings where necessary. To encourage participation in diversity workshops, the manager may need to communicate the importance of this knowledge base, or might choose to tie organizational rewards, where appropriate, to the development of diversity competencies; such rewards could include giving praise or recognition, or providing workers with opportunities to utilize diversity skills on desirable work assignments. The *controlling* function is the set of activities which make something happen as planned. Hence the evaluation activities necessary to assess diversity efforts are a part of the controlling role that managers play in shaping a multicultural workforce. Managers may find this aspect the most difficult to execute. It has been difficult to evaluate planned-change approaches in general and is particularly so when applied to diversity efforts. Many times the most successful diversity approaches simply reveal more problems and issues as employees begin to speak more openly about their concerns. In addition, the subtle attitudinal changes in one group's perception of another group are so difficult to measure. What can be accurately measured is the outcome variables of turnover, representation of underrepresented groups at all levels of the company, and legal problems stemming from inappropriate or illegal behaviors, such as discrimination or sexual harassment. A manager engaged in the controlling function with respect to diversity will provide ongoing monitoring of how well the unit is doing with respect to goals and standards. The manager will decide what measures to use (e.g., indicators of productivity, turnover, absenteeism, or promotion) and will need to interpret this information in light of diversity goals and standards.

From the complex set of skills needed to promote diversity, it becomes obvious that **managers themselves will need organizational support.** One important approach utilized by a large number of companies as a component of their diversity strategy is **diversity training.** Diversity training is a learning process implemented to raise manager's awareness and develop competencies concerning the issues and needs involved in managing a diverse workforce. As stated in chapter 11, training programs generally focus on the following five components or themes: (1) behavioral awareness, (2) acknowledgment of biases and stereotypes, (3) focus on job performance, (4) avoidance of assumptions, and (5) modification of policy and procedure manuals.

Donaldson and Scannell, authors of *Human Resource Development: The New Trainer's Guide*, have developed a **four-stage model** describing how managers progress in managing a diverse workforce. The first stage is described as *"unconscious incompetence,"* in which individuals are unaware of the behaviors they engage in that are problematic for members of other groups. The second stage, *"conscious incompetence"* refers to a learning process of discovering (or becoming conscious of) behaviors that create incompetence in interactions with members of diverse groups. The third stage is one of becoming *"consciously competent,"* where individuals learn how to relate with diverse groups and cultures by deliberately thinking about how to interact. The last stage is *"unconscious competence,"* in which the manager has internalized the new behaviors and is so comfortable relating to others different than him or herself that little conscious effort is required. Managers who have progress to the "unconscious competence" stage will be the most effective with respect to interacting in a diverse workforce.

In order for managers to respond to the challenges of working with diverse populations they must recognize employee difficulties in coping with diversity. These difficulties include resistance to change, ethnocentrism, lack of and misinformation about other groups, as well as prejudices, biases, and stereotypes. Some employees lack the motivation to invest energy in understanding cultural differences. This is because coping with and understanding diversity requires time and energy. At times one must take emotional risks necessary to explore issues of diversity with others who are different. There are not always social or concrete rewards. When diversity issues are ignored, however, or when they are mismanaged, interpersonal and intergroup conflicts arise. These conflicts very often affect the functioning of the workgroup, causing a lack of cohesiveness, communications problems, or employee stress.

There are a *number of supports available to managers* who are facing the challenges of diversity in the workplace. A primary source of support is education and training programs to assist employees with working through difficulties they may encounter in coping with diversity. Another source of support for diversity is managerial support from the top down within the company. When this top-down support exists, the organization is more likely to have, (1) managers who have skills in working within a diverse workforce, (2) effective education and diversity training programs, (3) an organizational climate that is supportive of diversity and which fosters peer support for exploring diversity issues, (4) open communication with one's manager about diversity issues, (5) recognition for employees' development of diversity skills and competencies, (6) recognition for employee contributions to enhancing diversity goals, and (7) organizational rewards for managers' implementation of organizational diversity goals and objectives.

Knowing You Know

True/False   *Directions: On the lines provided, place a T for True, and an F for false*

_____ 1. The "majority group" is always the group representing a numerical majority.

_____ 2. Diversity is the statistical characteristics of a population.

_____ 3. In health care organizations, white males are numerical minorities.

_____ 4. Diversity among managerial ranks might enhance company credibility.

_____ 5. Socialization in one's culture of origin can lead to misunderstandings in the workplace.

_____ 6. Reverse discrimination refers to inequalities affecting members of the minority group as an outcome of programs designed to help overrepresented groups.

_____ 7. Ethnocentrism is the belief that one's own group, culture, or customs are superior to others'.

_____ 8. Discrimination often stems from stereotypes and prejudice.

_____ 9. Role overload, defined as competing roles from two cultures, is a common characteristic of bicultural stress.

_____ 10. Because managers are responsible to see that older workers are valued for their contributions to the organization and are treated fairly, managers need to develop sensitivity to the very real physiological and psychological changes that older workers are adjusting to.

_____ 11. Human capital--knowledge, skills, organization, and leadership--is key to economic growth and competitiveness.

_____ 12. When an organization makes no effort to promote diversity and does not comply with affirmative action and EEOC standards, it sends a strong message to its employees that the dynamics of difference are not important.

_____ 13. Compensating for damages or disadvantages impacting blacks due to historical and existing inequalities is an example of application of the culture-specific approach.

_____ 14. Selecting diversity training programs for the organization or setting diversity goals for employees within the department are examples of organizing for diversity.

_____ 15. "Conscious incompetence" refers to a learning process of discovering (or becoming conscious of) behaviors that create incompetence in interactions with members of diverse groups.

Multiple Choice   *Directions: Circle the letter of the word or phrase that best completes each statement.*

16. Which of the following was *not* an advantage of diversity as outlined by Ann Morrison:
    a. Keeping and gaining market share
    b. Increased profitability
    c. Cost savings
    d. Better quality management
    e. Increased productivity and innovation

17. Which of the following was *not* one of the five "most important" demographic facts regarding workers and jobs by the year 2000?
    a. Minorities will make up a larger share of new entrants into the labor force.
    b. Immigrants will represent the largest share of the increase in population and the workforce.
    c. The population and the workforce will grow more rapidly than at any time since the 1930s.
    d. The average age of the population and the workforce will rise, and the pool of young workers entering the labor market will shrink.
    e. More women will enter the workforce.

18. A stereotype is:
   a. The belief that one's own group, culture, country, or customs are superior to others.
   b. A preconceived judgment, opinion or assumption about issues, behaviors, or groups of people.
   c. When one treats an issue, person, or behavior unjustly or unequitably.
   d. A positive or negative assessment or perceived attribute toward members of a group.
   e. None of the above are correct statements regarding stereotypes.

19. Tokenism refers to:
   a. being one of very few members of your group in the organization
   b. perceptions about people based on what our society believes are appropriate behaviors for their gender.
   c. an invisible limit to advancement.
   d. any unwanted sexual language, behavior or imagery affecting an employee.
   e. None of the above are correct statements regarding tokenism.

20. Which of the following is *not* one of the six strategies that corporations can undertake to implement diversity?
   a. Stimulate balanced world growth
   b. Improve the education and skills of all workers
   c. Accelerate productivity increases in service industries
   d. Recognize the conflicting needs of women, work, and families
   e. All of the above are strategies that corporations can undertake to implement diversity.

21. From Jean Kim's perspective, which of the following is *not* an approach or strategy to achieve effective workforce diversity?
   a. Righting the wrongs approach
   b. The multicultural approach
   c. The "TV test" approach
   d. The "Golden Rule" approach
   e. The assimilation approach

22. Which of the following is the final stage of Donaldson and Scannell's four-stage model for managing a diverse workforce?
   a. Unconscious incompetence
   b. Unconscious competence
   c. Conscious incompetence
   d. Conscious competence
   e. All four of the above are incorporated into stage four for managing a diverse workforce.

23. Minorities often experience stress associated with coping with membership in two cultures simultaneously. This type of stress is called:
   a. minority stress
   b. bicultural stress
   c. role conflict
   d. role overload
   e. ethnocentric stress

24. Most older workers:
   a. need to be watched closely because of the link between age and senility.
   b. are less cautious, more likely to take risks, and more open to change.
   c. should be viewed as "deadwood" and, wherever possible, "weeded out" through pension incentives, performance appraisals, or other methods.
   d. have their peak in performance around age forty-five to fifty and then find performance dropping off to retirement.
   e. None of the above are correct statements about older workers.

25. Pluralism refers to:
    a. shaping organization members to fit the existing culture of the organization.
    b. a group of people who lack critical power, resources, acceptance, and social status within the overall organization or system.
    c. characteristics of individuals that shape their identities and the experiences they have in society.
    d. an environment in which differences are acknowledged, accepted, and seen to be a significant contribution to the whole.
    e. a strategy that corporations can undertake to implement diversity.

Applying What You Know

Experience 22-1   Managing Diversity *Will* Be Your Business*

Introduction

Most basic management classes, such as the one you are registered for, are made up not only of individuals with diverse backgrounds (i.e., different culture, different ethnicity, etc.), but also with diverse professional interests or inclinations. From a university perspective, diverse professional interests or inclinations translate into different college majors. The chances are good that the person sitting to either side of you will be majoring in a specialization that is different than yours. In addition, the chances are good that none of the three of you (you or those sitting to either side of you) are management majors. While this class is made up of students with diverse backgrounds, including many different professional inclinations (from accounting, to marketing, to finance, to agri-business, to nursing, to library science, and so-on), and, in addition, most class members are non-management majors, there remains o*ne common thread* that binds together most, if not all, in the class. Strangely enough, this "thread" will forever link virtually all in the class to management. When I identify this factor (what all in the class have in common), your initial reaction will more than likely be: "Uh, uh, I don't believe that!" But the more you think about what I am going to tell you, the more you will *come to agree* with me. Ok, here it is:

No matter what your college major or specialty, if you have a desire to improve yourself, you *will* eventually become a manager. Your college degree, your technical specialty (i.e., accounting), will get you your first job or position; and your initial performance in that first position will get you your first promotion. But, *every other promotion throughout your entire career* will be primarily dependent on, not what you know about or how you perform in your technical specialty (i.e., accounting), but rather what you know and *how you perform as a manager.*

Think about it! With your first promotion, to *what* will you be promoted? Will you not be someone who now **manages** others that are doing the task that you once did so well? And even more importantly, if you cannot effectively manage that group that is doing what you once did so well yourself, someone else--*not you*--will be the prime candidate for the next higher job--the next promotion. You see, it is true; assuming that in your career you will seek more challenge, more responsibility, more authority, and more status, *you will be spending most of your working life managing other human beings*. **Managing diversity *will* be your business!!**

Exercise 1

An important step to effectively managing diverse work groups is understanding what others (possibly even potential future subordinates) want out of work and personal relationships. What people want, what they find rewarding, can very likely be what moves them to action--to be productive. Unfortunately, diversity is one factor that can significantly complicate a manager's ability to link rewards to performance. What do individuals with diverse backgrounds want from their jobs. If you polled people from a variety of different races, sexes, and ages, as well as able-bodied and disabled individuals, what do you think each of these different employee groups would say they want or value out of work and personal relationships?

---

*This exercise, coauthored by Lee A. Graf, Masoud Hemmasi, and Michael Winchell, was submitted to the 1994 Conference of the Association for Business Simulation and Experiential Learning, San Diego, California, March 16-18, 1994.

For each group below, list the three wants that you believe would be the most obvious and dominant:

a.   Younger and older employees want:

  1. _____
  2. _____
  3. _____

b.   Women want:

  1. _____
  2. _____
  3. _____

c.   Men want:

  1. _____
  2. _____
  3. _____

d.   People of color want:

  1. _____
  2. _____
  3. _____

e.   White people want:

  1. _____
  2. _____
  3. _____

f.   Disabled people want:

  1. _____
  2. _____
  3. _____

g.   Physically able-bodied people want:

  1. _____
  2. _____
  3. _____

h. Gay men and lesbians want:

1. _____

2. _____

3. _____

Exercise 2

Your instructor will share the research finding of two well-known researchers who, after conducting numerous workshops and interviews with the same diverse groups listed above, have identified the three most dominant themes for each group. Your next task is to compare your answers to the researchers' findings and then count up the total number of wants (out of a possible 24) that you correctly identified. Give yourself half-credit if you identified at least some component of each theme.

a. Write the number of correctly identified wants ("x" out of a possible 24) here. _____ (number correct)

b. What generalizations can you draw from the percent of themes ("x" out of a possible 24) that you correctly identified? Use the space provided below to record your response.

c. Form a discussion group with 4 or 5 of your fellow-classmates. Each member of this group needs to share his/her score in part "a" above (don't artificially inflate your score just to impress others in your group or protect yourself). Then discuss *why* some in your group may have done better than others in identifying dominant themes for the various groups listed above. Record, in the space provided below, the three reasons identified by your group that appear to most logically explain why some group members were more successful than others:

1. _____

2. _____

3. _____

d. In round-robin fashion, your instructor will call on groups to identify one of its listed reasons for members' lack of predictive accuracy. After a reason is called-out, the instructor will ask "how many other groups also identified this reason" and will record the reason and tally the number of groups identifying. This process will continue until all three reasons from all groups are called out. Record in the space provided below (using the instructor's tally) the three most identified reasons for lack of predictive accuracy:

1. _____

2. _____

3. _____

e.   Which text terminology/concepts reflect the technical definition/explanation for the reasons identified in part "d" above? Use the space below to record this terminology.

Exercise 3

Knowing your lack of predictive accuracy (and that of many members of the class) and some of the reasons for this lack of accuracy, what do you (a manager of the future) intend to do to overcome this shortcoming? Meet once again in your group and develop a short list of actions that could be taken to overcome identified shortcomings. Use the space below for your group's response. Once the class has discussed the various identified strategies for overcoming a lack of predictive accuracy, your instructor will share with the class her/his views and those of other experts.   Add other strategies and action plans (shared by other groups and your instructor) to the initial list below that your group generated.

Exercise 4

Explain what you have gained (learned about yourself and about others) from involving yourself in this experience.

Experience 22-2 Moving Your Company Toward A True "Multicultural Organization"

Introduction

A **Multicultural Organization** is one that has achieved high levels of diversity, is able to fully capitalize on the advantages of the diversity, and has few diversity-related problems.[*] As you might suspect from this definition, few, if any, true multicultural organizations probably exist. Yet, if one could identify the basic characteristics of such an *ideal organization*, one could compare any *actual organization* to these characteristics and, where significant differences exist, begin to set courses of action to bring the actual organization into coincidence with the ideal.

Exercise 1

Form a group with 4 or 5 other classmates. The group's assignment is to develop a list of the organizational characteristics that would make for the ideal multicultural organization. Use the space provided below to record the group's list of characteristics.

Exercise 2

Your group probably has relied primarily on text concepts to build your list of characteristics for the ideal multicultural organization. Meet once again in your group. This time *draw on the diversity within your own group to identify other creative suggestions not previously considered*. Use the space provided below to record other characteristics of the ideal multicultural organization not previously considered.

---

[*]Definition from Dinish D'Souza, "Multiculturalism 101," *Policy Review*, Spring 1991, pp. 22-30.

Exercise 3

Your instructor will share a list of characteristics for the ideal multicultural organization that were developed by one expert on the subject. Which of the characteristics from the expert's list were not considered by your group? Why were they overlooked? Use the space below to record your answers to these questions.

Exercise 4

Explain what you have learned from involving yourself in this experience. Use the space below to record your answer. Make sure that you utilize the text terminology in your explanations.

A THE EIGHTEEN THERBLIGS*

"Therblig" is a term invented by Frank and Lillian Gilbreth, who assured credit to themselves for their pioneering activity in this area by coining this term. It is *Gilbreth* spelled backward, except that the *t* and *h* of Gilbreth are not reversed. A therblig is a basic subdivision of work accomplishment, a minute element of a work operation that may be either a part of a motion or a combination of several motions. Originally, the Gilbreths created sixteen therbligs, but their followers have revised their work to establish the following eighteen:

1. *Transport Empty*, symbolized by "TE." This is the basic operation element required to move the hand or other transporting device unloaded and unresisted.
2. *Transport Loaded*, symbolized by "TL." This is the basic operation element required to move the hand or other transporting device loaded or when moving against resistance.
3. *Change Direction*, symbolized by "CD." This is the basic operation element required to change the line or plane of a transport motion, whether TE or TL.
4. *Grasp*, symbolized by "G." This is the basic operation element required to take hold of an object and bring it under the control of the operator or other transporting device.
5. *Hold*, symbolized by "H." This is the basic operation element required to retain control of an object after it has been successfully picked up.
6. *Release Load*, symbolized by "RL." This is the basic operation element employed in relinquishing one's hold on, and control over, an object.
7. *Preposition*, symbolized by "PP." This is the basic operation element required to prepare the transporting device and/or object to be moved from the next basic operation.
8. *Position*, symbolized by "P." This is the basic operation element utilized to line up one object in a predetermined position relative to another.
9. *Search*, symbolized by "S." This is the basic operation element utilized to locate a needed tool, part, or other object.
10. *Select*, symbolized by "SE." This is the basic operation element required for choosing between two or more items found by searching.
11. *Plan*, symbolized by "PL." This is the basic operation element utilized in deciding on the operating method to be used. Typically, with repetitive work, the operator will merely hesitate briefly and then go on.
12. *Inspect*, symbolized by "I." This is the basic operation element required for comparing a part with a predetermined standard--using the five senses, possibly assisted by an appropriate gauging device. Obviously, inspecting involves looking for desirable and undesirable characteristics. It is intended to tell whether the object is a good or bad product.
13. *Avoidable Delay*, symbolized by "AD." This is the basic operation element involved when the planned sequence of motions provides no delay, yet a delay occurs. A typical example is the operator who stops to wipe perspiration from his face and chin and, seeing a friend, calls to him to ask for a ride home that evening.
14. *Unavoidable Delay*, symbolized by "UD." This is the basic operation element represented by a work stoppage due to machine breakdowns, shortage of raw materials, waiting for work tickets to come from the production control office, or other such causes.
15. *Rest to Overcome Fatigue*, symbolized by "RTOF." This is the basic operation element required by a worker for recovery from excessive effort.
16. *Balancing Delay*, symbolized by "BD." This is the basic operation element occurring when two parts of the body must perform basic operations simultaneously and one is delayed by the slowness of the other. More specifically, the right hand may have to wait for the left hand to complete a motion before the right hand can resume productive work, or vice versa.
17. *Use*, symbolized by "U." This is the basic operation element required for actual processing of a part or a material (exclusive of assembly operations) to convert its form utility.
18. *Assemble*, symbolized by "A." This is the basic operation element required to bring two or more parts into a predetermined relationship and to join them permanently in these relative positions. It includes the converse operation of "disassembly."

---

*Source of Appendix A: From Broom, H. N., Production Management. © 1967 Richard D. Irwin, Inc. Reprinted by permission.

B METHODS ANALYSIS

| Part: | | Date: | | Part No.: |

Operation: Assembly of Shackle Bolt   Analyst:

Description-- Left Hand	Therblig Symbol	Time	Therblig Symbol	Description-- Right Hand
Total Time				

Ethical Behavior: Managers' Beliefs, Managers' Perceptions of Peers and Top Managements' Beliefs, Managers' Behavior Frequency, and Managers' Perceptions of Peers' Behavior Frequency[*]

Behavior:	Managers' Beliefs And Their Perceptions Of Peer And Top Management Beliefs			Managers' Self-Reported Behaviors And Their Beliefs About Peer Behavior	
	Managers	Peer	Top Management	Managers Behavior Frequency	Peer Behavior Frequency
1. Passing blame for errors to an innocent co-worker	1.22	1.90	1.69	1.98	2.57
2. Divulging confidential information	1.32	1.58	1.26	1.51	2.21
3. Falsifying time/quality/quantity reports	1.40	1.87	1.42	1.30	2.50
4. Claiming credit for someone else's work	1.47	2.18	1.90	1.88	2.77
5. Padding an expense account over 10%	1.50	2.23	1.55	1.45	2.60
6. Pilfering company materials and supplies	1.50	2.03	1.47	2.09	2.86
7. Accepting gifts/favors in exchange for preferential treatment	1.61	2.41	1.74	1.85	2.65
8. Giving gifts/favors in exchange for preferential treatment	1.74	2.40	2.00	1.26	2.62
9. Padding an expense account up to 10%	1.74	2.52	1.93	1.35	3.10
10. Authorizing a subordinate to violate company rules	1.85	2.16	1.66	1.31	2.39
11. Calling in sick to take a day off	1.98	2.50	1.81	1.24	2.75
12. Concealing one's errors	2.16	2.43	1.95	1.46	3.00
13. Taking longer than necessary to do a job	2.22	2.50	1.97	1.69	2.88
14. Using company services for personal use	2.45	2.85	2.27	1.86	3.31
15. Doing personal business on company time	2.46	2.85	2.25	1.26	3.26
16. Taking extra personal time (lunch hour, breaks, early departure, and so forth)	2.59	2.95	2.31	2.12	3.26
17. Not reporting others' violations of company policies and rules	2.73	2.65	2.02	2.38	2.98
Mean Score	1.88	2.35	1.84	1.65	2.81

Note: a low mean indicates that the behavior was believed to be highly unethical or that the behavior is practiced infrequently.

---

[*]From John W. Newstrom and William A. Ruch, "The Ethics of Management and the Management of Ethics," *MSU Business Topics*, Winter 1975, (Vol. 23, No. 1), pp. 29-37.

D   PRE-EMPLOYMENT INQUIRY GUIDE*

Subject	Permissible Inquiries	Inquiries That Must Be Avoided
1. Name	"Have you worked for this company under a different name?" "Is any additional information relative to change of name, use of an assumed name or nickname necessary to enable a check on your work and educational record? If yes, explain.	Inquiries about the name that would indicate applicant's lineage, ancestry, national origin, or descent. Inquiry into previous name of applicant where it has been changed by court order or otherwise. "Indicate: Miss, Mrs., Ms."
2. Marital and family status	Whether applicant can meet specified work schedules or has activities, commitments, or responsibilities that may hinder the meeting of work attendance requirements. Inquiries, made to males and females alike, as to a duration of stay on job or anticipated absences.	Any inquiry indicating whether an applicant is married, single, divorced, engaged, etc. Number and age of children. Information on child-care arrangements. Any questions concerning pregnancy. Any similar question that directly or indirectly results in limitation of job opportunity in any way.
3. Age	If a minor, require proof of age in the form of a work permit or a certificate of age. Require proof of age by birth certificate after being hired. Inquiry as to whether the applicant meets the minimum age requirements as set by law and indication that, on hiring, proof of age must be submitted in the form of a birth certificate or other forms of proof of age. If age is a legal requirement: "If hired, can you furnish proof of age?" or statement that hire is subject to verification of age. Inquiry as to whether an applicant is younger than the employer's regular retirement age.	Requirement that applicant state age or date of birth. Requirement that applicant produce proof of age in the form of a birth certificate or baptismal record. (The Age Discrimination in Employment Act of 1967 forbids discrimination against persons between the ages of forty and seventy.)
4. Handicaps	For employers subject to the provisions of the Rehabilitation Act of 1973, applicants may be "invited" to indicate how and to what extent they are handicapped. The employer must indicate to applicants that: (1) compliance with the invitation is voluntary; (2) the information is being sought only to remedy discrimination or provide opportunities for the handicapped; (3) the information will be kept confidential; and (4) refusing to provide the information will not result in adverse treatment. All applicants can be asked whether they are able to carry out all necessary job assignments and perform them in a safe manner	The Rehabilitation Act of 1973 forbids employers from asking job applicants general questions about whether they are handicapped or asking them about the nature and severity of their handicaps. An employer must be prepared to proved that any physical and mental requirements for a job are due to "business necessity" and the safe performance of the job. Except in cases where undue hardship can be proven, employers must make "reasonable accommodations" for the physical and mental limitations of an employee or applicant. "Reasonable accommodations" include alteration of duties, alteration of physical setting, and provision of aids.
5. Sex	Inquiry as to sex or restriction of employment to one sex is permissible only where a bona fide occupational qualification exists. (This BFOQ exception is interpreted very narrowly by the courts and EEOC.) The burden of proof rests on the employer to prove that the BFOQ does exist* and that all members of the affected class are incapable of performing the job.	Sex of applicant. Any other inquiry that would indicate sex. Sex is not a BFOQ because a job involves physical labor (such as heavy lifting) beyond the capacity of some women, nor can employment be restricted just because the job is traditionally labeled "Men's work" or "women's work." Sex cannot be used as a factor for determining whether an applicant will be satisfied in a particular job. Avoid questions concerning applicant's height or weight unless you can prove they are necessary requirements for the job to be performed.

---

*Source: *Personnel Practices for Small Colleges*--National Association of College and University Business Officers.

6.	Race or color	General distinguishing physical characteristics such as scars.	Applicant's race. Color of applicant's skin, eyes, hair, or other questions directly or indirectly indicating race or color.
7.	Address or duration of residence	Applicant's address. Inquiry into place and length of current and previous address, e.g., "How long a resident of this state or city?"	Specific inquiry into foreign addresses that would indicate national origin. Names or relationship of persons with whom applicant resides. Whether application owns or rents home.
8.	Birthplace	"After employment (if employed by this institution), can you submit a birth certificate or other proof of U.S. citizenship?	Birthplace of applicant. Birthplace of applicant's parents, spouse, or other relatives. Requirement that applicant submit a birth certificate or naturalization or baptismal record before employment. Any other inquiry into national origin.
9.	Religion	An applicant may be advised concerning normal hours and days of work required by the job to avoid possible conflict with religious or other personal convictions.	Applicant's religious denomination or affiliation, church, parish, pastor, or religious holidays observed. Applicants may not be told that any particular religious groups are required to work on their religious holidays. Any inquiry to indicate or identify religious denomination of customs.
10.	Military Record	Type of education and experience in service as it relates to a particular job.	Type of discharge.
11.	Photograph	Indicate that this may be required after hiring for identification.	Requirement that applicant affix a photograph to his or her application. Request that applicant, at his or her option, submit photograph. Requirement of photograph after interview but before hiring.
12.	Citizenship	"Are you a citizen of the United States?" "If you are not a U.S. citizen, have you the legal right to remain permanently in the U.S.?" "Do you intend to remain permanently in the U.S.?" "If not a citizen, are you prevented from lawfully becoming employed because of visa or immigration status?" Statement that, if hired, applicant may be required to submit proof of citizenship.	"Of what country are you a citizen?" Whether applicant or his or her parents or spouse are naturalized or native-born U.S. citizens. Date when applicant or parents or spouse acquired U.S. citizenship. Requirement that applicant produce his or her naturalization papers. Whether applicant's parents or spouse are citizens of the U.S.
13.	Ancestry or national origin	Languages applicant reads, speaks or writes fluently if another language is necessary to perform the job.	Inquiries into applicant's lineage, ancestry, national origin, descent, birthplace, or mother tongue. National origin of applicant's parents or spouse.
14.	Education	Applicant's academic, vocational, or professional education: school attended. Inquiry into language skills such as reading, speaking, and writing foreign languages.	Any inquiry asking specifically the nationality, racial affiliations, or religious affiliation of a school. Inquiry as to how foreign language ability was acquired.
15.	Experience	Applicant's work experience, including names and addresses of previous employers, dates of employment, reasons for leaving, salary history. Other countries visited.	
16.	Conviction, arrest, and court record	Inquiry into actual convictions that relate reasonably to fitness to perform a particular job. (A conviction is a court ruling where the party is found guilty as charged. An arrest is merely the apprehending or detaining of the person to answer the alleged crime.)	Any inquiry relating to arrests. Ask or check into a person's arrest, court, or conviction record if not substantially related to functions and responsibilities of the particular job in question.

17. Relatives   Names of applicant's relatives already employed by this company. Name and addresses of parents or guardian of minor applicant.

     Name or address of any relative of adult applicant, other than those employed by this company.

18. Notice in case of emergency   Name and address of persons to be notified in case of accident or emergency.

     Name and address of relatives to be notified in case of accident or emergency.

19. Organizations   Inquiry into the organizations of which an applicant is a member, providing the name or character of the organization does not reveal the race, religion, color, or ancestry of the membership. "List all professional organizations to which you belong. What offices are held?"

     "List all organizations, clubs, societies, and lodges to which you belong." The names of organizations to which the applicant belongs if such information would indicate through character or name the race, religion, color, or ancestry of the membership.

20. References   By whom were you referred for a position here? Names of persons willing to provide professional and/or character references for applicant.

     Require the submission of a religious reference. Request reference from applicant's pastor.

21. Miscellaneous   Notice to applicants that any misstatement or omissions of material facts in the application may be cause for dismissal.

Note: Any inquiry should be avoided that, although not specifically listed among the above, is designed to elicit information as to race, color, ancestry, age, sex, religion, handicap, or arrest and court record unless based upon a bona fide occupational qualification.

E   EMPLOYMENT APPLICATION BLANK

Application for Employment
(You must fill out this application
to be considered for employment
in this company.)

> **Photo**
>
> **Applicants: Your photograph should be submitted *only* after the interview has been conducted.**

1. Name:* Mr. Miss. Mrs. Ms._____
   Have you worked for this company under a different name? Yes_____ No_____
2. Marital status: a.*   Currently married_____ Currently unmarried_____
              b.*   Are you currently pregnant? Yes_____ No_____
3. If hired, can you submit proof of age? Yes_____ No_____
4. a.*   Are you handicapped? Yes_____ No_____
   b.*   If yes, what is the nature of your handicap?_____
5. a.†   Height: feet_____ inches_____   b.*   Weight:_____ lbs.
   c.*   Color of hair: _____   d.*   Type of hair:_____
6. Address:_____
7. Birthplace of parents:*_____
8. If employed, can you supply a birth certificate? Yes_____ No_____
9. a.*   Do you observe any particular religious customs? Yes_____ No_____
   b.*   If yes, what customs?_____

10. a.† What type of military experience do you have?

_____

   b.* What was the type of discharge you received?_____

      Honorable_____ Dishonorable_____ Why (explain briefly):

_____

11. a. Are you a citizen of the United States? Yes_____ No_____

   b.* If not, of what country are you a citizen?_____

12. a.† What languages do you speak fluently?_____

   b.* What is your native language_____

13. a. What is the highest degree you have earned?_____

   b. What school did you attend for your highest degree?_____

14. a. Work experiences: (1)_____

                          (2)_____

                          (3)_____

   b. Explain why you left each of your previous employers.

15.* Have you ever been arrested? Yes_____   No_____

16.† Have you ever been convicted? Yes_____   No_____

17. a. Do any of your relatives work for this company? Yes_____ No_____

   b.* If no, provide a name and address of a relative to be notified in case of an accident or emergency:

      Name_____

      Address_____

   c. If no relatives exist, provide the name and address of a person to be notified in case of an accident or emergency:

      Name_____

      Address_____

18.* List all organizations, clubs, societies, and lodges to which you belong.

_____

19.* Can you supply a recommendation from your pastor after the interview?

      Yes_____   No_____

20. Who referred you for this position?_____ .

I understand that any misstatements or omissions of material facts in this application may be cause for dismissal.

      Signature_____

      Date_____

F   ROLE FOR GEORGE STANLEY, SECTION HEAD*

You have evaluated all of the supervisors who report to you and during the next two weeks will interview each of them. You hope to use these interviews constructively to develop each person. Today, you have arranged to interview Tom Burke, one of the eight first-line supervisors who report to you. The following is the information and his evaluation as given in your files:

Thomas Burke: Twelve years with company, two years as supervisor, college degree, married, two children.

Evaluation: Highly creative and original, and exceptionally competent technically. His unit is very productive, and during the two years he has supervised the group, there has been a steady improvement. Within the past six months, you have given him extra work, and he has gotten this done on schedule. As far as productivity and dependability are concerned, he is your top supervisor.

---

*Source of Appendixes F, G and H: Reprinted from: N.R.F. Maier, A.R. Solem, and A.A. Maier, *The Role-Play Technique*, San Diego, CA: University Associates, Inc., 1975. Used with permission.

His cooperation with other supervisors in the section leaves much to be desired, however. Before you made him a supervisor, his originality and technical knowledge were available to your whole section. Gradually, he has withdrawn and now acts more as a one wolf. You've asked other supervisors to talk over certain problems with him, but they tell you that he offers no suggestions. He tells them he's busy, listens disinterestedly to their problems, kids them, or makes sarcastic remarks, depending on his mood. On one occasion, he allowed Jim Drake, one of the supervisors in another unit, to make a mistake that could have been avoided if he had informed Drake of the status of certain design changes that he knew about and had seen. Supervisors are expected to cooperate on matters involving design changes that affect them.

Furthermore, during the past six months, he has been unwilling to take two assignments. He said that the assignments were routine, that he preferred more interesting work, and he advised you to give the assignments to other supervisors. To prevent trouble, you followed his suggestion. However, you feel that you can't give him all of the interesting work and that if he persist in this attitude, there will be trouble. You cannot play favorites and keep up morale in your unit.

Burke's failure to cooperate has you worried for another reason. Although his group is highly productive, there is more turnover among his draftspeople than in other groups. You have heard no complaints yet, but you suspect that he may be treating his people in an arbitrary manner. Certainly if he talks down to you and other supervisors, he's likely to be even more that way with his people. Apparently, the high productivity in his group is not due to high morale, but to his ability to use his people to do the things for which they are best suited. This method won't develop good draftspeople. You hope to discuss these matters with Burke in such a way as to recognize his good points and at the same time point out some of his weaknesses.

G   ROLE FOR TOM BURKE, SUPERVISOR

One junior designer, six draftspeople, and two clerks report to you. You feel that you get along fine with your group. You have always been pretty much of an idea man and apparently have the knack of passing on your enthusiasm to others in your group. There is a lot of "we" feeling in your unit because it is obvious that your group is the most productive.

You believe in developing your people and always give them strong recommendations. You feel that you have gained the reputation of developing your employees because they frequently go out and get much better jobs. Since promotion is necessarily slow in a company such as yours, you feel that the best way to stimulate morale is to develop new people and to demonstrate that a good person can get somewhere. The two women in your unit are bright and efficient, and there is a lot of good-natured kidding. Recently, one of your women, Jane Wilson, turned down an outside offer that paid thirty-five dollars a month more because she preferred to stay in your group. You are going to get her a raise the first chance you have.

The other supervisors in George Stanley's section do not have your enthusiasm. Some of them are dull and unimaginative. During your first year as supervisor, you helped them a lot, but you soon found that they leaned on you, and before long you were doing their work. There is a lot of pressure to get out production. You got your promotion by producing, and you don't intend to let other supervisors interfere. Since you no longer help the other supervisors, your production has gone up, but a couple of them seem a bit sore at you. Frank, your junior designer, is a better person than most of them, and you'd like to see him made a supervisor. Since the company has some deadwood in it, you feel that Stanley ought to recognize this fact and assign to such units the more routine jobs. Then they won't need your help, and you could concentrate your efforts on jobs that suit your unit. At present, George Stanley passes out work pretty much as he gets it. Because you are efficient, you get more than your share of these jobs, and you see no reason why the extra work shouldn't be in the form of "plums." This motivates units to turn out work. When you suggested to Stanley that he turn over some of the more routine jobs to other supervisors, he did it, but he sure was reluctant about it.

You did one thing recently that has bothered you. There was a design change in a set of plans, and you should have told Jim Drake (a fellow supervisor) about it, but it slipped your mind. Drake was out when you had it on your mind, and then you got involved in a hot idea that Frank, your junior designer, had and forgot all about the matter with Drake. As a result, Drake had to make a lot of unnecessary changes, and he was quite sore about it. You told him you were sorry and offered to make the changes, but he turned down the offer.

H   HOW TO ROLE PLAY

All people are good actors when they make up their own lines. This is one of the most impressive facts one experiences in working with role playing. You can completely dispense with any consideration of training participants in voice intonation and gestures. Role players remain themselves and must merely behave in the situation described. If you are placed in the role of a union steward, you should consider yourself to be the steward for the group specified and not act the way you think a union steward behaves. In addition to finding themselves in specific positions, role players may be expected to accept certain facts about their length of service, sex, family ties, friends, and previous experiences. They should adopt these as their own and let their feelings and attitude change as these imagined events or factors seem to require.

All of us conduct ourselves differently, depending on the situation in which we find ourselves. As a supervisor on the job, your conduct is likely to be very different than when at home with the family. Similarly, appropriate behavior at a party is quite unlike accepted conduct at a movie. This does not imply that your personality changes, but rather that your behavior is altered in response to the situation, while you remain yourself.

The role-playing instructions describe the setting in which a particular frame of mind will be formulated. Because they set up a state of mind that serves as a point of departure, the roles should not be reexamined by the players once the interaction has begun. It is important to realize that the initial attitude adopted by a role player need not remain static. Subsequent events or experiences, as they occur in the process of role playing, may alter these attitudes and create pleasant or unpleasant feelings. As a result, the persons involved may have some of the same emotional experiences that occur in real-life situations. This emotional arousal is one of the most important values of role playing and makes it a form of rehearsal for practical problems. With experience in role-playing situations, you learn to feel the part; to the extent that this occurs, role-playing behavior becomes more and more authentic. The fact that role playing can simulate real-life situations makes it possible for you to try new ways of handling problems without suffering any serious consequences if the methods fail.

In the process of role playing, questions may be raised in the discussion that are not covered by the instructions to the participants. When this occurs, the person questioned should feel free to make up facts or experiences that are appropriate to the circumstances. For example, if the supervisor in a case asks a worker a question about the health of her children, she may answer it in any one of several ways without altering the spirit of the case. However, the player should not go out of her way to make up experiences or facts that are inconsistent with her role.

In conclusion, it is perhaps worthwhile to repeat points already stated to warn against two common role-playing mistakes:

1. Do not consult your role while playing a part. This practice tends to make an attitude a static condition and not subject to alteration. Real attitudes are dynamic forces and are subject to change in direction as well as in intensity.

2. Do not behave the way you feel a person in the position described in your role should behave. This ability to play the part of another person is perhaps a requirement for acting in a play but is a distinct disadvantage in successful role playing. A good role player need not be an accomplished actor.

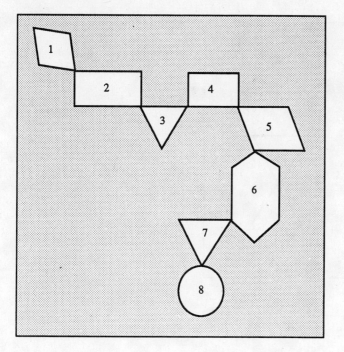

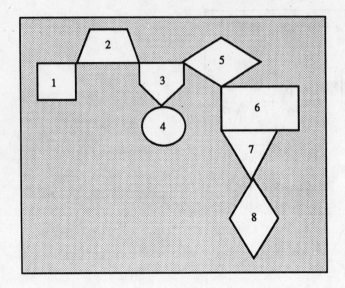

K STREET SCENE

L CAN YOU FOLLOW INSTRUCTIONS?

Three-minute timed test

1. Write your name in the upper left-hand corner of this paper.
2. Circle the word *corner* in sentence one.
3. Draw two boxes in the upper right-hand corner of this paper.
4. Write the letter *X* in each box.
5. Sign your name to the right of the title of this paper.
6. Draw a circle around sentence number *two*.
7. Write the letter *O* in the lower left-hand corner of this paper.
8. Draw a triangle around the letter *O* you just put down.
9. Draw a circle around the word *corner* in sentence number three.
10. Loudly call out your last name when you get to this point in the exam.
11. If you believe you have followed instructions carefully to this point, call out the words *I have*.
12. In the left margin of this paper, add 7,570 and 4,420.
13. Draw a box around your answer, and draw a circle around the box.
14. Count, in your normal speaking voice, from one to ten.
15. Write the name of your best friend in the lower left corner of this paper.
16. If you are the first person to get this far, call out the words *I am following directions*.
17. Circle the odd numbers on this side of the paper.
18. Say out loud the words *I am about to finish*.
19. Now that you have finished reading carefully, do *only what you were instructed to do in sentence one*.

M DISTRIBUTION OF REWARDS

In some organizations, a person's reward is tied explicitly to his or her output (for example, a piece-rate system); in others, salaries or bonuses may be partially tied to group efforts (athletic teams); still in other organizations, a fixed amount of money must be divided up among employees so that what one person stands to gain, another person may lose (academic salaries and raised are frequently from a fixed amount). These different reward structures historically have been classified along a cooperation-competition dimension.

The best summary to date on this literature was presented by Miller and Hamblin.[*] They pointed out that these concepts could be most usefully broken down on two dimensions rather than one as was previously thought. The dimensions they suggested were: (1) interdependence and (2) differential reward. By interdependence they meant the degree to which the group members needed each other to complete a task. By differential reward they meant the degree to which individual effort received compensation. A high differential reward situation would be one in which perhaps the most efficient member received twice the reward that the least effective member received from a somewhat fixed amount of resources. A low differential reward situation would be one in which everyone in the group received basically the same compensation. Dividing these variables into highs and lows produces a two-by-two matrix with four possible situations (see figure M.1). Miller and Hamblin felt that productivity would be lower in situations 1 and 4 than in situations 2 and 3. In situation 1, people are highly dependent upon one another, and yet to the extent that one person gains, another group member must lose. In situation 4, group members do not need each other to perform the job, yet everyone receives the same compensation (reward). Situations 1 and 4 seem to indicate a mismatch between how success is achieved and how rewards are distributed. Situations 2 and 3, however, show a consistent relationship between effort and reward. In situation 2, everyone is highly interdependent, and rewards are distributed equally among members. In situation 3, people work independently, and rewards are based upon one's individual contribution.

Figure M.1   Matrix relating interdependence and differential reward.

		Interdependence	
		High	Low
Differential	High	1	3
Reward	Low	2	4

The theoretical conceptualization of Miller and Hamblin was tested and generally supported. The implications of these findings suggest that organizations should be careful to match their reward structure with the degree of interdependence inherent in the task. To introduce what is traditionally called a competitive system (high differential reward) when employees are dependent upon each other may very well result in decreased, rather than increased, performance. On the other hand, giving everyone the same compensation on a task when employees work independently may also significantly detract from effectiveness.

N ROLE-PLAY SITUATIONS

Situation 1--I Am Joe Welch

I am Joe Welch. Bill Green is one of the men in my new office.

I haven't been in this office over three months, but in that period of time I've had a pretty good chance to look over the groups and study the operations. In that I'm new, I haven't instituted any changes as yet. However, there are a few things I have in mind, and one problem concerns Bill Green.

Bill, I understand, has been around for about fifteen years, four of them in this office. They tell me he knows the operation pretty well. Yet, he is on the reports job and doesn't seem to show much interest or initiative. I know that job must seem awfully routine, but Bill doesn't complain or seem to want anything different to do.

---

[*]I. Miller and R. Hamblin, "Interdependence, Differential Rewarding, and Productivity," *American Sociological Review* 28 (1963): 768-778.

The difficulty that I have today concerns the latest monthly report. It was due on the first, and it's very important that we have it in promptly for consolidation in the division report. A few minutes ago, my boss called me and said our report was late again. He wondered why we couldn't have it in on time like the other districts do. I told him that I was sorry and that we'd take care of it in the future.

It sort of burns me up. I'm trying awfully hard to make things click at this office, and a guy like Bill Green fouls things up. He doesn't seem to have too much to do--in fact, I've noticed him spending a lot of time on a new house project. Why can't he, at least, get his reports in or time?

Situation 1--I Am Bill Green

I am Bill Green. I have been with the company for fifteen years, am happily married, have just recently built a new home, and feel that I get along OK at the office.

I have been in this office for the last four years and have had several assignments. My latest assignment began last January. This job seems rather routine and unimportant, but I don't want to complain.

The group at the office is nice to work with. Our boss, Joe Welch, is new. He joined us only three months ago. I haven't had much contact with him. I guess he knows that my job is routine and that as long as I send in the reports every month there isn't anything to worry about. Once in awhile, I've been tied up on other things, and the reports have been a day or two late--in fact, that happened this month--but I guess it doesn't hurt anything. I always get them finished without any errors.

I've been awfully interested in my new house. When things are slow here at the office, I can get a lot of things done concerning the house--at least a few phone calls and letters.

I'd like to get to know Joe Welch better, but he always seems so buy.

Situation 2--I Am Carl White

I am Carl White, supervisor of an office in A Department.

Jim Webber is a young man in my office group. Jim has been with the company for a little over three years. For as long as I've known him, he has seemed like a nice lad, interested in his job and cooperative. He has a good future, I'm sure.

Lately, however, Jim has developed some rather bad work habits. For one thing, he comes in late almost every morning. At first it was only five or ten minutes. This past week it has been twenty or thirty minutes on an average. Then he seems to leave very promptly at our closing time.

Jim may have picked this habit up from Ed Olson. Ed has been with us thirty-five years and is one of the fellows who has been pretty much in the same job. Ed's desk is next to Jim's and, although they don't work on the same projects, I see them talk a lot together. Ed is going to retire next year, and I just don't know what to do about his work habits after all these years.

But I do know that I want Jim Webber to get on the ball. I think I'll have a talk with him when he gets in this morning (he's already late) and straighten this thing out!

Situation 2--I Am Jim Webber

I am Jim Webber. I work in Carl White's office in A Department. I have been with the company for thirty-eight months and like the job and the opportunity it offers.

Carl White is my boss. He seems like a nice fellow and helps me whenever I have a serious problem. Other than that, we don't spend much time together.

Ed Olson, the man at the next desk, is one of my best friends in the office. Although we do different types of work, he's been able to give me a lot of information about the company. Ed has been around over thirty-five years and seems to know a great deal. There are some things I've wondered about, however. He seems to get in late every day and takes a pretty long lunch hour.

Of course, I guess I'm having a little trouble about that myself. I used to ride the Main Street bus to work every day. I usually caught the one that got me to the office right about our starting time. Once in a while, we'd be a little off schedule because of traffic, or I'd be held up by the crowded elevators.

Because the bus was always so crowded, I decided to join a car pool and ride into town with the fellows on my block. It's certainly a lot easier and takes far less time. The only problem is that they don't have to be at work quite as early as I do, and it gets me in a little late. Then I have to be ready promptly at closing time to meet the car pool.

Mr. White hasn't said anything about my being late like this. Maybe he doesn't mind as long as I get my work done.

Situation 3--I Am Elmer Hill

I am riding in a company car with Al Jackson, one of our newer employees. Al is driving. We have been going through a good deal of heavy traffic, and it appears that we won't get back to the company garage by 5 P.M. (our quitting time). It is a very warm day, and both of us have had a busy schedule. This is the first time that I have been in a company car with Al. He has had the use of company vehicles about a year. I have never had any official complaints about his driving except that Roy Burns, one of my older staff men, remarked one day that he had had a "pretty fast ride with Jackson" and laughingly wondered if Jackson was a hot-rod enthusiast. I had answered that, considering the emphasis we are getting these days on safety, I would prefer that all our people would be safe-driving enthusiasts.

Al handled himself quite well this afternoon in the meeting we attended. He certainly has done a nice job in our group. I like his energy and initiative, although he obviously needs a great deal more experience. I understand Al is engaged to be married. At this moment, Al has swung the car into a right-hand lane to make a right-hand turn at the intersection. Another car is directly ahead of us approaching the intersection. As it reaches the corner, the light changes to red, and the car stops. There is a sign nearby indicating that right-hand turns are permitted at all times. Al starts to blow the horn on our company car and, before I can stop him, leans out of his window and shouts at the driver to keep his eyes open and to get his d--n car out of the way. The driver, with an angry look at us (and the company name on the car), turns the corner, whereupon Al "guns" our vehicle on around him and on toward the garage.

Situation 3--I Am Al Jackson

I am driving a company car with Elmer Hill, boss of our group, as a passenger.

It's near the end of a rough day, and with all the heavy traffic on the streets, we probably will be fifteen to twenty minutes late getting to the company garage. Of all the nights to have a prompt date with Ellen! I figured I could meet her at 5:00 P.M., and we could take a look at the furniture she had picked out before the store closed at 5:30 P.M. Now she'll be standing there waiting for me at the store, and I have no way of getting in touch with her. Of all the rotten luck! We have so darn many things to take care of before our wedding day. And look at these fool drivers! I can't understand why all these people who never seem to be in a hurry have to get out on the streets at the busy hours. There ought to be a law against them.

We certainly had a full day. I'll have to admit that I like this job more and more. And Mr. Hill seems like a top-notch fellow, too. Even though I'm pretty new, he seems to give me every chance to tackle a job my own way. And I've always liked to get things done in a hurry.

At this moment, I see the corner approaching where I want to make a right turn. I swing into the right lane just behind another car--one of those pokey drivers. This is one of the corners where you can turn right at any time. There's the sign there saying that you can. The light's turning red, and I'll bet that fool will stop. Sure enough, he does. Well, if I lay on the horn enough, he'll pull around. I honk repeatedly and then shout out the window: "Hey you! Why don't you keep your eyes open when you drive? Get the d--n car out of the way!" Honestly, I've never seen such dumb drivers. The driver gives me an angry look and turns the corner, whereupon I shift gears and rush past him.

A guy like that really burns me up!

O SUPPORTING INFORMATION FOR "PREPARING MANAGERS FOR OVERSEAS ASSIGNMENTS"

Profile of an Average Expatriated Manager*

- The person is usually male, although this is beginning to change as highly qualified women become managers.
- The person is typically well educated. Advanced degrees in law, business, engineering, or the sciences are common.
- The expatriate knows his/her company well. . . . Normally one needs five or more years of local experience before going abroad.
- The expatriate is a very tolerant and patient person. . . . Instead of finding the local culture alien and threatening, he (and his family) find it interesting and exciting.
- The expatriate knows the real need to make environmental/firm interlocks. . . and to be able to suggest policies that violate every rule in the book back home, but make good sense where he or she is.

---

*From Richard N. Farmer and Barry M. Richman, *International Business* (4th ed.; Bloomington, IN: Cedarwood Press, 1984), pp. 255-258.

- The manager abroad will be very well paid. Salaries range upwards of $50,000 per year, often way up. Fringe benefits, overseas allowances, and other allowances will cost another $50,000.
- He or she will be an American citizen if working for an American-based MNC, although this pattern is slowly changing.
- Expatriates from other-country-based MNCs will almost always be citizens of the MNC's home country.
- The expatriate may not know the local language. . . . The international business language is English. If a young Frenchman or German wants to move up in a MNC, he would be well advised to study English.
- The expatriate will be a good independent operator.

Reasons for American Expatriate Failures in Foreign Environments[*]

(In descending order of importance)

- Inability of the manager's spouse to adjust to a different physical or cultural environment.
- The manager's inability to adapt to a different physical or cultural environment.
- Other family-related problems.
- The manager's personality or emotional immaturity.
- The manager's inability to cope with the responsibilities posed by the overseas work.
- The manager's lack of technical competence.
- The manager's lack of motivation to work overseas.

P   EIGHT DIMENSIONS OF QUALITY[**]

Dimension	Explanation
1. *Performance*	A product's primary operating characteristic. Examples are automobile acceleration and a television set's picture clarity.
2. *Features*	Supplement to a product's basic functioning characteristics, such as power windows on a car.
3. *Reliability*	A probability of not malfunctioning during a specified period
4. *Conformance*	The degree to which a product's design and operating characteristics meet established standards.
5. *Durability*	A measure of product life.
6. *Serviceability*	The speed and ease of repair.
7. *Aesthetics*	How a product looks, feels, tastes, and smells.
8. *Perceived quality*	As seen by a customer.

---

[*]From Rosalie L. Tung, "Selection and Training for Overseas Assignments," Columbia Journal of World Business, Vol. XVI, No. 1 (Spring, 1981), pp. 68-78.

[**]Source: Adapted and reprinted by permission of *Harvard Business Review*. An excerpt from "Competing on the Eight Dimensions of Quality" by David A. Garvin, (November/December 1987). Copyright © 1987 by the President and Fellows of Harvard College; all rights reserved.

Q QUALITY ASSURANCE*

The term quality assurance is a general label applied to a company-wide effort by a business organization to enhance the quality of its products and/or services. Quality assurance is achieved through a combination of strategic commitment and improvements in employee involvement, materials, methods, and technology.

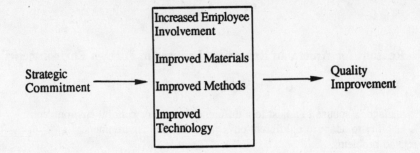

Strategic Commitment The beginning point for any real quality assurance effort is a strategic commitment by an organization's top management to make quality a top priority in all aspects of operations. This commitment is usually operationalized in four specific areas.

(1) **Employee Involvement**-Employee involvement and commitment are critical ingredients in any effort to enhance quality.

(2) **Materials**-Demanding higher quality materials from suppliers can have a significant impact on product quality.

(3) **Methods**-More efficient and effective methods of operation can significantly impact quality.

(4) **Technology**-Investing in automation and buying new equipment are also means of improving quality.

In a world with an ever-increasing quality emphasis, a very important outcome from the above mentioned strategic and operational commitments is **Quality Improvement.**

---

*Adapted from David D. Van Fleet, *Contemporary Management*, Boston: Houghton Mifflin Company, 1991, pages 531-532.

Answer Key for "Knowing You Know"

Chapter 1

True/False

1. F (p. 7)
2. T (p. 6)
3. T (p. 14)
4. F (p. 4)
5. T (p. 4)
6. F (p. 11)
7. T (p. 12)
8. T (p. 17)
9. F (p. 10)
10. T (p. 8)
11. F (p. 11)
12. F (p. 18)
13. F (p. 13)

Multiple Choice

14. c (p. 8)
15. c (p. 10)
16. a (p. 11)
17. b (p. 11)
18. b (p. 8)
19. c (p. 7)
20. e (pp. 6-7)
21. c (p. 6)
22. e (p. 4)
23. a (p. 4)
24. e (p. 8)
25. b (p. 9)

Chapter 2

Matching

1. a (p. 30)
2. g (p. 35)
3. l (p. 37)
4. j (p. 42)
5. i (p. 40)
6. e (p. 29)
7. k (p. 32)
8. m (p. 28)
9. n (p. 40)
10. f (p. 34)
11. c (p. 39)
12. h (p. 32)
13. b (p. 34)

14. o (p. 29)
15. d (p. 35)

Multiple Choice

16. a (p. 32)
17. e (p. 29)
18. a (p. 35)
19. e (p. 37)
20. c (p. 39)
21. c (p. 28)
22. a (p. 32)
23. b (p. 34)
24. a (pp. 40-41)
25. c (p. 41)

Chapter 3

Fill-in-the-Blank

1. social responsiveness (p. 61)
2. social audit (p. 70)
3. corporate social responsibility (p. 52)
4. social obligation approach (p. 64)
5. urban affairs, consumer affairs, environmental affairs and fairness in employment practices (p. 54)
6. Environmental Protection Agency (p. 60)
7. Utilitarian Principle (p. 74)
8. quality of life, social investment (p. 69)
9. social responsiveness approach (p. 64)
10. proposition four of the Davis model of social responsibility (p. 53)

True/False

11. T (p. 55)
12. T (p. 71)
13. T (p. 58)
14. T (p. 54)
15. F (p. 59)
16. F (p. 66)
17. F (p. 69)
18. F (p. 64)
19. T (pp. 73-74)
20. T (p. 69)
21. T (p. 59)
22. F (p. 52)
23. T (pp. 73-74)
24. T (p. 70)
25. F (p. 59)

CHAPTER 4

True/False

1. T (p. 92)
2. F (p. 92)
3. T (p. 93)
4. T (p. 94)
5. F (p. 95)
6. T (p. 96)
7. F (p. 98)
8. F (p. 100)
9. T (p. 102)
10. F (pp. 102-103)
11. T (p. 97)
12. F (p. 104)
13. T (p. 96)

Matching

14. i (p. 99)
15. d (p. 93)
16. j (p. 103)
17. a (p. 99)
18. c (p. 100)
19. e (p. 98)
20. g (p. 90)
21. h (p. 93)
22. f (p. 93)
23. b (p. 97)
24. k (p. 92)
25. l (p. 100)

CHAPTER 5

True/False

1. F (p. 119)
2. T (p. 120)
3. T (p. 118)
4. F (p. 123)
5. F (p. 121)
6. F (p. 125)
7. T (p. 120)
8. F (p. 122)
9. F (p. 124)
10. T (p. 125)
11. T (p. 122)
12. F (p. 115)
13. T (p. 122)
14. F (p. 126)
15. T (p. 125)

Multiple Choice

16. c (pp. 116-117)
17. a (p. 115)
18. d (p. 116)
19. c (p. 114)
20. c (p. 114)
21. c (p. 115)
22. d (p. 120)
23. e (p. 121)
24. d (p. 124)
25. e (p. 120)

CHAPTER 6

True/False

1. F (p. 135)
2. T (p. 139)
3. F (p. 140)
4. T (p. 143)
5. T (p. 145)
6. F (p. 145)
7. T (p. 140)
8. F (p. 146)
9. F (p. 134)
10. T (p. 140)
11. T (p. 134)
12. F (p. 136)
13. F (p. 143)
14. T (p. 145)
15. T (p. 137)

Matching

16. e (p. 134)
17. d (p. 139)
18. f (p. 136)
19. a (p. 145)
20. c (p. 137)
21. h (p. 144)
22. j (p. 139)
23. g (p. 144)
24. i (p. 141)
25. b (p. 134)

CHAPTER 7

Matching

1. l (p. 156)
2. c (p. 162)
3. f (p. 166)
4. i (p. 166)

5. a   (p. 156)
6. o   (p. 166)
7. d   (p. 167)
8. e   (p. 171)
9. n   (p. 174)
10. b   (p. 161)
11. g   (p. 168)
12. h   (p. 171)
13. j   (p. 175)
14. m   (p. 156)
15. k   (p. 158)

Multiple Choice

16. c   (p. 157)
17. b   (p. 158)
18. d   (p. 166)
19. b   (p. 166)
20. d   (p. 171)
21. b   (p. 174)
22. c   (p. 175)
23. a   (p. 156)
24. c   (p. 157)
25. b   (p. 156)

CHAPTER 8

True/False

1. F   (p. 186)
2. T   (p. 192)
3. T   (p. 198)
4. T   (p. 184)
5. F   (p. 186)
6. T   (p. 189)
7. F   (p. 187)
8. F   (p. 189)
9. F   (p. 199)
10. T   (p. 196)
11. T   (p. 190)
12. F   (p. 196)
13. T   (p. 196)

Multiple Choice

14. d   (p. 184)
15. a   (p. 194)
16. c   (p. 186)
17. d   (p. 199)
18. a   (p. 185)
19. d   (p. 189)
20. e   (p. 199)
21. e   (p. 198)
22. b   (p. 194)

23. d   (p. 192)
24. a   (p. 195)
25. c   (p. 198)

CHAPTER 9

Matching

1. d   (p. 218)
2. c   (p. 224)
3. i   (p. 226)
4. b   (p. 215)
5. j   (p. 214)
6. f   (p. 228)
7. e   (p. 219)
8. g   (p. 229)
9. h   (p. 224)
10. a   (p. 219)

Multiple Choice

11. c   (p. 217)
12. e   (p. 218)
13. e   (p. 219)
14. b   (p. 223)
15. a   (p. 224)
16. e   (p. 226)
17. d   (p. 226)
18. c   (p. 227)
19. b   (p. 228)
20. c   (p. 227)
21. d   (p. 215)
22. e   (p. 226)
23. e   (p. 218)
24. d   (p. 216)
25. c   (p. 224)

CHAPTER 10

Matching

1. e   (p. 238)
2. j   (p. 243)
3. i   (p. 247)
4. a   (p. 242)
5. h   (p. 249)
6. g   (p. 251)
7. d   (p. 246)
8. f   (p. 243)
9. c   (pp. 244-245)
10. b   (p. 242)

True/False

11. F   (p. 252)
12. T   (p. 253)
13. T   (p. 253)
14. T   (p. 238)
15. T   (p. 238)
16. F   (p. 239)
17. T   (p. 242)
18. T   (p. 243)
19. F   (p. 244)
20. F   (p. 246)
21. F   (p. 247)
22. F   (p. 242)
23. F   (p. 249)
24. T   (p. 252)
25. T   (p. 239)

CHAPTER 11

True/False

1. T   (p. 264)
2. F   (p. 267)
3. T   (p. 270)
4. F   (p. 270)
5. F   (p. 272)
6. T   (pp. 273-274)
7. F   (p. 274)
8. F   (p. 275)
9. F   (p. 279)
10. T   (p. 280)
11. T   (p. 265)
12. T   (p. 270)

Multiple Choice

13. c   (p. 264)
14. c   (p. 265)
15. a   (p. 270)
16. b   (p. 273)
17. b   (p. 273)
18. b   (p. 267)
19. d   (p. 276)
20. a   (p. 282)
21. d   (p. 278)
22. e   (p. 272)
23. a   (p. 269)
24. e   (p. 264)
25. a   (p. 267)

CHAPTER 12

True/False

1. F   (p. 292)
2. T   (p. 295)
3. F   (p. 307)
4. F   (p. 299)
5. F   (p. 301)
6. F   (p. 301)
7. T   (p. 303)
8. F   (p. 303)
9. F   (p. 305)
10. T   (p. 306)
11. T   (p. 301)
12. T   (p. 301)
13. T   (p. 305)
14. T   (p. 307)
15. F   (p. 298)

Fill-in-the-Blank

16. stability, adaptation (p. 293)
17. change agent (p. 295)
18. people, structure, technology (p. 296)
19. stressor (p. 308)
20. structural change (p. 297)
21. matrix organization (p. 298)
22. organization development (p. 300)
23. Grid OD (p. 300)
24. unfreezing, changing, refreezing (p. 304)
25. identification, internalization (p. 304)

CHAPTER 13

True/False

1. T   (p. 336)
2. F   (p. 337)
3. F   (p. 337)
4. F   (p. 322)
5. T   (p. 325)
6. T   (p. 328)
7. F   (p. 329)
8. F   (p. 330)
9. F   (p. 332)
10. T   (p. 332)

Matching

11. e   (p. 322)
12. a   (p. 325)
13. j   (p. 325)

14. b   (p. 326)
15. d   (p. 327)
16. h   (p. 327)
17. i   (p. 330)
18. c   (p. 332)
19. g   (p. 334)
20. f   (p. 334)
21. o   (p. 328)
22. l   (p. 334)
23. n   (p. 325)
24. k   (p. 336)
25. m   (p. 328)

Fill-in-the-Blank

1. leadership (p. 348)
2. structure, consideration (p. 357)
3. leader, follower, situation (p. 350)
4. follower maturity, leader task behavior, leader relationship behavior (p. 359)
5. leader flexibility (p. 362)
6. organizational situation, leader's style (p. 362)
7. leader-member relations, task structure, leader's position power (p. 363)
8. job-centered, employee-centered (p. 358)
9. type of organization, effectiveness of group members working together, problem to be solved, time available to make a decision (p. 351)
10. transformational leadership (p. 366)

True/False

11. T   (p. 359)
12. F   (p. 359)
13. T   (p. 359)
14. T   (p. 350)
15. T   (p. 359)
16. T   (p. 364)
17. F   (p. 364)
18. F   (p. 364)
19. F   (p. 359)
20. F   (p. 348)
21. T   (p. 355)
22. T   (p. 349)
23. T   (p. 351)
24. F   (p. 357)
25. F   (p. 359)

CHAPTER 15

True/False

1. F   (p. 391)
2. T   (p. 378)

3. F   (p. 392)
4. T   (p. 380)
5. T   (p. 378)
6. T   (p. 381)
7. T   (p. 382)
8. T   (p. 383)
9. T   (pp. 393-394)
10. F   (p. 389)

Multiple Choice

11. b   (p. 376)
12. b   (p. 376)
13. d   (p. 377)
14. d   (pp. 378-379)
15. d   (p. 388)
16. a   (p. 388)
17. a   (p. 380)
18. b   (p. 382)
19. c   (p. 384)
20. c   (p. 385)
21. d   (p. 389)
22. b   (p. 391)
23. c   (p. 392)
24. e   (p. 384)
25. d   (p. 385)

CHAPTER 16

Fill-in-the-Blank

1. people, dividing them into work groups (p. 402)
2. formal group (p. 402)
3. committee (p. 404)
4. groupthink (p. 407)
5. interest groups (p. 410)
6. linking pins (p. 403)
7. sociometry (p. 412)
8. command groups (p. 404)
9. informal groups (p. 410)
10. corporate culture (p. 418)

True/False

11. F   (p. 413)
12. F   (p. 414)
13. T   (p. 416)
14. T   (p. 416)
15. F   (p. 417)
16. F   (p. 417)
17. T   (p. 418)
18. F   (p. 418)
19. T   (p. 407)
20. T   (p. 409)

21. T (p. 402)
22. T (p. 417)
23. F (p. 418)
24. F (p. 414)
25. T (p. 407)

CHAPTER 17

Matching

1. d (p. 436)
2. h (p. 435)
3. b (p. 446)
4. e (p. 440)
5. c (p. 448)
6. f (p. 441)
7. a (p. 439)
8. j (p. 446)
9. i (p. 446)
10. g (p. 441)

True/False

11. F (p. 434)
12. F (p. 440)
13. T (p. 436)
14. T (p. 438)
15. F (p. 439)
16. F (p. 443)
17. T (p. 445)
18. F (p. 446)
19. T (p. 448)
20. T (p. 446)
21. F (p. 448)
22. T (p. 434)
23. T (p. 444)
24. F (p. 439)
25. T (p. 449)

CHAPTER 18

True/False

1. F (p. 474)
2. T (p. 475)
3. F (p. 478)
4. F (p. 480)
5. T (p. 475)
6. F (p. 460)
7. T (p. 475)
8. F (p. 463)
9. T (p. 472)
10. F (p. 473)
11. F (p. 470)

12. T (p. 465)
13. F (p. 460)
14. T (p. 472)
15. T (p. 470)

Multiple Choice

16. d (p. 474)
17. d (p. 458)
18. e (p. 458-459)
19. a (p. 474)
20. d (p. 476)
21. b (p. 470)
22. d (p. 466)
23. c (p. 471)
24. e (p. 479)
25. a (p. 479)

CHAPTER 19

Matching

1. h (p. 498)
2. d (p. 492)
3. a (p. 510)
4. c (p. 503)
5. g (p. 507)
6. f (p. 505)
7. e (p. 507)
8. i (p. 501)
9. j (p. 492)
10. b (p. 498)

True/False

11. F (p. 507)
12. F (p. 493)
13. T (p. 496)
14. F (p. 496)
15. T (p. 493)
16. F (p. 494)
17. F (p. 501)
18. F (p. 509)
19. T (p. 504)
20. F (p. 507)
21. F (p. 493)
22. T (p. 498)
23. F (p. 507)
24. T (p. 496)
25. T (p. 508)

CHAPTER 20

True/False

1. T   (p. 524)
2. F   (p. 527)
3. T   (p. 528)
4. T   (p. 530)
5. F   (p. 531)
6. T   (p. 531)
7. F   (p. 531)
8. F   (p. 533)
9. T   (p. 533)
10. F   (p. 533)
11. F   (p. 535)
12. T   (p. 536)
13. T   (p. 535)
14. F   (p. 537)
15. F   (p. 537)

Multiple Choice

16. b   (p. 537)
17. e   (p. 537)
18. c   (p. 534)
19. d   (p. 533)
20. e   (p. 528)
21. b   (pp. 528-529)
22. d   (p. 530)
23. e   (p. 530)
24. c   (p. 533)
25. d   (p. 536)

CHAPTER 21

True/False

1. F   (p. 544)
2. T   (p. 546)
3. F   (p. 556)
4. T   (p. 548)
5. T   (p. 545)
6. F   (p. 552)
7. T   (p. 547)
8. T   (p. 553)
9. F   (p. 555)
10. T   (p. 555)
11. F   (p. 555)
12. T   (p. 552)
13. T   (p. 554)
14. T   (p. 560)
15. F   (p. 555)

Matching

16. g   (p. 544)
17. d   (p. 544)
18. j   (p. 546)
19. a   (p. 548)
20. i   (p. 548)
21. e   (p. 550)
22. h   (p. 553)
23. b   (p. 551)
24. f   (p. 554)
25. c   (p. 558)

CHAPTER 22

True/False

1. F   (p. 570)
2. F   (p. 574)
3. T   (p. 570)
4. T   (p. 571)
5. T   (p. 578)
6. F   (p. 580)
7. T   (p. 576)
8. T   (p. 576)
9. F   (p. 578)
10. T   (p. 578)
11. T   (p. 580)
12. T   (p. 581)
13. F   (p. 584)
14. F   (p. 585)
15. T   (p. 587)

Multiple Choice

16. c   (pp. 571-572)
17. c   (p. 574)
18. d   (p. 576)
19. a   (p. 577)
20. e   (pp. 579-580)
21. c   (p. 583)
22. b   (p. 587)
23. b   (pp. 577-578)
24. e   (p. 578)
25. d   (p. 583)